WORLD® AIR POWER

J O U R N A L

Aerospace Publishing Ltd
AIRtime Publishing Inc.

Published quarterly by
Aerospace Publishing Ltd
179 Dalling Road
London W6 0ES
UK

Copyright © Aerospace Publishing Ltd

Cutaway drawings copyright
© Mike Badrocke/Aviagraphica

ISSN 0959-7050
Aerospace ISBN 1 874023 81 6
                (softback)
                1 874023 82 4
                (hardback)
Airtime ISBN   1-880588-07-2
                (hardback)

Published under licence in USA and
Canada by AIRtime Publishing Inc.,
USA

Editorial Offices:
WORLD AIR POWER JOURNAL
Aerospace Publishing Ltd
3A Brackenbury Road
London   W6 0BE   UK

Publisher: Stan Morse
Managing Editor: David Donald

Editors: David Donald
         Robert Hewson
Sub Editor: Karen Leverington
Editorial Assistants: Tim Senior
         Howard Gethin

Origination and printing by
    Imago Publishing Ltd
Printed in Singapore

Correspondents:
General military: Jon Lake
USA Washington: Robert F. Dorr
USA West Coast: René J. Francillon
USA Southwest: Randy Jolly
Europe: John Fricker
Russia/CIS: Yefim Gordon
Asia: Pushpindar Singh
Canada: Jeff Rankin-Lowe
Argentina: Jorge Nunez Padin
Chile: Patrick Laureau

All rights reserved. No part of this
publication may be reproduced, stored
in a retrieval system or transmitted, in
any form or by any means, electronic,
mechanical, photocopying, recording
or otherwise, without the permission of
the publishers and copyright holders.

The publishers gratefully acknowledge
the assistance given by the following
people:

Steve Harding for his invaluable
assistance with the OPTEC/'America's
Reds' article.

Rick Burgess, Hasse Vallas, Jeff
Rankin-Lowe, Salvador Mafé Huertas
and Peter Steinemann for their help
with the F/A-18 Hornet feature.

Robbie Shaw, Alec Moulton, Rob
Schleiffert and Corné Rodenburg for
their help with the Brazil Air Power
Analysis.

The editors of WORLD AIR
POWER JOURNAL welcome
photographs for possible publication,
but cannot accept any responsibility for
loss or damage to unsolicited material.

**World Air Power Journal is a
registered trademark in the
United States of America of
AIRtime Publishing Inc.**

**World Air Power Journal is
published quarterly and is
available by subscription and
from many fine book and hobby
stores.**

**SUBSCRIPTION AND BACK
NUMBERS:**

**UK and World (except USA and
Canada) write to:
Aerospace Publishing Ltd
FREEPOST
PO Box 2822
London
W6 0BR
UK**

**(No stamp required if posted in
the UK)**

**USA and Canada, write to:
AIRtime Publishing Inc.
Subscription Dept
10 Bay Street
Westport
CT 06880, USA
(203) 838-7979
Toll-free order number in USA:
1 800 359-3003**

**Prevailing subscription rates are
as follows:
Softbound edition for 1 year:
    $58.00
Softbound edition for 2 years:
    $108.00
Softbound back numbers
(subject to availability) are
$19.00 each. All rates are for
delivery within mainland USA,
Alaska and Hawaii. Canadian
and overseas prices available
upon request. American Express,
Discover Card, MasterCard and
Visa accepted. When ordering
please include your card
number, expiration date and
signature.**

**Publisher, North America:
    Mel Williams
Subscription Director:
    Linda DeAngelis
Retail Sales Director: Jill Brooks
Charter Member Services
 Manager:
    Janie Munroe
Shipping Manager: E. Rex Anku**

WORLD AIR POWER®

AIR POWER

JOURNAL

CONTENTS

Military Aviation Review

International

Eurofighter medium-range AAM bids invited

Requests for proposals (RFPs) were invited late last year by the UK Defence Ministry for its SR(A) 1239 requirement to select a future medium-range air-to-air missile (FMRAAM) as primary armament for the EF 2000 in the next century. Defence Procurement Minister James Arbuthnot said that the next-generation FMRAAM would give the RAF Eurofighters "a formidable beyond-visual-range interception capability," as well as complementing the Advanced Short-Range AAM already ordered.

Earlier MoD requests for information for the SR(A) 1239 programme brought responses by a European consortium led by BAe Dynamics, as well as from MATRA with a MICA development, and Daimler-Benz Aerospace/Bayern Chemie's A3M concept. BAeD has confirmed the intention of its team to respond to the SR(A) 1239 RFPs, for which renewed bids are also expected from the other European companies. RFP responses are further anticipated from Hughes, with an extended-range AMRAAM development propelled by an Atlantic Research/Alliant Techsystems variable-flow ducted rocket.

FMRAAM range requirements of up to 80 nm (92 miles; 148 km) have resulted in most submissions employing rocket/ramjet power, although long-term BAeD studies of its S225X projects, in conjunction with GEC-Marconi, Alenia and SAAB Missiles, encompass a range of rocket, ramjet and compound rocket/ramjet propulsion options. S225X sets out to provide fire-and-forget capability from datalink mid-course guidance and active radar homing, plus high ECM resistance, performance to meet agile evasion tactics, and stealth characteristics. S225X options, developed within the size constraints of EF 2000's FMRAAM conformal fuselage carriage, are quoted as including a dual-section 'boost-coast-boost' cycle rocket motor, to provide it with a high average velocity and optimum terminal speed. A wingless configuration is also specified for optimum aerodynamic and kinematic performance, with an electrically-actuated tail control system to provide a high degree of agility and minimum drag.

Alenia is now field-testing an active pulse-Doppler radar with a wide-band

gallium arsenide transmitter for its Agile Solid-State Seeker (AS3), in parallel with research by the other S225X partners, including active radar seeker work by GEC-Marconi. BAeD has been seeking to widen the partnership over the past year to include DASA and MATRA, to produce a unified European FMRAAM programme.

Eurofighter workshare agreement finalised

Agreement reached in London on 18 January between UK Defence Procurement Minister James Arbuthnot and his German opposite number Joerg Schoenbohm resulted in a final settlement of the recent dispute between Britain and Germany over Eurofighter workshares. Schoenbohm undertook to seek Parliamentary approval for follow-up orders for 40 Luftwaffe EF 2000s, optimised for ground attack as Tornado IDS replacements, in addition to the initial batch of 140 air defence Eurofighters planned by 2012. This was regarded as essential in Germany to ensure the continuation of an acceptable workshare in the overall Eurofighter programme for German industry. Its share of total production will now be reduced by only 3 per cent from its original 33 per cent, despite cuts in its planned EF 2000 procurement from the original 250 to 180.

Somewhat surprisingly, Britain's similar initial order was reduced at the same time by 20 EF 2000s to 230, although its workshare is to increase by 5 per cent to 38 per cent because of reductions in planned procurement by its other two partners. Italy has cut its original EF 2000 commitment from 165 to 130, and Spain from 100 to 87. The RAF has also indicated possible follow-up order requirements for another 70 or so EF 2000s, however, for long-term Harrier GR.Mk 7 replacements. If endorsed by the Bundestag, the revised orders and workshare agreement will clear the way towards the critical production investment phase commitment for Eurofighter due later this year.

More than 100 test flights had been completed in 1995 by the three

EF 2000 prototypes currently flying, most of which have been done by Britain's DA.2 development aircraft from Warton. DA.3 is also accumulating "highly satisfactory" experience with Eurojet's EJ200 turbofans in Italy, but progress with DASA's DA.1 continues to be slow, mainly because of its spares contributions to keep the two other prototypes in commission.

French funding doubts as NH-90 helicopter flies

While the European NH-90 utility helicopter prototype made a successful 40-minute first flight at Eurocopter France's Marignane facility on 18 December, French participation as prime contractor in the four-nation programme is threatened by recent major defence cuts. Reductions of 11.5 per cent in FY 1996 equipment appropriations to a revised total of FFr91 billion ($18.54 billion) resulted in a strategic procurement review scheduled for completion early in 1996, to provide the basis for a new and reduced long-term military spending programme for the 1997-2001 period.

Late last year, French Defence Minister Charles Millon gave assurances that funding for both the NH-90 and the Eurocopter Tiger helicopter programmes would remain in the revised FY 1996 defence budget. A National Assembly Defence Committee report at that time, however, claimed that the reduced budget would not allow simultaneous procurement of the NH-90 and the Tiger, and recommended that the former project should be cancelled.

Current indications are that French NH-90 participation could well be affected by the funding cuts, and accompanying delays in the original

Eurofighter EF 2000 DA.1 lands after a rare test flight from Manching. In early 1996 the future of EF 2000 seemed more secure following the increase of the German purchase by 40 aircraft to partially replace some of the Tornado fleet. Previously, the Luftwaffe was looking only at air defence aircraft to replace F-4Fs. The additional requirement has solved problems between the UK and Germany over workshare.

development time-scales. France plans to buy 220 NH-90s in the currently proposed 729-aircraft programme, compared with 272 by Germany, 214 by Italy and 20 by the Netherlands. French Eurocopter, however, has a 42.4 per cent share of the joint-venture NH Industries company, and its NATO Helicopter Management Agency (NAHEMA), as well as of the $2.18 billion total R&D budget. This compares with 26.9 per cent held by Agusta, 24 per cent by Eurocopter Deutschland, and 6.7 per cent by Fokker.

At the moment, Eurocopter France is responsible for the first three 'common' NH-90 prototypes (PT1, PT2 and PT3), all powered by twin Rolls-Royce/Turboméca RTM322 turboshafts. Eurocopter Deutschland is building PT4 as the first dedicated tactical transport helicopter version (TTH) with a rear loading ramp for vehicles and other cargo of up to 5,500 lb (2495 kg). Agusta has responsibility for PT5, the fifth and final prototype, which will be the first naval frigate helicopter version (NFH) for ASW/ASV roles with GE T700 engines for Italian requirements, and also for the 'Iron Bird' used for static testing.

Current plans are for Germany to acquire 120 army and 114 air force NH-90 TTH versions to replace Bell UH-1Ds, plus 38 NFHs as Sea King/Lynx replacements from 2002. France requires 160 TTHs to replace its army Pumas and Super Pumas, and 60 NFHs as Lynx/Super Frelon successors. Italy plans to acquire 150 TTHs and 64 NFHs to supersede army and naval Agusta-Bell 205/212/412s, while the Netherlands navy needs 20 NFHs as Lynx replacements.

With a maximum take-off weight of 8-10 metric tonnes, the NH-90 incorporates a number of advanced design features, including fly-by-wire controls, composite airframe panels and rotor blades, EFIS instrumentation, a titanium main rotor hub, and low acoustic, radar and infra-red signatures.

Bulgaria will operate this single Antonov An-30 on Open Skies missions, and in early 1996 was completing the necessary modifications. Bulgaria's main areas of interest are neighbours Turkey, Greece and Romania. A 10-km (6.2-mile) exclusion strip runs along the border with Yugoslavia and Macedonia, who were not signatories to the 16 February 1994 Open Skies treaty.

Europe

AUSTRIA:

New fighter evaluations

Evaluations have started by the Austrian air force (OeLk) of current lightweight fighters for replacement of its 20 or so Saab Drakens from the turn of the century. Main interest is in AMRAAM-armed ex-USAF or new Lockheed Martin F-16s, or the similarly-equipped Swedish JAS 39 Gripen. Twenty-four MiG-29s, plus six two-seat MiG-29UB combat trainers with BVR AA-10 or AA-12 AAMs, have also been offered in a counter-trade deal by MiG-MAPO.

BELGIUM:

ALFT relocated

Having withdrawn the last of its three squadrons from Germany on 30 October 1995, the FAeB's Aviation Légère de la Force Terrestre Belge (ALFT), or Belgian Light Army Aviation, is now fully established at Bierset, near Liege, in support of Belgium's 1st Mechanised Division within Eurocorps. Formerly based at Merzbrueck, near Aachen, the 18e Bataillon d'Helicoptères Anti-chars is ALFT's spearhead, with 15 Heli-TOW-armed Agusta A 109BA Hirundo anti-tank helicopters. It is backed at Bierset by the 17e Bn HATk, originally at Werl, near Düsseldorf, now operating as a tactical training unit with anti-tank and observation versions of the A 109 from the 46 originally ordered.

As the third former Germany-based unit, the 16e Bataillon d'Helicoptères de Liaison moved its 15 or so Aérospatiale SA 318C Alouette IIs and four Britten-Norman BN-2A-21 Islander light STOL twins from Butzweilerhof in September 1995, to Bierset, where the unit is continuing its liaison and light transport roles. Its Alouette IIs are now becoming overdue for replacement. ALFT also operates a second base at Brasschaat, home of its Ecole d'Aviation, also known as the 15e Escadrille, with Agusta A 109s and other army aviation types for basic training.

CZECH REPUBLIC:

MiG-21 upgrade debate

Recent selection by the Defence Ministry in Prague of Israel Aircraft Industries to upgrade 24 single-seat and six two-seat Czech air force MiG-21s represents a further stage in its long-running dispute with the Czech government on future fighter procurement policies. Parliament considers the upgrade of old military equipment to be a waste of money, but little funding is currently available to finance procurement of F-16s or similar modern combat aircraft, despite these now being offered to Central European countries by the US government. The

Polish technicians check one of the Czech air force's MiG-29s prior to its delivery to the Polish air force's 1.PLM 'Warszawa' fighter regiment at Minsk-Mazowiecki. In 1995 the Czech government took the decision to trade the MiGs, the deal including the supply of new W-3 Sokol helicopters. One MiG-29UB and four single-seaters flew to Poland on 21 December, two more on 29 December, and the remaining four followed in January 1996.

recent inclusion of lease prospects by the US for surplus F-16s in offers to the Czech, Hungarian and Polish air forces may possibly change this situation, although their refurbishment would also need to be funded, and would apparently not include combat equipment.

Backed by the Defence Ministry, the air force has regarded upgrading its existing aircraft as the only realistic financial option, and has been seeking to finalise a $100 million contract with IAI to modernise some of its 90 or so MiG-21s. Although suspended for the moment, this programme – if approved – would involve fitting Lavi-type avionics, including an Elta 2032 multi-mode radar and advanced nav/attack systems, plus other new equipment supplied and integrated by IAI, but installed locally by Letecke Opravny Kbely (LOK) and LOM Prague.

FINLAND:

New Russian SAMs

Three Ulyanosk BUK-1M Ural (SA-11 'Gadfly') mobile surface-to-air missile batteries valued at FMk850 million ($202 million) are being supplied to the Finnish defence forces through a Russian counter-trade programme. In Finland, the SA-11s will replace ageing S-125 Pechora (SA-3 'Goa') SAMs in 1996, their 9K37M1 missiles offering a range increase to about 17 nm (20 miles; 32 km). Their cost will be offset through some of Russia's $1.3 billion trade deficit with Finland.

FRANCE:

More CN.235s

Orders worth Pts13 billion ($104.2 million) were placed with CASA in February by the French air force for seven more CN.235 tactical transports. These will supplement an initial batch of six similar aircraft now operating with ETL 162 at Creil, plus two with GAM 82 in the Pacific. Delivery of the second batch is expected from 1997, this order being linked with follow-up purchases of the AS 532 Cougar by the Spanish army.

French missile export orders

Recent new MATRA contracts have included orders for Mistral air defence missile systems comprising one for naval use in the Asia-Pacific region, and the other in Latin America for

both maritime and shore-based air defence applications. This brings total orders for the fire-and-forget Mistral to more than 12,000 from 18 customers, including five in the Asia Pacific region. Negotiations are continuing for further orders from six more countries.

MATRA has also received a contract for the first time from an unspecified Central European country to equip its Soviet-supplied MiG-21, MiG-23 and MiG-29 combat aircraft with an initial batch of "some hundreds" of Magic 2 close-combat air-to-air missiles. This order is the result of negotiations with the Czech Republic, Hungary, Poland, Romania and Slovakia, some of which are still continuing. Successful infra-red seeker target acquisition trials, it may be recalled, were undertaken in mid-1995 with six captive MATRA 550 Magic 2s on two Czech air force MiG-23ML 'Flogger-Gs' at the French service flight-test centre at Mont-de-Marsan.

The new order is regarded by MATRA as particularly significant in resulting from competitive evaluations of both equivalent US AAMs and the Russian R 73/AA-11 'Archer', the latter with the reputation of being the best weapon in its class worldwide. With a helmet-mounted sight, however, Magic 2 can apparently match its off-boresight capability of up to 90°, and MATRA claims more autonomous capabilities than the Russian weapon.

Qatar is another recent Magic 2 customer. An order was also announced by MATRA in February from the British government for a new MATRA-Marconi Skynet 4 communications satellite. Aérospatiale has announced orders for three MM-40 Exocet Block 2 anti-ship missile batteries for coastal defence in two unspecified countries. With a 38-nm

The Luftwaffe contingent for UN operations over Bosnia, which set up base at Piacenza in Italy, consisted of eight Tornado ECRs from JBG 32 and six reconnaissance-configured aircraft from AKG 51, grouped together as Einsatzgeschwader (combat wing) 1. A new light grey scheme was applied in washable distemper (on reconnaissance aircraft, above), but when the first ECR returned to Lechfeld after six weeks of operations it was decided to adopt a permanent three-tone scheme (on ECR, below). Painting was undertaken at Erding.

The Monteprandone works (formerly BredaNardi) of the Agusta company licence-built 50 NH-500Es for the Italian air force's central helicopter training establishment, the Scuolo Volo Elicotteri at Frosinone. As demonstrated by this armed example, the school's aircraft wear the badge of the 72º Stormo.

(44-mile; 70-km) range, the latest Exocet incorporates enhanced ECM resistance and better target identification and tactical situation analysis.

ITALY:

Alenia/Lockheed launch C-27J Mini-Hercules

Alenia and Lockheed are offering a low-cost next-generation companion to the high-tech Hercules 2. The aircraft is a combination of the Allison AE2100D3 turboprops and Dowty six-bladed composite propellers powering the new Lockheed C-130J with the service-proved Alenia G222 tactical transport, now operated by the USAF as the C-27. Development and marketing of the proposed C-27'J' is being studied on a joint basis by Alenia and Lockheed as part of the industrial offset requirements of the Italian Defence Ministry for its planned purchase of up to 16 C-130Js.

More than 100 of the T64P4P- and Tyne-powered G222s have so far been sold by Alenia, including 10 C-27A Spartan versions to the USAF. When incorporated with the C-130J's power-plants each developing 4,200 shp (3130 kW) instead of the T64's 3,400 shp (2535 kW), and employing digital fuel control, the C-27J offers improvements in reliability and maintainability of up to 50 per cent, plus 30 per cent lower operating costs, 12 per cent shorter take-off run, 15 per cent faster cruise, 30 per cent higher cruise ceiling and 35 per cent more range.

With an increased maximum take-off weight of 66,140 lb (30000 kg), the C-27J would have a maximum speed of 305 kt (350 mph; 562 km/h), and a range increase from 675 nm to 1,150 nm (777 miles to 1324 miles; 1250 to 2130 km) with maximum payload of 13,600 lb (6168 kg) instead of 12,700 lb (5760 kg). It would also incorporate most of the C-130J's improved digital cockpit avionics, and would be available from late 1999 at about half the price of the Hercules 2, or $20 million, fly-away. A potential market for up to 120 C-27Js is foreseen over the next 10 years.

Aermacchi acquires Redigo trainer programme

Valmet's suspended L-90TP Redigo light turboprop trainer programme has been purchased by Aermacchi. The programme was completed in Finland in 1994 with delivery of the last eight off the line to the emergent air force of Eritrea, following 10 to the Finnish air force and a similar number to the Mexican navy. The Italian company intends to re-establish the Redigo production line at Venegono, and to offer the redesignated M-290TP as part of an all-through training package with its MB.339 advanced and lead-in fighter trainers. This suggests that Aermacchi, which plans to complete its first locally-produced Redigo next spring, may have a specific and major customer in mind with a positive requirement for a package of this type.

LITHUANIA:

More L-39s required

Finance is being sought by the Lithuanian government for the purchase of eight Aero L-39ZA armed light jet trainers from the Czech Republic for the newly-formed national air force (Karines Oro Pejegos). This already operates four L-39C jet trainers, plus nine ex-Polish MiG-21s, a few Antonov An-2, An-24V and An-26RV transport aircraft, and 12 Mi-8 utility helicopters inherited from the former Soviet Union.

NETHERLANDS:

Army UAV order

Four Sperwer unmanned air vehicle systems have been ordered by the Dutch army for tactical surveillance through a FFr400 million ($81 million) contract with SAGEM in France. Based on the lightweight Crécerelle UAV in service with the French army, Sperwer comprises a tailless delta airframe of mainly composite construction powered by a small piston engine in a pusher installation. Apart from eight reusable UAVs, each Sperwer system includes a catapult launch ramp, a recovery system and ground operations centre, operated by a four-man crew. The UAVs are fitted with Iris high-definition infra-red cameras offering a field of view under ground-station control. Their imagery is relayed to the command and control station for real-time analysis.

ROMANIA:

MiG-21 upgrade progress

Romanian air force plans to upgrade 110 of its MiG-21MF 'Fishbed-Js' are progressing on schedule since the programme was launched in 1993. The endeavour is being undertaken jointly by Israel's Elbit as prime contractor and Aerostar in Romania. Two standards of upgrade are involved for 85 ground-attack versions of Aviatiei Militare MiG-21s, a number of which are now flying, and 25 to be optimised for air-to-air roles. Both variants share a largely common 1553B digitised avionics suite, including single monochromatic and colour cockpit displays, HOTAS, and an El-Op head-up display. The air superiority version, however, has an Elta EL/M 2032 multi-mode radar with lookdown/shootdown capability instead of a ranging radar and enhanced weapon capabilities.

The Elta radar-equipped prototype of the Romanian air superiority version made its first flight in August 1995, two months ahead of schedule, and had completed 50 hours of successful development by February 1996. It is expected to have provision for Elbit's display and sight helmet (DASH), which may be used in conjunction with Rafael's advanced Python 3 all-aspect close-combat IR-guided AAM. For air-to-ground roles, Romanian MiG-21 armament is expected to include 500-lb (227-kg) Griffin Mk 82 laser-guided HE bombs and other precision munitions when carrying laser illumination pods.

C-130s expected

Four ex-USAF Lockheed C-130B Hercules are expected within the next few months for service with the Romanian air force, as part of US aid programmes. These will supplement 10 Antonov An-24s, six An-26s and three An-30s currently used by Romania as military freight transports.

Rapier SAM interest

Discussions were being finalised late in 1995 between the Romanian and UK governments for the purchase of a batch of Rapier low-level air defence missiles from British Aerospace Dynamics. Romania could therefore become the first Eastern European country to buy Rapier SAM systems, which are also being offered to the other Visegrad countries including the Czech Republic, Hungary, Poland and Slovakia. Clearance is expected for these to receive the Rapier B1X export version, which is generally similar to the Rapier Field Standard B, now being superseded in the British armed forces by the later Field Standard C or Rapier 2000.

On 28 September 1995 WTD 61 aircraft 98+01 made the Luftwaffe's last RF-4E flight, 25 years and 13 days after this example's first flight at St Louis. Previously serialled 35+01, the WTD 61 aircraft was the first of the Luftwaffe's order so it was fitting that it should be the last. Far from being retired, the aircraft was repainted in Turkish air force colours, and left Manching for its new operator on 21 November.

Above: Although the F-104G has not flown in German military hands since the last WTD 61 flight on 22 May 1991, a few remain on the strength of ground schools. This example is used by TSLw 1 at Kaufbeuren for technical training.

RUSSIA:

Western equipment considered for gunship upgrade

For the first time since World War II, the Russian army is considering acquiring Western weapons systems for a new upgrade programme launched for its vast fleet of Mil Mi-24 attack helicopters. Mil's First Deputy General Designer Gueorgi Sinelchikov has revealed that while the Mil group is going ahead with building two prototypes of the next-generation Mi-28N heavy attack-helicopter in competition with the Kamov Ka-52, its rotors and transmission systems are now to be retrofitted to upgraded Russian Army Aviation Mi-24Ms. A detailed mock-up of this installation has already been exhibited at the Paris air show on an Mi-24 which was also fitted with Sextant Avionique and Thomson-CSF avionics and night-vision sensors, for a proposed Mi-35M (the export designation) upgrade.

In effect, the Mi-35M modifications are now to be applied to Mi-24Ms, for which the final choice of mission systems avionics has still to be made. The French avionics package includes a navigation computer with GPS inputs, integrated with a Chlio FLIR, mounted alongside the radio command system's chin fairing for the anti-tank missiles of the 'Hind', plus a dedicated collimated display. Pilot and forward-seat weapons systems operator will each have cockpit display screens, with an additional Sextant CH-100 HUD for the aircraft commander and provision for Thomson-CSF NVGs.

Other changes in the Mi-35M will also be incorporated in the Mi-24M, including its weight-saving non-retracting landing gear, shortened stub wings and uprated Mi-28 main gearbox, to cope with power increases from the Klimov TV3 117VR turboshafts' emergency ratings of up to 3,000 shp (2237 kW). With a reduced equipped empty weight of 17,747 lb (8049 kg) compared with the original 19,004 lb (8620 kg), the Mi-24M will lift the same weapons load to an increased OGE hover ceiling of 9,843 ft (3000 m). The Mi-24M prototype is due to fly by the end of 1996.

Continuing the next-generation Mi-28 attack helicopter programme, the two prototypes are being built jointly by the Mil OKB and Rostvertol, with the first undergoing final assembly in Moscow and the second in Rostov (where Mi-24 production is still continuing for Russian Army Aviation). Mil's first Mi-28N was scheduled to fly in March or April 1996.

Display team loss

A bad weather accident in Vietnam on 11 December 1995 resulted in the loss of two Sukhoi Su-27 and one two-seat Su-27UB 'Flanker' fighters, plus all four pilots, of the Russian air forces (VVS). These were from the 'Russian

On 16 November 1995 MiG-MAPO chief test pilot Roman Taskaev accomplished the first wet refuelling of a standard MiG-29 from an Il-78 'Midas'. The retractable probe adds 65 kg (143 lb) to the aircraft's weight, and associated equipment a further 30 kg (66 lb). Maximum flow rate is 900 litres (238 US gal) per minute, and the aircraft needs approximately eight minutes to fill its tanks (including three drop tanks). The probe system is being fitted to Malaysian MiG-29s as part of an upgrade package.

Knights' (Russkiye Vityazi) national display team, comprising three Su-27s and two Su-27UBs, which were returning home from participation in the LIMA '95 air show at Langkawi, in Malaysia. All five Su-27s of the display team were formating on an escorting VVS Ilyushin Il-76 for an instrument approach in bad weather into Cam Ranh Bay airfield. The fact that the three aircraft which crashed into high ground were in tight formation on the starboard side of the Il-76 on its final right-hand approach turn to the runway at about 1,800 ft (548 m), with the remaining two Su-27s on its left, would appear to indicate that the other two aircraft escaped similar destruction by a matter of a few yards. Minimum descent altitude at that point was apparently 4,500 ft (1372 m). Russian air force C-in-C Colonel General Piotr Deneiken castigated both the Il-76 crew and the approach radar controller for incorrect procedures which resulted in this accident.

SPAIN:

Second-batch Hornets delivered

Delivery took place on 28 December to Zaragoza air base in Spain of the first six of 24 ex-US naval McDonnell Douglas F/A-18A/B Hornets recently ordered by the EdA at a cost of $300 million. They were flown from NAS Cecil Field, Florida, following structural refurbishment and the installation there of new General Electric F404-400 powerplants. The EdA is expecting to receive its remaining 18 Hornets over the next three years, to supplement original 1986 deliveries of 60 EF-18As and 12 two-seat EF-18B combat trainers.

Thomson-CSF gains Mirage F1 upgrade contract

Thomson-CSF has been nominated as prime contractor, with CASA and Amper Programas in Madrid, for a FFr700 million ($142 million) programme to upgrade 55 Dassault Mirage F1CE/EE/BEs (C.14A/Bs and CE.14As) of the Spanish air force (EdA). Sextant Avionique will provide much of the equipment to modify the Mirages to a new tactical ground-attack configuration, while extending their useful service lives to around 2015. This will include liquid crystal cockpit and head-up displays, laser gyro INS/GPS, Have Quick 2 com-munications systems and encrypted Mode 4 digital IFF. A radar ranging function will also be added to the Mirage F1s' Cyrano IV fire-control radar.

SF-5B upgrade completed

After some delays following a partnership dispute with Bristol Aerospace, CASA had completed the upgrade of 22 EdA licence-built two-seat Northrop SF-5B (AE.9) combat trainers by November 1995. These aircraft are now back in operation with EdA's Ala 23 wing at Talavera, following the installation of new structural components and new VOR/ILS/DME-40 navigation systems, AN/APX-101 IFF and RWR/chaff/flare equipment.

More army Cougars

Spanish army aviation (FAMET) has selected the AS 532UL Cougar from Eurocopter France for its new transport helicopter requirement, and in February 1996 was seeking government approval for the purchase of 15, costing Pts26 billion ($206 million). This was expected to be a formality, since the French government had agreed to buy another seven CASA CN.235 tactical transports for the EdA as offsets for additional Spanish military Super Puma (Cougar) procurement. The Cougar was chosen in preference to the Sikorsky Black Hawk, FAMET having operated 18 AS 332B1 Super Puma versions since 1988. Delivery is scheduled from 1997 at about four per year.

SWEDEN:

Third Gripen production batch discussed

Negotiations have begun between the Swedish Defence Materiel Administration (FMV) and the JAS Industry Group to finalise price and delivery details of a third batch of up to 80 JAS 39 Gripen advanced multi-role fighters for the Swedish air force. These are required to equip the 12 SAF fighter wings planned for service in the early 2000s, and could increase total Gripen procurement to 220 aircraft. Details still to be decided include the number of third-batch Gripens that available funding will permit, and whether these would incorporate upgrade improvements to the proposed JAS 39C standard.

SWITZERLAND:

More Hornets required

Flight testing started early in 1996 of the first two Hornet air superiority fighters, of 34 on order for the Swiss air force at a cost of $2.3 billion. These were two-seat F/A-18D combat trainer versions (J-5231/2) built by McDonnell Douglas in St Louis, and are being followed by the remaining 32 (26 Cs and six Ds) assembled by the

The small Tu-160 'Blackjack' fleet has returned to Russian soil at Engels AB, but operations have been severely hampered by lack of fuel and essential maintenance items. Operational aircraft wear this all-white scheme.

Tupolev Tu-134s are used in small numbers by the Russian bomber force as trainers. The Tu-134UBL supports the Tu-160 fleet, while the Tu-134BSh trains Tu-22M crews. Both variants have long pointed nose extensions, unlike this otherwise similar aircraft, whose bloated radome suggests fitment of a different type of radar, perhaps that of the Tu-95MS.

Swiss Federal Aircraft Factory at Emmen. Delivery of these AIM-120 AMRAAM-armed fighters is due for completion in 1999, and SAFAAC C-in-C Lieutenant General Fernand Carrel has indicated a requirement for a similar follow-up batch to fulfil ground-attack and reconnaissance roles previously undertaken by the recently-retired Hawker Hunters.

UAV orders

Four ADS 95 Ranger unmanned air vehicle systems are to be supplied to the Swiss armed forces by Oerlikon-Contraves for battlefield surveillance from a recent $200 million contract. These have been developed in conjunction with Israel Aircraft Industries from IAI's 551-lb (250-kg) twin-boom all-composite Ranger UAV, powered by a 38-hp (29-kW) pusher piston engine, for initial delivery in mid-1998. Apart from several air vehicles, each Ranger system includes duplicated truck-mounted catapult launchers, communications terminals and ground control units.

TURKEY:

French F-5 upgrade contract

France's SOGERMA/SOCEA subsidiary of Aérospatiale has joined the ranks of Northrop F-5 upgrade specialists with the award of a $250 million three-year contract as prime contractor to modernise 70 F-5A/Bs of the Turkish air force (THK). According to the US Triton Systems Corp., as financier

of the Turkish programme, 36 of the upgraded F-5s will be retained for THK service and the remaining 34 offered for sale elsewhere to recoup much of the overall programme costs. New avionics to provide lead-in training for F-16 and similar fighters will be incorporated by Israel's Elbit company during the upgrade, which will also involve airframe structural reinforcements to extend the fatigue lives of the Turkish aircraft. Development of an upgraded THK F-5 prototype is due to start in June.

UNITED KINGDOM:

Hercules 2 delivery plans

Somewhat surprisingly, the prototype Lockheed Martin C-130J Hercules 2 (c/n 5408), which is also the first RAF aircraft, was in full USAF markings and overall grey paint scheme when it was formally rolled out at Lockheed Martin's Marietta plant on 18 October 1995. It also carries the USAF tail number 93-3026, and the only clue to its RAF identity is from the '865' flanking its nose, derived from its British serial, ZH865. Still more curiously, the USAF had its own C-130J roll-out two days later, on 20 October, when the first short-fuselage version (c/n 5413) emerged with similar ceremony from the Martin Marietta line. After initial flight tests, both USAF C-130Js will undergo operational evaluation with Air Combat Command's 314th Airlift Wing at Little Rock AFB, Arkansas.

Formally accepted by deputy C-in-C Strike Command (and well-

known warbird pilot) Air Marshal Sir John Allison, the first C-130J was due to begin its year-long flight development in December. RAF project pilot Flight Lieutenant Mark Robinson is participating in this alongside Lockheed Martin and USAF test crews. Service trials with the Defence and Test Establishment are then due to start at Boscombe Down before the end of 1996, to be followed by CA clearance and initial RAF service.

This will be with No. 24 Sqn at Lyneham, which will receive most of the first 15 RAF Hercules 2s from July 1997. These will all be stretched Dash 30 (C.Mk 4) versions, after which No. 70 Sqn will then re-equip at a later stage from the same base with the remaining 10 RAF C-130Js on order. A decision will then have been made as to whether these, plus options on another five, will be short- (C.Mk 5) or long-fuselage variants, or a mixture of both. All RAF C-130Js will be equipped for air refuelling, with a new removable probe flanking the port flight-deck, and swing-down head-up display screens for tactical operations.

Nimrod R.Mk 1 replacement started

As anticipated, a Royal Air Force BAe Nimrod MR.Mk 2, XV249, is being

modified by British Aerospace at Woodford to replace the Nimrod R.Mk 1P special missions aircraft lost in a ditching accident off Kinloss on 16 May 1995. Most of the Nimrod R.Mk 1's special ECM equipment had been removed for a major airframe inspection and had not been replaced when the aircraft ditched on a flight test after completion of this work, and is now being used for the current conversion programme.

RAF Tornado losses

Three RAF Tornados were lost over a two-day period in January, in three discrete accidents. On 10 January, two of a formation of three Tornado F.Mk 3s from No. 56 (Reserve) Sqn, which is the ADV Operational Conversion Unit at Coningsby, collided at an estimated 700-800 ft (213-244 m) near Sleaford during air combat training. All four crew members ejected with minor injuries, and were airlifted by RAF Sea King to Lincoln County Hospital for overnight observation. Both Tornados crashed in open farmland near Digby, with no ground casualties. On the following day, a Tornado GR.Mk 1 from No. 14 Sqn at RAF Bruggen crashed into a wood near Albachten, south of Munster. Once again, both crew members made successful ejections.

Middle East

EGYPT:

Black Hawk purchases

An FMS contract was being finalised late in 1995 by the Egyptian air force for two Sikorsky UH-60L Black Hawk transport helicopters. These would follow the earlier EAF acquisition of two generally similar Sikorsky S-70A-21s.

ISRAEL:

Aircraft disposals

Phase-out plans for a number of first- and second-line Israeli military aircraft have been revealed by SIBAT, which is the Foreign Defence Assistance and Defence Export Organisation of the Defence Ministry in Tel Aviv. This is the sole government agency in charge of licensing, control and supervision of Israeli defence exports. Current disposals include unspecified totals of J-79-GE-J1E-engined Kfir C-2 and C-7

fighter-bombers with M-2001 ranging radars, and F-4 Phantoms with APQ-120 fire-control radars. Up to 150 surplus IDF/AF Kfirs were in storage at one time. Also offered for disposal are a number of Douglas A-4H/N Skyhawks with Pratt & Whitney J-52-408 turbojets and extended tailpipes to minimise their infra-red signatures.

Support aircraft retirements include six Douglas C-47s, built between 1941-1944 but with flying times of only 9,357-21,478 hours; 10 MDH 500D and five MD 500E armed helicopters with Allison 250C-20B turboshaft engines; and nine Bell UH-1Ns with Pratt & Whitney Canada PT6T3 engines.

In addition to the primary operational equipment of Canberra PR.Mk 9s, No. 39 (1 PRU) Sqn also operates two PR.Mk 7s. This variant is retained for the chaff-laying role, using modified wingtip tanks previously used by the T.Mk 17.

Tornado in a strange environment: in the winter of 1995/96 eight GR.Mk 1s were deployed to MCB Yuma, Arizona, for Exercise Arid Thunder, in which Tornado crews utilised the large range areas and excellent weather to practise live weapon drops. While at Yuma the RAF detachment (manned in rotation by various squadrons) was invited to participate in the major USMC exercise Scorpion Wind.

Sino-Pakistani Super 7 development of the MiG-21, the FC-1, powered by a single MiG-29-type Klimov RD-93 turbofan, and without fly-by-wire controls, represents a relatively modest and low-cost advance in technology, although with a high planned performance. First flight of a prototype is still planned for 1997.

New turbofan developed for China's K-8 trainer

CATIC's K-8 Karakoram jet trainer shown at Asian Aerospace '96 in Singapore was the first example to production standard from the Nanchang factory. It was a follow-on to one of the four flight prototypes which appeared at Changi in 1994. Like six more pre-production examples being evaluated by the Pakistani air force, the prototype and initial production K-8s are all powered by AlliedSignal/Garrett TFE731 turbofans. Political and financial difficulties, however, may lead to replacement of the PAF's current powerplant and Collins EFIS equipment in K-8s planned for service with the air force of the People's Liberation Army (AF/PLA).

Development of an indigenous turbofan in a similar thrust category to the K-8's 3,600-lb (16-kN) TFE731-2A is being undertaken in Hunan Province by the Zhuzhou Power Manufacturing factory within the South Motive Power & Machinery Complex. The Wopen WS-11 appears to be at a relatively early bench-running stage, however, so either the first K-8s to be ordered for the AF/PLA will be Garrett-powered or they will not enter service until the turn of the century.

As joint developer and first customer for the K-8, the Pakistani air force has completed its initial evaluation of the six pre-production K-8s at the PAF Academy, Risalpur, which shows that they meet the specified requirements to replace the current Cessna T-37s as a basic trainer. Further flight testing has also been continuing with one of the original K-8 prototypes at Pakistan's Aeronautical Complex (PAC) at Kamra, where fin and tailplane production is part of the PAF unit's contribution to the joint programme. Second stage evaluation is now in progress to assess the K-8's capabilities in advanced training roles and its suitability to take over these tasks from China's Shenyang FT-5 developments of the MiG-17 in current PAF service at Mianwali.

Six more K-8s expected to arrive in Pakistan later in 1996 will incorporate some of the minor changes in cockpit

JORDAN:

F-16s in US arms package

As expected, an initial batch of 12 ex-USAF Lockheed Martin F-16A and four two-seat F-16B Fighting Falcon advanced air superiority fighters, together with M60A3 main battle tanks and other military equipment, have been included in a military assistance package worth over $300 million authorised in January for the Jordanian armed forces. That country has requested up to 72 F-16s to replace the RJAF's current Northrop F-5E/Fs and Mirage F1s, as well as 200 M1A2 MBTs and more Improved Hawk surface-to-air missile systems, as part of US military assistance totalling up to $10 billion sought over the next decade. FMS notifications are still awaited for the initial RJAF batch of F-16s, which are expected to include associated weapons, support equipment and training.

Far East

BRUNEI:

New equipment orders

Confirmation of Brunei's long-awaited order for three IPTN CN.235MPA twin-turboprop maritime patrol aircraft came late in 1995 with selection of Boeing ARGOSystems as prime contractor for their mission avionics systems integration. Selection is still awaited of the main avionics components, including the search radar, forward-looking infra-red, electronic support measures, IFF and related systems. The Air Wing of the Royal Brunei Armed Forces is not expecting its first CN.235MPA until 1999, but has ordered a single transport version for earlier delivery to use for training and general utility roles.

Royal Brunei Armed Forces Air Wing transport helicopter requirements are now expected to be satisfied by a late 1995 order for four Sikorsky S-70A (UH-60L) Black Hawks. Delivery is scheduled in 1997-98.

CHINA:

Su-27 production planned

A major shift in the balance of air power in the Far East seems probable from China's reported deal with Russia's state-owned Rosvooruzhenye arms sales agency for the licensed production of Sukhoi's formidable Su-27 'Flanker' long-range advanced air superiority fighter. Signed late in 1995, the new licence agreement follows China's initial acquisition of 26 Su-27s in 1992. These aircraft were recently deployed in military manoeuvres in the Dongshan Island area, and an additional 24 are expected later in 1996.

According to Russian air force C-in-C General Piotr Deneikin, reported by the Interfax news agency, China's Su-27 production programme has a potential long-term value of up to $2.5 billion. It will include the construction of a new factory in China, as well as assistance with the training of Chinese technicians and management personnel. Su-27 output from China is therefore not expected to begin until the turn of the century. It could then involve considerable numbers, since the Chinese armed forces have requirements to replace 2,500 combat aircraft by about 2005.

FC-1 fighter plans continue

Discussions are approaching finalisation between China, Pakistan and several European and Russian avionics companies concerning the equipment (including a fire-control radar) for the joint CATIC/PAF FC-1 lightweight fighter project. This is designed to replace MiG-21s, F-7s, A-5s, Mirages and F-5s in the early 2000s. Target deadline for equipment selection is late June, if agreement can be reached, to complete the design stage.

As a follow-on to the proposed

24 November 1995 marked the end of an era when the last dedicated transport VC10 C.Mk 1 (XR808) departed its base at Brize Norton for Bournemouth-Hurn. When it returns to service with No. 10 Sqn it will be in C.Mk 1K tanker/transport configuration, having been modified by FR Aviation.

Military Aviation Review

layout and equipment required by the PAF from its initial evaluation. This has totalled about 2,000 flying hours, in which is included initial flight testing. Similar evaluation procedures with small batches of K-8s are planned by the AF/PLA, although no orders have yet been received from China, where decisions are still awaited on the AF/PLA's choice of powerplant and avionics installation. K-8s are also being offered for export, at a fly-away unit cost of around $3.5 million.

INDONESIA:

PAF F-16 interest

Indonesia has responded to a mid-1995 offer by US State Secretary Warren Christopher, made also to the Philippines, of the 28 F-16A/Bs ordered by Pakistan through the Peace Gate III and IV programmes for $658 million, but embargoed by Congress before delivery. Negotiations have been reported by the Indonesian air force for up to 12 of the ex-Pakistani Block 15 F-16s, which incorporate Operational Capabilities Upgrades and are of a similar standard to the eight F-16As and four two-seat F-16Bs delivered to the TNI/AU from late 1989.

JAPAN:

F-2s reduced in defence cuts

Plans by the Japanese Air Self-Defence Force (JASDF) to buy 141 Mitsubishi FS-X developments of the F-16, now designated F-2s, have been curtailed by recent budgetary cuts in the new Y25.15 trillion ($235.5 billion) 1996-2000 medium-term military procurement programme. On 15 December 1995, the Japanese Cabinet approved a production programme for 130 F-2s, deleting 11 two-seat F-2s from the originally planned total; this reduces JASDF procurement of this variant to 47, plus 83 single-seat versions.

Nine of the deleted F-2s had been intended for the JASDF's 'Blue Impulse' aerobatic display team, and the other two for planned reserves. The revised total will still allow three squadrons operating 74 Mitsubishi F-1s from Misawa to re-equip with a similar number of F-2s, plus 12 for an OCU, eight for the Tactical Fighter Training Group, two for maintenance training and the remainder for rotational reserves. The two prototypes so far flown had achieved 15 test flights by 1 February. First flight of the prototype FS-X took place at Nagoya on 7 October 1995, followed by the second aircraft on 13 December.

Funding has now been approved for the first 47 F-2s in the new five-year defence plan. Other main aircraft totals include (with previous five-year procurement in parentheses) four Mitsubishi/MDC F-15DJ fighters (29), 59 Kawasaki T-4 intermediate trainers (68), and six Kawasaki/Boeing CH-47J transport helicopters (two) for the JASDF; 37 Mitsubishi/Sikorsky SH-60J ASW helicopters (31) for the JMSDF; and four Fuji/Bell AH-1S attack helicopters (18), plus 12 Kawasaki/Boeing CH-47J helicopters for the JGSDF (12). JASDF proposals to acquire four long-range tanker/transports have been deferred for about

Photographed while visiting Kunsan AB is a RoKAF F-16C Block 52. The aircraft serves with the 161st Fighter Squadron of the 19th Fighter Wing, based at Jungwon AB near Chungju. Unlike USAF Block 50/52s, the Korean aircraft are LANTIRN-capable.

In November 1995 deliveries of the McDonnell Douglas F-15S began to the Royal Saudi Air Force. The aircraft is based on the F-15E but with a slightly downgraded capability (but not as dramatically cut as originally envisaged). The order totals 72.

three years. FY 1996 defence spending will now total Y4.85 trillion ($45.42 billion), an increase of 2.6 per cent over the previous year.

Fratricidal shoot-down

The pilot of a Japanese Air Self-Defence Force F-15J Eagle ejected safely over the Sea of Japan on 22 November 1995, after his aircraft was hit by an AIM-9L Sidewinder AAM launched by accident from an accompanying F-15 during air combat training. Both F-15s, plus four others taking part in the exercise, were from the 303rd Squadron of the 6th Air Wing at Komatsu. After obtaining a lock-on to the target F-15 at a range of 5,900 ft (1798 m), and confirming his missile arming switch was off, Lieutenant Hino Junya made a 'simulated' AIM-9L launch, which turned into the real thing. Some 336 JASDF F-15J, F-4EJ and F-1 fighters were then briefly grounded for inspections of their fire-control and related sub-systems, while training procedures with live missiles were also reviewed. This was the JASDF's eighth F-15J loss from about 190 Mitsubishi-built Eagles delivered since 1982, of 220 on order.

SOUTH KOREA:

KTX-2 supersonic trainer design changes

Lockheed Martin influence is evident in the most recent design concepts of South Korea's ambitious $1.5-2 billion KTX-2 supersonic trainer project, which has been scaled down from Samsung's original twin-tailed Model 401, and now has a single vertical tail surface. Having progressively evolved to the current Model 406, the aircraft now resembles a slightly smaller F-16, with a similar fuselage-stowed main landing gear and inner leading-edge strakes, but has lateral intakes for a so-far unspecified 'new' turbofan in the GE F404 thrust category.

Its F-16 relationship is hardly surprising, since the KTX-2 design was evolved over a three-year period at Fort Worth by a joint Lockheed Mar-

tin/Korean engineering team, as part of the trade-off for the Korean Fighter Programme for the licensed production of 120 F-16C/D Block 52s. Samsung has been teamed with the government's Agency for Defence Development and other Korean aerospace companies, including Daewoo and Korean Air Lines, for the conceptual and preliminary design studies of the KTX-2. It is still looking for a risk-sharing partner to launch full-scale development, planned for 1997, and eventual production. First flight is scheduled for the year 2000.

Other KTX-2 design features includes digital triplex fly-by-wire flight controls, a nav/attack system with a mission computer for lead-in fighter training and light ground attack, seven hard points for external stores including wingtip air-to-air missile rails, and an internal 20-mm (0.787-in) cannon. Student and instructor have twin MDC ACES II ejection seats in stepped high-visibility cockpits, with twin head-down displays, and the front seat also has a head-up display. Maximum design speed is Mach 1.4, initial climb rate is 27,000 ft/min (137.16 m/sec), and service ceiling is 43,000 ft (13106 m). Dimensions include span of 29.9 ft (9.1 m), length of 42 ft (12.8 m) and height of 14.4 ft (4.4 m). Airframe design load factors are +9g and -3g.

MALAYSIA:

BAe Hawks' service units

The 18 two-seat Hawk 100 lead-in fighter trainers and 10 single-seat Hawk 200 light strike/interceptors recently delivered by British Aerospace to the Royal Malaysian air force are now operated by three RMAF squadrons. These appear to have mixed complements of both types, and comprise Nos 6 ('Dragon') Squadron at Kuantan, 9 ('Civet') Sqn at Labuan, in Eastern Malaysia near Brunei, and 15 Sqn, which operates as the Hawk OCU at Butterworth. Their wide dispersal and type mix have resulted in some maintenance teething troubles, further complicated by shortages of trained technicians, although these are now being overcome.

Large contingents of Russian ground and flight personnel have ensured

Seen shortly after an overhaul at Fokker's Woensdrecht plant is a Philippine air force F28. The aircraft is on the strength of the 250th Presidential Airlift Wing.

fewer problems with initial operation of the RMAF's 18 Kuantan-based MiG-29Ns. Contrary to earlier reports, these aircraft do not appear to be current MiG-29SE export versions, although they do incorporate many similar modification. MiG-29SEs are likely to be specified for the second batch of 18 now being actively considered by the RMAF to equip a second 'Fulcrum' squadron.

New helicopters evaluated

Following its recent acquisition of new combat and support equipment, including five of the last nine production Lockheed Martin C-130Hs, the Royal Malaysian air force is now concentrating on large-scale helicopter procurement. The 10 SA 316B Alouette IIIs of the newly formed Army Air Corps (AAC) are to be supplemented by 12-24 RMAF-operated attack helicopters, for which a wide range of international contenders is currently being evaluated. These are headed by MDH's AH-64D Apache, probably initially without its Longbow radar, in competition with Denel's CSH-2 Rooivalk. Evaluations have also been made of the Bell AH-1W Cobra, Eurocopter Tiger and Kamov Ka-50.

South Africa is also competing strongly with its Oryx upgrade of the SA 330 Puma for the army's six to 10 transport helicopter requirement, against the Bell 412, Boeing CH-47D, Eurocopter AS 532 Cougar and EH101. Another six helicopters of up to 14,000 lb (6350 kg) take-off weight are being sought for Malaysia's 10 ANZAC frigates and additional offshore patrol craft, from current evaluations of the Eurocopter AS 555SN Fennec, AS 565 Panther, Kaman SH-2G Super SeaSprite, Sikorsky SH-60B and S-76N, and Westland Super Lynx.

Fixed-wing transport plans

While awaiting six IPTN CN.235M tactical transports from Indonesian production, the RMAF has decided to upgrade its remaining dozen or so DHC-5 Caribou STOL transports, because of their extended range and capability to carry up to 40 troops. RMAF Caribou refurbishment is being undertaken in Malaysia by Airod, now independent of its former Lockheed shareholder, with help from Australia's Hawker de Havilland group.

PHILIPPINES:

Pinto jet trainer revival?

The possibility of a new lease of life for a 40-year-old US basic jet trainer design was recently raised by the chief of staff of the Philippine air force, Lieutenant General Arnulfo Acedera Jr, as part of PhilAF modernisation plans involving increased self-reliance and advances in technology. The first of 14 tadpole-shaped Temco TT-1 Pinto light trainers, powered by Continental J-69-T-9 turbojet of only 920

lb (4.1 kN) thrust, made its initial flight on 26 March 1956. Built for evaluation by the US Navy (which subsequently rejected the type), it was taken over 12 years later by Aeronca and American Jet Industries, who produced a Super Pinto development that was more realistically powered by a 2,850-lb (12.7-kN) General Electric CJ-610-4 turbojet and that had a 2-ft 6-in (0.76-m) longer rear fuselage.

Design and production rights, plus the sole AJI T-610 Super Pinto prototype, passed in the mid-1970s to Self-Reliance Development Wing of the Philippine air force at Nichols Air Base, where it was known as the Cali. Apart from planned PhilAF procurement, export prospects were explored in conjunction with the Philippine Aerospace Development Corporation. Interest flagged, however, when the prototype crashed in the early stages of flight testing.

General Acedera now maintains that the revival and eventual production of this project could provide considerable economies, amounting to about 33 per cent of the costs of the SIAI-Marcheti S.211 light jet trainers in current PhilAF service. These aircraft have experienced heavy attrition, five of the 18 originally delivered having been lost to date in mostly pilot-related accidents.

TAIWAN:

Last C-130H customer?

Taiwan was expected to finalise the purchase in December 1995 of the last four C-130H Hercules off Lockheed Martin's Marietta production line, before output changed to the radically new C-130J. These C-130H-30s would be the first stretched versions operated by the RoCAF, which had previously taken delivery of at least 14 standard C-130Hs.

THAILAND:

Hornet/AMRAAM procurement approved

Royal Thai air force insistence on acquiring the Hughes AIM-120 AMRAAM active radar-homing medium-range air-to-air missile to arm its initial batch of eight MDC F/A-18C/D Hornets has apparently paid off, and the initial $578 million procurement package will reportedly include 58 of these advanced weapons. Provision is also made for five MDC AGM-84 Harpoon anti-ship missiles, plus AIM-7M Sparrow and AIM-9L Sidewinder AAMs, FLIR, targeting and ECM systems. Contract signature was expected in April 1996, but delivery is not expected to start until the late 1990s.

In Thailand, the four F/A-18C and four two-seat F/A-18D Hornets will supplement the RTAF's F-16s, of which delivery began late in 1995 of its second batch of 12 new-build Lockheed Martin Block 15OCU F-16A and six two-seat F-16B fighters, to double its establishment of this type. The new F-16s are replacing the

Above: Wearing the lightning bolt badge of No. 19 Sqn, one of Malaysia's 18 MiG-29Ns streams its brake chute. At present the aircraft is fitted with the NO19ZM radar and is armed with R-73 'Archer' and R-27 'Alamo' missiles. In 1996/97 the Vympel R-77 missile will be integrated, together with an upgraded radar capable of engaging two targets simultaneously.

A new military type to appear is the SME Aerospace MD3-180, built in Malaysia as a light trainer for the RMAF. The design originated in Switzerland as the Datwyler MD3. The first Malaysian-built aircraft flew on 25 May 1995, and the first two were handed over to the RMAF on 7 December.

Northrop F-5E/Fs of No. 403 Sqn at Takhli, and supplementing 103 Sqn's F-16s at Korat.

More equipment orders

Having recently completed delivery of 36 L-39ZA armed light jet trainers to the Royal Thai air force, Aero Vodochody in the Czech Republic has received follow-up orders for four more. These will be delivered in two batches later in 1996. The RTAF has also indicated a requirement for another eight Pilatus PC-9 turboprop trainers, increasing its total procurement to 30.

Three AS 332L2 Super Puma Mk 2 helicopters have been ordered from Eurocopter by the Thai government for VIP transport operations with the RTAF. Two will be delivered in October, and the third by mid-1997. 1996 budget requests for the Thai armed forces have included Bt700 million ($27.64 million) for army helicopter gunships, and Bt418 million ($16.5 million) for unspecified RTAF missiles.

Six specially-modified Sikorsky S-76B helicopters, powered by two Pratt & Whitney Canada PT6B-36B turboshafts, have been ordered by the Royal Thai navy. They will be mainly land-based, and used for shore-to-ship naval support and utility missions, rep-

resenting the first S-76 applications of this kind. Delivery to the RTN is scheduled for 1996, followed by six Sikorsky S-70B Seahawks in 1997 to operate alongside the RTN's AV-8A(S) Harriers from the V/STOL carrier Chakri Naruebet.

Sikorsky is also developing an ASW/ASV version of its twin Turboméca Arriel 2S1-powered S-76C, with optional GEC-Marconi Seaspray 3700 L-band surveillance radar, FLIR Systems AN/AAQ-22 thermal imager, a towed Texas Instruments AN/ASQ-208(V) magnetic anomaly detector, Griffin G500-NH ESM, a Spectrolab SX-16 Nitesun searchlight and Honeywell SPZ-760 automatic flight control system with auto-hover. Twin 675-lb (306-kg) capacity stores pylons can accommodate BAeDD Sea Skua anti-ship missiles, homing torpedoes, depth charges, rockets or other weapons.

G222 delivery begins

Delivery started in the latter part of 1995 to the RTAF of the first of six Alenia G222 twin-turboprop tactical transports. These were ordered in late 1993 for a cost of Bt2.9 billion (then $117 million), with requirements for another six at a later stage to replace the RTAF's last Douglas C-47s and Fairchild C-123s.

Southern Asia

BANGLADESH:

Mushshaks delivered

Recent new equipment deliveries have included eight to 10 MFI-17 Mushshak primary trainers from extended Pakistani production from the Aeronautical Complex at Kamra. This has also resulted in deliveries of up to 24 Mushshaks to Iran.

INDIA:

More Su-30MKs sought

While Indian negotiations are nearing finalisation with the Russian government for the purchase of Sukhoi Su-30MK two-seat multi-role fighters, the IAF requirement is believed to have been increased from the original 40 to around 100 aircraft. Su-30MK acquisition, together with associated precision-guided munitions, is apparently preferred by the IAF to procurement of additional MiG-29s to supplement the 80 already delivered. The most recent batch of 10 includes two two-seat MiG-29UB combat trainers. It is not yet known whether Indian Su-20 procurement will extend to licensed production, which would probably replace current manufacture of the variable-geometry MiG-27M by HAL's Nasik Division. This organisation has now built over 1,500 MiG-21FL/M/bis, two-seat MiG-21Us, and MiG-27Ms, and is continuing their repair, overhaul and spares manufacture.

LCA roll-out

India's Light Combat Aircraft (LCA) programme reached a significant milestone on 17 November 1995 with the long-awaited roll-out of its technology demonstrator. Four prototypes of seven planned have so far been authorised of this MiG-21 replacement, designed jointly by India's Aeronautical Development Agency in conjunction with Dassault, and built by Hindustan Aeronautics Ltd. Claimed to be the world's smallest lightweight supersonic multi-role fighter, its first flight is expected within a year, and work is continuing on the second and subsequent prototypes. These are powered by the GE F404-F2J3 turbofan, although later versions will be fitted with the indigenous flat-rated Kaveri low-bypass turbofan, developed by the Gas Turbine Research Establishment at Bangalore.

Among other design features of the tailless delta LCA are relaxed static stability with quadruplex digital fly-by-wire controls, an advanced digital cockpit with integrated avionics, a HAL/LRDE multi-mode radar, and extensive use of advanced carbon composite materials for the wing, fin and rudder. Basic specification of the LCA includes a span of 26.9 ft (8.2 m), length of 43.3 ft (13.2 m), height of 13.4 ft (4.4 m), maximum take-off weight, clean, of 18,740 lb (8500 kg), maximum external load of 8,818 lb (4000 kg) on seven hardpoints, and fixed armament of one 23-mm (0.9-in) GSh-23 twin-barrelled cannon. The LCA is quoted as having a fly-away unit cost of around $22 million, and its initial operational capability is now planned for 2002.

Naval ALH flies

The fourth prototype of Hindustan Aeronautics's Advanced Light Helicopter joined the flight development programme on 23 December 1995. It was powered by 1,200-shp (895-kW) LHTEC CTS-800 turboshafts in place of the 1,000-shp (746-kW) Turboméca TM333-2Bs in earlier ALHs. This was also the first naval prototype with a retractable tricycle undercarriage instead of skid landing gear, plus other changes.

More than 300 hours of development flying had then been completed by the three preceding prototypes, covering the full flight envelope including turns of up to 3.2g at a weight of 4.5 tonnes. Production is planned to start in 1997, initially for an Indian Army Aviation order for 10, although deliveries are eventually expected to all three services plus the coast guard. A civil version is also under development, with two engine options now available.

Mirage 2000 upgrade approved

Thomson-CSF in France has been selected by the Indian Air Force as prime contractor for an avionics upgrade of the IAF's 46 Dassault Mirage 2000H interceptors. These are planned to be given multi-role and night combat capabilities from the installation of the Thomson-CSF RDY multi-mode radar and some of its associated advanced avionics and weapon integration systems from the next-generation Mirage 2000-5. Eventual contract value could be up to $33 million.

PAKISTAN:

Spanish Mirage III purchase planned

To help offset the Pts17.88 billion ($150 million) cost of its avionics upgrade of 55 Mirage F1CE/EE (C.14A/B) fighters by Thomson-CSF in France, the Spanish air force (EdA) is selling 22 older Mirage IIIEE/DEs (C.11/CE.11s) to Pakistan. These have been in storage at Torrejon since their retirement from EdA service in August 1991, and their acquisition by Pakistan follows earlier purchases for upgrading

In December 1995 the Kenyan air force took delivery of this Fokker Executive Jet 70 for VIP work. The aircraft's interior was fitted by Fokker Aircraft Services and Hunting, the cabin consisting of a VIP section, utility section and staff seating area. The Executive Jet has extra fuel tanks compared to the standard airliner Fokker 70.

or cannibalisation of 50 ex-RAAF Mirage IIIOs from Australia, and nine low-houred Mirage IIIELs from Lebanon in 1995. About half of the Mirage IIIOs have been refurbished for PAF service, with the remainder being stripped for spares.

SRI LANKA:

New combat aircraft delivered

Recent equipment deliveries to the Sri Lankan air force have included the promised eight ex-IDF/AF Kfir C2s from Israel, as the SLAF's most effective combat equipment. Supplied through a $50 million package including weapons, spares and support equipment, the Kfirs will supplement the survivors from 10 Chengdu F-7B (MiG-21) fighters and a similar number of Nanchang A-5-III ground-attack aircraft supplied from China.

Three Mil Mi-24 'Hind' helicopter gunships are also reported to have arrived from unknown but probably surplus CIS sources. With their heavy weapon loads or alternative capability of airlifting up to eight fully armed troops, the Mi-24s will be used in support of the Sri Lankan army offensive against Tamil rebel forces.

Australasia

AUSTRALIA:

RAAF becomes third C-130J customer

The Royal Australian Air Force confirmed in December its long-standing intention to follow the RAF and USAF to become the third customer for Lockheed Martin's new C-130J Hercules II. Its initial order is for 12 stretched Dash 30 versions, costing $A900 million ($675 million), to replace its dozen C-130Es in 1997-98. Options are also included to add another 24 for later replacement of its dozen C-130Hs, plus RAAF tanker and AEW requirements, together with eight replacement C-130Js for Royal New Zealand Air Force C-130Es in a

ENAER delivered its T-35 basic trainer to Chile, Spain, Panama and Paraguay. The latter's air force (illustrated) bought 15 designated T-35D.

joint procurement programme.

These could increase eventual Australian and New Zealand C-130J purchases to 44 which, based on the initial programme unit price of $56.25 million, could cost $2.5 billion. With the first RAAF order, Lockheed Martin is claiming sales in 1995 of 39 C-130Js, including 25 for the RAF and two evaluation aircraft for the USAF. Italy is expected to become the next C-130J customer, with an order for 12 as interim equipment pending planned procurement of the Future Large Aircraft in about 2005.

The RAAF is now interested in replacing its 14 remaining DHC-4 Caribou STOL transports through its Project Air 5190 requirement. This involves 10-15 twin-turboprop aircraft, for which the Alenia/Lockheed Martin C-27J development of the G222 is proving of interest, although submissions are also being made by CASA and IPTN of the CN.235M-200/330, and by ATR for its proposed rear-loading ATR-52C. Boeing is also proposing eight CH-47D Chinooks and four more C-130Js as another possible alternative.

Adour replaced by F124 for MDC's Hawk bid

Long-standing efforts by AlliedSignal to replace the McDonnell Douglas/BAe T-45A Goshawk's Rolls-Royce/Turboméca Adour powerplant by its non-afterburning F124 turbofan, rejected by the US Navy in 1994, may finally show some success. In its submission for the RAAF's Project Air 5367 requirement for 35-45 new two-seat lead-in fighter (LIF) trainers to replace its ageing Aermacchi MB.326Hs from mid-1999, MDC is now offering the T-45 with the F124, rated at 6,300 lb (2.8 kN) as its primary engine. MDC and the International Turbine Engine Co. (ITEC), which is jointly owned by AlliedSignal Engines and Taiwan's Aero Industry Development Corporation, plan to share the development costs of the T-45's F124 installation.

Derived from the TFE1042/F125, which develops 9,460 lb (42.08 kN) maximum thrust with afterburning in the AIDC's Ching-Kuo indigenous defence fighter, the F124 has also been specified for installation in the single-seat Aero L-159 light fighter on order for the Czech air force. MDC will continue to offer the Adour-powered T-45A as an alternative submission to the RAAF, which has also short-listed the standard BAe Hawk 100 as one of its final contenders. Deadline for the PA 5367 bids was 14 March 1996.

To match the RAFF's LIF requirements, MDC's RAAF bids may also be expected to include the T-45's planned 'Cockpit 21' upgrades. These

Bringing a splash of colour to the otherwise drab US Navy Seahawk fleet is this SH-60F Ocean Hawk of HS-4 'Black Knights'. Shore-based at NAS North Island, California, the squadron is part of Air Wing 14 assigned to USS Carl Vinson.

Under Project Sure Strike, 38 F-16C Block 40s of the 31st Fighter Wing were fitted at Aviano with Improved Data Modems. This allows ground forces to transmit the locations of ground targets digitally into the aircraft's weapons system. The programme was completed at short notice by 13 December 1995, enhancing the F-16's effectiveness in the close air support role over Bosnia.

include twin Elbit monochrome multi-function cockpit displays, linked with a Litton LN-100G RLG with embedded Collins GPS, and a Smiths Industries HUD, and are due to fly in prototype form in the 37th production Goshawk in October 1996. They are then intended to become standard in all production T-45s from the 73rd.

ASMs short-listed

New air-to-surface missiles sought by the RAAF through its Project Air 5398 programme, mainly for its F-111C/G force, have been narrowed down to a short list of two. One is Rafael's TV-guided Popeye, which has an 800-lb (363-kg) warhead, and a version produced in conjunction with Martin Marietta is carried by USAF B-52s as the AGM-142. It is also cleared for use with the F-111, F-4, F-15 and F-16. Rockwell International's AGM-130E is the second contender, with TV or a new improved modular infra-red guidance, incorporating GPS, and is compatible with the Rockwell GBU-15 glide bombs already in used by the RAAF.

NEW ZEALAND:

ASW helicopter submission deadline

Kaman's SH-2G and the Westland Super Lynx have also been short-listed for the final phase of the requirement by the Royal New Zealand navy for six Westland Wasp replacements for the RNZN's new ANZAC frigates. With completely new USN-funded integrated missions systems avionics and weapons, T700-GE-401 turboshafts, and upgraded surplus SH-2F airframes, the SH-2Gs combine a high degree of ASW and ASV operational capabilities. They offer a useful cost advantage within the RNZN's $NZ200 million ($131 million) budget, which poses tough competition for Westland's best and final offers in February.

Africa

SUDAN:

More F-7s supplied

Six CAC F-7Bs (MiG-21) have recently been supplied from China via Iran to the Islamic government of Sudan, supplementing earlier deliveries of about a dozen similar fighters. With a number of ex-Soviet combat aircraft, these are being used for operations against secessionist Christian forces in southern Sudan.

ZIMBABWE:

Buffalo transport transfers

Recent transport reinforcements of the Air Force of Zimbabwe (AFZ), hitherto mainly reliant on 10 or so CASA C.212-200s, reportedly include six heavier DHC-5 Buffalos. These were transferred from eight CC-115 Buffalos withdrawn earlier last year from Canadian Armed Forces service, and delivered from September 1995.

South America

CHILE:

New IAI air tanker contract

Israel Aircraft Industries Bedek Aviation Group has received an $11 million contract from the FACh to convert an ex-airline Boeing 707-300C transport into an inflight-refuelling tanker. The conversion will be undertaken in Chile by ENAER in Santiago, from a customised kit supplied by Bedek Aviation. This will include two wingtip hose-and-drogue refuelling pods; new navigation systems, incorporating GPS; and other new avionics, for the support of the FACh's Mirage 50s, Northrop F-5s and Cessna A-37s. The contract also includes options for similar conversions of two FACh Lockheed C-130s.

ECUADOR:

More Kfirs from Israel

The air force of Ecuador (FAE) is expecting delivery of an attrition batch of four IAI Kfir C2 fighters from Israel, following US government approval for release of their GE J79 engines. The FAE had previously received a total of 32 Kfir C2s and four two-seat CT2 combat trainers from Israeli deliveries, but had lost numbers of these in border disputes with Peru.

With Sikorsky pilot Russ Stiles and Boeing pilot Bob Gradle at the controls, the Boeing/Sikorsky RAH-66 Comanche made its first flight at West Palm Beach, Florida, on 4 January 1996. Basic handling was demonstrated, the 1996 flight test programme being initially aimed at expanding the flight envelope.

North America

CANADA:

Helicopter requirements clarified

The Canadian Armed Forces have now separated their SAR and ASW helicopter requirements, for which 50 EH101s were at one time on order. Bids for 15 replacements for the 13 tandem-rotor Vertol CH-113 Labradors currently equipping CAF rescue units were invited early in 1996. Some $C600 million ($445 million) has been allocated for this programme, which may involve either lease or purchase, with civil maintenance but CAF flight personnel.

Specifications include a 120-kt (138-mph; 222-km/h) cruise speed with five crew and at least 10 passengers over a 500-nm (576-mile; 927-km) range, plus a 6,000-ft (1829-m) hover ceiling and single-engine recovery ability. Current contenders include the Boeing CH-47D Chinook, Eurocopter AS 532 Cougar Mk 2, a joint Canadian/Kamov Ka-32 submission, the Sikorsky HH-60J or S-92, and Westland/Agusta AW 520 Cormorant version of the civil ramp-equipped EH101-500. Deliveries would be required between 1998-2001. A decision on the 32 ASW helicopters needed to replace the navy's Sikorsky CH-124 Sea Kings was promised in March.

UNITED STATES:

Longbow Apache progress

McDonnell Douglas Helicopters brought one of its six AH-64D Longbow Apache heavy attack helicopter prototypes to the Asian Aerospace air show in Singapore in February 1996, having completed a three-month US Army Initial Test and Evaluation exercise in late 1995 at Fort Hunter Liggett, CA. This demonstrated multiple increases in the effectiveness of the AH-64D weapons systems when matched against the original Apache, amounting to four times its lethality while improving its survivability by a factor of seven.

Later in 1996 MDH will begin remanufacturing 728 US Army AH-64As to AH-64D standard, with mast-mounted Longbow radar capability, from an initial contract for 18, with first deliveries starting in early 1997. New-build construction is also continuing to meet total orders to date for 1,034, of which 937 had been delivered. In addition to 821 for the US Army, these included 116 to Egypt, Greece, Israel, Saudi Arabia and the United Arab Emirates. Orders have been placed for 30 AH-64Ds without radar by the Netherlands, and a contract for 67 fully-equipped Longbow Apaches is being finalised with the UK. Interest in the Apache has also been expressed by several other countries, including Singapore, Malaysia and Japan in the Asia Pacific area.

Production of the Hellfire fire-and-forget attack missile version, with an internal millimetric-wave guidance radar, to be used with the AH-64D's Longbow radar has been started by Lockheed Martin/Westinghouse's joint Longbow Limited Liability Company from an initial $165 million contract. This covers production of 123 launchers and 352 missiles, although follow-on contracts for up to 13,000 similar missiles are expected by 2003.

Comanche stealth helicopter flight development begins

Long-delayed flight development of Boeing-Sikorsky's RAH-66 Comanche low-observable scout/reconnaissance helicopter began on 4 January with a successful 34-minute sortie from Sikorsky's flight-test centre at West Palm Beach, FL. Initially flown by Sikorsky test pilot Russ Stiles, who then handed over to his Boeing colleague in the rear (weapon-systems operator's) cockpit, the Comanche proved the basic validity of its fly-by-wire flight control system and sidearm control stick, incorporating twist-grip yaw control in place of rudder pedals, in low-speed and hover manoeuvres, within the limitations of its currently downgraded transmission system.

The Comanche's fly-by-wire controls had previously been tested in a modified Sikorsky S-76, and responded very much as expected. A second prototype is planned to join the flight development programme in September 1998, to be followed by six demonstrator Comanches, as well as a static test airframe and a propulsion system testbed for the LHTEC T800 turboshaft engines. US Army procurement is currently planned of 1,292 Comanches, compared with the original requirement of 2,096, and programme funding cuts of some $2 billion have stretched planned initial operational capability dates to around FY 2006.

U-2s leave the UK

Three Lockheed U-2R high-altitude reconnaissance aircraft from the USAF's 9th Operations Group, whose home base is Beale AFB, CA, were transferred in January from their overseas deployment at RAF Fairford to the French air force base of Istres, near Marseilles, for surveillance missions over Bosnia. At Istres, they are operating alongside six USAF Boeing KC-135R tankers of the 100th Air Refueling Wing, normally based at Mildenhall, which are also operating in support of Bosnian air operations.

US Air Force EA-6B Prowler crew

Four US Air Force officers underwent training to fly the EA-6B Prowler at NAS Whidbey Island, WA in late 1995, reflecting a Pentagon decision to have the EA-6B take over the mission of the US Air Force's EF-111A Raven radar-jamming aircraft. The men are the first USAF members of newly-formed VAQ-134, established on 29 September 1995. The USAF has an authorised strength of only 12 EF-111As in Fiscal Year 1996 and expects to retire the aircraft in 1997, despite criticism that the Prowler is slower and has less range.

First flights for new MDD aircraft

McDonnell Douglas test pilot Fred Madenwald reported that the FA-18E Super Hornet (BuNo. 165164) handled "very well" on its first flight on 29 November 1995. The flight ended earlier than planned when a warning light illuminated. Madenwald said the 20-minute flight in the prototype, known as E-1, "was smooth, precise, and easy to control." A warning light signalled a bleed air malfunction and Madenwald returned to St Louis airport as a precaution. The second Super Hornet, E-2, flew in January 1996. Twelve F/A-18E/Fs are to be ordered in FY 1997; the eventual requirement is for more than 1,000 Super Hornets by 2015.

Also on 29 November 1995, McDonnell Douglas conducted the first flight of the remanufactured AV-8B Harrier II-Plus with night attack capability. The Harrier flew for one hour and 16 minutes at St Louis. AV-8B remanufacturing work is split between MDC and the Naval Aviation Depot at Cherry Point, NC, and will cover 73 aircraft. The rework involves a new fuselage, night attack capability (a forward-looking infra-red system, night-vision goggles, and related cockpit systems), Hughes APG-65 radar and Rolls-Royce F402-RR-408 engine.

F/A-18C/D Hornets for Finland

The Finnish air force took delivery on 7 November 1995 of its first four of 64 McDonnell Douglas F/A-18C/D Hornets at Tampere-Pirkkala, where the Hornets will serve with HavLlv 21. All four were two-seat F/A-18D models. The Hornets used callsigns ZESTY 41-44 during the delivery flight. American and Finnish pilots ferried the aircraft on the 9 1/2-hour flight, during which the aircraft were flight refuelled by a KC-10 over the North Atlantic.

In May 1992, Finland chose the F/A-18C/D Hornet to replace the MiG-21bis and J 35 Draken, in preference to three other aircraft candidates: the F-16C/D Fighting Falcon, Mirage 2000, and JAS 39 Gripen. The F/A-18C/Ds are powered by two 17,700-lb (78.74-kN) thrust General Electric F404-GE-402 EPEs (Enhanced Performance Engines) and have Hughes APG-73 radar and

This KC-10A serves with the McGuire-based 305th Air Mobility Wing, two squadrons of Extenders flying alongside three of C-141Bs. The aircraft is one of 20 fitted with Mk 32B wing-mounted refuelling pods.

Above: On 29 November 1995 BuNo. 165305 made the first flight from St Louis of a remanufactured AV-8B Harrier II Plus. The USMC currently has plans to rework 73 day attack Harriers to the new radar-equipped standard.

Based at Holloman AFB, New Mexico, is the 586th Test Squadron 'Roadrunners', which operates a pair of AT-38Bs (with 'HT' – 'Holloman Test') tailcodes. The unit is parented by the Eglin-headquartered Air Force Development Test Center.

Hughes APG-73 radar and AIM-120A AMRAAM capability. The US manufacturer was scheduled to deliver seven F/A-18Ds by the end of 1995, after which Valmet at Halli was to assemble the remaining 57 F/A-18Cs of which the first is to be delivered in September 1996.

T-1A flying milestone

Raytheon T-1A Jayhawk trainers logged their 100,000th hour of US Air Force flying time in November 1995. The first of 180 Jayhawks was delivered in January 1992 to Reese AFB, TX. The 100th aircraft was delivered early in 1995 and number 180 is slated for delivery in May 1997. More than 1,000 pilots have trained on the military version of the Beechjet 400A business jet.

T-38 Talon upgrade

On 14 December 1995, the USAF issued a Request for Proposals for an avionics upgrade system for the service's fleet of Northrop T-38 and AT-38 Talon trainers. Northrop Grumman, which manufactured the Talon, was regarded as front-runner for a February 1996 contract award which will result in production of about 425 rebuilt T-38s lasting through September 2004.

K-MAX completes sea trials

The US Navy's Military Sealift Command completed a two-month demonstration of the Kaman K-1200, or K-MAX 'aerial truck', helicopter in the VertRep mission to supply warships at sea. The helicopters flew in September-October 1995 to and from USNS Saturn and Sirius and USS Enterprise (CVN-65) and Theodore Roosevelt (CVN-71). The K-MAX utilises two side-by-side, intermeshing, counter-rotating main rotors and requires no tail rotor. It has a maximum hook lifting capacity of 6,000 lb (2722 kg) at sea level. The K-MAXs flew 52 shipboard sorties with average external loads of 2,700 lb (1226 kg). They carried a maximum load of 5,300 lb (2406 kg). Kaman and the US Navy are interested in K-MAX as a replace-

ment for the Boeing CH-46 Sea Knight, although Congress has not appropriated funds for a new VertRep aircraft.

F-16 Mid-Life Update

During the late 1980s General Dynamics (now Lockheed Martin) proposed a Mid-Life Update (MLU) for the F-16A/B series intended to provide the aircraft with capabilities similar to the F-16C/D. After a period of evaluation of the proposal, the programme was authorised in May 1991 with a plan to convert 130 US, 110 Belgian, 63 Danish, 172 Dutch and 58 Norwegian aircraft. One year later the US withdrew, and the European air arms reduced their planned quantities to 48 Belgian (with options on 24 more), 61 Danish, 136 Dutch and 56 Norwegian conversions.

The modification work includes the fitment of a wide-angle head-up display, conversion of the cockpit instruments to enable compatibility with night-vision goggles, a single modular mission computer in place of the three installed at present, digital terrain-following radar, a hardpoint adjacent to the air intake, replacement of the APG-66 radar with the advanced APG-66(V2A) model, a digital acquisition target display, a pair of 4-in (10-cm) colour display screens, a microwave landing system, a forward-looking infra-red pod, and provision to perform a limited suppression of enemy air defences (SEAD) role with the AN/ASQ-213 HARM targeting system.

The US Air Force earmarked F-16A 80-0584 of the 412th Test Wing, Air Force Flight Test Center for the project, although this aircraft was not converted. Three Europe-based aircraft were flown to Fort Worth, TX to be modified, consisting of Norwegian F-16A 299, Dutch F-16B J-650 and Danish F-16B ET-204. The latter made its public debut on static display at Edwards AFB air show displaying 'MLU' on the fin along with the flags of the five nations involved. The conversion kits will start to be delivered in October 1996 for installation at the two European F-16 production facilities at Gosselies in Belgium (SABCA) and at Schiphol (Fokker) in the Netherlands. The programme is due to be completed by 1999.

US Army Europe forces to police Bosnian agreement

US Army forces from Europe are to be included in the multi-national force of 60,000 contributing troops which will come under NATO control to police the agreement reached between the opposing factions in the former Yugoslavia. The agreement was worked out between the heads of the various groups during meetings staged at Wright-Patterson AFB, OH. The Implementation Force will patrol Bosnia itself, which will be divided into three sections, with the UK, Belgium, Canada and the Netherlands taking responsibility for the southeastern area that includes Sarajevo and Mostar, while the US and Russia will police the northeastern area centred on Tuzla. The remaining western areas will be the responsibility of other nations. The plan was agreed in London during early December, with the official peace signing taking place in Paris one week later.

The US Army contribution was formed around the 1st Armoured Division, with this unit's 4th Battalion already forward-based in Germany. Troops from Germany began being airlifted by C-130s immediately, with their armour following by rail from various sites. The battalion was expected to be boosted by a substantial helicopter force with assets drawn from Hanau and Budingen. Front-line forces will be unable to perform the duty on a open-ended basis, so more than

2,000 reservists will probably be called to active duty on a rotational basis.

Globemaster III wins approval with DAB

The Defence Acquisition Board (DAB) approved the funding of an additional 80 C-17A Globemaster IIIs when it met on 3 November. The decision removes previous concerns over the C-17, and enables Air Mobility Command to plan the introduction of the full 120 aircraft which will see the 437th Airlift Wing at Charleston AFB, SC operate 48 aircraft within four squadrons of a dozen aircraft each. The 62nd AW at McChord AFB, WA has been selected as the next unit to convert, with a similar number of aircraft, commencing in 1997. The 62nd AW is the only other AMC unit which at present operates solely the C-141B StarLifter.

The 437th and 62nd AW account for 96 of the planned buy of 120 aircraft; eight of the remainder are to be stationed at Altus AFB, OK with the 97th Air Mobility Wing, which will train Globemaster aircrew. While at Altus the aircraft will be part of Air Education and Training Command, with airframes rotated for periods of duty in much the same way as the 97th AMW operates the C-5 and C-141 at present. This procedure helps equalise flying hours, particularly as those aircraft stationed at Altus perform dozens of practice overshoots and fewer long-distance airlift sorties than those which are operated by AMC. The 97th AMW will commence receiving the

C-17 in the spring of 1996.

Six aircraft will be assigned to a Reservist unit, joining either the Air National Guard or Air Force Reserve directly, in addition to those being operated on an associate basis by the AFRes at present. The final 10 C-17s will serve as spares while the authorised strength receive major overhaul.

The 80 new aircraft will be funded between 1997 and 2002, although budget restrictions may well see the planned purchase extended over a longer period. The decision to obtain the full number of aircraft will enable McDonnell Douglas to offer the C-17 for export. Several NATO countries have expressed an interest in a possible acquisition, although the high unit cost will probably rule out the majority from operating the aircraft under their own banner. Consideration is being given to these nations forming a collaborative venture, with a fleet operated in a similar manner to the E-3 Sentries flown by NATO.

The Boeing proposal for its 747-400F, designated the C-33, to be considered as an alternative to the C-17 under the Non-Developmental Airlift Aircraft (NDAA) programme was rejected outright. The 747 freighter would have been a dedicated military version with widened doors and a strengthened floor enabling outsized loads, such as heavy armour, to be transported. Lockheed Martin had proposed an upgraded version of the Galaxy as the C-5D, with this too being rejected.

The decision by the DAB to approve the purchase of the C-17 in full was based on many aspects, including an analysis of all three aircraft types, using performance predictions for the C-33 and C-5D, and actual performance data from the C-17. One parameter within which the C-17 was notably far superior was the maximum number of aircraft on the ground or, to be more precise, the number of aircraft which could occupy a confined area. This could include a small runway and limited parking space, enabling rapid on and off loading and refuelling. The figures produced a greater that two to one advantage to the C-17. According to the Pentagon, eight C-17s could operate in an area that could accommodate only three C-5s and C-33s. The payload of the C-17 would be 3,852 tons per day compared to 1,754 for the C-33 and 1,443 for the C-5D. The Pentagon used these figures to evaluate a mixed force of Globemasters and one of the other two contenders to the NDAA programme, including 100 C-17s and 18 others versus a force of 120 C-17s and no C-5Ds or C33s. While there was not much variance between the operating costs, there was a huge variance in the payload per aircraft, per day.

Approximately six C-17As were assigned to the 412th Test Wing at Edwards AFB, CA for test and evaluation duties, although this was completed in December 1994. Several of these aircraft have been flown back to the manufacturer at Long Beach, CA where they will probably be refurbished to enable them to enter operational service. The prototype C-17A 87-0025 has been retained at Edwards AFB for an ongoing operational test and evaluation programme.

Third Marine Air Wing commences helicopter moves

The Third Marine Air Wing (3rd MAW), which is the controlling element for front-line US Marine Corps aviation assets located on the western side of the United States, has begun the next stage of its relocation programme involving almost all of its aircraft and helicopters. Fixed-wing types began moving from MCAS El Toro, CA to NAS Miramar in August 1994, with five F/A-18 Hornet squadrons having completed the process by September 1995. During autumn 1995 the first of the helicopter squadrons based at MCAS Tustin began to move the short distance to El Toro. The CH-46Es of HMM-166 commenced the move during October 1995, with the remaining dozen or so squadrons due to follow during the next two years. The move will only be temporary, as El Toro is also due to be closed once it is vacated. When the move of Marine Corps fixed-wing assets to Miramar is completed, and the remaining Navy squadrons at Miramar have moved elsewhere, the 3rd MAW will then evaluate the possibility of centralising the helicopters from El Toro. However, the helicopter squadrons at MCAS Camp Pendleton are unaffected by the move as space limitations at Miramar will preclude a complete centralisation. The F-14 squadrons at Miramar will eventually be consolidated at NAS Oceana, VA, with the first unit due to move in the spring of 1996. The Naval Fighter Weapons School ('Top Gun') will move to NAS Fallon, NV.

E-3 Sentry crashes in Alaska

Early on the morning of 22 September an E-3B Sentry of the 962nd Airborne Air Control Squadron, 3rd Wing crashed shortly after take off from Elmendorf AFB, AK. The aircraft came down in a thickly wooded area 2 miles (3.2 km) from the end of the runway at Elmendorf, sadly killing all 24 US and Canadian personnel on board. This was the first loss of an E-3. The crash will be investigated to determine the exact cause, although preliminary analysis suggests the aircraft, which was fully laden with fuel for its surveillance training mission, ingested a number of Canada geese into an engine. The unit operates two E-3s which are detached from the 552nd ACW at Tinker AFB, OK and replaced periodically. During 1994 the unit was operating 77-0354 and 79-0002, both displaying a green tail stripe and tailcode 'AK' (for the resident 3rd Wing), while 77-0351 was assigned in June 1995. The aircraft lost is believed to be 77-0354.

Bottom-Up Review II

In late 1995 the 190th Fighter Squadron adopted the famous 'WW' ('Wild Weasel') tailcode for its F-4Gs. The aircraft were slated for retirement in early 1996.

The US military could face yet another comprehensive force structure review to establish whether further cuts can be made. An announcement made by the Air Force's Principal Deputy Assistant Secretary for Acquisition during September will have to be reduced to free funds needed to modernise the services through the purchase of new equipment. However, the Under Secretary of Defense for Acquisition and Technology, who in effect is the Pentagon's top weapons official, denied the impending review and stated instead that the Department of Defense would adjust its forces through normal procedures.

Critics of the possible review have expressed concern that the current force structure, which was dictated following the 1993 Bottom-Up Review, would not be able to fight and win two near-simultaneous major regional conflicts. The pressures of repeatedly deploying to support peacekeeping and humanitarian operations have reduced funding which would otherwise have been made available for new weapons.

B-52 sets world record

A B-52H from the 2nd Bomb Wing at Barksdale AFB, LA broke existing speed records during a sortie on 25 August. The records in question were for an aircraft weighing between 440,000 and 550,000 lb (200000 and 250000 kg), with a payload of 11,000 lb (5000 kg) flying unrefuelled for more than 5,400 nm (6,210 miles; 10000 km). Flight time was 11 hours and 23 minutes, with an average speed of 556 mph (895 km/h). The original route was to have seen the bomber fly from Edwards AFB, CA to Greenland, although weather conditions at its destination resulted in the aircraft being redirected to land in Alaska instead.

Reserve bomber crews test accuracy

Aircrew of the 93rd Bomb Squadron, 917th Wing, Air Force Reserve at Barksdale AFB, LA have participated in an evaluation to help improve the accuracy of gravity bombs. A major factor used to determine accuracy has traditionally been wind velocity, which could be inaccurate at various levels

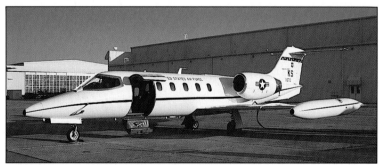

Having been deactivated as an A-10 operator in USAFE, the 81st number resurfaced on 1 July 1994 at Keesler AFB, Mississippi. The wing operates the 45th Airlift Squadron, equipped with four Beech C-12Cs (below) and four C-21A Learjets (above), acting as the training unit for both types.

and thereby play havoc with conventional munitions. The 93rd BS aircraft delivered 52 500-lb inert bombs on the Utah Test and Training Range during July using wind measurements provided by the Light Detection and Ranging (LIDAR) laser system. The bombs impacted with extreme accuracy, enabling officials to declare the LIDAR as 100 per cent effective. The system involves a laser beam being directed through the atmosphere to determine wind velocity at various levels all the way to the ground. At present, crews can only calculate the wind speed at their flight altitude, which can vary considerably between that and ground level. The project was conducted under the control of the 49th Test Squadron at Barksdale AFB.

F-15 Eagles in retirement

The 128th Fighter Squadron at Dobbins Air Reserve Base, GA performed its final sortie with the F-15 Eagle on 30 August 1995. The flight was performed by an F-15A, possibly 75-0024, which carried appropriate art work to commemorate the event. The retirement of the Eagle will enable the squadron to relocate to Robins AFB before commencing the lengthy process of converting to the B-1B.

The F-15B achieved a milestone on 22 September when the final example was withdrawn from active duty with the USAF. The last aircraft in front-line service was 77-0156 operated by the 325th FW at Tyndall AFB, FL with Air Education and Training Command. The aircraft departed Tyndall for Sheppard AFB, TX where it has been relegated to ground training duties with the 82nd Training Wing as a GF-15B.

EF-111A and F-4G retirements

The Air Force has begun to retire its SEAD aircraft in earnest. F-4Gs from the 561st FS, 57th Wing at Nellis AFB, NV and the 190th FS/Idaho Air National Guard at Boise commenced entering storage with AMARC at Davis-Monthan AFB, AZ earlier in the year, although both squadrons were still actively flying throughout the early winter of 1995. Both units will progressively wind down Phantom operations during the winter, with the final aircraft from Idaho due into storage by the spring of 1996. The 561st FS has a similar retirement timescale. The role of SEAD is to be gradually transferred from the USAF's EF-111As to the Navy, with the EA-6B community gaining this task. It is almost certain that this transfer will go ahead as planned, even though the EA-6B will need to have new tactics devised to enable it to perform the escort role. The EF-111A with its supersonic capability could perform this task effectively, although the subsonic Prowler may find it difficult to keep up.

The EF-111s will be withdrawn from service in due course, with a gradual reduction enabling the type to be out of service by 1999. The first example to be retired to AMARC was seen on the arrivals pad in October 1995, the aircraft being a former test airframe which saw service with the 46th Test Wing at Eglin AFB, FL.

The Air Force still intends to perform the SEAD mission, even though its two dedicated types will be retired from service. In their place will be two F-16Cs paired in the hunter/killer role. The hunter will consist of an F-16C (or F-16D) fitted with the AN/ASQ-213 HARM targeting system pod, which will acquire the enemy emitter; the second aircraft, armed with the Texas Instruments AGM-88 HARM, will destroy the source. The use of the F-16s is seen as economical, and the aircraft will operate in combination with stealthy fighters and the Navy jammers.

The 190th FS has six F-4Gs deployed to Incirlik, Turkey for Operation Provide Comfort, and had the honour of performing the 50,000th combined task force mission on 26 September with a pair of Phantoms. The selection of the F-4G to perform this mission was rather appropriate, as the six aircraft are among the oldest in the Air Force inventory. The six F-4Gs were due to have arrived back at Boise Air Terminal by 15 December, thereby ending the role of the US Air Force Phantom in United Nations' peacekeeping operations.

SR-71 news

The Air Force programme manager overseeing the refurbishment of the SR-71s has stated that the two aircraft have been restored to better than original condition for less than half the $100 million that Congress anticipated spending. The Reconnaissance Aircraft Systems Group, which is part of the Aeronautical Systems Centre at Wright-Patterson AFB, OH, played a part in helping to reduce costs dramatically. Among the tasks was to find spare parts, some of which had been consigned to scrap yards close to the bases associated with the SR-71 programme. Personnel toured the yards to recover the necessary parts. The bases included Norton AFB, CA, the Marine Station at Yermo near Barstow, CA, and Eglin AFB, FL where SR-71 defensive systems had been stored. Norton AFB, which housed an SR-71 support element, closed some time ago, with the equipment and spares being moved to Barstow. The SR-71s are being fitted with a datalink, which is a feature the aircraft did not have during its previous service career. The aircraft should have commenced operations with Det 2, 9th Reconnaissance Wing at Edwards AFB in January 1996.

Aggressor role reducing

The first surplus F/A-18A/B Hornets arrived at AMARC in October 1994, with a number of former aggressor aircraft being placed in temporary storage. As reported in World Air Power Journal Volume 25, the Spanish air force will receive 24 of these aircraft with deliveries due to begin early in 1996. The USN aggressor role is gradually being phased out at some air stations, although it will not disappear completely. VFA-127 at NAS Fallon, NV is to disestablish in 1996 with its aircraft being retired or transferred elsewhere. However, the unit will not cease operations until the Naval Fighter Weapons School ('Top Gun') has completed the move from NAS Miramar to Fallon.

USAF C-130J

The prototype C-130J performed its maiden flight at Marietta in December prior to entering the test and evaluation phase. The aircraft was a -30 which will be delivered to the RAF. The second and fourth aircraft will be for the US Air Force and will join the 412th Test Wing, Air Force Flight Test Center at Edwards AFB, CA. The tests should be completed by 1997, enabling deliveries to be made to the 314th Airlift Wing at Little Rock AFB, AR. Air Combat Command had an initial requirement for 150 aircraft which will join the 314th AW as well as the 7th Wing at Dyess AFB, TX. Others will probably be assigned to the two composite units, with the 23rd Wing at Pope AFB, NC and the 347th Wing at Moody AFB, GA. The C-130J will replace the C-130E and H models within ACC.

USAF C-12 Hurons join the Army

The majority of US Air Force C-12F versions of the Huron, which were employed for the Companion Trainer Program with Air Mobility Command, have been transferred to the US Army. A number of former Air National Guard C-12Js have also joined the Army. Twenty-one C-12Fs and six C-12Js were seen in September and October 1995 at Craig Field, near Selma, AL, where the Raytheon Corporation has an overhaul facility. Following repainting with Army titles and an overhaul, the aircraft were ferried to their new homes, with 15 being delivered to Europe between mid-October and mid-November. These replaced a similar number of C-12Cs which returned to the USA following the arrival of the newer equipment at bases in Germany, Italy and Turkey.

Raytheon also had a large number of U-21s, including 41 U-21As, three U-21Fs, four U-21Gs, two U-21Hs and 10 RU-21Hs, at Selma during the same period.

Above: New markings appearing recently in the US Navy fighter community include the skull-and-crossbones on the Tomcats of VF-103 (previously the 'Sluggers') who have adopted the 'Jolly Rogers' tradition from deactivated VF-84.

Right: Two new squadrons in the Naval Air Warfare Center organisation are the Weapons Test Squadron China Lake 'Dust Devils' (markings on F/A-18) and the Weapons Test Squadron Point Mugu 'Bloodhounds'. The latter unit has an eagle badge, depicted here on an NF-14D Tomcat.

BRIEFING

Ilyushin/Myasishchev Il-22M *Bizon*/'Coot-B'
Russian airborne command post

Above: The Il-22M cockpit is fairly typical of a 1960s turboprop airliner. More engine instruments are grouped at the flight engineer's station behind the two pilots.

Below: Looking aft, this is the main compartment which would accommodate the force commanders during a mission. Note the telephones.

On 4 July 1954, the prototype of the Il-18 four-engined turboprop airliner (registration CCCP-L5811, c/n 1870 000 01) made its first flight from Moscow's central aerodrome, with Ilyushin's OKB chief test-pilot Vladimir Konstantinovich Kokkinaki at the controls. It carried the OKB designation TsKB-30. The aircraft was powered by four Kuznetsov NK-4 engines, the same engines used on the Tu-4 'Bull'. Series production took place exclusively at GAZ (Gosudarstvennyy Aviatsionyy Zavod, State Aircraft Factory) number 30 'Znamya Truda' (Banner of Labour) at Moscow-Khodinka. The aircraft made its first revenue passenger flight for Aeroflot on 20 April 1959, from Moscow to Adler. Production ran from 1957 to 1969 and a total of 569 airframes is known to have been manufactured, of the Il-18A, Il-18B, Il-18V, Il-18D and Il-18E versions. During the course of production, the number of passenger seats increased from 75 to 122, range increased by 30 percent, and maximum payload by 35 percent.

The Il-18D is powered by four Ivchenko AI-20M turboprop engines rated at 4,250 ehp (3,169 kW) with AV-68I four-blade reversible pitch propellers. It is thought that production of the specialised variants, such as the Il-20 'Coot-A' for electronic and signals

Unmistakeable thanks to its antenna array, underfuselage fairing and fin-tip bullet, the Il-22M 'Coot-B' fulfils a similar function as the USAF's EC-135. This aircraft is based at Minsk-Machulische, and is now operated by Belarus.

intelligence (ELINT/SIGINT), Il-22 'Coot-B' long-range communications platform and Il-38 'May' maritime patrol/reconnaissance aircraft commenced after the cessation of production of the commercial Il-18 variants. The Il-38 was first identified by western observers in 1971, the Il-20 in 1978. Specialist variants include the Il-20RT for space test support, the Il-24N which features an underfuselage SLAR (similar to that fitted to the Il-20) for fishery and ice reconnaissance, and the Il-18D 'Cyclone' with specialised meteorological reconnaissance equipment.

Development of the original Il-22 was undertaken in about 1970 by the Myasishchev OKB, in competition with the An-12BK-VKP. Both aircraft were known as the Zebra. The original Il-22 had a very long canoe fairing under the fuselage. This was shortened considerably in the Il-22M Bizon upgrade along with other minor antenna differences.

The Il-22M Bizon is operated as a Vozhduzhnyy Punkt Upravlenya (Airborne Control Post). It may be safely assumed that the 'Coot-B' is a development of the longer range Il-18D (D for dalnosty, long range) airframe. 'Coot-B' is easily distinguished from the basic Il-18 airframe by the underfuselage container, the multitude of external fairings and antennas, and a bullet fairing at the fin tip. The cabin entrance is located on the port side aft of the cockpit. The flight deck of the Il-22M accommodates a crew of five: the aircraft commander occupies the left-hand seat; the

co-pilot the starboard seat; the radio operator has a work station located behind the co-pilot; the navigator behind the aircraft commander's seat; the flight engineer occupies a seat between the pilots' seats. The 24-m (79-ft) long cabin, with a diameter of 3.5 m (11 ft 6 in), is divided into several compartments. The largest compartment occupies the central section of the fuselage, and is equipped with four

large tables and two smaller desks, several telephones and small consoles, and at least nine swivelling chairs. Between this section and the flight deck is another compartment, which is taken up by the radio operators and their multitude of radios and associated consoles. In both compartments, there are numerous overhead baggage stowage lockers.

Mission details are scant, other

than that a routine mission is flown with a flight crew of seven and nine or ten operators. Missions last up to nine or ten hours and are flown at a cruising altitude of 8000 to 9000 m (26,250 to 29,500 ft).

A specification for the Il-22M remains unknown. The Il-18D on which it is based is quoted with a take-off weight of 64000 kg (141,100 lb), empty weight of 35000 kg (77,160 lb), max payload of 13500 kg (29,750 lb), range with maximum payload of 4300 km (2,300 miles), maximum range of 7100 km (4411 miles) and a cruise speed of 675 km/h (419 mph). By comparison, the Il-24N is credited with a range of 4800 km (2,982 miles) at a cruising speed of 600-655 km/h (373 to 407 mph) and operating altitude of 7000 m (22,965 ft). Thus, for all-weather operation, the mission coverage is 360000 km^2 (139,000 sq mi) and a mission duration of 10 hours. Furthermore, the Il-38, which has an empty weight of 36000 kg (79,367 lb) and a gross weight of 63500 kg (141,000 lb), is quoted with a patrol mission endurance of 12 hours, based on a patrol speed at 600 m (2,000 ft) of 400 km/h (248 mph), and maximum range of 7200 km (4,473 mi).

According to official figures, only 20 Il-20/-22 airframes are currently operated by the Russian Air Force and PVO (Air Defence Forces), with an additional three Il-20s and 36 Il-38s in service with the Russian Naval Air Forces. It appears that single 'Coot-Bs' were assigned to the headquarters of Military Districts (MD) and the Western Group of Forces, headquarters of Strategic Directions (TVD), commands of the Strategic Rocket Forces (SRF) and Long-Range Aviation (LRA) and, incidentally, other commands. All Il-22Ms wear the standard Aeroflot

The navigator occupies this station behind the aircraft commander, complete with chart table.

On the starboard side of the flight deck sits the aircraft radio operator. The console at the right of the photograph is for the flight engineer.

This station is located on the port side at the front of the main cabin, occupied by a mission radio operator. The main display has been covered for security purposes.

livery and are designated Il-18 on the blue cheatline, just aft of the cockpit.

Up to 1994, Il-22Ms were known to be based at the following airfields: Alma-Ata (one, Turkestan MD, to Kazakhstan); Baku-Kala (one, Trans Caucasus MD, ex HQ Southern Strategic Direction, to Azerbaijan?); Irkutsk (one, Trans-Baikal MD, LRA); Kalinovka (one, Carparthian MD, SRF); Leningrad (now St Petersburg)-Levashovo (one, Leningrad MD); L'vov-Skilnov (one, Carpathian MD, to Ukraine); Minsk-Machulische (one, Belorussian MD, to Belarus); Vinnitsa-E (one, Carpathian MD), Moscow-Shelkovo (Chkalovskii) (at least seven, Moscow MD, Air Force HQ); Moscow-Ostafyevo (one, HQ Long Range Aviation); Moscow-Zhukhovskii (several, Flight Research Institute); Omsk SW (one, Siberian MD, SRF); Orenburg SW (one, Volga-Ural MD, SRF); Severomorsk (one, Northern Fleet Air Force);

Smolensk (one or two, Moscow MD, HQ Western Strategic Direction resubordinated to Moscow HQ – and/or LRA); Ulan-Ude (one, resubordinated to Moscow HQ).

Up to 1991, one aircraft was based at Sperenberg (former German Democratic Republic), and further aircraft were occasional visitors at the base until the final withdrawal. In addition, 'Coot-Bs' are/were based at unidentified airbases in the Trans-Baikal MD (two, including one SRF) and the Far Eastern MD (one). Furthermore, it is assumed that the Il-22s (registered SSSR-75899 and 75901) which were photographed at Pushkin in May 1990 (see *World Airpower Journal* Volume 6), among other specially adapted Il-18 airframes, were either normally based elsewhere but were detached to the Pushkin Red Star Higher Command PVO and Electronics School, or were undergoing upgrade to Bizon standard.

Reports of one 'Coot-B' having been based at Osla (Krzywa, 4th Air Army, Headquarters Northern Group of Forces) require confirmation. Known Il-22 'Coot-Bs' by registration are:

SSSR-75898 – Omsk SW
  (c/n 0393607950)
SSSR-75899 – (Pushkin)
SSSR-75900
SSSR-75901 – Zhukhovskii (Pushkin)
SSSR-75902 – Irkutsk (c/n 0393610226)
SSSR-75903 – Kubinka (a regular Il-18
  also with the registration
  SSSR-75903 is based at Ryazan)
SSSR-75904
SSSR-75905
SSSR-75906 – Chkalovskaya
SSSR-75907
SSSR-75908
SSSR-75909 – Chkalovskaya
SSSR-75910
SSSR-75911
SSSR-75912
SSSR-75913 – (formerly at Sperenberg)
SSSR-75914
SSSR-75915 – Alma Ata (Almaty)
SSSR-75916 – Minsk-Machulische
  (c/n 2964017102)
SSSR-75917 – Chkalovskaya
SSSR-75918 – L'vov
SSSR-75919 – Moscow-Ostafyevo
  (c/n 2964009805)
SSSR-75920
SSSR-75921
SSSR-75922 – Zhukhovskii
SSSR-75923 – Chkalovskaya
SSSR-75924 – Chkalovskaya/Zhukhovskii
SSSR-75925 – Chkalovskaya
SSSR-75926 – Chkalovskaya
SSSR-75927
SSSR-75928
SSSR-75929 – Kishinev SE
  (Il-18 conversion)

Many of these have subsequently taken up the new civil country designators, with at least five having been seen with Russia's 'RA-' suffix.　**Frank Rozendaal**

Il-22s have always been seen in full Aeroflot livery. It is thought that they were built specially for the command post role after the Il-18 production was completed.

Antonov An-26RT and An-26L

Special mission 'Curl' variants

In 1990, the reunification of Germany allowed much greater access to the air forces of the CIS/Soviet Union, resulting in many new variants of aircraft to be identified. Among these was the Antonov An-26 'Curl-B', which was seen operating from Sperenberg, near Berlin. Two of these electronic variants operated with the 226 OSAP, flying alongside various ECM/Elint-configured aircraft which included an An-12PP 'Cub-C', a specially-equipped Tu-134A-3 and several special mission helicopters. Two Il-20 'Coot-As', an Il-22 'Coot-B' were operated by the co-located 390 ORAE.

'Curl-B' differed significantly from the standard 'Curl-A' transport version by the addition of several large blade aerials along the top and bottom of the fuselage. The designation An-26RTR was given for the type, and a role of electronic intelligence gathering was widely

reported. This assumption was logical given the company the aircraft kept at Sperenberg.

Further disintegration of the former Soviet Union in the early 1990s allowed access to newly-independent republics, some of whom have been more open about the aircraft they inherited from the dispersal of the massive Soviet air arms. At least one 'Curl-B' was based at Minsk-Machulische, and this has been adopted by the Belarus air force after independence.

This aircraft is designated An-26RT, the suffix standing for ReTranslyator, or radio relay. This accounts for the primary role of the aircraft, which is to supply an airborne relay station for communications. In this role An-26RTs saw service during the Afghan campaign, extending the range across which tactical communications could be broadcast.

At least two configurations of the An-26RT have been noted. The aircraft seen at Sperenburg (Yellow 06 and Red 11) were fitted with an antenna fit consisting of large blade aerials grouped on the upper and undersides of the fuselage around the centre of the aircraft, with a further large aerial on the lower starboard side level with the nosewheel. A number of smaller blade and hook aerials are above and below the forward fuselage. A long blade antenna and a small domed fairing

Black 58 was seen at Kubinka in 1993, equipped with bomb racks on the fuselage. An-26s were reported to have been used as makeshift bombers during the Afghan war.

are situated forward of the main-wheels on the underside of the cabin. A long wire trailing from above the flightdeck to the fintip supports three vertical wires, completing the communications fit.

The Belarus aircraft at Minsk-Machulische (Yellow 24) has a similar fit to the Sperenberg aircraft apart from two large fairings scabbed on to the lower sides of the fuselage level with the wing's trailing edge. The flat-sided fairings have a side-facing array consisting of six racks, with what appears to be an airflow-deflecting baffle upstream. Each rack contains infra-red flares.

Several 'Curls' are in service for the calibration and checking of navigation aid systems. These are described as 'An-26RT variants'. Belarus operates at least one of these aircraft (Yellow 23). Among the special equipment is a forward-looking video camera, carried in a fairing on the lower port side of the forward fuselage. This is deployed during calibration approaches to record the forward view so that the alignment of the ILS can be checked. None of the blade aerials carried by the radio-relay An-26RT is carried, and the wire array has only one vertical element. One new blade aerial is situated just inboard and ahead of the camera pod. Several operator consoles are mounted on rails within the cabin, equipped with oscilloscopes and meters to measure the strength of navigation aids.

A related variant is the An-26L (Laboratornyy, laboratory), a single example of which (Yellow 14) operated from Sperenberg during the early 1990s with the 226th OSAP. This aircraft was regularly

Above: Black 22 is a standard An-26RT, similar to the two aircraft based at Sperenburg. The aerials serve the onboard communications relay suite, used for both receiving and transmitting signals.

Below: A close-up of the Belarus An-26RT reveals details of the fuselage fairing, including the small airflow baffle and the six flare racks.

Belarus operates at least one An-26RT. Under the Soviet air force structure these aircraft had been stationed at various HQ bases to aid the local commanders. What appears to be an extra whip aerial above the observation window is in fact a rod used to remove the pitot cover from ground level.

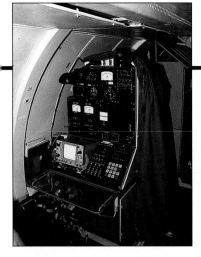

Above and right: These are the two main operator consoles in the flight check variant of the An-26. The instruments measure the strength of navaid signals.

Left: The principal external characteristic of the flight check 'Curl' is this large pod attached to the port forward fuselage. The pod contains a retractable video camera for recording landing approaches while instrument landing systems are under test.

Above: The cockpit of the An-26 reveals a simple layout, the flight check aircraft having an additional scope on the top of the dashboard connected with the mission. Note the three thrust levers, the right-hand lever controlling the auxiliary jet engine housed in the rear of the starboard nacelle.

Below: With engine access doors open, this is the Minsk-based 'An-26RT variant' used for flight checking by the Belarus air force.

seen at Russian bases in Germany checking landing aids. It featured a prominent astrodome above the flight deck, but lacked any cameras.

Other military 'Curls' are used for a variety of trials and special missions. Some have been used as bombers with fuselage bomb racks, combat action having been seen in Afghanistan and Angola. The An-26M is an emergency response version with resuscitation equipment, while the An-26Sz is a navigation trainer.

Frank Rozendaal and David Donald

The 16th Air Army in East Germany used this Sperenberg-based aircraft, designated An-26L, for checking its airfield aids. Externally the principal difference was the astrodome above the flight deck.

BRIEFING

McDonnell Douglas C-17 Globemaster III
Airlift to Tuzla

On 14 December 1995 the Dayton peace treaties were signed to bring an end to the four-year war in Bosnia. On the next day, the new NATO Implementation Force (IFOR) was assigned by the UN to go in, not just to save but to create peace in the region. By far the most powerful element within the IFOR is the US Task Force 'Eagle', which has its main base at Tuzla. A huge effort to get airlift missions underway began at the unprepared base, in the middle of winter. The operation also marked the combat debut of the new McDonnell Douglas C-17 Globemaster III.

In a short ceremony at the base on 20 December, the task force commander Major General William Nash took over command and the former peacekeeping duties from UNPROFOR's Norwegian General Haukland. Around Christmas time the airlift started to run steadily and other examples of AMC's airlifters arrived regularly. From 21 to 24 December almost 100 C-130s, plus the first C-17 transports, landed at the base. To mark the type's debut, one of the first cargoes unloaded from a McDonnell Douglas C-17 was hundreds of Christmas turkeys for the growing numbers of US personnel in the area. Also in that cargo – and rather less festive – were a 26-ton self-propelled 155-mm howitzer and its 14-ton support vehicle.

Twelve out of the initial 24 Globemaster IIIs of the 437th AW, Charleston, South Carolina were deployed to Rhein Main in mid-December to start the first real combat evaluation. Out of 1,030 missions flown by AMC transports up to 11 January, the 12 C-17s

flew 326 and the C-141s, 304. The new type delivered 8,148 tons, against 3,551 tons by the StarLifter. The C-17's ability to perform strategic airlifts into tactical targets has given new possibilities to the operational cell at Rhein Main, the 626th Air Mobility Support Squadron.

As the C-17 mission commander in Rhein Main, the 14th AS/437th AW's Lieutenant Colonel J. Reheiser, pointed out, it very soon became clear that the army had a lot of oversized equipment that had to be flown in. Threats to US interests have changed in recent years, and the size and weight of US mechanised firepower and equipment have grown in response to improved capabilities of potential adversaries.

The area of heavy outsized cargo, in particular, makes increasing demands on air mobility, and the C-17's 26.50 x 5.50 x 4.10 m (86.95 x 18.0 x 13.45 ft) cargo bay is the only one able to carry it. Another advantage is that two wheeled vehicles or trailers can fit side-by-side, so that more can be carried. Special attention is paid to the cargo floor by the loadmasters, who have their compartments in the starboard front side of the cargo deck. Depending on the demands of particular loads, the floor can be configured up to 10 different ways. All of the strengthened easily-turned aluminium strips that make up the floor's surface are laid side-by-side and have at least two different surfaces. Anti-skid strips, roller conveyors, tie-down hooks for chains, and seat fittings are among the available attachments, some of which can be rotated up 30° to allow cargo to be slipped in longitudinally. In one hour, strate-

gically placed strips can be changed with railway tracks. Using this sophisticated floor with attachment points in the aircraft's sides, special vehicles or tall items with a high centre of gravity no longer cause loadmasters concern as they did in the past. Although taller items are no problem for the C-5, either, the Galaxies cannot be used in Tuzla because they are much too heavy for the concrete surfaces there. One outgrowth of the C-17's advanced storage facilities is the potential for an increase in female loadmasters, due to the reduced physical demands of the job.

Asked about initial experiences in reliability and maintainability during the first weeks of rotating C-17 operations, Reheiser revealed figures very near USAF requirements. A mission completion success rate of 90 per cent, approximately 19 maintenance man-hours per flying hour, and a full mission-capable rate of 75 per cent had been calculated for 100,000 flying hours by 437th AW technicians. At the Rhein Main ramp it transpired that eight C-17s could be operated in the same space required for three C-5s.

To AMC crews, the aircraft has clearly proved itself in the air and during landings at Tuzla. The flying crew of two works in the most sophisticated cockpit layout of any

The C-17's cockpit offers an excellent view for such a large aircraft, especially downwards. Each pilot has a primary multifunction display, with two further screens in the centre of the dash, while head-up displays provide essential flight information and landing cues.

of today's multi-engined non-combat aircraft. Flown almost entirely with HUDs and controlled by fighter-like sticks, the experience is closer to flying a fighter than ever before in a transport, as one pilot said during a mission. Four large colour CRTs dominate the front console, two of which can present all of the various data: that from flying instruments, plus navigational and technical figures. Below, the middle console houses four FMS screens, and all navigation and communication elements.

The mission to Tuzla from Rhein Main at the aircraft's cruising speed of Mach 0.77 (450 kt) takes precisely two hours' flying time, compared to 2 hours 20 minutes in the C-141. After crossing the airspace of Austria and Slovenia at 23,000 to 29,000 ft (7010 to 8840 m), the C-17 heads over the Croatian coastline towards Krajina. When Bosnian airspace is entered, the aircraft turns sharply northeast, at which point all an board put on their protective gear and the two additional seats in the cockpit are emptied. As all landings into Tuzla are performed as combat landings with a strong nose-down attitude, combined with intelligence-based evasive manoeuvring, the result is a relatively brutal corkscrew descent. This is where the differences between the two jet transports are most obvious to the casual observer. In the C-141 the navigator receives special approach briefings for Bosnian airspace and the final part of the flight; the same task is

Six 437th Airlift Wing C-17s can be seen in this view of the ramp at Rhein Main during the January 1996 airlift to Tuzla. With the opening of a land route from Hungary, the C-17s are mainly used for the transport of high value cargo.

accomplished in the C-17 by programming the necessary daily information into the aircraft's navigation system. In the C-141 such a combat landing involves movement and noise as the airframe exits the corkscrew with loud cranks and moans, especially when heavy loads are shipped; in the C-17 the same procedure is much quieter and smoother. The steady fighter-like descent does not require changes in approach speed, even when the nose is lifted in the final stage. Thanks to the 29 control surfaces and the blown flaps, soldiers transported in the new aircraft repeatedly have to be woken up during taxiing by the loadmaster's voice in the speaker. Such sleep is almost impossible in a C-141! A few seconds after raising the nose, the wheels touch the runway, and the immediate thrust reverse is much more strongly felt because the P&W F-117-100s reversers direct the flow upward and forward to prevent the ingestion of dust and debris.

Preparations for the long-awaited peace enforcement operation have been underway since the end of November 1995. In addition to the transfer of combat aircraft from Deny Flight operations into the new mission, the effort of airlifting all the necessary troops and their equipment began on 15 December. The first unit deployed to Tuzla by the C-130Hs of the 37th AS/86th AW where squads of the 325th Airborne Infantry Brigade from Vicenza, Italy. Their job was to secure the former JRV fighter base, used for years only by helicopters and as a refugee camp. Conditions on the field hampered the quick deployment of larger forces for about two weeks, compounded by a particularly hard winter with alternating blizzards and fog periods.

The first task was to establish the initial cell of the future 4100st Air Group (Provisional). Airlift operations are run by this unit with its 600 to 700 specialists, headed by the former deputy commander of the 16th Air Force, Colonel G. Patton. Their first job was to install and operate a navigation system to allow aircraft to land safely in the less-than-optimal weather conditions. In the first days 50 per cent of the C-130s had to turn back to Germany, so it took the team of the 1st CCS some days to collect the necessary equipment to put a TACAN system on the infield grass between the 3,100-ft (945-m) runway and the taxiway. It was certified by FAA officials on 18 December. Pilots where able to

lock on to the signal from 90 miles (145 km) out, 30 miles (48 km) being the required minimum. Two days later an additional antenna increased the range of the military-ATC radio from 7 to 85 miles (11 to 137 km). One day later a precision approach radar was in operation near the TACAN site. Near the end of 1995 rotating operations began; on the peak day of 29 December, 42 aircraft of all three types delivered more than 1 million lb of cargo.

The initial work was heavily hindered by the latent danger of land mines. Several examples from the former JNA mines inventory were laid in thousands on the airfield and around the base. After the frozen dirt turned into mud, it became even more difficult to create mine safe-areas. Even today, only a space of 50 ft (15 m) around all used surfaces is free, the forest between the taxiway and the outside of the base being still off limits.

After the bridge over the Save was finished at the first day of 1996, the mass of troops and most of the armour rolled in by road from the Hungarian bases around Kaposvar and Taszar. The nature of the airlift to Tuzla changed to a higher value supply from mid-January.

Direct operations around the aircraft are less obstructed by mines and mud than are the patrolling and living conditions for the personnel. A total of about 20,000 servicemen and women have been forming the US Task Force within the IFOR since early February 1996. After security and airfield operations, quarters were the last main demand. About 150 Air Force engineers from the Florida-based 823rd 'Red Horse' Squadron erected a total of 1,000 tents at a rate of one per hour. Currently, three major tent cities accommodate the mass of troops and specialists. The remaining Bosnian Serb and Muslim forces had retreated 2 km (1.2 miles) from each other by 20 January, and the created 4-km (2.4-mile) wide corridor is now controlled by IFOR units. As such, the direct threat to the air base itself has become almost negligible. Despite that, some lone mortar grenades and single rounds have fallen within the base's boundaries. Colonel Patton's staff considers these to be only mishaps and not direct targeted fire. In case this situation worsens, a US Army artillery unit with four 105-mm Howitzers is dug in at the southwestern end of the runway, guided by an artillery tracking radar unit.

The base itself, a typical Eastern

Above: Heavy equipment can be rapidly unloaded from the C-17, as demonstrated by this aircraft on the ground at Tuzla. Turnround times at the base are often less than 10 minutes.

Below: Although the C-17s have grabbed the limelight on the Tuzla airlift effort, the venerable C-130 and C-141 have also played a huge part. This 'USAFE'-emblazoned aircraft is from the 86th AW at Ramstein.

European fighter field layout which housed Oraos and MiG-21s in the past, is now run with three little flight lines, each for different kinds of aircraft. At the southeastern end, on the enlarged turn between runway and taxiway, is the jet transport turning and reloading point. Here the C-17s and the C-141s from 62nd AW (McChord AFB) are handled within 10 minutes of ground time. During reloading, engines are kept on 15 per cent thrust, with reversers deployed. In the centre of the taxiway, where it connects the former flight line through a junction exit to the runway, are two positions for the C-130s. In addition to the 86th AW aircraft, some Hercules of the Danish, Norwegian and Swedish air forces are accommodated. And every day, several -30 series from well-known Southern Air Transport fleet can be seen here.

In the base's northwestern corner, the taxiway is used by the large fleet of US Army Aviation

helicopters. A strong contingent of more than 20 AH-64C Apaches was observed there in January. Together with some AH-1 Cobras, they are forming the key element in pursuit of treaty violators of all sides, fire support of IFOR patrols and cover for transport and medevac flights. These are performed by UH-60 Blackhawk machines, some armed, some L versions with ESSS stub wings and drop tanks, and some UH-60Q medevac variants. Heavy lifting of equipment to inaccessible areas is performed by several CH-47s. All the helicopters have self-protection and IR jammers fitted. They flew into the area in formations of up to eight along prior-negotiated routes through Austria and Hungary. Refuelling stops between their bases in middle Germany and the US-run airfield of Taszar in southeastern Hungary were made at the two Austrian Fliegerdivison airfields of Linz Horsching and Tulln Langenlebarn, the former in particular catering to the CH-47s.   **Georg Mader**

23

Croatian Air Force Update

Photographed by Dragiša Brašnović

In November 1995 the Croatian air force (HZS) held an air show to celebrate its fifth anniversary at the air base of Zemunik, near Zadar. This show provided an excellent opportunity to view all of the types in service with the air arm, together with much of the weaponry employed by the aircraft. Combined with the article published on the HZS in *World Air Power Journal* Volume 24, this photo-feature provides a complete guide to the various aircraft in service with this growing air arm.

Above: Yugoslavia procured five Canadair CL-215 amphibians for fire-fighting purposes. Croatia now operates three of these, and is believed to have a fourth on order.

Below: A number of MiG-21UM trainers are included in the HZS line-up. The MiG-21s of the Zagreb-based Fighter Squadron 21 wear the black knight emblem.

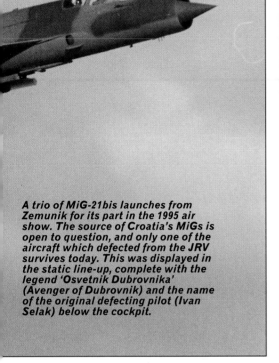

A trio of MiG-21bis launches from Zemunik for its part in the 1995 air show. The source of Croatia's MiGs is open to question, and only one of the aircraft which defected from the JRV survives today. This was displayed in the static line-up, complete with the legend 'Osvetnik Dubrovnika' (Avenger of Dubrovnik) and the name of the original defecting pilot (Ivan Selak) below the cockpit.

Above: An Mi-24V 'Hind-E' took part in the short air show at Zemunik, displaying the type's power and manoeuvrability. The fairing on the port wing usually houses a gun camera.

Above: A second 'Hind-E' in the static display was shown surrounded by a wide array of ordnance, including rocket pods and various bombs. Of special interest were these torpedoes, which appear to be Mk 44 weapons.

Below: HZS 'Hips' on display at Zemunik covered both the Mi-8MTV (Mi-17) and the earlier Mi-8T variants. One Mi-8MTV (H-205) flew during the display, while another (H-210, named 'Sveti Ivan'/'St John') was positioned in the static, both equipped with nose radar. This aircraft is the first of Croatia's Mi-8s, still wearing its original camouflage scheme. Croatia also operates the Mi-8S VIP transport.

Above: For observation and liaison duties, the HZS operates the McDonnell Douglas MD500D. Aircraft of this type are also believed to operate with the police air wing.

Above: The Mi-8 (shown right) carries this nose art, the legend translating as 'Old Girl'. The aircraft also wears the tiger's head badge and 'Tigrovi' legend carried by other 'Hips' in the Croatian helicopter squadron.

Below: A type little known outside of former Yugoslavia is the **UTVA-75**, a primary trainer. This example was flown in action during the Croatian war by Matko 'Caos' Raos, armed with twin launchers for the locally made M-90 rocket.

Above and right: Another ex-Yugoslav rarity is the **SOKO J-20 Kraguj**, which served on territorial defence force units in the old federation. This example was captured by the Croatians and now undertakes training and light attack duties.

Left: With the capture of Udbina airfield, the HZS acquired a small number of SOKO G-2A/N-60 Galebs, which have been overhauled, repsrayed and placed into service in the training role. The aircraft are armed with two 12.7-mm guns and have underwing pylons.

Right: Also captured at Udbina were a number of SOKO IJ-21 Jastrebs. This variant has small cameras in the wingtip pod for reconnaissance, but retains its full light attack capability.

Left: Parked next to a civilian-registered UTVA-75 is this Albatros microlight. Two microlights were on display at Zemunik, both painted black. These aircraft were used during the war as makeshift raiders and for special forces duties. This aircraft is displayed with four small bombs and equipped with bomb racks.

Below: Although wearing a civilian registration, this Do 28D Skyservant is believed to be an HZS aircraft. The colour scheme would suggest that it had been in previous use with the Luftwaffe's FBS VIP transport squadron. The bombs are in use as tiedown points.

Above: A pair of Antonov An-32Bs is in use for transport tasks, wearing civilian registrations. More transports are sought by the HZS.

Below: The An-2 'boiler bomber' occupies a special place in the HZS inventory, having been one of the mainstays of the limited bombing effort during the war with JNA forces. This aircraft has recently been repainted, and is displayed with the small bombs it could carry underwing, and the larger weapons which were manually dropped from the cabin. The tiedown bombs are believed to be M72 (FAB-250) fragmentation weapons.

AIDC
Ching-Kuo

The Indigenous Defence Fighter

The tiny island nation of Taiwan has overcome international indifference and arms embargoes to produce one of the most advanced combat aircraft in service today. Its development began when the US prevented the delivery of F-20 Tigersharks, ironically forcing the Republic of China to develop an even more advanced and capable fighter. Some believe that the US so feared the emergence of a powerful Taiwanese aerospace industry that F-16s were supplied expressly to force the early termination of the IDF programme and to remove a potential competitor.

C onceived in desperation, when it seemed that deliveries of the latest US hardware would be denied, Ching-Kuo has been sidelined by history and especially by the delivery of F-16s. Technical problems, crashes and groundings have undermined confidence in the aircraft (though in truth it has suffered no more than was expected) and production has been cut back. Some Taiwanese pilots are reportedly

lukewarm about the aircraft, fearing that its home-grown design somehow ensures mediocrity. In fact, the IDF (Indigenous Defence Fighter) was designed and built with a great deal of help from US aerospace giants like Lockheed Martin, and for Taiwanese requirements the aircraft represents perhaps the best combat aircraft available, although its small production run also makes it one of the most expensive. Its only real

Taiwan is only 70 miles (112 km) from mainland China and so maintains a constant state of readiness. The RoCAF relies on an extensive system of hardened shelters to protect its combat aircraft at its limited number of airfields.

disadvantage is its high cost, since the main threat offered by Communist China lies more in the sheer numbers of combat aircraft which it can field than in the quality of those aircraft. Taiwan must therefore be able to field relatively large numbers of fighters in order to deter (or even combat) the threat. The delivery of Su-27s to the Chinese makes it essential for Taiwan to be able to field a high quality BVR–capable fighter

Taiwan owes its origins as an independent nation to the events of 1949, when Chiang Kai Shek's Nationalist forces were finally forced to flee the Chinese mainland by Mao's Communists, following the brief but bitter and bloody civil war. Formosa (and a handful of

Above left: Wearing smart AIDC house colours, the first IDF flew on 28 May 1989. Though often viewed in the West as an unsophisticated lightweight aircraft, the IDF can fairly claim parity with several of the so-called 'fourth generation' fighters (still) under development today. With substantial US assistance, AIDC beat them all into the air.

Above: A very public mishap marred the early career of 10001 when it burst a tyre and suffered a gear collapse on take-off during a demonstration for the Taiwanese President in October 1989.

Left: After its accident, 10001 was quickly repaired and returned to the flight test programme. It was soon joined by the remaining three FSD aircraft, which all took to the air between September 1989 and July 1990.

smaller islands) became the Nationalist's last stronghold, and the foundation stone of a new, pro-Western, anti-Communist Republic of China. The island of Formosa had been ceded to Japan in 1895 and had been liberated by Nationalist forces in 1945. It is seen by both sides as being an integral part of China as a whole, although the Taiwanese believe that their National government should rule the whole country, while the Communists on the mainland naturally see the very existence of a separate Nationalist China as evidence of unfinished business. The People's Republic therefore hoped to 'liberate' what it saw as part of its legitimate territory. During the early years of the Cold War, Communist China and Soviet Russia were seen (perhaps simplistically) as close allies, and on the basis of 'My enemy's enemy is my friend' the West saw support of Nationalist China as a duty of honour. Taiwan became a fortress nation on the Cold War's front line, garrisoned by the USA, with its own armed forces generously equipped with the latest American weaponry.

However, even at the height of the Cold War, Taiwan's total reliance on the USA for the supply of weapons brought great instability. Every time relations between Peking and Washington improved Taiwan felt the effect, with restrictions being imposed on delivery of the latest weapons. Its value as a bulwark against Communism, and as an example of a stable Western-style capitalist democracy, was reduced by the emergence of many equally stable and

The first two-seat Indigenous Defense Fighter to fly, 79-8004/10005, was also the first to adopt the three-tone, grey and white, RoCAF Ching-Kuo camouflage – unique among Taiwanese air force aircraft. This photograph shows 10001 in its original radarless configuration, when it was in use as an aerodynamic and flight envelope testbed – hence the recovery parachute for spin trials, mounted on the rear fuselage.

arguably more democratic pro-Western nations within Asia, from Singapore and Malaysia to South Korea. Following the end of the Cultural Revolution, the thaw in Sino-American relations became more permanent and the position of the island republic of Taiwan became more tenuous. The US withdrew its forces from Taiwan in stages from 1974, and began scaling down its military assistance. In 1979, the USA actually broke off diplomatic relations with Taiwan. This marked the low point in Taiwan's relations with the USA, but from 1974 it was clear that Chinese objections would always threaten to prevent deliveries of the latest military equipment from the USA.

The breakdown in relations could not have come at a worse time for the Taiwanese air force, since its first effect was to prevent the re-equipment of its F-104 Starfighter squadrons and to close off many of the options for replacing the F-5. Both types were effective enough in

the day fighter role, but improvements in People's Liberation Army Air Force fighter forces (notably the introduction of the J-7 MiG-21 copy) led the Taiwanese to look for a more capable fighter, with all-weather and beyond-visual-range capability. Before Washington dumped its former client, Taiwan could have expected to be an early recipient of F-16s, and to have been able to obtain surplus F-4E Phantoms at a bargain price.

Taiwan had been a major user of the F-5, starting with the A and B model Freedom Fighters before licence-building most of the 242 F-5Es and two-seat F-5Fs acquired between 1973 and 1986. The aircraft's maintainability and high readiness figures had won it much support, and Taiwan's requirement was behind the Northrop studies of an up-engined AIM-7 Sparrow-equipped derivative which eventually culminated in the F-5G (later F-20) Tigershark. This aircraft would have been perfect for

Left: A Sky Sword I-armed, single-seat Ching Kuo seen on short finals to Ching Chuan Kang AB. Note the small airbrakes inboard of the tailplanes. The F-5E-style centreline drop tank can carry 275 US gal (1041 litres).

Left: The IDF was intended as an F-5 and F-104 replacement. F-104s, such as this ex-Luftwaffe TF-104G, are a small part of today's RoCAF, remaining in service with a single wing, the 2nd TFW. Substantially larger numbers of F-5s serve with four front-line wings and another training wing (alongside T-38s). The original requirement for 420 Ching-Kuos was a reflection of the need to replace these more elderly types.

A key element of the AIDC Ching-Kuo programme is its suite of Taiwanese-designed weapons. Sky Sword I (left) is an AIM-9L-class AAM, while Sky Sword II is allegedly comparable to the AIM-120, though this is thought by many to be an exaggerated claim. Seen here test firing a Sky Sword I, FSD aircraft 10001 has gained a GD-53 radar and a modified rudder – fitted after its October 1989 crash.

Taiwan (especially if licence-built), offering a degree of commonality with the five existing wings of F-5Es (and ease of training and conversion) and representing a useful means by which local industry could gain experience in manufacturing a more advanced fighter type.

In the event, Taiwan was specifically excluded from the list of potential Tigershark and Fighting Falcon customers, and even from the list of customers approved for redundant F-4 Phantoms. Instead, Taiwan received a batch of 150 tired Starfighters from Germany, Denmark and Japan in a transfer deal organised and allegedly part-funded by the USA. This was a useful boost for the Taiwanese air force, allowing the 3rd Fighter Wing to be restored to full strength and allowing the 2nd Fighter Wing to finally discard its last F-100s. Some 107 Starfighters had been delivered between 1960 and 1975, but many had been lost, or were becoming structurally tired. It did nothing to address Taiwan's requirement for a modern fighter with true BVR capability, however.

Search for the next-generation

During the late 1970s there were few alternatives to the F-16 and F/A-18 for free world nations. Israeli attempts to export the Kfir were frustrated by the need for US approval (for its General Electric J79 engine), while Britain's Tornado ADV was handicapped by its high price, by its lack of close-in dogfighting capability and by early problems with its radar. France was

aggressively marketing its Mirage 2000 and upgraded versions of the Mirage III/5/50 family but, in the end, Taiwan decided on a bolder step – the development of an entirely indigenous fighter aircraft. This was made possible by the ambiguous nature of the restrictions placed on the supply of arms to Taiwan by the USA. Brokering the supply of aircraft from elsewhere was fine, as was the provision of components and assistance for Taiwanese licence-production programmes. In fact there was little restriction on technical assistance of any sort, and it was clear that Taiwanese industry would be able to collaborate with US partners in designing and building the proposed new fighter.

Industrial collaboration had already been successfully demonstrated in the programme which produced the indigenous AIDC AT-3 jet trainer, which benefited from Northrop's work on the T-38 trainer and on the unsuccessful YA-9 close support aircraft, while companies like Garrett and Smiths Industries had helped with powerplants and avionics. The production of an entirely new combat aircraft was nevertheless an ambitious project for AIDC, despite its experience in designing and building the AT-3 trainer and in building the majority of the F-5Es and F-5Fs delivered to the Republic of China Air Force.

Development and production of an indigenous fighter was not only driven by the needs for self-sufficiency and for the reduction of the potential damage of arms embargoes. The

programme also promised to act as a prototype for the kind of high-technology projects which the country's changing economy demanded. Taiwan's economic success had led to increased labour costs, reducing its competitive advantage in the production of relatively low-technology, low-cost goods. The aerospace industry was an attractive area for expansion, offering a product in which labour and raw material costs represent a relatively small proportion of the total price. The Ching-Kuo promised to be insulated from commercial realities (it was a priority defence programme) which would allow personnel to gain valuable experience of aircraft design and construction.

Project launch

The IDF programme was formally initiated in May 1982, although initial studies had begun during 1980. The 1982 launch allocated US$150 million for engine development. The programme was initially known by the code-name An Hsiang (Safe Flight). The aim was to produce an aircraft with significantly increased air-to-air and air-to-ground capability and, moreover, to produce an aircraft with a low life cycle cost, improved maintainability, reliability and supportability. The aircraft was originally

The first Ching-Kuo squadron to form was No. 7 'Seed' ('Wolf') Sqn which was followed by No. 8 'Dragon' Sqn. The 'Dragon' was commissioned during the ceremony seen here on 28 December 1994, at Ching Chuan Kang AB.

conceived as a very lightweight 'hot-rod', akin to the F-20 Tigershark, and capable of speeds in excess of Mach 2. This aim was wisely abandoned as weight increased, and the opportunity was taken to simplify the engine intakes. The overall programme was managed by AIDC and the Ministry of National Defence through four distinct subsidiary programmes dealing with the four vital elements of the aircraft – airframe, powerplant, avionics and armament. These programmes took in more than 1,000 vendors and sub-systems contractors. Even in 1989, sub-contract work was estimated to be worth US$27 billion (NT$739 billion). Like many 'besieged' nations (Israel being the best example), Taiwan feels itself to be permanently 'at war', and distrust of the outside world has created an atmosphere in which concern for national security has almost reached the level of paranoia. Thus, each of these subsidiary programmes was similarly codenamed in order to maximise security.

Soaring Eagle

The Ying Yang (Soaring Eagle) airframe development programme was undertaken with considerable assistance from General Dynamics Fort Worth (now Lockheed Martin Tactical Aircraft Systems). Design, development and production was undertaken at AIDC's sprawling Factory One adjacent to Ching Chuan Kang air force base, although described as Taichung (a nearby city which is home to AIDC's headquarters). The factory at Taichung was involved in the IDF programme, where canopy forming, bonding work, machining and sheet metal forming was conducted. General Dynamics' consultancy (which cost Taiwan US$50 million) included the provision of technical specifications and drawings from the F-16, and the modification of these to conform with the IDF's twin-engined configuration and slightly different role priorities. About 50-60 General Dynamics engineers and technicians were sent to work in Taiwan, forming an integral part of the AIDC team.

Unsurprisingly, the Ching-Kuo bears some external resemblance to the F-16, albeit with its blended wing set higher, and with the single chin inlet replaced by F/A-18-style canted oval intakes under the wing roots, and with twin engines in the rear fuselage. Some small details could almost have been lifted directly from the F-16, including the characteristic UHF antenna on the fin root fairing, the navigation lights on the intake sides, the external lightning conductor strips on the radome and the position of the cannon in the port LERX. The aircraft is dimensionally small (smaller than the F-16, and similar in size to the A-4, F-5E or MiG-21), and its twin-engined configuration closely follows in the tradition of the F-5E which the Taiwanese have operated for so many years.

It would be entirely wrong to think of the IDF as being some kind of scaled-down F-16 analogue, despite the similarities between the two aircraft. The designers of the IDF were much more concerned with limiting weight and drag than those of the F-16, who could rely on a higher thrust-to-weight ratio, and who had to accommodate 50 per cent more fuel, as well as more avionics equipment. The F-16 also required stressed pylons for air-to-ground weapons, and a substantially stronger undercarriage for operation from forward bases. Nevertheless, the requirement for agility at

Above: With a load of two Sky Sword Is a 3rd TFW Ching-Kuo taxis from its HAS for departure. Aircraft carry no squadron markings, which appear only on flying suit patches.

Right: The Ching-Kuo cockpit is outfitted with two Bendix/King MFDs and a Bendix/King HUD. Weapons, radar modes, and chaff/flares are controlled with the main sidestick. The throttle, just visible in the lower left hand corner, also controls undercarriage, some radar functions and control surfaces.

subsonic and supersonic speeds led to very similar configurations.

A highly blended wing and fuselage gave low drag and reduced radar cross-section, while massive LERXes (Leading Edge wing Root eXtensions) both destabilised the aircraft in pitch (by producing lift ahead of the centre of gravity and centre of pressure) and generated powerful vortices which helped keep airflow attached to the wing and tailfin during high-Alpha flight. High-Alpha capability is further enhanced by the positioning of the elliptical intakes, below the LERX. The use of twin intakes on the IDF allows a relatively simple and clean, straight-through intake duct. The wing leading edge is moderately swept, but broad chord (and trailing-edge taper on the IDF) give generous area and thus relatively low wing loading. The use of a single tailfin dictates that it be of relatively large size.

Construction and composition

Designed with a fatigue life of 8,000 flying hours (and at least 12,000 landings), and with a normal service load factor limit of 6.5 g, the IDF airframe is of conventional all-metal (aluminium alloy) construction, with steel used in areas of high load intensity, or where particularly high temperatures would be encountered. Titanium was restricted to the jet pipe nozzles. Composite materials (graphite epoxy) were restricted to fin and tailplane skins, access panels, speed brakes

and trailing-edge flaperons. Composite tailplanes were introduced only after the loss of the second FSD aircraft following a fatigue failure of the port tailplane. The limited use of advanced materials was a deliberate decision, imposed by damage repair and durability requirements. All material selection was a careful balance between considerations of cost, weight and maintainability. The flightless fourth prototype served as the structural test aircraft and has demonstrated a fatigue life in excess of 16,000 hours.

A true lightweight fighter

The undercarriage of the Ching-Kuo is much simpler and lighter than that of the F-16, reflecting the fact that the Taiwanese do not expect to have to operate from primitive forward airstrips, and also reflecting the difference in role between this aircraft and the F-16, which might be expected to launch as a fighter-bomber carrying up to 20,000 lb of weapons. Even in the air-to-ground role, the IDF's maximum external load was 9,000 lb (4082 kg). The tricycle undercarriage folds forward, the mainwheels rotating through 90° to lie flat in the bottom of the intake ducts.

Most Western pilots would find the cockpit cramped, but it was designed around the anthropometric measurements of the typical Taiwanese pilot, and was never intended for 6-ft 4-in, 200-lb Texans! Moreover, a large cockpit would have demanded a larger, heavier aircraft,

Left: Armed with a single Sidewinder, this is the thirteenth production Ching-Kuo, and the fifth two-seater to be built in that batch. Note the large landing lights, both in the nosewheel and main undercarriage bays.

Right: The fourth FSD Ching-Kuo (nearest the camera) formates with the first pair of pre-production aircraft. The weathering on this aircraft is obvious – the even more toned down national markings on the newer aircraft less so.

and in modern military aircraft weight means cost. Apart from its slightly compact dimensions, the cockpit of the production Ching-Kuo is very similar to that of the latest models of the F-16, with a pair of multi-function display screens, a modern Bendix-King wide-angle HUD and a sidestick controller. Full HOTAS control is assured through use of sidestick and throttle-mounted input buttons plus the HUD and MFD keyboards. As in the F-16, the ejection seat (a Martin-Baker Mk 12, capable of zero-zero operation and usable at speeds of up to 600 kt/690 mph/1110 km/h) is canted back by 30°.

Mission avionics

Taiwan requested proposals for an upgraded cockpit for the IDF during 1992. This was to include a raster-capable wide-angle HUD compatible with displaying imagery from a FLIR, as well as colour MFDs to replace the monochrome CRTs in the original cockpit. The upgrade was also to include a programmable display processor and a video recorder for the HUD and displays. Sources suggested that the cockpit upgrade was to be incorporated as a part of a block change which would also include the provision of a FLIR, perhaps broadly equivalent to the LANTIRN system, and was described as being equivalent to the change from F-16A to F-16C. The IDF is being procured in blocks of 60 aircraft (presumably excluding the four FSD aircraft and 10 pre-production machines) with two blocks currently funded to give a total of 130 aircraft (plus four FSD examples). It will be interesting to see whether the second block will incorporate the new cockpit.

Under the skin, the IDF has a pair of independent and separate hydraulic systems, each operating at 300 psi (2068 kPa) and actuating the flight control surfaces, the leading-edge flaps, wheel brakes, undercarriage retraction and nosewheel steering, fuel flow adjuster and the air brakes. Both systems provide power to the flight control surfaces but can each supply sufficient power for full operation of the system in the event of the failure of the other hydraulic system, providing the necessary redundancy.

The fuel system is similarly dual-redundant, with a backed-up transfer system whose purpose was to balance fuel centre of gravity within stability limits. Internal tankage comprised full-span, full-chord integral wing tanks, a tank in the forward fuselage immediately aft of the cockpit, with a larger tank in the centre-section, which spread out over the intake ducts and which extended aft over the foremost part of each engine. All tanks were pressurised using the inert gas Halon, which would also suppress fire or explosion caused by electrical shorting or battle damage.

Internal fuel can be augmented by jettisonable external fuel tanks. The centreline and inboard underwing hardpoints are plumbed for the carriage of drop tanks, which are available in two sizes. The larger of these is a 275-US gal (1041-litre) tank almost identical to that carried by F-5Es, sloping upwards at the trailing edge and with three fins – two horizontal, and one vertical (on top) – while the smaller tanks had a capacity of only 150 US gal (568 litres). Use of the centreline hardpoint makes it impossible to use the tandem missile recesses below the fuselage, thereby preventing carriage of the BVR Sky Sword 2. This position is thus little used for the carriage of fuel tanks in the air defence role, when underwing tanks are more common.

Cloud Man

Engine development was conducted under the Yun Han (Cloud Man) programme, which was largely delegated to AlliedSignal/Garrett, since the engine chosen was to be an afterburning derivative of the tried and tested Garrett TFE73 family of turbofans. The engine programme was nominally undertaken by ITEC (International Turbine Engine Co.) which combined staff and assets from both Garrett and AIDC, and was headquartered at AIDC's Factory Two in the Kang Shan suburb of the southern city of Kaohsiung. Some components were made at Kang Shan, but the plant was mainly concerned with engine assembly, using US-built parts and assemblies. The basic TFE731 is a twin-spool geared turbofan which has primarily been used as the powerplant for a range of biz-jets. The TFE731-3 has even found military applications, in both the CASA C.101 trainer and in the FMA IA-63 Pampa trainer, although still without reheat. The most significant use for the engine, at least insofar as the Ching-Kuo was concerned, was its application (in 3,500-lb st/15.57-kN, non-afterburning TFE731-2-2L form) to the indigenous AT-3 advanced jet trainer. One further advantage of the engine was that it could be portrayed as being a relatively 'harmless' civilian biz-jet engine, and not something to worry those concerned about arms transfers to Taiwan.

Engine overhaul

For the IDF, Garrett completely redesigned the TFE731, more than doubling its length (to 140.2 in/356.1 cm) by adding a fully variable augmentor. This gave reheat in the bypass and core flows, with a 10-flap fully variable nozzle driven by three mechanical actuators. The engine's fan and turbines were also significantly changed, with the TFE731's single-stage fan giving way to a three-stage fan with a rotating spinner, and with the single-stage HP and three-stage LP turbines giving way to two single-stage turbines.

Initial flight release of the new engine was obtained in February 1989, with full qualification following in September 1991. The engine underwent more than 5,000 hours of testing (some of it perhaps in a modified AT-3 testbed) before it flew in the IDF. Production deliveries began in October 1991. The resulting AlliedSignal/Garrett TFE1042-70 was qualified to US Mil-E-87231 standard and was later allocated the US service designation F125. At the beginning of the Ching-Kuo programme, afterburning thrust was quoted as being 8,400 lb st (37.37 kN), but development allowed this to be increased significantly. The current IDF production engine weighs in at 1,360 lb (617 kg), develops 6,060 lb (26.96 kN) dry and 9,500 lb (42.26 kN) with afterburning, with a bypass ratio of 0.46, an overall pressure ratio of 19 and a mass flow of 92.6 lb/sec. The specific fuel consumption was 0.79 lb/hr/lb in military power and 1.98 lb/hr/lb in afterburner.

Production-standard, single-seat aircraft feature a revised canopy – a one-piece upwards hingeing unit, instead of a two-piece sideways opening one.

In early specifications, thrust ratings of the TFE1042 were given as 6,025 lb st (26.80 kN) dry and 9,460 lb st (42.08 kN), perhaps indicating that production engines produce slightly higher thrust. The engine is of modular design, with eight major sections which can be separately built, bought, shipped, stored and installed, and which are interchangeable between engines. The engine does not need to be balanced following module replacement or exchange.

One hundred and twenty-five examples of the 9,500-lb st (42.26-kN) TFE1042 were ordered for the first 60 pre-production and production aircraft, the first 10 being built at Garrett's Phoenix facility. The same engine was re-ordered for the subsequent batch of 60 aircraft during December 1991.

Many felt that the thrust of the TFE1042 was still inadequate and plans were made for a succession of more powerful engines to be fitted. One of the earliest engines to be mentioned as a potential TFE1042 replacement was the 14,000-lb (62.28-kN) Garrett TFE1088 nominated for the IDF II. Efforts have also been made to upgrade the existing powerplant as the TFE1042-IPE. One option was the replacement of the existing multi-crystal turbine blade with a directionally solidified crystal turbine blade, or even by a single-crystal turbine blade. Either would allow

the engine to run at higher temperatures, thereby generating extra thrust. The F125X was another TFE1042 derivative promoted for the IDF, with an increased airflow fan, new high-pressure compressor and turbine, an increased-durability afterburner, a higher-pressure ratio and increased operating temperatures. These provided 30 per cent extra thrust and 5 per cent better specific fuel consumption. The F125X had 88.9 per cent commonality with the basic F125.

General Electric engine option

General Electric developed a private venture fighter engine, the 12,900-lb st (57.38-kN) J101/SF, which was the same size as the TFE-1042, to within a few millimetres. The engine was an 86 per cent scale derivative of the F404, developed specifically for lightweight twin-engined fighters, and for single-engined jet trainers like the BAe Hawk. With the same airflow requirements as a pair of J85 turbojets, 20 per cent more thrust, and offering a considerable reduction in specific fuel consumption, the engine was also seen as a potential F-5 power-plant. General Electric made an unsolicited bid to AIDC, which was warmly received, and the American company even supplied a J101 mock-up for installation and fit checks.

Whatever increased thrust engine was selected was intended to be fitted to the 161st and subsequent production aircraft, i.e. those aircraft destined for the planned third and fourth IDF wings. It was felt that such engines might then be retrofitted to the earlier aircraft. Unfortunately, the increased-thrust engine programme was cancelled in August 1992, as a result of the decision to purchase F-16s, although the idea may still be revived.

Interestingly, the afterburning F125 has been developed into the non-afterburning F124 which has been offered as an alternative power-plant for the McDonnell Douglas/BAe T-45 Goshawk. By comparison with that aircraft's existing Adour Mk 871, the new powerplant was claimed to offer a higher maximum take-off rating and faster acceleration time, as well as cheaper operating and purchase costs.

The two TFE1042-70 turbofans form part of an integrated power system (also developed by Garrett), which also includes an APU and an EPU (Emergency Power Unit). In the unlikely event of a double engine failure, or if hydraulic or electrical problems occurred, the EPU would start automatically and supply electrical and hydraulic power until the Garrett GTC36-120 APU could complete its more protracted autostart cycle. The APU's normal functions

These two *Ching-Kuos* admirably display the differences in canopy design between the initial 10 pre-production aircraft (foreground) and the 60 aircraft included in main production Block 1. Deliveries of the (anticipated) additional 60 aircraft of Block 2 have not yet begun.

were to supply high pressure air to the air turbine starter and could be used for the full ground checkout of aircraft systems requiring the electrical generator, hydraulic pumps and cooling from the ECS without starting the engines or using external power.

Sky Thunder

IDF avionics were developed by a team led by Smiths Industries under the Tien Lei (Sky Thunder) programme. Smiths Industries was a natural choice for the IDF's Sky Thunder programme, not least because the company had already played a similar role in developing and integrating the avionics of the AT-3 trainer. The requirement demanded a sophisticated avionics system, with the need for a look-down multi-mode radar and with provision for IR and BVR missile armament. It also required 360°

RHAWS coverage and both active and passive countermeasures. The agility required of the IDF dictated that the aircraft be inherently unstable in pitch, and this in turn necessitated the use of a modern triple-redundant full authority fly-by-wire control system. The need for avionics integration (and redundancy), and the need to provide for growth, made it

inevitable that the avionics suite was based around modular architecture, with dual-redundant, high-speed MIL STD 1553B digital MUX buses. The X MUX was primarily used by the defensive avionics, BVR missile system, the radar and laser INS, while the Y MUX was primarily used by the CNI (communications, navigation and identification) system, the

AIDC Indigenous Defence Fighter (IDF) Ching-Kuo

1 Pitot head
2 Glass-fibre radome
3 GD-53 multi-mode radar
4 Incidence probe
5 Lower VHF/UHF antenna
6 Radar equipment racks
7 Dynamic pressure probes
8 Forward avionics equipment bays
9 Mission computer
10 Formation lighting strip
11 Rudder pedals
12 Pilot's head-up-display (HUD)
13 Instrument panel with multi-function CRT displays

14 Side-hinging cockpit canopy
15 Sidestick controller
16 Martin-Baker Mk 12 'zero-zero' ejection seat
17 Engine throttle lever, HOTAS controls
18 Forward-retracting nosewheel
19 Hydraulic steering jack
20 Digital flight control computer, fly-by-wire control system
21 Liquid oxygen converter
22 Rear avionics equipment bays
23 Blast-suppressing cannon muzzle aperture
24 Ground test panel
25 Fixed-geometry engine air intake
26 Port navigation light
27 Forward radar warning antennas, port and starboard

28 Forward fuselage fuel tank
29 M61A1 Vulcan gun
30 Ammunition magazine
31 APU exhaust
32 Integrated Power System (IPS) comprising Auxiliary and Emergency Power Units (APU & EPU)
33 Leading-edge flap hydraulic drive motor
34 Air conditioning pack
35 Centre fuselage fuel tanks
36 Machined wing attachment bulkheads
37 Tank access panels

38 Inboard wing pylon
39 Outboard wing pylon
40 Starboard wing integral fuel tank
41 Wingtip missile launch rail
42 Starboard flaperon
43 Upper VHF/UHF antenna
44 Radar warning receivers
45 Flight control system memory unit
46 Fin root joints

47 Conventional fin structure with composite skin panels
48 Formation lighting strip
49 Fintip antenna fairing
50 Anti-collision strobe light
51 Rear radar warning antenna
52 All-composite rudder
53 Rudder hydraulic actuator
54 Radar warning signal processor
55 Tail navigation light
56 Starboard all-moving tailplane

57 Variable-area afterburner nozzles
58 Runway arrester hook
59 Split trailing-edge airbrakes
60 Airbrake hydraulic jack
61 Port all-moving tailplane
62 All-composite tailplane structure
63 Tailplane pivot mounting
64 Tailplane hydraulic actuator
65 Machined fin attachment bulkheads
66 International Turbine

Engine Corporation (ITEC) TFE1042/F125 afterburning turbofan engine
67 Full-Authority Digital Engine Control (FADEC) unit
68 Formation lighting strip
69 Engine oil tank
70 Airframe-mounted accessory equipment gearbox with hydraulic pump, generator and air turbine starter
71 Flaperon hydraulic actuator
72 Port flaperon
73 Wingroot attachment joints
74 Main undercarriage leg strut and hydraulic retraction jack

75 Forward-retracting mainwheel
76 Port wing integral fuel tank
77 Pylon attachment hardpoints
78 Multi-spar wing structure
79 Flaperon composite structure
80 CBU-87 Rockeye sub-munition dispenser
81 Fuselage centreline pylon

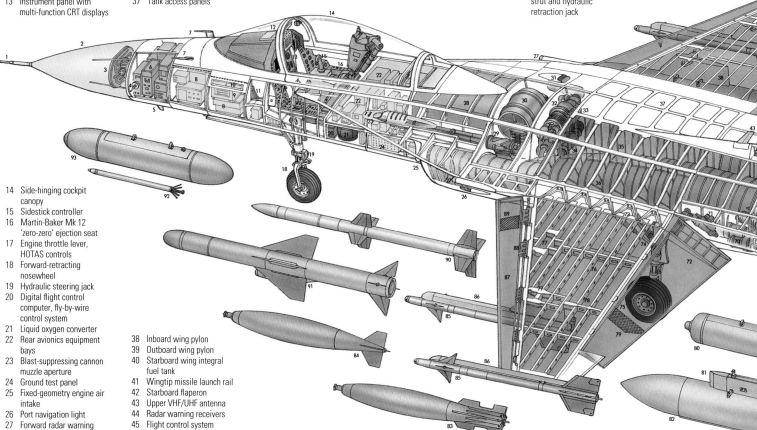

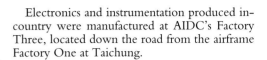

HOTAS system, the gun, stores jettison, IR missile system, the flight control system and the sensor data acquisition system.

The aircraft is equipped with a new Kam Lung (Golden Dragon) GD-53 multi-mode pulse-Doppler radar. This is based on the Westinghouse AN/APG-67 (V) developed for the F-20 but incorporates some technology from the Westinghouse AN/APG-66 (used by the F-16A). This is a true monopulse radar, and the use of monolithic microwave devices and high-density integrated circuits has made possible a lightweight and extremely compact package. The capabilities of the APG-67 were first demonstrated in the F-20. Despite its small size and relatively small flat plate antenna, the radar proved quite comparable with the F-16's larger APG-66, with almost identical detection ranges. In some respects it even proved superior. In the larger nose of the IDF, the antenna has probably been increased in size, which would infer a significant increase in detection range, while development since the demise of the F-20 has almost certainly led to major improvements in other areas.

82	275-US gal (73-litre) external fuel tank
83	Mk 82 SE Snakeye retarded bomb
84	Mk 82 500-lb HE bomb
85	TC-1 (Sky Sword-1) short-range air-to-air missile
86	Missile launch rail
87	Leading-edge manoeuvre flap
88	Leading-edge flap torque shaft and rotary actuators
89	Flap aluminium skin panel with honeycomb core structure
90	TC-2 (Sky Sword-2) beyond-visual-range (BVR) air-to-air missile, two carried on fuselage centreline
91	Hsiung-Feng air-to-surface anti-shipping missile
92	2.75-in (68-mm) air-to-surface rocket
93	LAU-69, 19-round rocket launcher

Coherent pulse-Doppler processing provides good lookdown capability, while Doppler beam sharpening gives better angular resolution for the identification of ground targets. The radar has a very low parts count and a high level of integration, giving extraordinarily reliability illustrated by a 235-hour MTBF. Digital pulse compression and expansion techniques allow low peak power to be used, which in turn reduces the aircraft's signature, improves signal-to-clutter ratio and reduces susceptibility to jamming or interference. The aircraft's avionics system also incorporates a Honeywell H423 INS, TWS-95 RHAWS and Bendix-King multi-function and head-up displays. AlliedSignal's AiResearch Division provided the environmental control system.

The Lear-Astronics flight control computer provides automatic stability augmentation, and automatically limits angle-of-attack and *g*. It also incorporates an independent triplex analog backup. The control surfaces are actuated by a limited-movement, pressure-sensing sidestick controller on the starboard console, and by rudder pedals. The single-piece rudder is driven by a single Direct Drive Valve (DDV) actuator, while the slab horizontal tailplanes are driven by two DDV actuators. The flaperons occupy the inboard three-quarters of each trailing edge and are similarly powered. The leading-edge flaps are each powered by four rotary actuators.

Electronics and instrumentation produced in-country were manufactured at AIDC's Factory Three, located down the road from the airframe Factory One at Taichung.

Sky Sword

As if developing an entirely new indigenous fighter were not ambitious enough, it was decided from an early stage that the aircraft would not have to rely on US-supplied weapons (or even on licence-built versions of existing weapons), and that new missiles would be developed. Accordingly, the IDF's indigenous primary missile armament was developed in the Tien Chien (Sky Sword) programme. As a modern fighter interceptor the IDF would require both an agile short-range missile for dogfighting and for use when rules of engagement dictated visual identification of the target, and a longer-range missile which could be fired at beyond visual range.

Although the Taiwanese were keen to avoid simply copying existing weapons, there is little point in trying to reinvent the wheel, and it was inevitable that the short-range indigenous missile would resemble the excellent AIM-9 Sidewinder in concept and configuration, not least since the IDF would be expected to be compatible with both types of missile. It would thus be sensible if both weapons could use a common launch rail. Furthermore, it was

Martin-Baker undertook sled tests for the Ching-Kuo's Mk 12 ejection seats, using a mock-up forward fuselage mounted on a trolly. AIDC have rejected the tried and tested system of explosive ejection through the canopy in favour of a rocket assisted canopy that disposes of the entire canopy unit before the seat is fired.

Sky Sword II (Tien Chien II) is carried in pairs by the Ching-Kuo and, it is believed, will also be integrated on the RoCAF's F-16s and Mirage 2000s. The missile is fractionally shorter than an AIM-7, with the same diameter, and slightly longer fins. It has a blast-fragmentation warhead, of unknown size and is fitted with an active laser fuse.

Sky Sword I (Tien Chien I) was first test fired by a Taiwanese F-5 in 1986 and entered production for the RoCAF in 1989. It seems virtually interchangable with the various models of Sidewinder license-built in Taiwan. Sky Sword II appears to have undergone subtle modifications of its forward fin and seeker head design, over its operational life, as its manufacturer (the Chung Shian Institute) has sought to improve its performance.

The badges of the three component squadrons of the 3rd TFW are seen here. They include the wolf of No. 7 Sqn (note the position of its jaws), the golden dragon of No. 8 Sqn (again echoing the squadron designation in its form) and the strange concoction of No. 28 Sqn, which began to transition from the F-104 in late 1995

This Ching-Kuo sports a typical air defence load of four Sky Sword Is, two Sky Sword IIs and two 275-US gal (1041-litre) drop tanks. Ching-Kuo is designed to allow an 'in-cockpit' scramble time of three minutes when on QRA.

always intended that the Sky Sword 1 (also known as the Tien Chien 1 or TC-1) would also be compatible with other Taiwanese fighters, and that the new missile would serve as an alternative to US-supplied AIM-9s.

The AIM-9 had already been licence-built in Taiwan, and prime contractor, the Chung Shan Institute of Science and Technology (Taipei), almost certainly used many AIM-9 components virtually unchanged. The end result is that the Sky Sword 1 closely resembles the AIM-9L in appearance, dimensions and weight. Even the moving forward control fins are similar in shape, although without the reduced sweep at the tips. The missile has the same kind of HE fragmentation warhead wrapped in a skin of pre-formed rods, and triggered by a laser proximity fuse with a ring of eight laser diode emitters and silicon photodiode receivers.

Development of the Sky Sword 1 proceeded smoothly, and the first test firing was made from an F-5E in April 1986, destroying the Beech target drone against which it was fired. Firings from the IDF were initially conducted by the rebuilt first FSD aircraft, after it had been retro-fitted with radar. Initial production of the missile began in 1989, and it entered service in 1991. The AIM-9L and MATRA Magic 2 have been

ordered for Taiwanese F-16s and Mirage 2000s, but Sky Sword 1 is likely to remain the primary short-range weapon of the IDF. AIM-9L/Ps have also been seen on operational IDFs.

Sky Sword II – Taiwan's AMRAAM?

Less is known about the Sky Sword 2 (also known as the Tien Chien 2 or TC-2) long-range air-to-air missile, with little information having been released by the prime contractor (the Chung Shan Institute of Science and Technology) or AIDC. Photos showing the missile being launched from the Ching-Kuo (actually from the third FSD aircraft) have been released, but the dates of firings remain unknown, and it is uncertain how many live,

guided firings have been attempted, or with what results. Interestingly, the photo shows the rear missile being fired first, apparently after having been explosively ejected downwards away from the aircraft by pyrotechnic rams. This would make sense, since it removes any possibility of the rear missile being damaged by rocket motor efflux from the front missile. The Sky Sword 2 missile bears some resemblance to the AIM-7 Sparrow, although it has distinctive cropped short-span, long-chord trapezoidal wings forward and squared-off trapezoidal fins aft. The aft fins on the Sky Sword 2 are the moving control surfaces, and taper on both leading and trailing edges, while the forward fins (little more than broad strakes) are fixed. On the AIM-7 Sparrow both sets of fins are tri-angular in shape and are moving forward and fixed aft. The missile is estimated to have the same body diameter and length as the Sparrow, and a similar launch weight. Details of the fuse, warhead and seeker have not been released, and sources even differ as to whether the missile employs semi-active or active radar homing.

In 1989 Military Technology's Taiwanese correspondent described the missile as being in the same class as AMRAAM, with a maximum speed of Mach 4, a range of about 50 km (31 miles) and a fire-and-forget guidance package.

Specification
AIDC IDF Ching-Kuo

Wing: span over wingtip missile rails 9.46 m (31 ft 0.45 in); area 24.26 m² (261.1 sq ft)
Fuselage and tail: length including probe 14.21 m (46 ft 7.37 in), height 4.65 m (5 ft 3.38 in)
Powerplant: two ITEC (Garrett/AIDC) TFE1042-70 (F125) each rated at 6,060 lb st (26.96 kN) dry and 9,500 lb st (42.26 kN) with afterburning
Weights: empty operating 14,300 lb (6486 kg), normal take-off 21,000 lb (9525 kg), maximum take off weight 27,000 lb (12247 kg)

Fuel and load: internal fuel 4,650 lb (2198 kg), normal weapon load 2,000 lb (9078 kg) air-to-air, or up to 8,600 lb (3900 kg) air-to-ground
Speed: (estimated) maximum level speed 'clean' at 36,000 ft (10975 m) more than 688 kt (792 mph; 1275 km/h); limiting Mach Number 1.8
Performance: (estimated) maximum rate of climb at sea level 50,000 ft (15240 m) per minute; (estimated) service ceiling 55,000 ft (16760 m)
g limits: basic design gross weight; 9 g; maximum design gross weight +6.5 g

Aero Industry Development Center (AIDC)

AIDC was established in 1969, replacing the previous Bureau of Aircraft Industry, which dated back to 1946. The first aircraft built in Taiwan, between 1968 and 1974, was the PL-1B Chien-Shou piston-engined, primary trainer (based on Ladislo Pazmany's US-designed Pazmany PL-1 lightplane). Subsequently, 118 Bell UH-1Hs were assembled for the Army and nearly 300 F-5E/Fs were assembled for the Air Force. AIDC's first 'home' design was the T-CH-1 Chun-Hsing turboprop trainer, which made its maiden flight in November 1973. This was followed by the twin turbofan-powered AT-3A/B Tzu-Chung trainer/light attack aircraft, which first flew in September 1980 and remained in production until 1990. In January 1995 local press reports reports suggested that AIDC might be about to re-open the AT-3 production line for a potential domestic and export order. In 1994 a three-year privatisation programme for AIDC was announced, and a 42-month privatisation bill was finally approved by the national legislature in May 1995.

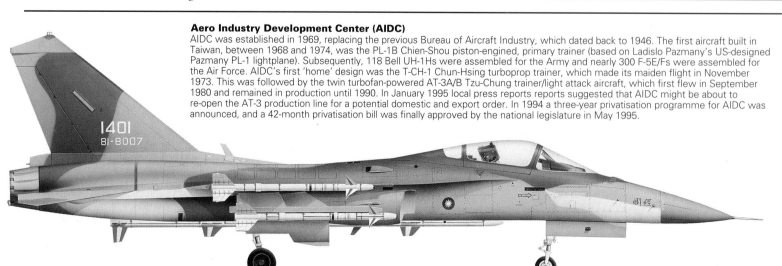

Cannon armament
The Ching-Kuo is fitted with an M61A1/A2 Vulcan 20-mm cannon in the port LERX. The gun is tied into a Photo-Sonics gun camera, operated by a switch on the pilot's main sidestick control.

The two-seat Ching-Kuo
Only one of the initial batch of four FSD Ching-Kuos was a two-seat aircraft (79-8004). This aircraft was lost, and its pilot killed, in a crash caused by transonic airframe/powerplant vibrations on 12 July 1991 (which forced several design changes). Six pre-production two-seaters are now being followed by 28 production aircraft (from the current authorised run of 130 IDFs, in total). The rear cockpit is not stepped and replaces the forward fuel tank, cutting down on the single-seater's maximum internal fuel load of 665 US gal (2517 litres; 554 Imp gal). The second rear cockpit is not equipped with a HUD, but displays from the front cockpit HUD are repeated on one of the rear cockpit MFDs. The two-seat aircraft, which has no known change in designation, also shows no evidence of airframe changes to compensate for the extra cockpit and resultant aerodynamic differences.

The Chinese dimension
In October 1995 the President of the People's Republic of China stated on television, that "The peaceful reunification of the two sides of the Taiwan Straits is the unshakable determination of the entire Chinese people, however, one cannot rule out the military option."

ITEC TFE1042 engine
The International Turbine Engine Co. (ITEC) is a joint venture by AIDC and Allied Signal (formerly Garrett AiResearch) which builds a developed, afterburning version of the TFE731 engine, the TFE1042-70. This a twin-shaft, augmented turbofan with a maximum power output of 41.15 kN (9,260 lb). Initial flight release was achieved in February 1989, with full qualification in September 1991. Each Ching-Kuo is fitted with two TFE1042-70s (US military designation F125-GA-100), and ITEC is also offering a non-afterburning version, the F124-GA-100, for other uses. Future developments of the IDF may benefit from proposed F125X and F125XX growth versions, which may ultimately increase the engine's thrust to 54.49 kN (12,250 lb) and 71.17 kN (16,000 lb), respectively.

AGM-65B Maverick
AGM-65B is an early member of the Maverick ASM family fitted with the missile's original TV seeker, but with a scene magnification optics upgrade, to improve target identification at range. The weapon is fitted with a 57-kg (125-lb) shaped charge HE warhead.

Cockpit
All versions of the Ching-Kuo are fitted with Martin Baker Mk 12 ejection seats. Cockpit avionics include Bendix King MFDs and HUD coupled with a Honeywell INS. The digital FCS was supplied by Lear Astronics.

AIDC Indigenous Defence Fighter (IDF) Ching-Kuo

This is the second of the pre-production batch of four two-seat Ching-Kuos, which entered production in October 1990. Six single-seat aircraft were also included in this batch, and all were delivered to the Republic of China Air Force by November 1993. The RoCAF's Ching-Kuos are all flown by the 3rd Tactical Fighter Wing, based at Ching Chuan Kang Air Base, in northwest Taiwan.

Structure and flying controls
Early production Ching-Kuos were all-metal, but composites have now been introduced in the tailplanes and flaperons. The almost full-span flaperons and all-moving tailerons are linked to the leading edge flaps by the digital flight control system.

Golden Dragon 53 radar
The Ching-Kuo's GD-53 multi-mode fire control and AI radar is based on the APG-67, developed by Martin Marietta for the ill-fated F-20 Tigershark. APG-67 is a coherent pulse Doppler I-/J-band radar, with ±60° scan capability in azimuth and elevation, now optimised for air-to-air modes. GD-53 also incorporates elements of the Westinghouse APG-66, which has been ordered by Taiwan for its 150 F-16A/Bs (in its APG-66V3 version).

Air-to-air missiles
Taiwan has developed a range of indigenous AAMs, while also acquiring weapons from abroad. The Tien Chien 1 (Sky Sword 1) is a Sidewinder lookalike, with an active laser fuse and all-aspect capability – making it broadly comparable with the AIM-9L. Tien Chien 2 (Sky Sword 2) is a Sparrow-class BVR missile, with a 40-km (25-mile) range and 30-kg (66-lb) warhead (approximately). Reports differ on whether TC-2 has semi-active or active radar guidance (like the AIM-120 AMRAAM). This aircraft is carrying AIM-9L Sidewinders and Taiwan has ordered not only AIM-9s and AIM-7s (for the F-5, F-16 and Ching-Kuo) but MATRA Magic 2 and Mica AAMs for its Mirage 2000-5s.

Ching-Kuo: The Indigenous Defence Fighter

Above and left: Two-seat Ching-Kuos have entered service alongside single-seat aircraft in a seemingly random fashion, though a high proportion of the early deliveries in Batch 1 were training aircraft. AIDC have plans to develop a dedicated (simplified) lead-in fighter trainer version of the Ching-Kuo. The flying suit badge worn by all IDF pilots is seen opposite.

The IDF is intended to carry Taiwanese equivalents of the 500-lb Mk 82 and 1000-lb Mk 84 HE bombs as well as napalm canisters and CBUs. Seen here is a Mk 20 Rockeye II CBU which is filled with 247 Mk 118 bomblets.

an excellent air-to-air weapon with a high rate of fire and high muzzle velocity, although many non-US aerospace companies believe that using a higher calibre (25 mm, 27 mm or 30 mm) offers a balance of advantage.

The IDF carries its weapons on nine hardpoints, although not all can be used at once. They are numbered roughly according to American practice, in ascending order from the port wingtip to the starboard. The wingtips (stations 1 and 9) carry Sidewinder-type missile launch rails, which may be permanently fitted. AIM-9, TC-1 or similar light AAMs can also be carried under the outboard underwing pylons (stations 2 and 8), which can also accommodate a single CBU or 500-lb bomb. The inboard underwing pylons (stations 3 and 7) were stressed for the carriage of two Mk 82s or CBUs, or for the carriage of rocket pods or external tanks. The centreline could either carry a single pylon (on station 5) or a pair of tandem pylons mounted in the missile recesses (stations 4, forward, and 6, aft). The latter could carry a single CBU or Mk 82, while station 5 could accommodate a Mk 84, a pair of CBUs, a pair of Mk 82s, a centreline tank or rocket pod.

Current training fit

At this stage of its career, the Ching-Kuo flies mainly in the training role, and the most common configuration consists of wingtip missiles (usually dummies or inert acquisition rounds) and a centreline fuel tank, usually with underwing pylons removed entirely. AIM-9L/Ps seem to be as common as the indigenous TC-1. When flying in operational configuration, the standard load-out appears to be a pair of wingtip-mounted IR-homing missiles, with two more underwing, 275-US gal (1041-litre) inboard underwing fuel tanks and TC-2 long-range missiles in the centreline recesses.

For the anti-shipping role the aircraft is said to be able to carry three of the new indigenous turbofan-powered, 520-kg (1145-lb) Hsiung Feng 2 (Male Bee 2) under the centreline and on the inboard underwing pylons, although these are not listed in the current IDF brochure, nor have they ever been publicly displayed

This, he averred, had an INS for mid-course guidance, and an active radar seeker for terminal homing. The missile itself decided whether to use its proximity fuse or its impact fuse. Seven rounds had been ground launched even before the IDF was rolled out, with 'impressive results'. The missile may now be in front-line service. If the missile is an AMRAAM-class weapon, this is a miraculous achievement for a nation with a population of only 20 million, since elsewhere in the Western world only the USA and France have attempted development of a long-range fire-and-forget missile. Unfortunately, reliable sources indicate that the missile was indeed planned as a fire-and-forget weapon, but that delays and difficulties led to

the development of an interim semi-active radar homing version which is the Sky Sword 2 missile now in service. Reports that development has been abandoned are almost certainly erroneous, since the missile is a common sight at Ching Chuan Kang.

In addition to the IDF's purpose-designed missile armament described above, the aircraft was fitted with a single six-barrelled General Electric M61A1 Vulcan cannon. This is located in the port LERX, with the cylindrical ammunition tank lying lengthways across the fuselage to its right. This appears to be the same size as the ammunition tank fitted to the F-16, which contains 515 rounds of 20-mm ammunition. Despite its relatively small calibre the M61A1 is

Early Ching-Kuos (perhaps all pre-production aircraft) were fitted with the M61A1 Vulcan cannon. From 1993 onwards, all aircraft may have been fitted with an improved version of the Vulcan, the M61A2, which weighs 105 lb (93 kg) compared to the 252-lb (114.5-kg) M61A1.

alongside a service Ching-Kuo. The Hsiung Feng 2 was developed from the Hsiung Feng 1, which was itself derived from the Gabriel 2 ship/surface-launched missile. The air-to-surface version of Hsiung Feng 2 began development during the mid-1980s, and may not yet be complete. Identified ground attack weapons seen with the Ching-Kuo include AGM-65B Maverick EO ASMs, Mk 82 500-lb bombs with slick and retard tails, the Mk 84 AIR 2,000-lb bomb (probably carried only on the centreline), and 19-round LAU-5003 2.75-in rocket pods. The GBU-12A Paveway I laser-guided bomb has also been described as a potential IDF weapon.

Development and test programme

The IDF design was frozen in 1985, following a comprehensive design review. It was announced that the research, development and production budget was US$1 billion although, by 1989, Taiwanese sources suggested that this had escalated to US$5 billion. AIDC has stated that it decided to bypass the prototype stage, and instead decided to proceed directly to the production of what it called Full Scale Development (FSD) aircraft. These first four aircraft differed from later IDFs, however, and are best regarded as prototypes. On 10 December 1988, the aircraft was formally named Ching-Kuo after the late Chiang Ching-Kuo, who was the son of Chiang Kai Shek and former C-in-C of the armed forces in addition to serving as Taiwanese President; it was he who had authorised the aircraft's development. By then the first FSD aircraft was complete enough to taxi under its own power and to form the centrepiece of a formal naming ceremony. For the roll-out the aircraft was armed with a pair of Sky Sword 2s under the centreline, with underwing and wingtip Sky Sword 1s in an attempt to underline the type's combat persistence and BVR capabilities.

The first FSD aircraft (77-8001/10001, A-1) made its maiden flight on 28 May 1989, in the hands of Colonel Wu Kang-Ming and followed 7,000 hours of testing in AIDC's supersonic wind tunnel. The aircraft wore a smart red, white and blue colour scheme and was without radar. The first flight was delayed from late April to allow for checks of the flight control system, whose similarity to the control system of the Saab JAS 39 Gripen (whose prototype crashed due to FCS problems on its sixth flight) prompted concern. The aircraft almost certainly flew with engines which produced only 8,500 lb st (37.81 kN) each in reheat, and it is understood that these conferred a maximum level speed of Mach 1.2. The second and third aircraft (78-8002/10002, A-2 and 78-8003/10003, A-3) made their maiden flights on 27 September

Ching-Kuo has a service design life of 8,000 hours (12,000 landings) and has been fatigue tested to over 16,000 hours by AIDC. Its largely metal construction and twin-engined configuration underline AIDC's commitment to building a robust, easily maintainable/repairable airframe that can survive combat damage to get home safely with its pilot.

1989 and 10 January 1990, and were painted in a similar scheme, although both aircraft had grey radomes indicating the presence of radar. The fourth FSD aircraft (79-80004/10004, B-1) flew for the first time on 10 July 1990 and was the first aircraft painted in camouflage. It was also the first two-seat Ching-Kuo.

All four FSD aircraft were fitted with comprehensive telemetry equipment, with 300 real-time relay channels and 1,000 data recording channels for playback post-flight. They were built on production tooling to reduce cost and overall programme timescale. This was a gamble, relying on the fact that major modifications would not be required, and luckily it paid off. Each of the aircraft was assigned its own specific responsibilities within the flight test programme, and within AIDC the aircraft were referred to

simply by their construction numbers. A-1 was assigned to handling and stability testing, including high-Alpha flying. It also cleared the Mach and altitude envelope to its pre-planned limits. The second aircraft, A-2, was used primarily for structural load tests (up to 9 *g*), while A-3 was assigned to high-altitude testing, gunnery and external stores clearance. B-1 was used for test pilot training, radar tests and avionics integration, and for proving of the rear cockpit operation.

The two-seat IDF was a minimum-change version of the single-seater, with no increase in fin height to compensate for the increased keel area forward, and with no discernible increase in fuselage length to accommodate the second cockpit, which instead replaced the forward fuselage fuel tank. The rear seat was not appreciably raised, so that the instructor does not have a particularly good view straight forward. This is not too much of a problem, since the IDF two-seater is scarcely intended as anything but a conversion and continuation trainer. The tandem cockpits are covered by a single-piece canopy, hinging open to port, with a separate fixed windscreen. The two-seater's canopy was only marginally longer than that of the single-seater.

Problems in the public eye

It was unfortunate that the first view many had of the Ching-Kuo was a press photo of the first aircraft suffering a landing accident, resulting from a burst tyre. This happened on 29 October 1989 when AIDC test pilot Lieutenant Colonel Wu Kang Ming was demonstrating the aircraft in front of President Lee Tung Hui. The accident resulted in damage to a wingtip and a collapsed nosewheel. The aircraft was soon repaired and restored to flying status, the opportunity being taken to add radar. Unfortunately, the accident resulted in the cancellation of the Ching-Kuo's planned international debut, which had been scheduled for the 1990 Hannover air show. The addition of radar to the first FSD aircraft helped compensate for the loss of the radar-equipped second prototype on 12 July 1991, during tests intended to assess the IDF's performance during short sprints. The aircraft suffered severe vibration as it approached Mach 1, as the pilot reported that he was climbing through 5000 m (16,500 ft). The port horizontal stabiliser suffered a fatigue fracture and separated, causing an uncommanded roll to starboard. Test pilot

Above: Ching-Kuo will remain an important element in Taiwan's defence system for many years to come. Taiwan has a sophisticated air defence radar system, which is currently being upgraded, and integrated with E-2T Hawkeyes.

Left: The Ching-Kuo conversion training syllabus includes 30 to 40 hours flying training, including air combat sorties over the RoCAF's own instrumented ACMI range.

Colonel Wu Ke Chen ejected at about 2000 m (6,500 ft) but had drowned before the SAR team reached him, only 10 minutes after the accident. Swift-flowing currents in the Taichung Straits frustrated efforts to recover the wreckage.

The four flying FSD aircraft (including the single twin-stick trainer) were followed by a 10-aircraft pre-production batch (including four two-seaters). Final assembly of the first of these 10 aircraft began in April 1990, and the first was delivered to the RoCAF on 9 March 1992. All 10 had been delivered by 19 November 1993. Manufacturing techniques changed during the construction of the pre-production batch, with increasing automation of the production process reducing the production time. From A-6 (82-8011/1403) most sub-systems, wiring and pneumatics were pre-installed in the wings, forward and centre fuselage sections prior to assembly. The use of increasingly sophisticated computerised testing equipment reduced forward fuselage wiring tests from 25 days (when performed manually) to 14 and finally 10 days. One pre-production aircraft (81-8007/1401) was bailed back to AIDC to replace the crashed A-2 in the flight test programme, flying avionics and radar tests. The FSD aircraft were funded between 1988 and 1990 (1977 to 1979 in the Chinese calendar), while the pre-production aircraft were funded during 1992 (two single-seat, two trainers) and 1993 (two trainers, four single-seaters). IDF funding in 1989 alone amounted

to US$702 million. The pre-production aircraft wore much the same grey/blue air superiority colour scheme as the fourth, two-seat prototype.

The first of the 10 pre-production aircraft was rolled out on 9 March 1992, and it introduced new cylindrical RWR fairings on the LERXes. Deliveries to the air force began soon afterwards, considerably earlier than the expected date of January 1994. By March 1992 the aircraft had made 830 flights and clocked up 500 flying hours, in the hands of eight AIDC and five RoCAF pilots. On 10 February 1993 the first unit, No. 7 'Seed' Squadron, publicly unveiled its aircraft at Chin Chuan Kang air base, which included two production single-seaters (81-8007/1401 and 81-8008/1402) and two production two-seaters (81-8006/1601 and 81-8010/1604). Also present and apparently temporarily on charge with the unit were the rebuilt first prototype and the fourth prototype. Weapons on display included the GBU-12 500-lb LGB, the CBU-87 Rockeye, the AGM-65B TV Maverick ASM, the AIM-9P Sidewinder IR-homing AAM and the indigenous Sky Sword I and Sky Sword II AAMs. The last of the pre-production batch (82-8014/1406) was delivered to Chin Chuan Kang on 19 November 1993, with the first production aircraft (83-8015/1605) following in January of the following year. The squadron was responsible for instructor training, and for producing a cadre of pilots for future units, while also performing operational evaluation and tactical development.

The production single-seaters varied slightly from the six single-seat aircraft in the pre-production batch. They had a reconfigured canopy, which became a single-piece, upward-hinging unit (albeit with a canopy frame which appeared to divide it into separate canopy and windscreen sections). The pre-production aircraft had featured a three-part canopy, with fixed windscreen and rear section and a port-hinging middle section. Some of the pre-production aircraft may also have had a slightly different intake, with a reconfigured intake splitter plate, but no evidence can be found to support statements that any of the pre-production aircraft ever had a dorsal fin.

Production reduction

Planned production of 256 aircraft was dramatically cut back in March 1993, following US promises to supply Lockheed Martin F-16s. Taiwan's eventual requirement for Ching-Kuos was even higher, standing at 420 aircraft. Even with a production run of 256, the Ching-Kuo was an expensive aircraft, and cost had escalated dramatically. Engines originally budgeted at $2 million were actually costing $5 million, for example. Taiwan's legislature, the Yuan, announced that total procurement would be reduced to only 130 Ching-Kuos, including 28 two-seaters. At the same time, the Taiwanese Minister of Defence announced that the aircraft would be available for export, giving AIDC the slim chance of restoring the production run to its original level. The aircraft would make an ideal choice for many nations, although in competition with aircraft like the F-16, and with major upgrades of earlier-generation fighters, the price would have to be right. The aircraft's best hope might be to attract orders from those nations unable or unwilling to buy 'American' due to the danger of arms embargoes or sanctions, although the aircraft's very high US content would almost certainly necessitate US approval for any exports in any case. Otherwise,

Ching-Kuo: The Indigenous Defence Fighter

Israeli F-16D Fighting Falcons, plus a centreline pod, and is apparently intended as a defence-suppression 'Wild Weasel' aircraft. Another planned variant was an unarmed two-seat trainer intended as an advanced and lead-in trainer, rather than as a simple conversion and continuation trainer for the single-seater Ching-Kuo. Other planned sub-variants included a dedicated night attack version, a specialised reconnaissance model and even an adversary trainer. Even more advanced was the proposed IDF II, which was to have been an entirely new fighter, of F-15/Su-27 configuration with twin fins, widely spaced engines and a large dorsal airbrake. The engines were to have been Garrett TFE-1088s, versions of the TFE-731-5A each developing 12,000 lb (53.38 kN) with afterburning.

By the end of 1995 production totalled at least 55 aircraft, four FSD 'prototypes' (one a twin-sticker), 10 pre-production aircraft (four of them two-seaters) and 41 of the first batch of 60 production aircraft (11 of them two-seaters). The high proportion of two-seaters in the early batches reflects the early need for these aircraft for pilot conversion training. They have not been produced at fixed intervals, sometimes being interspersed between single fighters, and sometimes between blocks of up to 13 single-seaters. The accompanying table gives known serial number, construction number and build number details. FSD aircraft used five-digit numbers commencing with 10001, regardless of whether they were single- or two-seaters, while production and pre-production aircraft had four-digit build numbers commencing 1401 (single-seat) and 1601 (two-seat). The aircraft also wore USAF-type serials, with a year prefix (but based on the Chinese calendar, to which 11 has to be added to obtain the Western year) and a four-digit serial. Single-seaters were allocated construction numbers from A-1, while two-seaters were numbered from B-1, but these numbers were not displayed externally.

Many analysts have taken the planned premature cessation of production as evidence of the Ching-Kuo's supposed 'inferiority' but, in fact, the small production run has been imposed by economic realities. The F-16s now being supplied by the USA are quite simply cheaper than the cost of new Ching-Kuos. In Nationalist China a lower price means a higher quantity, and numbers mean a great deal when you are facing the might of the People's Republic of China. Despite limited international assistance or interest (and hostility from those nations attempting to gain friendlier relations with mainland China), Taiwan has succeeded in producing a truly modern advanced jet fighter. The aircraft is arguably no less advanced than Sweden's JAS 39, yet is already in front-line service with more than 50 aircraft delivered. The Ching-Kuo is in every respect a superb achievement, and it is also an impressive performer and a worthy successor to the F-5. **Jon Lake**

nations like Pakistan might be ideal customers for the Ching-Kuo. Cynics might assume that the Ching-Kuo's export chances would hardly have been helped had AIDC accepted Lockheed Martin's 1993 offer to help market the aircraft, since it is inconceivable that the US firm would have pushed the Taiwanese aircraft rather than its own F-16. The damage to AIDC was further reduced by Taiwan's investment in BAe's BAe 146 as the Regional Jetliner.

RoCAF service

The cut-back production run is now intended to allow the re-equipment of only two fighter wings, instead of the four originally planned and the seven which the RoCAF had hoped to re-equip. In early 1996 even the first of these, the 3rd Tactical Fighter Wing, was not fully equipped. The wing's second squadron, No. 8, completed conversion on 28 December 1994 and was declared operational on the first day of 1995. The third and last F-104 squadron of the wing, No. 28 Squadron, commenced conversion at the end of 1995. Delays had been imposed by a grounding order which followed at least two losses. These necessitated modifications to the fuel management system (cited as the cause of both crashes), and the recall of 40 aircraft. Although the 3rd TFW's three squadrons have distinct identities, with their own badges, squadron and wing insignia is not carried by the aircraft, but is worn by the pilots. This reflects a centralised servicing arrangement which is likely to give way to a more traditional squadron set up, with individual units performing their own engineering when conversion is complete.

The reduced production run is likely to kill off most of the planned sub-variants of the Ching-Kuo. The aircraft delivered will provide a high-quality BVR-equipped air defence fighter for the Taiwanese air force, augmenting F-5Es and the planned F-16s. Planned performance upgrades may still be incorporated in production Ching-Kuos (perhaps by retrofit), but the 'Special Missions' Ching-Kuo illustrated in AIDC's own brochure is unlikely to see the light of day. This aircraft features a square-section fuselage spine similar to that fitted to

Current RoCAF plans call for the 3rd TFW to be joined by one other Ching-Kuo-equipped Wing, the 1st TFW, currently based at Tainan and operating three squadrons of F-5Es.

AIDC IDF Ching-Kuo production list

Serial	C/n	Build number
FSD aircraft (four aircraft, plus one static test airframe)		
77-8001	A-1	10001
78-8002	A-2	10002
78-8003	A-3	10003
79-8004	B-1	10004
Pre-production (10 aircraft)		
81-8005	B-2	1601
81-8006	B-3	1602
81-8007	A-4	1401
81-8008	A-5	1402
82-8009	B-4	1603
82-8010	B-5	1604
82-8011	A-6	1403
82-8012	A-7	1404
82-8013	A-8	1405
82-8014	A-9	1406
Production block 1 (60 aircraft)		
83-8015	B-6	1605
83-8016	A-10	1407
83-8017	B-7	1606
83-8018	A-11	1408
83-8019	B-8	1607
83-8020	A-12	1409
83-8021	B-9	1608
83-8022	A-13	1410
83-8023	A-14	1411
83-8024	A-15	1412
83-8025	A-16	1413
83-8026	A-17	1414
83-8027	B-10	1609
83-8028	A-18	1415
83-8029		
83-8030		
83-8031		
83-8032	A-21	1418
83-8033	A-22	1419
83-8034	A-23	1420
83-8035	B-12	1611
83-8036	A-24	1421
83-8037	B-13	1612
83-8038	A-25	1422
8?-8039	B-14	1613
84-8040	A-26	1423
84-8041	B-15	1614
84-8042	A-27	1424
84-8043	A-28	1425
84-8044	A-29	1426
84-8045	A-30	1427
84-8046	A-31	1428
84-8047	A-32	1429
84-8048	A-33	1430
84-8049	A-34	1431
84-8050	A-35	1432
84-8051	A-36	1433
84-8052	A-37	1434
84-8053	A-38	1435
84-8054	A-39	1436
84-8055	B-16	1615
Further serials unknown.		
Production block 2 (60 aircraft)		
Not yet delivered.		
Serial tie-ups for B-11 (1610), B-12 (1613), A-19 (1416), A-20 (1417) and A-23 (1420) are unknown..		

America's 'Reds'
Threat support for the US Army

Away from the better known 'Aggressor' units of the Air Force Navy and Marines, the US Army has established its own dissimilar training programme. OPTEC's fleet of 'threat support' Soviet helicopters gives US combat troops a taste of just what it feels like to be on the receiving end of an attack by 'enemy' air forces.

The use by the US Army of former Soviet and Warsaw Pact aircraft owes its existence to long-standing requirements to simulate and train against these systems in the event of their employment by potential adversaries. During the mid-1970s, Army planners were faced with the emerging threat to their ground forces from increasingly greater numbers of second-generation attack helicopters that had proliferated with the air forces and army aviation units of Eastern Bloc and Third World countries. American infantry and armour units could expect to face potential adversaries that fielded increasingly deadly close combat threats that would perform as airborne artillery, along with the expected ground-based threats and high-speed strike aircraft. At the time, there was little attention paid to the use of these rotary-wing platforms in air-to-air combat against American helicopter aviators, any thoughts on these matters being relegated to think tanks and theoretical scenarios.

In the same time frame, the US Army began to focus on the ability of its battalion- and brigade-level units to synchronise their battle-field systems in various contingency scenarios. Studies by the Training and Doctrine Command (TRADOC) indicated that new and sophisticated training systems would be needed to improve the future record of success of America's land warfare assets. As analysts evaluated

the service's successes and failures through past operations they came to several conclusions, one being that there was a need to activate combat training centres (CTC) where the service could train its personnel in realistic, advanced warfighting skills using the equipment and tactics that they would be expected to employ in any future conflict.

The first CTC, the National Training Center (NTC), was activated in 1981 in the high desert of Fort Irwin, California, in order to train heavy armoured forces in a realistic manoeuvre warfare environment. The centre was tasked with supplying an opposition force (OPFOR) cadre to provide very realistic training by studying and employing Soviet and Warsaw Pact tactics.

Early training at the NTC

Actual training of battalion-sized armoured and mechanised units began in 1982 against the OPFOR, which was in reality a combat-capable, US Army mechanised battalion that represented a Soviet mechanised 'rifle infantry' unit. NTC planners took great pains to provide OPFOR with a variety of armour and infantry fighting vehicle (IFV) systems, including some actual Soviet tanks and IFVs acquired through international sources. In addition, some American systems received visual modifications for disguise and to add optimal realism to the exercises.

The only thing missing were helicopters that could simulate Soviet-built attack helicopters such as the Mi-24 'Hind'. The centre funded the modification of at least six standard 'Hueys' with visual modifications and camouflage that allowed the aircraft to simulate the 'Hind'. These aircraft were originally operated by the Operations Group of NTC since at least 1984. The aircraft were later reassigned to an Army Reserve unit, 'C' Company/3rd Battalion/159th Aviation Regiment (C/3-159 AVN) by 1987. This unit has continued to operate the aircraft, designated as JUH-1Hs, alongside standard assault-configured 'Hueys' that also support other NTC requirements. The 'Hind' surrogates are equipped with MILES tracking gear that allows the recording and playback of engagement profiles as the aircraft simulate anti-armour attacks. At least one JUH-1H has also been operated by the Joint Readiness Training Center, located at Fort Polk, Louisiana.

Another critical need for the Army was to provide extensive training for its personnel to aid in the visual identification of Soviet-designed aircraft likely to be encountered on the modern battlefield by the Air Defence Artillery (ADA) branch. The use of electronic systems such as Identification Friend or Foe (IFF) would be relied upon to sort out fast-moving strike aircraft moving across battle lines, but the movement of slower aircraft posed different problems.

Above: The JUH-1Hs of 159th Aviation Regiment are equipped with MILES tracking gear and painted in Soviet-style camouflage. Such converted 'Hueys' were a poor substitute for the Mi-24, as they differed so substantially in size, shape and even sound. Their shortcomings led to the Orlando QS-55 VISMOD prgramme, but it was obvious even then that the best threat 'simulator' would be a 'Hind' itself.

Above left: The worldwide proliferation of Mi-24 'Hinds', still in many ways a helicopter without equal, was one of the biggest incentives to the US Army to develop an effective threat simulation programme. OPTEC performs a vital role within a larger opposition forces establishment including 'enemy' ground forces.

Helicopters could easily hide behind obstacles such as trees, or move along terrain features such as mountain ridges to mask their movements by adversaries. Air-to-ground communications can be difficult when such tactics are employed and these factors present a whole series of problems concerning fratricide, or 'friendly fire'.

Drone targets

Concurrently, requirements were also being drafted to utilise unmanned, drone aerial targets as realistic simulation platforms that could assist in the testing and development of ground-to-air missile systems and sensors for several programmes, including the Stinger, Patriot and the next-generation FAAO and THAAD, now in development.

The Air Defence Artillery forces are equipped with a variety of guns, hand-held infra-red missiles, and several self-propelled or towed, IR- and radar-guided surface-to-air missile systems. The forces must prepare to deploy for a wide variety of potential conflicts, from low-intensity insurgencies to large, force-on-force attacks conducted on delineated battlefields, employing land, air and sea forces. Any future engagements will likely involve a great variety of fixed- and rotary-winged aircraft including American, Western European and Russian designs, all of which would be very difficult to differentiate and positively identify during the heat of battle (as bitter experience has shown).

The service began to explore further options to find a more suitable 'Hind' surrogate than the ubiquitous UH-1H. Most proposals included the use of sub-scale models, radio-controlled aircraft, or unmanned aerial vehicles that would be used to simulate numerous, high-threat opposition systems such as the Mil Mi-8/-17, Mi-24 or other attack helicopters. By 1985 the US Army Missile Command (MICOM) approached several major helicopter manufacturers for bids to develop and build an initial lot of 15 special helicopters that would closely mimic many of the characteristics common to the 'Hind', including similar infra-red, radar and visual signatures. Their bids were reported to be in the neighbourhood of $20 million to provide MICOM with the desired systems, which was higher than the Army expected to pay for aerial targets.

Synthetic 'Hinds'

In early 1986, executives of Orlando Helicopter Airways, Inc. (OHA) were approached by personnel from MICOM's head-quarters at the Redstone Arsenal, Huntsville, Alabama. A contract was closed that year with the selection of OHA as the sole source for the production of the 'Hind' surrogate, which was an aircraft designed around surplus Sikorsky S-55 airframes. The aircraft, designated as H-19s when operated by the US military services, carried the new designation of QS-55 and were extensively redesigned. The main rotor system was changed from a three-bladed to five-bladed system, the physical shape was altered by visual modifications (VISMODs) including the addition of fibreglass panels on the fuselage to copy the planform of the Mi-24 fuselage, and winglets were added to simulate the weapons-carrying ability of the 'Hind' design (see *World Air Power Journal* Volume 18).

An unusual line-up at Fort Polk consisting of the unit's Antonov An-2 (Red Baron) and a Mil Mi-24 and Mi-8 in the background. The An-2 has a number of useful assets including a very good STOL capability and the ability to fly at low enough speeds to allow 'terrain masking' flight profiles for special forces insertion and battlefield liason.

By 1989, all 15 QS-55s had been delivered to MICOM for a cost of about $7 million, with most of the aircraft being assigned to perform at the White Sands Missile Range (WSMR), the huge test range that covers hundreds of square miles of western Texas and southern New Mexico. The aircraft performed their assigned tasks with exceptionally high availability rates.

Orlando ran into legal troubles, due to a 'whistle-blower' suite initiated in November 1989, and events conspired to negate further conversions of the QS-55, despite avowed customer satisfaction. The Army had little choice but to investigate alternative systems. Some of the QS-55s continued to be employed through the mid-1990s with at least one being attached to a long wire cable, mounted high in the San Andreas Mountains west of White Sands and secured to the desert floor, a length of several miles. This target could be configured

with various threat systems to aid in the development of ADA systems such as Stinger, Patriot and the next-generation FAAO and THAAD systems. The aerial target role has now been taken over by the Simulation, Training, Instrumentation Command (STRICOM)

Emerging threats

At the same time, newer attack helicopter designs began to appear in the Soviet Union, particularly the Kamov Ka-50 'Hokum' and the Mi-28 'Havoc', either of which could be operationally deployed in the near future. MICOM had to deal with these emerging threats along with the older Mi-24 family that had proliferated around the world. The command speculated that the single-pilot Ka-50 would be the choice of the Soviets and so began to study which twin-engined helicopter design could be converted to resemble it with external sheet metal

This An-2 definitely shows its age as it puffs smoke from its Shvetsov radial during an engine start. Despite its vintage, the An-2 remains in production with PZL-Mielec in Poland, and is still a useful utility aircraft.

changes and the right amount of paint. Interestingly, the USAF is reported to have negotiated with a 'commercial' firm to acquire new production Ka-50s in the early 1990s, with little success. To date, it appears that the Mi-28 and Ka-50 are still a long way from volume production.

STRICOM, working with MICOM, decided to take up a US Air Force offer of surplus Sikorsky CH/HH-3Es. From 1991-92, the service took delivery of nine CH-3Es (redesignated JCH-3E), and 12 HH-3Es, (redesignated JHH-3E). The Army took proposals from several contractors in anticipation of awarding a contract to perform the VISMOD modifications. While the programme gained momentum, only three aircraft were maintained in flying status to support various projects of the Aviation Technical Test Center (ATTC), one of the Army's principal aviation test units, based at Cairns Army Airfield, Fort Rucker, Alabama. The remaining airframes literally sat around the busy airfield until 1993, when STRICOM shelved the project. The aircraft were supposed to have been trucked to AMARC at Davis-Monthan AFB, Arizona for storage by late 1993. Any future attempts to replicate a full-scale target programme is likely to be performed by adapting an aircraft such as the AH-1 'HueyCobra', now leaving the Army's inventory in rapidly increasing numbers.

There has been no relevant data released publicly about the Army's efforts to secure secondhand Soviet-built helicopters, and great

This head-on view of OTSA's Mi-24P 'Hind-F' shows its armament of B-8 80-mm rocket pods on the wing pylon, with a simulated AT-6 'Spiral' ASM mounting on the wingtips; the muzzle of the GSh-30-2 cannon is covered by a guard. The 'Hind' has performed with commendable reliability in US Army service and is well liked by the pilots lucky enough to fly it.

A gunner in an OTSA Mi-2 searches for targets. The unit's gunners are provided by 1st Battalion/509th Infantry Regiment, part of the Joint Readiness Training Center based at Fort Polk. His Minimi GPMG is fitted with a MILES laser system and a very improvised mount.

sensitivity remains about both the source and dates of acquisition of the types employed by the service. That position probably is more a result of honouring political realities than preventing assimilation of technical capabilities of aircraft performance and systems. It is possible that one or more aircraft could have been on charge during the 1980s, perhaps based with the ATTC or one of its operating directorates, such as the Aviation Qualification Test Directorate (AQTD), formerly known as the Airborne Engineering Flight Activity (AEFA), when that unit was assigned to the Aviation Systems Command (AVSCOM), now known as ATCOM. In this capacity, the aircraft may have operated in a classified status, much in the same way as the Air Force is reported to have flown Soviet-built, fixed-wing strike aircraft, allegedly with a unit designated as the 4477th ('Red Hats') Test & Evaluation Squadron based at an airfield located on the Tonopah Test Range, near Nellis AFB, Nevada.

Finding 'Hinds'

The need for acquisition of an Mi-24 surrogate, or a real example, continued to be a high priority for Army analysts and weapons systems programme managers. US intelligence agencies were constantly probing for ways to learn more about the aircraft's performance, including its advantages and liabilities. Prior to 1989, opportunities to gain access to these weapons systems were few and far between. Two Afghani, Mi-24s were acquired during the early 1980s, after the Pakistani intelligence service contacted two pilots wishing to defect. The 'Hinds' flew over the border safely, with clearance given that the Pakistan Air Force would not intercept them. At least one Libyan Mi-24 was captured intact by Chadian forces during fighting in early 1987;

it was apparently secured by both US and French intelligence experts and removed from the country to an unknown destination. Unofficial accounts from the UK suggest that a Libyan 'Hind' was tested at RAF Boscombe Down in the late 1980s. Still other reports have stated that a handful of Soviet-built aircraft were captured intact during Operation Desert Storm, from airfields in Kuwait and Iraq; if true, it is likely that they were brought to the United States, initially for technical evaluation by intelligence analysts, prior to their being employed for other missions.

The collapse of East Germany generated considerable excitement in the intelligence community and raised its expectations of the acquisition of more detailed flight and technical data on the Soviet aircraft. With the reunification of Germany, the government found itself with a

varied collection of Soviet-designed aviation assets, including Mi-8s, Mi-14s and Mi-24s, many of which were declared surplus to the country's needs. With the crumbling of the 'Iron Curtain', the flood gates opened and suddenly systems that could only be reviewed vicariously, just two years before, could suddenly be examined under close scrutiny and at the right price. The change from centrally-controlled to market-driven economies in the Soviet Union, its former allies and many of its clients, led to numerous opportunities to exploit the financial requirements of cash-strapped government ministries and agencies. These entities have found themselves in competition to set up export agencies since 1989, and they quickly began to form market alliances with commercial firms to develop market niches, for the helicopters in particular, for police, agriculture, air ambulance,

Right: This Mi-25 (replete with 'Tasmanian Devil' nose-art), is known as the Devil to its crews. It carries a 20-mm cannon from a Bell AH-1 Cobra in place of the Yak-B 12.7-mm machine-gun. This aircraft also carries MILES equipment on the nose turret and underwing pylons.

Patience is the nickname of OPTEC's only Mi-24 (the other 'Hinds' being Mi-25 export variants). This machine is probably one of the two aircraft that defected to Pakistan from Mazar-I-Sharif, Afghanistan.

This Mi-25 'Hind-D' (export Mi-24D) is equipped with ASO-2V chaff/flare dispensers under the tailboom. The aircraft wears a camouflage scheme similar to that used by Libyan forces operating in Chad. However, pictures of captured Libyan 'Hinds' show aircraft fitted with the Ispanka IR jammer behind the rotor mast, which is not carried by this aircraft.

fire-fighting, and aerial logging roles. Many of these helicopters were constructed specifically for export and came complete with both English and Russian language instrumentation and maintenance instructions. This 'capitalist' technique has proven a viable route to acquire even the most sophisticated technology from the former Soviet Union and it has allowed the US Army to make acquisitions at acceptable prices.

OPTEC is established

The different command elements within US military services each had their own priorities and requirements for the acquisition of numerous classes of systems operated by potential adversaries. By late 1990, the Army had been given primary responsibility for the co-ordination of the myriad requirements for threat analysis and the development of tactics to counter air-defence systems and aircraft likely to be encountered at the forward edge of battle area (FEBA). The activities were consolidated under the Operational Test and Evaluation Command (OPTEC), which was established in November 1990. The command, headquartered

in Alexandria, Virginia, was established from assets of the former Operational Test and Evaluation Agency, a Field Operating Agency (FOA), and the Test and Experimentation Command (TEXCOM), which was then assigned to TRADOC (Training and Doctrine Command). OPTEC became responsible for the creation and funding of a single organisation that would operate and maintain the service's fleet of Soviet-designed, ground-based air defence systems, helicopters and fixed-wing aircraft. The result was an organisation known as OTSA (OPTEC Threat Support Activity), which was established at Fort Bliss, Texas, which borders the immense White Sands Missile Range. When OTSA was organised it was staffed by civilian contractor personnel, many of whom had prior Army or DoD service.

Links with the 'customer'

The unit has only recently taken active Army aviators on staff and they provide the ability to accommodate a closer liaison to the 'customers', in addition to their regular flying duties. The pilots conduct mission briefings to the 'customers' concerning the features and capabilities of the systems, particularly to other aviators who train against them. OPTEC also has technical analysts on staff to assist when more technical presentations and briefings are required for commanders, intelligence experts and planning staffs.

The 'customers' that fund the missions flown

by the OTSA aircraft include Army commands such as components of the Army Material Command (USAMC) including ATCOM (Aviation and Troop Command), MICOM (Missile Command), and STRICOM (Simulation, Training & Instrumentation Command). Other major users include the Army Special Operations Command (USASOC), Forces Command (FORSCOM), Training and Doctrine Command (TRADOC) and, very likely, the Army intelligence community as well.

Foreigners from Fort Bliss

The aircraft that are operated by OTSA are based at Biggs AAF, Fort Bliss, and they have operated from many Army bases including Fort Bragg, North Carolina; Fort Rucker, Alabama; Fort Polk, Louisiana; and Fort Irwin, California, the home of NTC. In 1993, OTSA established a permanent detachment to work with the Joint Readiness Training Center (JRTC), when that command relocated from Little Rock AFB, Arizona to Fort Polk. JRTC is the premier light infantry warfighting training centre and the command was formally activated at the new base in August 1993. This detachment was originally based at Lake Charles Regional Airport located 70 miles (112 km) south of Fort Polk. By 1994, the unit had relocated to DeRidder/Beauregard Parish (county) Airport, an old World War II training base 15 miles (24 km) southwest of JRTC headquarters. By the summer of 1995, the unit had relocated once again to Polk AAF, located on the post itself. This detachment supports the JRTC's assigned OPFOR, the 1st Battalion/509th Infantry Regiment (Airborne) and the battalion furnishes the OTSA detachment with personnel to perform as helicopter door gunners.

When these aircraft were acquired in the early 1990s they were initially evaluated by the ATTC, formerly known as the Aviation Development Test Activity (ADTA). From its base at Cairns, this Test and Evaluation Command Unit (TECOM) evaluated performance characteristics to build recommended flight envelopes and develop flight procedures that conform to Army standards. ATTC also supervises and contracts for technical documentation and maintenance procedures.

Crews operating these aircraft have largely

The OTSA 'Hind-F', Patience, wears only a small US Army serial number on the tail. This aircraft was most likely obtained via the Luftwaffe from its stock of former East German Mi-24Ps.

favourable comments about the design and operating characteristics of these generally simple but rugged machines. Many of the original systems remain, but the aircraft have been upgraded with MILES (Multiple Integrated Laser Engagement System) and US communication systems. Some of the cockpits feature instrumentation and maintenance instructions in both English and Cyrillic, owing to their purposeful production as export variants, and an astute Soviet understanding of international flight operations procedures.

The well-travelled aviators of OTSA must live out of a suitcase, as they have also been tasked to support numerous other Department of Defense organisations, including the other services. The Marine Corps and the Air Force have been especially receptive to the employment of the aircraft in exercises and demonstrations. Teams of the aircraft have participated in Red Flag exercises, staging out of Nellis AFB and one of its satellite airfields, Indian Springs AFAF, Nevada.

Wide-ranging exercises

OTSA was heavily tasked to support the Air Force-sponsored, joint service air defence technology demonstration known as ASCIET (All-Source Combat Identification Evaluation Team) during September 1995. The demonstration was a series of multiple engagements including low-intensity and force-on-force scenarios. The motto of this event was 'When Friendly Fire Isn't', which clearly reflects the urgent need of the military services to find ways to eliminate friendly fire incidents. The Blue Force staged from the ANG CRTC (Combat Readiness Training Center) at the Gulfport-Biloxi Regional Airport, Gulfport, Mississippi and the opposition Red Force staged from Eglin AFB, Florida. OTSA provided a detachment for the Red Force (that operated from Gulfport) which included an Mi-2, Mi-14, Mi-25 and An-2. These aircraft flew multiple aggressor missions against Army and Marine defenders located at Camp Shelby, Mississippi, and the aircraft also conducted mock special operations insertions against elements of the USS *Eisenhower* (CVN-68) battle group deployed in the northern Gulf of Mexico. Since the carrier was undergoing main-

*This Mi-8, one of two in service with the OTSA fleet, is named **Dave's Deluxe**. The aircraft has had its rear clamshell doors removed and cabin door-guns fitted.*

*Above: This Mi-14, known as **Orca**, is an unusual component of the OPTEC force. The origins of the aircraft remain unclear, but it is likely to be one of the aircraft inherited by the Luftwaffe after the reunification of Germany.*

*Left: The crew of Mi-2 **Lite Action** fly a variety of missions, including armed scouting, medical evacuation and laying defensive smokescreens. The rear cabin window is fitted with a 5.56-mm M249 machine-gun, a variant of the Belgian-made FN Minimi, used as a section light machine-gun.*

tenance, the 'Aegis'-class cruisers USS *Anzio* (CG-68) and USS *Cape St George* (CG-71) were present to represent the command's assets.

OTSA's primary threat assets consist of a wide variety of ground-based air defence and electronic warfare systems including ZSU-23/4 anti-aircraft guns, SA-8 missile batteries, and the Giraffe target acquisition radar system. Many of these assets were used during ASCIET, operating from dispersed sites at the Mississippi Army National Guard's training base, Camp Shelby, located southeast of Hattiesburg, Missouri.

Actual threat systems and contractor-built simulators have been employed by the other services to improve the training of their strike aircraft during combat exercises for at least 20 years. The Air Force's (Tactical) Fighter Weapons Center at Nellis AFB has had a 'petting

zoo' of non-working threat systems, semi-hidden behind a walled compound, used to brief personnel prior to executing missions during major exercises such as Red Flag. Visiting aircrews then fly their missions on the Nellis ranges against a collection of actual and simulated threat systems that provide a very high degree of realism. Additional threat systems are also assigned to Eglin AFB, Florida, and at selected sites in the United States, primarily to test and evaluate countermeasures. The Navy has also employed numerous air defence and electronic warfare threat systems at facilities located on the China Lake and Point Mugu, California ranges, primarily to emulate those systems that would be found on the warships of potential adversaries. All these systems are designed to put aviators through 'air defence hell' while they operate on their respective ranges.

Total authenticity

It is not known to what extent OTSA either complements or replaces those systems. The demonstration at ASCIET clearly indicates that the Army systems are mobile and represent a greater training value since their ability to relocate, or 'shoot and scoot', forces aviators to hunt down these systems in order to neutralise or avoid them during exercises and demonstrations.

The unit also maintains threat systems for the Army in other areas of interest including field artillery, manoeuvre systems that include armour and IFVs, and ground target vehicles. All the OTSA systems make up an extensive threat force capability with actual and simulated systems that closely emulate the operating parameters, characteristics and electronic emissions. The crews and operators are fully trained in the hardware, software and tactics used to maximise the system's effectiveness. They are constantly updated with the latest intelligence estimates that detail system

America's 'Reds': Threat support for the US Army

A posting to OTSA is one of the most rewarding for US Army aviators, offering a chance to fly unique helicopters in intense simulated combat scenarios. The unit's aircraft are constantly in demand, and take part in a wide variety of exercises such as special operations insertions and main-force assaults with armoured forces.

enhancements and changes in doctrinal employment. The ground and air systems work together or separately, depending on the requirements of the customers. The Soviet-designed aircraft are used to simulate a variety of roles including anti-armour/anti-personnel attacks and special operations insertion/extraction of forces, and they have also been used to 'dust' ground troops with coloured water spray that is used to simulate the dispersal of chemical weapons on the battlefield. The use of these systems against units in training is predicated on the training objectives of any exercise and the combat instructions given to the OPFOR.

The exercises that OTSA assets support are all well organised, but the simulated battles are particularly fast-moving and fluid, with operations changing with the situation and weather. Each aircraft is unique and considerable planning goes into picking the right aircraft for each mission.

By 1995 the OTSA fleet consisted of at least 11 aircraft. Most of the aircraft are upgraded with American communication and navigation systems but are otherwise left in their 'stock' or original condition. The weapons systems carried by the fleet are equipped with MILES gear to

The Ka-28 'Helix' remains the only Kamov aircraft in the OTSA fleet, despite attempts to buy a Ka-50 'Hokum' through commercial sources. The lack of a radome indicates that the aircraft may have been a civil model (Ka-32) rather than a military one.

provide maximum realism and feedback on the performance of the aircraft. Likewise, the aircraft are equipped with sensors to indicate if they have been hit by anti-aircraft fire. Once 'downed', the aircrews often choose to shoot it out with ground forces until the aircraft and its operators have been judged to be destroyed.

OPTEC Aircraft

Type	Serial	Nickname
An-2	00074	Red Baron
An-2	16555	
Mi-2	00221	Lite Action
Mi-8	00528	Dave's Deluxe
Mi-8	12053	
Mi-14	13790	Orca
Mi-17	01192 (Iraqi markings)	
Mi-24F	22270	Patience
Mi-25	80616	Devil
Mi-25	32472 (Iraqi markings)	Warlord
Ka-28	00218	Double Trouble

The aircraft carry a variety of paint schemes, replicating those that might be encountered in future conflicts. Their markings are limited to a 'US Army' presentation on the tail and a five-digit serial number. It is not known if the serial number listing above correlates to specific fiscal years of acquisition or programme acceptance.

The Antonov An-2 aircraft are presently the only fixed-wing aircraft assigned to OTSA. These large, single-engined biplanes were

designed by the Antonov OKB (design bureau) in Kiev, in what is now Ukraine. The first prototype flew on 31 August 1947 and was initially designed for agricultural spray duties. It was adapted for numerous other roles, primarily military, and the type remains in production today, nearly 50 years later. Over 15,000 An-2s have been produced, including large numbers that were built under licence in China and Poland. There are over 25 international military operators of the type including North Korea, which is reported to have a fleet of over 200, principally for special operations missions.

Versatile 'Colt'

The An-2 is utilised for numerous missions including transport, aerial ambulance, aerial and photo reconnaissance, and as a 'crop-duster' spray platform for agriculture. Its excellent low-speed handing characteristics and the ability to operate fully loaded from unprepared, remote locations, approximately the length of two football fields, make the aircraft unique. Take-offs and landings can be executed in less than 600 ft (183 m) with a full load, owing to the full-span, slotted trailing-edge flaps and ailerons. The An-2 is reported to be somewhat 'stealthy', since its wings are covered in fabric material; this characteristic, along with its low speed, actually allows the aircraft to penetrate to its targets while hugging terrain features, much like a helicopter. When employed as a troop transport, the cabin can carry 12-14 paratroopers or considerable cargo into forward operating locations, when employed for scout, supply or infiltration missions.

OTSA operates at least one Kamov Ka-27 (export Ka-28) 'Helix' twin-turbine, co-axial rotor helicopter. This aircraft is used by several countries for ASW and surveillance roles, and was originally designed to deploy aboard warships. However, OTSA's example closely resembles the civilian Ka-32 'Helix-C' variant, as it is not fitted with radar or any obvious external military equipment.

The Mil/PZL Mi-2 'Hoplite' was one of the first Eastern Bloc, turbine-powered helicopters.

Below: OTSA's 'Helix' is known as Double Trouble, no doubt a reference to its distinctive twin-rotor configuration (the nose-art depicts cartoon crows 'Heckle' and 'Jeckle'). Unlike OTSA's other aircraft, Double Trouble may have been quietly acquired on the commercial market.

This OH-58 is used by the National Training Centre at Barstow. The large 'OC' painted on the fuselage stands for Operations Control.

Above: This OTSA Mi-25 is armed with four UV-32 rocket pods and, unlike the unit's Mi-24, it retains its original gun instead of the American M197 20-mm cannon. The markings and camouflage indicate that it was captured from the Iraqi forces which operated over 40 Mi-25s.

Below: Rumours abound of a windfall of hidden Iraqi aircraft found after Desert Storm. Many aircraft were hidden well away from airfields, in villages, near schools and other 'off-limits' target areas. Certainly, this Mi-17 'Hip-H' seems to have survived the fighting in good condition.

The ungainly shaped aircraft is nonetheless very versatile. Besides being used as a primary training helicopter, the type is operationally used for medical evacuation, armed scout, target acquisition/aerial observation and utility roles. The helicopter was designed in Moscow by Mil OKB, and that design bureau completed two prototypes before production was shifted to Poland. The first Polish-built Mi-2 made its first flight in November 1965, being built by WSK-Swidnik, now known as PZL (Panstwowe Zaklady Lotnicze) in Swidnik, Poland. The aircraft is employed by over a dozen nations and is used by OTSA primarily for armed scout and for laying smoke screens.

'Hip' assault

The Mil Mi-8/-17 aircraft are among the most widely used assault and attack helicopters in the world. More than 10,000 of the type have been procured and more than 50 countries continue to operate it in numerous roles including transport, attack/CAS, medical evacuation, electronic warfare and SAR. The aircraft first flew in 1961 and production versions are equipped with twin-turbine engines that allow the aircraft to carry up to 24 troops. The Mi-17 variant is a designation for export aircraft that are powered by uprated engines to allow for better hot-and-high operating performance. The aircraft are flown by OTSA for transport, attack and chemical-spray missions. Like their US-built counterparts – the Bell UH-1 or Sikorsky UH-60 – the Mils can be armed with machine-guns in the cabin and stub wing pylons that can be outfitted with rockets and missiles.

OTSA also operates a single Mi-14, which is a derivative of the Mi-8 optimised for ASW and SAR roles. The fuselage of this large helicopter features an amphibious boat hull and sponsons that enable it to operate from water if necessary. The type offers significant range. The OTSA aircraft retains the magnetic anomaly detector (MAD) 'bird' mounted against the rear of the fuselage. This aircraft is operated by about a dozen countries around the world.

Flying tank

Most intimidating of the OTSA fleet, owing to its legendary status as a flying tank, is the Mil Mi-24/-25 'Hind'. The type made its first flight in 1970 and entered operational service with the Soviet air armies in 1973. The 'Hind' was based on the Mi-8, but introduced shorter rotors and a new Isotov powerplant, that were later applied to the Mi-17. The pilot sits in the raised, rear seat with the co-pilot/gunner in the front. A flight engineer is carried in the rear cabin. The type is operated by at least two dozen different international military services and it gained notoriety from its employment in Afghanistan from 1979, in Chechnya during 1995/96 and in numerous civil wars and insurgencies in such countries as Algeria, Angola, Chad, Ethiopia, Georgia, Iraq, Kazakhstan, Lebanon, Peru and Yemen. The OTSA examples have had their original nose-mounted cannon replaced with one from the Bell AH-1 'Huey Cobra', since that system is integrated with the MILES target identification system; the aircraft currently have no laser designation capability.

The 'black helicopters' myth

Various reported sightings indicate that another Mi-2 and An-2 may be assigned to the organisation, but no photographs or identifications have been forthcoming. The existence of these aircraft has made the Army sensitive to the fact that a small element of Americans firmly equate the use of these airframes with the alleged 'occupation' of the US by international mercenary forces, supposedly led by elements of the UN! One can only imagine informed readers rolling off their chairs with laughter at this thought but, sadly, many Americans are totally ignorant of the diplomatic, economic and military realities that exist in the world. Thankfully, there are enlightened personnel at high levels in the Army who have chosen to display these aggressor aircraft at numerous public forums and to encourage knowledge of the benefits gained by American and allied forces as they study and work with these systems. This is not to say that the appearance of these unique platforms has become routine, but they have been making an increasing number of well-appreciated guest appearances at widely dispersed air show locations throughout the continental United States. The aircraft usually make solo appearances and they often turn up in smaller or remote locations.

OPTEC in the public eye

One of the first indications of the presence of these aircraft in the Army inventory came during an air show at Fort Bragg/Pope AFB, North Carolina in 1992, when an An-2 was seen. In early 1993 a 'Hip' and a 'Hind' were operating openly from Yuma, reportedly on tests with General Electric. An Mi-17 made an appearance at NAS Corpus Christi's air show in the spring of 1994, while was undergoing sea-level testing. By 1995, additional aircraft had been noted on public exhibition at OTSA's Fort Bliss home. An An-2 assigned to the JRTC detachment was even used as a jump platform for Army parachutists from that command's OPFOR, during the September 1995 air show at the former England AFB, in Alexandria, Louisiana.

All indicators point to OTSA being a prudent and necessary investment to realistically train and prepare American soldiers for modern warfighting. The unit is effective in portraying real-world threats and gives American and allied troops the chance to see and fight against the actual systems they are likely to face on future battlefields. This effort greatly increases the odds that they will survive and win in combat. The organisation has plans to broaden its client base while concurrently increasing the quantity and quality of its threat systems over the next few years. OTSA personnel and their aircraft will certainly remain in demand for a long time to come.

Tom Ring

With Special Thanks to Photographer Steve Harding

McDonnell Douglas
F/A-18 Hornet

In another era the Hornet might not have made it. Early F/A-18s
were derided for their poor performance and many felt that they
were not worthy successors to the aircraft they were supposed to
replace on the carrier decks. That the Hornet has survived,
prospered and become a great combat aircraft now much in
demand is a tribute to the designers and engineers who worked
hard to get the best from the airframe. New weapons and avionics
have also combined to make it a sophisticated fighting machine.
Furthermore, the launch of the next-generation F/A-18E/F heralds
the arrival of a new 'Super Hornet' for the 21st century.

Spain acquired 72 F/A-18 Hornets from the St Louis production line and is now preparing to introduce an additional 24 aircraft from ex-US Navy stocks. Since their introduction, the Spanish Hornets have been comprehensively upgraded to virtual F/A-18C standard and have played an increasingly important part in NATO operations over Bosnia.

The scene is a top-secret meeting of McDonnell Douglas executives, some time in 1974. The senior man has the floor.

"We are going to monopolise the Navy tactical aircraft business. In 20 years, we'll have the only Navy fighter in production, and in 30 years there will be carriers going to sea without a single fighter or attack aircraft that doesn't say 'McAir' on the side. This is the plan.

"We're not going to design our own aircraft. We'll modify somebody else's design, and when they try to sell the original version for export, we'll beat them.

"Our design won't work very well when it enters service, and we'll keep having to change it and fix it. Eventually, the Navy will pay for a complete redesign and use our aircraft to replace the F-14 and A-6, even though it won't go as fast as an F-14 or carry as much as far as an A-6."

It is a fair guess that no such meeting ever happened and that no such outrageous plan was ever concocted. However, as the historical record will show, that is exactly what happened in the case of the McDonnell Douglas F/A-18.

While the end of the Cold War has played a part in reversing the Hornet's fortunes, McDonnell Douglas Aerospace (MDA) has made an important contribution through steady development and refinement of the design, mostly during production of the F/A-18C and its two-seat equivalent, the F/A-18D. It is primarily with these aircraft – the bridge between the frankly disappointing F/A-18A/B and the almost entirely new F/A-18E/F – that this article is concerned.

Hornet history

The development and early career of the F/A-18 were covered in detail in the first issue of *World Air Power Journal* (Spring 1990). For newer readers, however, it is worthwhile to recapitulate the Hornet's complex history.

The F/A-18 design has its roots in 1966, at Northrop's advanced projects office in Hawthorne, not far from Los Angeles airport. The leader of the design team, Lee Begin, had been responsible for the F-5 fighter. With the latter established in production, Northrop was looking at ideas for a follow-on fighter which would eventually replace the F-5 and other widely used fighters of the same vintage. As in the case of the F-5, Northrop had the international market very much in mind.

The first designs resembled a scaled-up, high-wing F-5, with two engines and the same thin, minimally swept wing with leading-edge manoeuvring flaps. The design evolved between 1966 and 1969 in the light of market surveys and

Canada is the largest export customer for the Hornet, acquiring 138 single-seat CF-188As and two-seat CF-188Bs from 1982. However, recent deep cuts in the Canadian defence budget have reduced Fighter Group's fleet of Hornets to just 60 operational aircraft.

combat lessons from Vietnam. Begin's goal was to develop a relatively small fighter which could easily out-turn older, large-winged subsonic aircraft like the MiG-17, while retaining supersonic speed and the ability to carry large external weapons loads. The new fighter's wing span and aspect ratio increased. The design thrust/weight ratio approached 1:1 at combat weights. Leading-edge root extensions (LERXes) appeared and grew steadily larger and more complex with each iteration of the design. The LERXes affected the airflow over the tail, so the single vertical tail was replaced by twin canted surfaces.

Together with Northrop president Tom Jones, Begin believed that the Pentagon's main fighter competitions of the late 1960s would lead to large and costly aircraft which most countries could not afford. Northrop was never a front-runner in the contest to develop the USAF's F-4 replacement, won by McDonnell Douglas' F-15. By 1971, however, Begin's new fighter, the P-530, was far enough advanced to be shown in the form of a full-scale mock-up at the Paris air show. Northrop named it Cobra, because of its hood-like LERXes. The company's plan was to develop the Cobra in collaboration with one or more European partners, as a replacement for ageing F-104s and Mirages.

F-17 versus F-16 for LWF

Northrop fell victim to its own success in promoting the idea of the lighter, more agile fighter. A group of analysts, engineers and Air Force pilots, nicknamed the 'Fighter Mafia', managed to attract the attention of budget-conscious, innovative civilian leaders at the Pentagon. The US Air Force was still unconvinced of the value of a smaller fighter, but was persuaded to sponsor a programme under which two designs would be built and flown as prototypes. This was enough to bring other competitors into the ring – most significantly, General Dynamics, which was awarded a contract to build two YF-16 Lightweight Fighter (LWF) prototypes in April 1972. Northrop, to no one's surprise, was the other winner, with a Cobra derivative known as the YF-17.

By the time the prototypes flew, the stakes had been raised dramatically. The Department of Defense, facing post-Vietnam budget cuts, directed the Air Force to buy 650 new fighters based on the winning LWF design, and four NATO nations looking for an F-104 replacement (Belgium, Holland, Norway and Denmark) agreed to buy their aircraft as a single package. In the absence of a credible European alternative, it appeared most likely that the winner of the USAF contest would scoop the European market too.

Most observers agreed that the bomber-builders of Fort Worth stood little chance against Northrop, with its extensive light-fighter experience and years of work on the P-530, so it was all the more surprising when the YF-16 out-pointed its rival in tests and won the USAF contest.

The US Navy takes a different route

The competition was not quite winner-take-all, however. Congress had directed the US Navy to use a version of one of the LWF designs to meet its requirement for a new fighter/attack aircraft, formerly known as VFAX but now identified as the Navy Air Combat Fighter (NACF). The Navy's requirement was stiffer than the USAF's: for instance, it called for the ability to carry AIM-7 medium-range air-to-air missiles, and the radar specification was tougher, calling for a larger antenna than would fit in the YF-16 or YF-17. Both factors tended to make the NACF into a larger aircraft than the USAF design. Either aircraft would need a new engine: the fact that the F-16 had the same engine as the F-15 was an advantage in the USAF

The Hornet has always acquitted itself well in ACM training. Until now, the aircraft was only cleared to a 7.5-g limit – significantly less than the 9-g limit of the F-16 and other rivals. The first F/A-18C 9-g clearance is expected in early 1996 after FCS and minor airframe changes have been made.

Above: A VMFA-451 F/A-18A carrys an AGM-62 Walleye II ER/DL glide bomb under its outboard pylon. Walleye has always been almost exclusively a USN and USMC weapon, although some Walleye Is were exported to Israel. The 2,490-lb (1130-kg) Walleye II ER/DL combines the massive shaped-charge warhead of Walleye II with an Extended Range/Data Link system. This requires the AWW-9 guidance pod visible under this Hornet, though operationally the pod is often carried by a second aircraft. Some Walleye IIs have been fitted with an imaging infra-red seeker head to replace the standard TV seeker.

Above right: The Mk 7 CBU dispenser was developed by the US Navy's Naval Weapons Center but has been adopted by the USAF and air forces worldwide. It is most widely used in its Mk 20 Rockeye II form – containing 247 Mk 118 anti-armour bomblets. It can also be configured for anti-personnel bomblets, fragmentation mines and Gator anti-armour mines. Naval Mk 7s (Mod 6 and later) carry a distinctive double yellow band signifying that they have a fire-resistant coating for extra safety onboard ship.

contest but was of no help in NACF. It was also clear from the outset that the Navy preferred a twin-engined aircraft.

The Navy insisted that the NACF prime contractor be a company with experience in carrier fighters. GD teamed with a Texas neighbour, Vought, while Northrop joined forces with McDonnell Douglas. Of the two prime contractors, only McDonnell Douglas had recent supersonic fighter experience; the company had lately worked with Hughes on the sophisticated radar for the F-15.

McDonnell Douglas and Northrop were announced as winners in May 1975, and the first F/A-18 flew in November 1978. It was a new aircraft, sharing only its general layout with the YF-17. Compared with its predecessor, it was larger and more powerful, incorporating the stronger structure and landing gear required for carrier operations.

In many respects, the F/A-18 was technologically more advanced than the F-16A. Its fly-by-wire flight control system used digital rather than analog processors. It used more composite materials (in the wing skins, for example). It had a multi-mode radar, and a cockpit which used cathode-ray tube (CRT) displays in place of conventional dial-and-pointer instruments. It was designed from the ground up to accept pods for electro-optical navigation and targeting aids, and the AIM-7 medium-range air-to-air missile, neither of which could be carried on the F-16. McDonnell Douglas touted the new fighter as a true multi-role type, as opposed to the simpler F-16A.

Canada and Australia, both with large fleets of older supersonic fighters, were persuaded by these arguments and selected the F-18A over the F-16 before the new fighter had finished its flight tests. One of the F/A-18's rivals was Northrop's land-based F-18L, similar in size to the F/A-18 but with an almost completely redesigned structure. Unfortunately for Northrop, the export customers found that the lower risks of the F/A-18A, already in full-scale development for the US Navy, outweighed the higher performance promised by Northrop.

Advantages of the F/A-18

Canada, with its large expanses of Arctic terrain, and Australia, with its overwater interception mission and the need to overly the Australian interior (known to pilots as the GAFA, or the Great Australian ****-All), assigned some value to the F-18's twin engines. In fact, the new fighter's General Electric F404 was proving to be trouble-free, in sharp contrast to the F-16's F100 engine.

The F/A-18's new-technology cockpit was also widely acclaimed, and its radar and weapons integration drew no criticism. This was just as well, because other important attributes of the new aircraft were drawing sharp criticism.

During development, the F/A-18 underwent some major changes. Dog-teeth disappeared from the wing and stabiliser leading edges. The wing itself was reinforced and the lateral controls were revised, because the long, thin

Soviet navy's land bases. All these aircraft were expensive, and would not be built soon, or in large quantities – but the Navy's carrier fleet was expanding, and ageing F-4s and A-7s, dating back to the Vietnam War, had to be replaced. Cancelling or delaying the F/A-18 would leave the Navy short of modern aircraft, so the Navy decided to put the aircraft into production without attempting to fix the range problem.

The end of the F/A-18A

The F/A-18A garnered a total of three export customers – Canada, Australia and Spain. They were in a rather better situation than the US Navy, because the limitations on the Hornet's range and bring-back capability could be alleviated when it was operated from land bases. Canada, for instance, developed a 480-US gal (1800-litre) external tank to supplement the 330-US gal (1250-litre) tanks used by the US Navy. The US Navy did not adopt them because the larger tank would not fit on the centreline. Nevertheless, the F/A-18's problems, combined with the arrival on the scene of the F-16C/D, ushered in a long sales drought.

Pilots were – as always – enthusiastic about the F/A-18A/B when it entered service in 1983. However, historical fact tells a different story. Some 410 of this initial version were built until production switched to the F/A-18C/D in 1987. By 1995, the Navy had retired most of the A/B models from carrier-based service, the shortest first-line career of any modern fighter. Apart from a small top-up batch of aircraft delivered to Spain from Navy stocks in 1995, there are no plans to offer these aircraft for export, or to upgrade them – unlike the older and more austere F-16A/B.

The fact was that VX-5 had been right. The F/A-18A/B was a somewhat inadequate aircraft which validated the adage "Jack of all trades, master of none" in its full and not altogether complimentary sense. It took a series of upgrades to produce a Hornet variant which could be called the master of most of its many missions. This process started with the first F/A-18C/D, delivered from September 1987. Basically designed to accommodate new technologies and weapons, the first F/A-18C/Ds have formed the basis for a series of Hornets whose exterior resemblance to the original A/B is entirely deceptive.

Airframe development

The F/A-18C/D airframe is not very different from that of the A/B, and has not changed significantly since it entered production in 1987. The reason was not so much that the original design was perfect, as that it had run into a hard limit on its growth.

wing proved insufficiently stiff – leading to a severe shortfall in roll rate. Long slots in the LERXes were sealed along most of their length, to reduce drag.

Even these measures, however, barely touched the basic problem. The F/A-18 was failing, by a large measure, to meet its warload and radius specifications. Both of the aircraft which it was supposed to replace (the F-4 and A-7) could carry larger loads over a greater distance. Weight and drag increases also meant that the F/A-18 was limited in its 'bring-back' capability. With normal fuel reserves, the new fighter could not land aboard a carrier at an acceptable approach speed with more than a minimal ordnance load.

In 1982, Navy test squadron VX-5 recommended that the F/A-18 programme be suspended until some way of alleviating the range shortfall could be found. Among other measures, McDonnell Douglas proposed a thicker wing and an enlarged dorsal spine, which would have improved the aircraft's range at the expense of transonic acceleration and speed.

The Navy, however, rejected these suggestions and over-rode VX-5's recommendations. By that time, the service had other priorities, including the development of modernised versions of the A-6 and F-14 and the definition of a long-range, stealthy bomber to carry the war to the

The Walleye family of glide bombs is built around the basic Mk 83 (Walleye I) and Mk 84 (Walleye II) bombs, to which are added control fins and a guidance system. At the nose of the bomb is a TV camera, which relays the scene ahead, via a tail-mounted datalink, to the controlling aircraft. Using an onboard TV display the Walleye is flown to its target by means of a joystick controller. Only Walleye II remains in the US Navy and US Marine Corps inventory. The longer-range ER/DL versions are fitted with extended wings to improve their gliding performance. This former NAS Fallon-based Naval Strike Warfare Center F/A-18 is carrying a basic AGM-62 Walleye II (which is always only carried on the outboard stations 1 or 5) along with the associated AWW-9 on the centreline (station 3).

more, making a full-afterburner take-off and climb to regain flying speed from a few hundred feet of deck. Because of this, the Navy requires large fuel reserves at the point where the aircraft makes its first landing attempt: for the F/A-18, up to 3,000 lb (1360 kg) in the daytime and 4,000 lb (1815 kg) at night.

The difference between the maximum landing weight and the fighter's empty weight, minus the fuel reserve, is the 'bring-back': the ordnance load with which the fighter can land aboard the carrier. Bring-back was not much of a concern until the 1970s and 1980s. Air-to-air missiles were relatively light in weight, while Mark series bombs were 'cheaper than hamburger' (these days, about a dollar a pound) and it mattered little if they had to be jettisoned into the sea before landing. Heavy precision-guided weapons were another matter. Even the carrier's magazines could not store enough of these bulky and expensive weapons for them to be loaded on to an aircraft in the knowledge that they will have to be dropped if the target cannot be hit.

Unseen limits

On a typical day, a Lot 19 F/A-18C in an interdiction configuration (with an AAS-38 pod attached) approaches the carrier at 145 kt (270 km/h) with a maximum payload of 5,500 lb (2495 kg), including its fuel reserves. With night-time reserves, the fighter cannot bring AGM-84E SLAM or AGM-88 HARM missiles aboard the carrier. The F/A-18D is in an even tighter situation, with a second crew member and ejection seat, plus a heavier canopy. (It is worth noting that the Marine Corps, operating from land bases, makes more use of the F/A-18D in the interdiction role than the Navy.)

Bring-back weight is a difficult limit to circumvent. Most fighters, after they enter service, follow the same development path: take-off and landing weights and engine thrust are all steadily increased. At the same time, the empty weight also increases, because new equipment is added and the more powerful engines are heavier, but the rise in empty weight is more than offset by the greater take-off and landing weight and the extra thrust, so the aircraft is still as fast and manoeuvrable as ever. The F-16 is typical, gaining 20 per cent in thrust and weight during development.

The F/A-18 could not follow this path because any increase in empty weight reduced the already limited bring-back weight. Major airframe changes have, therefore, been avoided.

Apart from some antennas, the only visible modification to be made during the F/A-18's service career was the addition of a pair of strakes or 'billboards' above the LERX. At angles of attack above 45°, the strakes help to break up the vortices generated by the LERX, which otherwise cause buffeting around the vertical tails. This is uncomfortable and hard on the structure. The strakes have been retrofitted to most F/A-18s.

Hornet stealth measures

One significant change, however, is very far from visible. It is conventional wisdom, and correct, to state that a conventional fighter cannot be modified into a stealthy aircraft. This is not to say that stealth technology cannot be usefully applied to a conventional design.

An all-out stealth aircraft is designed for an extremely low radar cross-section (RCS) over a wide band of radar frequencies, and with a near-equal RCS from any direction. The goal is to delay detection as long as possible. But a smaller reduction in RCS, aimed at a narrower bandwidth and concentrated on the most sensitive aspects – typically, head-on – will also yield some tactical advantages. In a beyond-visual-range missile engagement, it reduces the range at which a hostile fighter can detect and track the aircraft, giving the reduced-RCS fighter the first look and first shot. It gives surface-to-air missile systems less warning

Above: On a mission over Bosnia this VMFA-224 F/A-18D drops a flare – on this occasion more for display than defence. NATO pilots quickly learned that chaff and flares and jamming were essential to their survival in the dangerous Bosnian skies.

Right: VAQ-34 were 'electronic aggressors' who flew sorties against the fleet and ground targets rather than individual aircraft. Here, one of the 'Flashbacks' F/A-18Bs taxis out with an AN/ALQ-167 METE jammer, underwing.

Below: HARM launch by a USMC F/A-18D. A Hornet can carry a maximum of three AGM-88s for a SEAD mission.

The F/A-18 had been designed for an approach speed of 125 kt (231 km/h), but development problems increased this to 134 kt (250 km/h) on a standard day – a respectable figure for a land-based fighter, but on the high side for a carrier-based aircraft. This in turn set a cap on the F/A-18's maximum landing weight. The problem was complicated by the requirements of carrier operations. In bad weather or at night, a pilot may miss the wires once, twice or even

time and reduces the range at which their radars can 'burn through' defensive jamming (that is, the range at which the natural return energy from the target exceeds the power of the jammer).

Stealth programmes in the late 1970s and early 1980s spurred the development of new types of radar-absorbent material (RAM) which were lighter, more durable and more effective than their predecessors, along with analytical tools and test facilities which took some of the trial and error out of designing or modifying an aircraft for low RCS. As a result, the USAF and US Navy both initiated programmes to reduce the RCS of their most widely used fighters. The USAF's low-RCS programme for the F-16 was known as Have Glass, and the equivalent F/A-18 configuration has been referred to as a 'Glass Hornet'.

The F/A-18 modification package designed by the Navy and McDonnell Douglas, and first incorporated in the Lot 12 night-attack aircraft, have not been described in detail. However, they are almost certainly similar to those used on the F-16. Glass Hornets can be identified by a gold-tinted canopy, coated with a thin layer of indium–tin-oxide (ITO). This makes the canopy reflect radar signals, which may seem a strange way of making an aircraft stealthy. From the most critical aspects, though, the canopy reflects radar signals away from the transmitter, and it has a much lower RCS than the many reflective objects (such as the seat headrests and HUD frame) inside the cockpit.

Another key area is the flat bulkhead behind the radar antenna. The radome itself is transparent at radio frequencies, so the radar bulkhead and the antenna drive can generate some strong reflections. A plastic RAM panel mounted in front of the bulkhead suppresses some of these echoes.

The engines and engine inlets are also strong radar reflectors. Paint-type RAM, consisting of carbonyl iron particles in a polymer binder, is probably applied to the inlet lips and to the interior of the duct, helping to absorb signals which bounce off the face of the engine. Other 'hot spots' are also treated.

Above: Rockets remain effective, and spectacular, weapons which still have role to play in a world of stand-off, precision-guided munitions. For concentrated and accurate firepower, they are hard to beat – especially in a benign air defence scenario. This Hornet is unleasing 5-in Zuni rockets from a four-round LAU-10 pod.

Canada has developed the CRV-7 rocket system specifically for use against hardened targets. CRV-7 has been widely exported and was used successfully in Operation Desert Storm.

McDonnell Douglas F/A-18 Hornet

Top: Seen aboard the USS Theodore Roosevelt in July 1995, this HARM-armed F/A-18C of VMFA-312 was one of those involved in Operation Deliberate Force the following month. Roosevelt had embarked three Hornet squadrons (including one Marine unit) and only a single F-14 squadron for its Adriatic 'combat' cruise. When it was replaced on station by the USS America, in early September, this air wing make-up was retained.

Above: A second VMFA-312 Hornet aboard Roosevelt carries a single AGM-88, 500-lb GBU-12 Paveway II, Sidewinders and a lot of extra fuel. The smaller LGBs were of value in Bosnia where it was critical to avoid all and any collateral damage.

US gal/1800-litre tanks under the wings and one 330-US gal/1250-litre tank on the centreline) but with lower drag and the centreline station free. Originally offered to Israel, these tanks were due to be tested in early 1996.

Navy Hornets have a maximum load limit of 7.5 *g*. Although Navy operators would argue that the difference between this limit and the F-16's 9 *g* boundary is not tactically significant, it has been used as a selling point by Lockheed. McDonnell Douglas accordingly launched a programme of analysis and flight tests to ensure that the F/A-18 could be flown to 9 *g* at typical air-to-air combat weights without compromising the longevity of the airframe. The aircraft being delivered to Switzerland are the first to feature flight control system (FCS) software which permits 9 *g* loadings, and Thailand's aircraft also incorporate this option.

Engine development

Although the airframe has changed relatively little, some significant improvements have been made to the Hornet's engine. One of the features which made the new generation of agile fighters possible in the 1970s was the development of fighter engines which offered a much higher thrust/weight ratio than their predecessors. This in turn contributed to the high thrust/weight ratio of the aircraft itself, allowing a fighter with the large wing required for manoeuvrability to accelerate quickly at transonic and supersonic speeds.

The first engine in this class, the Pratt & Whitney F100, was not initially an unqualified success, suffering from stall problems which took several years to fix across the fleet. Against this background, the performance of the General

The change was not free from penalties. The later F/A-18s carry almost 250 lb (113 kg) of RAM, further reducing their bring-back load. Also, the carbonyl iron is subject to corrosion in the saltwater-laden carrier environment. This did not affect the 'lossy' RCS-suppressing characteristics of the material, but did require frequent corrective maintenance. It is likely that future F/A-18s will have the new corrosion-resistant RAM which was developed for the F/A-18E/F.

Some more recent airframe improvements use technology drawn from other programmes. For the F-15E, McDonnell Douglas used thinner, more flexible polyurethane fuel bladders in the fuselage tanks, replacing the Nitrol rubber material used earlier. The new tanks are not only easier to install (they have to be pushed into the completed fuselage through an access panel, unfolded and fitted with internal plumbing) but, because they are more flexible and less subject to cracking, they can be installed without some of the foam padding which had to be used with the older tanks. These tanks are being used for the F/A-18E/F and will be used on F/A-18C/Ds from 1998.

Also, for land-based export Hornets, McDonnell Douglas has obtained approval for a smaller ullage allowance: that is, space left empty at the top of the tank to reduce the risk of spilled fuel. Together with the new tanks, the result is a 500-lb (227-kg) increase in the internal fuel capacity, a 5 per cent improvement.

McDonnell Douglas has also designed 600-US gal (2270-litre) underwing tanks for the F/A-18. This allows the Hornet to carry as much fuel in two identical tanks as it could previously carry in three dissimilar tanks (two 480-

Left: A VFA-37 F/A-18C departs the USS Eisenhower *in February 1995. VFA-37 'Bulls' (previously VA-37) transitioned to the Hornet, from the A-7E, on 13 December 1990.*

Electric F404 stood out like a good deed in a naughty world. The engine was relatively free of handling limits from the outset. By 1988, the basic F404-GE-400 engine had accumulated 700,000 flight hours, and reliability and maintainability statistics were good: 1.8 shop visits, from all causes, every 1,000 flight hours; less than one inflight shutdown in every 6,500 hours of engine operation (so that a pilot could well spend his entire career on F-18s and never have a shutdown); and 0.8 manhours of maintenance per engine flight hour. All these numbers were a fraction of those for the larger F100. The F404 low-pressure system (fan and turbine) was scaled up for GE's F110, which was adopted as an alternative to the F100 in the F-16.

Some problems did surface as the F404 fleet approached the million-hour mark. The afterburner nozzle outer flaps suffered from premature joint wear, caused in part by the aerodynamics of the F/A-18 boat-tail and linked to the LERX-induced vibration of the vertical tails. An improved design was incorporated, based on the F110 nozzle. Some incidents in which the afterburner liner buckled in high-Mach, low-altitude flight were recorded in 1988, and the afterburner was strengthened to avoid a repetition of the problem.

F404 fire risk

The most serious problem cropped up in 1987, when fires broke out in a number of high-time engines. The fires broke through the outer bypass duct into the airframe, causing the loss of several aircraft. Failures in the front end of the compressor, caused by vibration, foreign object damage (FOD) or maintenance errors, produced debris which jammed in the tight clearances between the aft compressor blade tips and the compressor casing. This eroded the wear coating on the casing, and allowed the titanium blades, debris and case to rub together. Under these circumstances, titanium will burn away merrily.

Below: The USS America *ended its last cruise in early 1996 on patrol in the Adriatic, before returning to the USA. The* America *had CVW-1 (Carrier Air Wing 1) onboard, which included the Hornets of VFA-82, VFA-86 (as seen here) and VMFA-102. It too followed the emerging pattern of deploying just a single F-14 unit (VFA-102).*

Thermal imaging pod
The Night-Attack F/A-18D usually carries a Hughes AN/AAR-50 NAV/FLIR on the starboard shoulder station. This provides a TV-quality picture of the terrain and is fixed to stare ahead.

Flying controls
The F/A-18 has a digital fly-by-wire flight control system, with outboard ailerons and differential tail for roll control. The inboard flaps acting as flaperons at low speeds. Pitch control is provided by symmetrical tailplane movement.

Powerplant
The F/A-18D is powered by a pair of 16,000-lb st (71.17-kN) General Electric F404-GE-400 afterburning turbofans. Many may be re-engined with the 17,600-lb st (78.29-kN) F404-GE-402 EPE (Enhanced Performance Engine) already fitted to Kuwaiti and Swiss Hornets.

Rear cockpit
Marine Corps F/A-18Ds are normally configured for the night attack role. The rear cockpit has no stick, but has two sidestick weapons/system controllers and a new colour multi-purpose display mounted between the two standard MFDs. It can be quickly reconfigured for the training role, with the control column and throttles reinstated, and with the colour multi-purpose display replaced by the normal multi-purpose display repeater.

FLIR/Laser
The F/A-18D can carry a Loral (Ford Aerospace) AN/AAS-38 or AAS-38A NITE Hawk targeting pod on the port underfuselage 'shoulder' station.

Colour scheme
US Marine Corps and US Navy F/A-18s generally wear an overall two-tone grey colour scheme, with toned-down unit and national markings.

Reconnaissance
The reinstigation of the USN/USMC ATARS (Advanced Tactical Air Reconnaissance System) project will add an all-new reconnaissance role to the Hornet's already impressive list of capabilities. Designated F/A-18D(RC), 31 Marine Corps Hornets will be modified to carry a range of EO and IR sensors in the nose, replacing the Vulcan cannon. The F/A-18D(RC)'s improved APG-73 Phase 2 radar will have a significant SAR capability, and the aircraft may also gain a podded EO/LOROP system, if funding allows.

ITT/Westinghouse ASPJ
F/A-18Ds and F/A-18Cs are fitted with a number of antennas for the cancelled AN/ALQ-165 Airborne Self Protection Jamming (ASPJ) system, which was cancelled because it failed to meet its (very demanding) specification. Twenty-four test sets were used over Bosnia, and proved much better than existing equipment, and there is a faint chance that the programme may be reinstated. ASPJ antennas include bulged fairings on the nose (above the formation-keeping 'slime light'), on the spine behind the cockpit, and on the nosewheel and gun-bay doors. These antennas are essentially hexagonal in shape, with the parallel upper and lower sides being stretched to form a rectangle with pointed ends. ASPJ transmitting and receiving antennas also 'straddled' the ALR-67 antenna on the trailing edge of the port tailfin, with another below the position light and ALR-67 fairing on the starboard fin.

McDonnell Douglas F/A-18D Hornet
VMFA(AW)-225 'Vikings'
US Marine Corps
MCAS El Toro

The two-seat Night-Attack F/A-18D has replaced the A-6 Intruder, OA-4M Skyhawk and RF-4C Phantom in the US Marine Corps all-weather attack squadrons, fulfilling secondary Fast FAC and (soon) reconnaissance roles. VMFA(AW)-225 was the third of six USMC squadrons to receive two-seat Night Attack Hornets, taking delivery of its first aircraft during July 1991. VMFA(AW)-121 had been the first unit, re-equipping in May 1990.

Wingtip missile launch rails

The F/A-18 was designed with a pair of wingtip AIM-9 Sidewinder launch rails. These allowed the aircraft to carry at least two IR-homing AAMs without sacrificing an underwing hardpoint, contributing to the fighter's capability as a 'swing' fighter. The wingtip launchers also act as anti-flutter masses. In the air-to-air role the Hornet can carry up to six AIM-9 Sidewinders, with two each on twin LAU-7 launchers on the outboard underwing pylons, and with single missiles on the wingtips. A pair of AIM-7 Sparrow or AIM-120 AMRAAM missiles can be carried on the fuselage 'shoulders', while the use of LAU-115 adaptors on the outboard underwing pylons allows an extra pair of Sparrows to be carried underwing. A Hornet has been loaded with a pair of wingtip 'Winders and 10 AIM-120 AMRAAMs – two on the fuselage stations and two under each underwing pylon. Aircraft undertaking dissimilar air combat training often carry a single inert AIM-9 Sidewinder with no warhead and no motor, but with a 'live' seeker head. This allows the dummy missile to be used as an acquisition round, forcing the pilot to follow realistic target acquisition procedures to lock-up his target, and to follow the normal routine for a missile launch up until the moment of launch itself. Sidewinder acquisition rounds sometimes lack the rear control fins, and sometimes even have the forward fins removed as well, but they often look externally similar to a live missile. On USAF combat aircraft, a blue-painted body indicates an inert weapon.

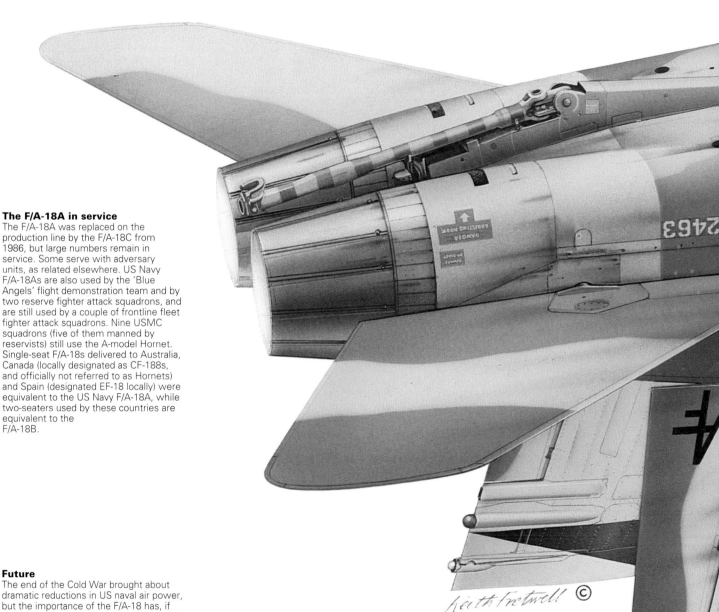

The F/A-18A in service

The F/A-18A was replaced on the production line by the F/A-18C from 1986, but large numbers remain in service. Some serve with adversary units, as related elsewhere. US Navy F/A-18As are also used by the 'Blue Angels' flight demonstration team and by two reserve fighter attack squadrons, and are still used by a couple of frontline fleet fighter attack squadrons. Nine USMC squadrons (five of them manned by reservists) still use the A-model Hornet. Single-seat F/A-18s delivered to Australia, Canada (locally designated as CF-188s, and officially not referred to as Hornets) and Spain (designated EF-18 locally) were equivalent to the US Navy F/A-18A, while two-seaters used by these countries are equivalent to the F/A-18B.

Future

The end of the Cold War brought about dramatic reductions in US naval air power, but the importance of the F/A-18 has, if anything, increased. The cancellation of the A-12 left the Navy without a replacement for its A-6 Intruder bombers, a gap filled by the development of the new-generation F/A-18E and F/A-18F, chosen in preference to derivatives of the Grumman F-14 Tomcat. The virtual disappearance of the Soviet-type long-range bomber/long-range stand-off cruise missile threat has reduced the importance of the F-14 Tomcat as a fleet defence fighter, and the number deployed aboard carriers has steadily declined. In their place are an increasing number of the more versatile F/A-18 Hornets (usually three squadrons per carrier), with regular deployments by US Marine squadrons. When the threat to the carrier is posed primarily by Exocet-type weapons, the F/A-18 has adequate range and its versatility is highly prized by Air Group commanders.

Tailfins

Early experience with the F/A-18 revealed that the Hornet's vertical fins were not as strong as they should have been. The aircraft's remarkable high Alpha capability encouraged its pilots to exploit it, and they did. Vortices generated by the LERXes during slow-speed, high-angle-of-attack dogfighting took a toll on the structure, and in 1985 three braces were added to the inner face of each fin root. This provided a partial solution to the problem, but fences were added above the LERXes from 1988 to modify the vortex flow. The strengthening plates and fences were added on the production line and were retrofitted to earlier Hornets.

33 Rear instrument console with multi-function CRT displays
34 Single-piece upward-opening cockpit canopy
35 AWW-7/9 datalink pod for Walleye missile, fuselage centreline pylon-mounted
36 AGM-62 Walleye II ER/DL air-to-surface missile, starboard outboard pylon only
37 Naval flight officer's helmet with GEC-Marconi Avionics 'Cats Eyes' night-vision goggles
38 Naval flight officer's SJU-5/A ejection seat
39 Sidestick radar and weapons controllers, replacing dual flight control system
40 Liquid oxygen converter
41 Ventral radar warning antenna
42 Rear avionics equipment bays, port and starboard
43 Cockpit rear pressure bulkhead

44 Canopy actuator
45 Starboard navigation light
46 Tailfin aerodynamic load-alleviating strake
47 Upper radar warning antennas
48 Forward fuselage bag-type fuel cell
49 Radar/avionics equipment liquid cooling units
50 Fuselage centreline pylon
51 Boundary layer splitter plate
52 Port navigation light
53 Fixed-geometry engine air intake
54 Cooling air spill louvres
55 Cabin air conditioning system equipment
56 Leading-edge flap drive motor
57 Boundary layer spill duct
58 Air conditioning system heat exchanger exhaust
59 Centre fuselage fuel cells

60 Wing panel root attachment joints
61 Central Garrett GTC36-200 auxiliary power unit (APU)
62 Airframe-mounted engine accessory equipment gearbox, port and starboard
63 Engine bleed air ducting to conditioning system
64 Fuel tank bay access panels
65 Upper UHF/IFF/datalink antenna
66 Starboard wingroot joint
67 Starboard wing integral fuel tank
68 Stores pylons
69 Mk 83 1,000-lb LDGP bomb
70 Leading-edge flap
71 Starboard secondary navigation light
72 Wingtip missile launch rail
73 AIM-9L Sidewinder air-to-air missile
74 Outer wing panel, folded position
75 Drooping aileron
76 Aileron hydraulic actuator
77 Wing-fold hydraulic rotary actuator
78 Drooping flap vane
79 Starboard slotted flap, operates as flaperon at low speeds
80 Flap hydraulic actuator
81 Hydraulic reservoirs

82 Reinforced fin-root attachment joint
83 Multi-spar fin structure
84 Fuel jettison pipe
85 Graphite/epoxy tail unit skin panels with glass-fibre tip fairings
86 Tail position light
87 AN/ALR-67 receiving antenna
88 AN/ALQ-165 low-band transmitting antenna
89 Fuel jettison
90 Starboard all-moving tailplane
91 Starboard rudder
92 Radar warning system power amplifier
93 Rudder hydraulic actuator
94 Airbrake panel, open
95 Airbrake hydraulic jack
96 Fin formation lighting strip
97 Fuel venting air intake
98 Anti-collision beacon, port and starboard
99 Port rudder

100 Port AN/ALQ-165 antenna
101 AN-ALQ-67 receiving antenna
102 AN/ALQ-165 high-band transmitting antenna
103 Variable-area afterburner nozzles
104 Nozzle actuators
105 Afterburner duct
106 Port all-moving tailplane
107 Tailplane bonded honeycomb core structure
108 Deck arrester hook
109 Tailplane pivot mounting
110 Tailplane hydraulic actuator
111 Full-authority digital engine controller (FADEC)
112 General Electric F404-GE-400 afterburning turbofan engine
113 Rear fuselage formation lighting strip
114 Engine fuel control units
115 Fuselage side mounted AIM-7 Sparrow air-to-air missile
116 Port slotted flap
117 Control surface bonded honeycomb core structure
118 Wing-fold rotary hydraulic actuator and hinge joint

126 Port wing stores pylons
127 Pylon mounting hardpoints
128 Multi-spar wing panel structure
129 Port wing integral fuel tank
130 Leading-edge flap shaft driven rotary actuator
131 Port mainwheel
132 Levered suspension main undercarriage leg strut
133 Shock absorber strut
134 Ventral AN/ALE-39 chaff/flare launcher
135 330-US gal external fuel tank
136 Strike camera housing
137 AN/ASQ-173 laser spot tracker/strike camera (LST/SCAM) pod
138 Fuselage starboard side LST/SCAM pylon adaptor
139 Port side FLIR pod adaptor
140 AN/AAS-38 forward-looking infra-red (FLIR) pod
141 CBU-89/89B 'Gator' sub-munition dispenser
142 GBU-12 D/B Paveway II 500-lb laser-guided bomb
143 LAU-10A Zuni four-round rocket launcher
144 5-in FFAR
145 AGM-88 HARM air-to-surface anti-radar missile
146 AGM-65A Maverick air-to-surface anti-armour missile

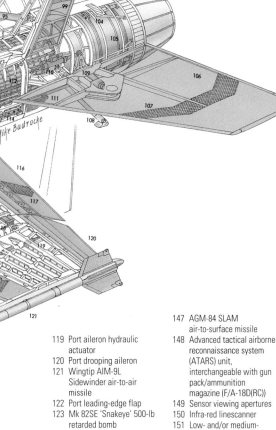

119 Port aileron hydraulic actuator
120 Port drooping aileron
121 Wingtip AIM-9L Sidewinder air-to-air missile
122 Port leading-edge flap
123 Mk 82SE 'Snakeye' 500-lb retarded bomb
124 Mk 82 500-lb LDGP bombs
125 Twin stores carrier

147 AGM-84 SLAM air-to-surface missile
148 Advanced tactical airborne reconnaissance system (ATARS) unit, interchangeable with gun pack/ammunition magazine (F/A-18D(RC))
149 Sensor viewing apertures
150 Infra-red linescanner
151 Low- and/or medium-altitude electro-optical scanner

When it first appeared, the cockpit of the basic F/A-18A (above right) was the most advanced fighter cockpit in service, dominated by three monochrome CRT displays and featuring comprehensive HOTAS controls to allow head-up operation. The front cockpit of the F/A-18D (above) is little changed, and the rear cockpit of the all-weather F/A-18D (below) is similarly equipped. The next generation of fighter cockpits will dispense with analog instruments on the main panel altogether, using small LCDs or CRTs as back-ups, and with full-colour display symbology.

McDonnell-Douglas F/A-18D Night-Attack Hornet

1 Glass-fibre radome, hinged to starboard
2 Planar radar array radar scanner
3 Scanner tracking mechanism
4 Cannon port and gun gas purging intakes
5 Radar module withdrawal rails
6 Hughes AN/APG-73 radar equipment module
7 Formation lighting strip
8 Forward radar warning antennas
9 UHF/IFF antenna
10 Pitot head, port and starboard
11 Incidence transmitter
12 Canopy emergency release
13 Ammunition drum, 570 rounds
14 M61A1 Vulcan 20-mm rotary cannon
15 Retractable inflight-refuelling probe
16 Single piece wrap-round windscreen
17 Pilot's Kaiser AN/AVQ-28 raster HUD

18 Instrument panel with multi-function colour CRT displays
19 Control column
20 Rudder pedals
21 Ammunition loading chute
22 Ground power socket
23 Nose undercarriage wheel bay

24 Catapult strop link
25 Twin nosewheels, forward-retracting
26 Retractable boarding ladder
27 Nosewheel hydraulic jack
28 Nosewheel leg-mounted deck signalling and taxi lights
29 Forward avionics equipment bays, port and starboard
30 Engine throttle levers
31 Pilot's Martin-Baker SJU-6/A ejection seat
32 Rear cockpit rudder pedals (dual flight control system interchangeable with radar and weapons controllers)

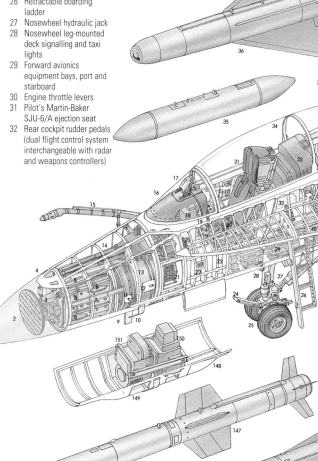

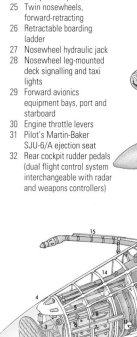

Range instrumentation pod
Aircraft using an instrumented air combat range
inevitably carry a streamlined datalink pod which
allows details of aircraft position, altitude and speed to
be transmitted to the ground throughout the flight,
together with key events such as simulated missile
firings, to allow accurate and complete 'playback'
during post-flight debriefings. These pods are usually
designed to be carried on a standard AIM-9
Sidewinder missile launch rail, and some are actually
packaged inside former AIM-9 airframes.

Boarding ladder

A retractable four-step boarding ladder is stowed in the port LERX. This incorporates a series of support tubes which brace it to the fuselage when extended. The built-in ladder removes the need for another item of ground support equipment and makes the F/A-18 more autonomous on the carrier deck or away from its home airfield.

Intakes

Mach 2 performance was never required, so the F/A-18 can get away with a simple fixed-geometry air intake, without variable intake ramps. The oval intake incorporates a rectangular splitter plate. This has four rows of tiny perforations, which allow sluggish boundary layer air to be extracted before it can be ingested by the engine. The Hornet's General Electric F404-GE-400 has proved to be a remarkably pilot-friendly engine, tolerant of throttle mishandling and disturbed airflow in the inlets. Part of the reason for the F404's docile handling characteristics is the excellence of the inlet design.

Above: A 'Hummer' tows a bomb truck laden with low-drag general purpose Mk 82s and Mk 82Rs with their BSU-86 retard tails.

Left: An F/A-18 of VFA-83 'Rampagers' waits for launch, carrying a 500-lb Mk 82R bomb with a BSU-86 retard tail, an alternative to the Snakeye.

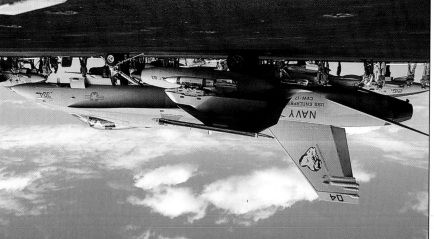

The US Navy and Marines use the Mk 7 CBU dispenser to carry a variety of cluster munitions – resulting in the Rockeye, Gator or CBU-59 bombs, for example.

Right: Two pods of five-inch Zuni rockets (each with four unguided rocket projectiles) wait to be loaded aboard a waiting F/A-18D. The unguided rocket is especially suitable for use against soft and area targets.

Designing the M61A1 gun installation for the F/A-18 was a major task, as its proximity to the radar set presented sizeable vibration problems.

This 250-kg ALD-250 GP bomb is one of a range produced in Spain by International Technology SA, which also makes CBUs and retarded bombs.

Spanish F/A-18s which saw action over Bosnia carried a mix of weapons on each sortie, including AIM-9s, GBU-12s and AGM-88 HARM.

Australian Hornets also carry AGM-65D Mavericks, a relatively recent addition to the RAAF's armoury. AGM-65D is an imaging infra-red version of the Maverick, which is highly accurate both day and night.

This Hornet from No. 75 Sqn, RAAF, is carrying an unusual warload of three CRV-7 rocket pods on its centreline pylon, coupled with a 500-lb GBU-12 Paveway II LGB. GBU-10s (2,000-lb LGBs) are also available.

McDonnell Douglas F/A-18C Hornet

No. 9 Squadron
Kuwait Air Force
Ali Salim Sabah Air Base

Kuwait signed a contract for 32 F/A-18Cs and eight F/A-18Ds in September 1988, but deliveries were delayed by the Gulf War. No. 25 Squadron received its first aircraft in January 1992, and deliveries were completed (to No. 9) in September 1993. Although the F/A-18A and F/A-18C differ very little externally, the later version is considerably more capable, with a host of modifications and improvements. These include a new stores management system, changes to the APG-65 to give AMRAAM compatibility and provision for the AN/ALQ-165 ASPJ. Later F/A-18Cs (from BuNo. 163985) are Night-Attack Hornets, with a gold-tinted canopy, an AN/AVQ-28 faster HUD and provision for the AN/AAR-50 Thermal Imaging Navigation Set. Their cockpits are compatible with the use of MXV-10 Catseye NVGs. Kuwaiti F/A-18s have not been supplied with AMRAAM, but would carry AIM-7F Sparrow semi-active radar homing missiles, and IR-homing AIM-9L Sidewinders for the air-to-air role. AGM-65G Maverick and AGM-84 Harpoons were supplied for the air-to-ground and anti-ship roles.

Colour scheme
The Kuwaiti Hornets wear a three-tone disruptive pattern camouflage. National insignia is restricted to a small flag on the tailfin and there is a small toned-down squadron badge on the tailfin.

Ejection seat
Beginning with BuNo. 164196 F/A-18Cs and Ds were fitted with the Martin-Baker SJU-17/A ejection seat. Prior to this, single-seat F/A-18s used the SJU-5/A and two-seaters used the SJU-6A. The seat is rocket powered and capable of zero-zero operation. The headrest incorporates canopy penetrators.

Powerplant
Kuwaiti Hornets were the first fitted with the General Electric F404-GE-402 EPE powerplant whose higher fan speed and higher operating temperatures conferred extra thrust.

Antenna
From Lot 14, F/A-18Cs and F/A-18Ds had a taller, swept UHF/IFF antenna on the spine, aft of the smaller TACAN antenna.

Tailplane strengthening
On the upper surfaces of the LERXes are a pair of fences which was added to all F/A-18s from March 1988 to modify vortex flow over the tailfins and cure a fatigue cracking problem. The fences were designed with three pairs of attachment points (forward, central and aft) but the aft pair is not used because they are on the central section of the fuselage originally produced by Northrop. Two pairs of attachments were deemed to be sufficient, modifications to only one section of the fuselage saved a considerable sum of money (and time)!

McDonnell Douglas F/A-18A Hornet
VFA-127 'Cylons'
US Navy
NAS Fallon, Nevada

Force drawdowns following the end of the Cold War left many relatively new F/A-18As surplus to US Navy requirements, while the fatigue problems suffered by the F-16N left a requirement for a new aircraft for the adversary squadrons. The F/A-18A was pressed into service, and has proved an excellent simulator for fourth-generation Soviet fighters like the MiG-29 and Su-27, with similar aerodynamic performance and with a radar easily capable of simulating Soviet radars in range discrimination and performance. Because the Hornet is a major current fleet fighter type, its value as a pure dissimilar air combat adversary for fleet Hornet pilots is limited, while many F-14 pilots are familiar with the F/A-18's salient characteristics. Its opponents usually fly with a more representative fuel load, and with pylons (and sometimes external tanks), but the adversary Hornets usually fly clean and thus enjoy a significant performance advantage. The aircraft does mark a major improvement over the recently retired A-4, and over the radarless F-5E, whose numbers are steadily declining. F/A-18s are used as adversary aircraft by the Navy Fighter Weapons School ('Top Gun') at Miramar, by VFA-127 at Fallon, and by reserve adversary squadrons VFC-12 at Oceana and VFC-13 at Miramar. Most are painted in colour schemes designed to mimic those of potential adversaries, while colour is also used to attempt to change the apparent shape of the F/A-18. This aircraft has its wings and tailfins painted to mimic the shape of the MiG-29/MiG-25, with new intake positions suggested by bold black chevrons on the fuselage sides, although the two-tone brown camouflage has not been seen on either of the Soviet types. Other adversary Hornets wear a more realistic blue-grey camouflage, similar to that applied to MiG-29s and Su-27s. Features like false canopies on the underside are used as a means of disorientating opposing pilots. The US Navy's adversary community has been in a state of steady decline for several years, and there is a possibility that further reductions will occur, perhaps leaving only a single reserve squadron with the Pacific and Atlantic fleets. Whatever happens, the F/A-18 seems likely to continue to play a pivotal role in providing realistic air combat training for US Navy fleet fighter pilots.

Cannon

The internal armament of the F/A-18 consists of a single six-barrelled M61A1 Vulcan cannon, which can be used in the air-to-air or air-to-ground roles. Its high rate of fire makes it extremely effective, though many believe that a 30-mm cannon, firing heavier shells, is a better choice for most purposes. The barrels and breech rest above a cylindrical ammunition drum containing 570 rounds of ammunition, forming a single unit. The weapon is capable of rates of fire of up to 6,000 rounds per minute and has a muzzle velocity of 3,400 ft (1036 m) per second. In principal, this highly effective modern weapon is an adaptation of Dr Gatling's original machine-gun The cannon is mounted in the top of the nose, a position which makes for easy aiming with no need for harmonisation, but posed major vibration problems so close to the radar and other delicate avionics black boxes. The designers worked miracles in sealing the avionics bays against gun gases and smoke, and in providing sufficient cooling and vibration damping. The gun system (including the ammunition tank and feed mechanism) can be quickly removed for servicing by being winched down through the underside of the nose. Ease of servicing and the need for fast operational turnarounds were stressed during the initial design process. The various (as-yet) unbuilt reconnaissance versions of the Hornet (the single-seat RF-18 for the Navy and the F/A-18D(RC) for the Marines) can each replace the cannon with a reconnaissance pallet, with camera access doors and integral sensor windows replacing the gun bay doors.

The AGM-62 Walleye II ER/DL (seen here on a USMC F/A-18D) is an unpowered glide bomb which employs an imaging infra-red seeker, like that fitted to the AGM-65 Maverick and AGM-84E SLAM. Use of the AWW-9 datalink pod (usually carried by an accompanying designator aircraft) allows lock-on after launch. The guidance pod and weapon can be carried by two separate aircraft.

Above and left: The AGM-84E Stand-off Land Attack Missile (SLAM) was derived from the AGM-84 Harpoon anti-ship missile to meet a US Navy requirement for a versatile stand-off weapon. The missile has a lengthened airframe and employs imaging infra-red homing instead of the Harpoon's active radar seeker. The missile was combat-proven during Operation Desert Storm, although it was still undergoing operational evaluation. An extended-range SLAM-ER is now under development.

Among the laser-guided bombs carried by US Navy and Marine Corps Hornets is the GBU-16, effectively a 1,000-lb Mk 83 bomb with a long-winged Texas Instruments Paveway II guidance kit attached. The F/A-18 regularly carries laser-guided versions of the 500-lb Mk 82 and the 2,000-lb Mk 84 bombs, too, with Paveway I and Paveway II guidance kits.

Above and below: The McDonnell Douglas AN/ASQ-173 LST/SCAM is a laser spot tracker similar to the Pave Penny pod fitted to USAF A-10s, although it also incorporates a strike camera. The starboard station can carry a Hughes AAR-50 NAVFLIR pod.

The Hornet's original APG-65 radar was once regarded as the best fighter radar in the world, and forms the basis of the APG-73 fitted to current production Hornets (including the aircraft for Finland, Malaysia and Switzerland). The improved radar incorporates a new data processor, a new receiver module, and a new power supply system giving much improved performance and reliability with no increase in weight. The retrofit of existing F/A-18s with APG-73 has allowed US Marine Corps Harrier II Pluses to be fitted with surplus APG-65 radars.

since performed well, sustaining its reliability and maintainability through the 2 million and 3 million hour marks.

One area in which the original F404 has been outperformed by the F100 is in its ability to be upgraded. The F404 control system was designed to maintain the engine's handling characteristics and reliability throughout its service life. As the engine ages, the control system automatically opens the exhaust nozzle wider at given throttle settings. This maintains a constant fan speed and turbine exhaust temperature, but results in a gradual loss in thrust. Unlike Pratt & Whitney's F100-PW-220E, there is no cost-effective upgrade kit available to restore the lost power. This is why the Spanish air force acquired new engines for the ex-USN F-18s which it placed in service in 1995.

A Pratt & Whitney F404?

One major change in the F404 programme was proposed in 1988, when the Navy was planning to produce or modify more than 300 Grumman A-6Fs with F404-GE-100D non-afterburning engines. The Navy planned to qualify Pratt & Whitney to produce the F404, and to split production between the two companies, as a way of reducing cost. The move displeased GE, which saw it as a way of rewarding its competitor for GE's own efforts. The plan was dropped in 1989 after the A-6F was cancelled.

"Develop or perish" is a watchword in the engine business. In the late 1960s, GE Aircraft Engines had developed the 'building block' approach to engine development. Instead of meeting each requirement with a completely new engine, GE planned to develop families of engines around common cores, and to work on technology which could be applied to a variety of engine types.

From 1983, GE worked on a series of demonstrator engines based on the F404, which was used to test new fans, compressors and cores, combustors, turbines and augmentors. Most of these were funded by the Pentagon's Joint Technology Demonstrator Engine (JTDE) programme.

The first uprated version of the engine to enter full-scale development was the F404/RM12 for Saab's JAS 39

Above: A line-up of VFA-137 and VFA-151 Hornets seen on the USS Constellation in 1994. Constellation was the first carrier to host an operational deployment of Hornets, in February 1985.

Not only have Hornets been displacing Tomcats on carrier decks, but USMC F/A-18 squadrons have been increasingly deployed at sea as part of the regular CVWs.

Although this particular problem was solved by redesigning the blades in the front of the compressor, it was clear that titanium fires could still result from FOD or different types of damage. The first step was to develop a fire-resistant Viton rubber coating for the inner wall of the outer bypass duct, which was retrofitted across the fleet. Later F404 engines have a compressor case made of M152 steel alloy, which eliminates the risk of titanium fires. Because the steel case is heavier than the original titanium component, these engines also have a lighter bypass duct made of carbon-fibre composite material. The duct uses a new high-temperature polymer matrix material called PMR-15. With the steel case and composite duct, the engine weighs almost exactly the same as the original all-titanium F404. The engine has

Gripen. This 18,000-lb (80.07-kN) thrust engine had a higher-airflow fan than the basic F404-GE-400, material changes to allow the engine to run at higher temperatures, and a more efficient augmentor.

The Enhanced Performance Engine

Much of the same technology was transferred to a follow-on powerplant for the F/A-18C/D, the F404-GE-402 Enhanced Performance Engine (EPE), which was originally developed to meet the Swiss air force's performance requirements and went on to become the standard engine from 1992. The EPE delivers about 10 per cent more static, sea-level thrust than the basic GE-400 engine, but, as in the case of the improved versions of the F100 and F110, static thrust is only part of the story. Jet engines are usually limited by their maximum operating temperature in the 'lower left-hand corner' of the envelope – that is, at high speeds and low to medium altitudes. Under these circumstances, the EPE can provide up to 20 per cent more thrust than the earlier engine, sharply improving acceleration, time to climb, and speed with a heavy weapon load.

The EPE uses the same basic fan design as the GE-400, because the original version was limited by temperature, rather than airflow, in the most important parts of the envelope, and because using the RM12 fan would have required more flight testing. Improved materials include single-crystal alloys in both turbine stages and higher-temperature alloys in the compressor.

With the EPE, the F/A-18 has up to 18 per cent more specific excess power at Mach 0.9 and 10,000 ft (3048 m). Transonic acceleration (from Mach 0.8 to Mach 1.6 at 35,000 ft/10668 m) is 27 per cent better. A typical runway-launched interception profile, from brake release to Mach 1.4 at 50,000 ft (15240 m), takes 31 per cent less time because it is dependent on achieving the greatest possible acceleration at low altitude.

Kuwait and Switzerland were the first customers for the new engine; the US Navy committed to it later, after deciding that the EPE's higher performance outweighed the slight loss of commonality with the earlier engine.

The EPE is expected to handle the F/A-18C/D's thrust requirements for the remainder of the type's career. Most of GE's current engineering work on the F404 is aimed at improving the engine's durability and reducing its manufacturing and ownership costs.

Avionics

If the airframe looks the same, and the engine has been improved but not redesigned, why do its operators think of the F/A-18C/D as a new aircraft? Most of the answer lies in the avionics.

The original F/A-18 full-scale development programme was accomplished with 11 aircraft. Remarkably, a decade and a half later, there are more F/A-18s engaged in flight tests at Patuxent River and China Lake than there were

Top: The tiny 'blue bombs' (Mk 76 25-lb practice bombs) seem out of place on the TERs of these VMFA-314 aircraft. Despite its small size, the Mk 76 accurately replicates the ballistic characteristics of a 500-lb Mk 82 bomb.

Above: VFA-37 Hornets seen aboard the USS John F. Kennedy. The Kennedy returned to the fleet in September 1995 after a SLEP in the Philadelphia naval yard.

McDonnell Douglas F/A-18 Hornet

Right: A VFA-83 F/A-18C lands at NAS Dallas in 1994, with empty TERs (triple ejector racks). Despite its prowess as a fighter, the accent on US Hornet operations is very definitely on the 'A' rather than the 'F', and the aircraft are firmly committed to the light attack role.

Below: Snuggling under a tanker, a group of VFA-15 'Valions' F/A-18Cs poses for the camera. Note the black walk panels that extend along the LERXes. These Hornets are all Lot 14 night-attack aircraft.

then: as many as 20 Hornets are assigned full-time to flight tests, not including the new F/A-18E/F.

Some of these aircraft are assigned to the development of new weapons. Because it can carry such a wide range of stores, most Navy weapon development offices pick the Hornet as their initial test aircraft. Most of the test fleet, however, are engaged in developing improvements to the F/A-18 itself.

The F/A-18 was the first true 'digital aircraft'. Many aspects of the Hornet – what the pilot sees on the cockpit displays, how the aircraft and its systems respond to stick and switch inputs, and how the onboard sensors work – are influenced if not actually determined by software, either in the aircraft's main mission computer or in processors built into the other avionics subsystems. Because of this, the F/A-18's capability has grown steadily and substantially through apparently minor hardware upgrades, combined with regular updates to the mission software – a new package is released to the operator about once every two years.

Core mission computer

The core of the avionics system is the Control Data International AYK-14 mission computer. This has been the standard Navy airborne computer throughout the 1980s; however, while the newest AYK-14s share some external interfaces with older units, the circuit boards inside have been largely revised. The first version fitted to the F/A-18, the XN-5, has been completely replaced in service by the XN-6. All F/A-18C/D versions have the XN-8 version, which has 2 million words of memory. This has been retrofitted to Lot 8 and Lot 9 A/B models and will also be fitted to at least the first F/A-18E/Fs. Its capacity is expected to be adequate until around 2002-03.

By today's standards, the AYK-14 is not a high performer. It is rugged and reliable – and unlike the case in the commercial world, the development of airborne military computer systems is paced by the rate at which software can be designed, thoroughly tested and introduced fleet-wide. Also, a restrained rate of advance in computing capacity means that, by the time a new mission software package is released, most of the aircraft in the fleet can use it.

The most important change in mission software to be released in the last few years is called multi-sensor integration (MSI). Introduced with the night-attack versions of the Hornet, MSI is intended to keep the crew's workload at a reasonable level despite the addition of new sensors and new weapons. With MSI, the computer receives inputs from different sensors, correlates them and displays them so that one target appears on the pilot's display.

In the air-to-air mode, for example, MSI will match a target detected by radar with the same target's signature on the targeting FLIR. The radar provides range and velocity information, which the FLIR cannot supply; but the FLIR

provides more accurate elevation and bearing data and is better at resolving several closely spaced targets. MSI can select the best data from both sensors and display it to the pilot. Alternatively, the system can be put into a passive, 'quiet' mode in which targets are located with FLIR and the radar is used in bursts for ranging.

MSI can be used in air-to-ground operations as well. If the radar warning receiver (RWR) detects an emitter, it will provide accurate bearing information but only a rough estimate of range, based on signal strength. MSI can automatically point the radar at the target area in its high-resolution mode and locate it.

The first software package to incorporate MSI reached the fleet in October 1991, and the third MSI release is just entering service. One area which is likely to see improvements is the suppression of enemy air defences (SEAD) mission, where the HARM seeker, radar and RWR could be integrated to locate threats and display them to the crew.

The F/A-18A/B cockpit set a pattern for a generation. Its multi-function displays ringed by bezel switches, the up-front control beneath the head-up display, and the hands-on-throttle-and-stick (HOTAS) controls have all been widely emulated. It has also lasted very well. The only major change came with the Lot 12 night-attack variant, in which the monochrome displays were replaced by Kaiser Kroma displays. These combine a monochrome CRT with a three-colour liquid-crystal display (LCD) 'shutter' over the screen, allowing them to display colour stroke information. Lot 12 also saw the introduction of a Honeywell digital map, based on an optical disk reader, which replaces the former film-based map. The new display is easier to read and more flexible - tactical information can be overlaid on it - and changing maps is much easier.

The F/A-18E/F cockpit takes advantage of active matrix LCD (AMLCD) technology. This has made it possible to produce large-format, sunlight-readable displays which can

This appropriately badged F/A-18 of VMFA-122 'Crusaders' is carrying live Mk 82 bombs on a weapons training sortie. On the Hornet's starboard 'shoulder' station can be seen a Lockheed Martin ASQ-173 LST/SCAM (Laser Spot Tracker/ Strike CAMera). ASQ-173 can target weapons on the launch aircraft's HUD, using laser designation from another source (on the ground or in the air) – but only during daylight. It also houses a strike camera for bomb damage assessment. ASQ-173 is often carried in favour of the AN/AAS-50 navigation FLIR. When fitted, the larger AN/AAS-38 NITE Hawk FLIR and laser designator is always carried to port.

A Lemoore-based F/A-18C from VFA-137 'Kestrels' is seen with a single GBU-16 Paveway II. GBU-16 is based around the 1,000-lb Mk 83 GP bomb, mated with a set of (second-generation) guidance fins and seeker head. The US Navy does not yet use the more advanced Paveway III system. Interestingly, during Operation Desert Storm US Navy aircraft dropped more British-designed Paveway II LGBs than US-designed ones. The British bombs (1,000-lb CPU-123s, developed by Portsmouth Aviation) reportedly had greater penetration capability against hardened targets.

McDonnell Douglas F/A-18 Hornet

Above: During FWIT 95 (Fighter Weapons Instructor Training) F/A-18s of VFA-105 were deployed to snow-covered Leeuwarden AFB, in the Netherlands, to exercise alongside other NATO forces.

Right and below: The Hornet is stealing back orders from the F-16 on account of its now-proven ability and sophistication. Meanwhile, F-14s are being steadily edged off the carrier decks by Hornets and revised US Navy doctrine that calls for increased 'in-shore' (littoral) operations.

fit in the tight confines of a fighter cockpit, so the new version has a 200 cm-square (78.74 in-square) tactical situation display (also made by Kaiser) in the centre of the panel. It also features a clearer, touch-sensitive up-front control. AMLCD screens, meanwhile, are dropping steadily in price, and eventually will probably replace the Kroma displays in the C/D, being both better and cheaper.

Another change in the works is the replacement of the optical disk map with an all-digital map, both for the E/F and for late-production C/Ds. The Navy programme office plans to run a competition to select a new map. It will be an open-architecture unit, so that other features can be added by inserting new modules. In particular, the Navy is interested in adding a terrain-referenced navigation (TRN) system, which constantly updates the aircraft's position relative to the ground by matching radar altimeter readings with stored terrain data. TRN can be used as a safety device, to warn the pilot of ground collisions, or it can be used for tactical terrain-following flight without the very un-stealthy use of a terrain-following radar.

Helmet-mounted sight technology

Another new feature for the cockpit will be the Joint Helmet-Mounted Cueing System (JHMCS), a future helmet-mounted display under development for all three US fast-jet operators. The F/A-18 will be the first Navy aircraft to be fitted with the JHMCS. At the time of writing, the JHMCS programme office at Wright-Patterson AFB plans to issue a request for proposals (RFP) covering the JHMCS in March 1996. All the principal Western manufacturers – Honeywell, Kaiser, GEC Avionics, Sextant and Elbit – are expected to compete. The JHMCS is likely to be a display which attaches to a pilot's standard helmet and can be used to designate airborne and ground targets for the fighter's weapon control system. It will meet stringent specifications for symbol brightness and quality, head-tracking accuracy, ejection safety, wearability and supportability – issues which have hampered the deployment of helmet-mounted displays in the past. A three-year engineering and manufacturing development programme is due to start in 1997, leading to service entry in the year 2000.

The F/A-18 has flown with other helmet-mounted displays, because McDonnell Douglas in general, and the company's resident cockpit guru Gene Adam in particular, have been strong advocates of what Adam calls "the HUD on your head" since the early 1980s. The aircraft has been used to test several of the Kaiser Agile Eye HMD prototypes. In 1993, while the F/A-18 was in competition for an Israeli air force order, McDonnell Douglas signed an agreement with Elbit to market the Israeli company's DASH (Display And Sight Helmet). DASH has been flown by US Navy pilots, and was also demonstrated in flight evaluations for the Israeli and Singaporean air forces. Early in 1996, it was used by the Navy in tests of Hughes and Raytheon off-boresight missile seekers at China Lake. As far as is known, no export customer has ordered the DASH helmet or any other HMD.

Other elements of the basic avionics system have seen changes during production. The digital flight control system has been continuously upgraded, sometimes to improve the aircraft's handling qualities but usually in order to handle new weapons configurations: by early 1996, the DFCS software had reached Version 10.5. In the early 1990s, the DFCS computers were modified with larger programmable memory modules to make the update process easier. Industry mergers have created a remarkable situation for the DFCS. The General Electric division

which originally developed the system was acquired in 1990 by Martin-Marietta, which in turn merged with Lockheed in 1995. As a result, the most critical avionics system on the F/A-18 is now produced by Lockheed Martin.

All-new inertial nav

The original Litton mechanical-gyro ASN-130 inertial navigation system (INS) was replaced with a lower-mainte-nance Litton ASN-39 ring-laser-gyro (RLG) INS in aircraft delivered from 1991. Aircraft handed over since September 1995 have also had a P-Code Global Positioning System (GPS) receiver, and this will eventually be retrofitted to all F/A-18s in service. The next step is the introduction of an integrated GPS/INS, which offers better accuracy and integrity than either system alone. The GPS corrects the long-term drift in the INS, while the INS can detect GPS errors caused by poor satellite signals. A Litton GPS/INS was starting tests in a King Air in early 1996 before being installed on an F/A-18.

The combination of GPS/INS and a TRN system provides a near-ultimate navigation capability, with three largely independent and different sources of position data. As the software is developed to integrate all three systems aboard the aircraft, the operator will see improvements in weapons delivery accuracy, in-weather capability and flight

A VFA-94 'Mighty Shrikes' F/A-18C is pictured in the empty skies over Nevada. The US has learned hard lessons about 'blue-on-blue' kills in less friendly environments. An improved IFF system is currently undergoing tests at the Naval Air Warfare Weapons Division, China Lake, on an F/A-18D. The new AN/APX-111 or Combined Interrogator Transponder (CIT) will be fitted to 500 US Navy and Marine Corps Hornets, allowing their crews to survey airspace up to 100 miles (160 km) from their aircraft. The CIT will provide identification, azimuth and range information on all targets in that zone.

The F/A-18 has become a popular mount for the US Navy's adversary squadrons. While the Navy has steadily cut back its aggressor training units (to the horror of many) those that survive operate mostly early-model Hornets in a variety of vivid colour schemes. This VFC-12 MiG-29 'lookalike' is one of those which replaced the squadron's former mount, the A-4F/M, at its East Coast base of NAS Oceana.

safety. The new navigation devices are also a very good match for low-cost 'semi-precise' GPS/inertial weapons such as JSOW and JDAM and – in the air-to-ground role – for a helmet-mounted display. If a pilot sees a target on the ground, he needs only to look at it – that is, point his helmet 'pipper' at it – to designate it. The weapons system can compute the target's exact location from the aircraft's attitude and direction (INS), its exact position relative to the ground and the elevation of the target (TRN) and the boresight of the HMD. The data can then be used for an over-the-shoulder attack with JDAM or JSOW, without overflying the target or even being within line-of-sight of it.

Connected to the core avionics – the computer, displays and navigation equipment – are two main groups of 'peripherals', which are sensors that help find targets and defensive avionics which defeat threats. These, too, have been steadily improved since the Hornet entered service.

The world's best fighter radar

As in the case of any fighter, the Hornet's most important and expensive sensor is its radar. The GM-Hughes Electronics APG-65 radar fitted to the F/A-18A/B was an effective and flexible system for its day, drawing on much of the technology that had been developed for the F-15's APG-63. During the 1980s, the radar was progressively modified with more memory and faster processors, but by the end of the decade its growth potential had been fully realised. Later Hughes radars, such as the APG-70 fitted to later F-15s, had demonstrated new technologies and components which could be incorporated at low risk into an improved radar for the F/A-18.

The new radar, designated APG-73, was flown on an F/A-18 in April 1992, and deliveries started in May 1994, to VFA-146 and VFA-147 at NAS Lemoore, California. All subsequent F/A-18s, including export versions for Finland, Switzerland and Malaysia, have the APG-73, and the Navy plans to retrofit all Block 12 and later aircraft – that is, all the night-attack variants – with the new radar. (The APG-65 radars removed from these aircraft will be fitted to USMC Harriers as they are remanufactured into the AV-8B Plus configuration.)

The basic APG-73 uses the same antenna and travelling-wave-tube (TWT) transmitter as the APG-65, but the rest of the hardware is new. The receiver/exciter unit is more sophisticated and provides much faster analog-to-digital conversion, allowing the radar to cut the incoming signal into smaller fragments and thereby achieve better range

resolution. The radar data processor replaces two units in the older radar (the signal processor and the data processor); signal processing speed is increased almost tenfold, and both functions can use much more memory. The third new unit is the power supply, which uses new solid-state techniques to provide much more reliable power conversion. Power supply reliability has been the bane of the radar designer's life for many years, but the new APG-73 unit ran for 2,500 hours on tests with only one failure.

All the new electronic units comprise racks that accommodate 5 x 9-in (12.7 x 22.9-cm) modules. These electronic units snap into the racks, which provide them with power, cooling and connections to the other modules and to the radar. Built-in test modules will isolate any fault to an individual module, which can be changed quickly without removing the rack from the aircraft. Future hardware upgrades can be carried out in the same way.

The APG-73 offers higher resolution in its air-to-ground mapping and bombing modes ("My grandmother could win Gunsmoke with the APG-73," is one comment) and is better at discriminating between closely spaced airborne targets for raid assessment. Air-to-air detection and tracking ranges are up between 7 and 20 per cent. One of the biggest single benefits is a wider receiver bandwidth which allows it to use more advanced electronic counter-counter-measures (ECCM) techniques to defeat jamming and confuse an adversary's radar warning receiver.

Phase 2 reconnaissance capability

The current APG-73, though, is the first of three phases in radar development. The main change in Phase 2 will be the addition of a high-resolution synthetic aperture radar (SAR) mode in the radar. SAR is a radar technique which uses the movement of the aircraft between pulses to emulate the resolution of a very large antenna. On the F/A-18, SAR has been a problem because the inertial navigation system, which is needed to measure the movement of the aircraft, is in the middle of the fuselage. In flight, the body flexes between the nose and mid-section, introducing errors into the antenna pointing accuracy and thereby limiting the resolution that SAR can achieve. The Phase 2 radar will incorporate a small Honeywell RLG inertial measurement unit to overcome this problem. It will be fitted first to the USMC's reconnaissance-capable F/A-18D(RC) in 1997, and will be standard from 1999.

The APG-73 Phase 3 radar will have an active array, which is a physically fixed antenna comprising hundreds of

transmit/receive modules. Advantages include virtually instantaneous mode changes and beam steering, and the elimination of components, such as the gimbal drives and transmitter, which can render the radar inoperative with a single failure. An active array can also be shaped so that it adds very little to the aircraft's total radar cross-section. Phase 3 is not yet funded, so it has no firm timetable and is unlikely to appear on the F/A-18C/D. One possibility is that it could share its antenna design with the JAST (Joint Advanced Strike Technology) programme.

One of the features of the F/A-18 which has distinguished it from its competitors is that it has always been offered with infra-red navigation and targeting systems, which are attached to the body-side Sparrow/AMRAAM mounts. The first systems to be offered were the Hughes AAR-50 Thermal Imaging Navigation System (TINS), a wide-angle forward-looking infra-red (FLIR) imager which was designed to project an IR picture on the pilot's HUD, and the Ford Aerospace AAS-38 NITE Hawk (Navigation IR Targeting Equipment) FLIR, a steerable sensor which could track a target on the ground automatically as the aircraft moved. Ford, which became a division of Loral in

1990, delivered more than 300 AAS-38 pods to the USN and USMC by 1992, and they were used on more than 10,000 sorties in the Gulf War.

NITE Hawk, Laser Hornet

From 1992, the F/A-18 acquired the ability to designate targets for laser-guided bombs, as NITE Hawk production shifted to the AAS-38A FLIR-LTD/R (Laser Target Designator/Ranger). The new pods were issued to VFA-37 and VFA-105 and went to sea aboard the *Kennedy* in October 1992, and are now being widely used by USN and USMC squadrons, including those in Bosnia. With the new pod, the F/A-18 can deliver LGBs without the help of a laser-carrying forward air controller on the ground. Once the target has been acquired on the FLIR and the auto-tracker has locked on, the bomb is released and guided automatically as long as the aircraft does not manoeuvre outside the FLIR gimbal limits or exceed the system's range. The LTD/R also provides more precise range and velocity information for the delivery of unguided weapons.

The latest NITE Hawk version, the AAS-38B, has a new Texas Instruments signal processor and a laser spot tracker

On a sortie from MCAS Yuma, a Marines F/A-18C rolls in on a target with a live load of four 500-lb Mk 82 'slicks' and a pair of Zuni rocket pods. In Operation Desert Storm the US Marines used their F/A-18Ds as Fast FACs and these tactics have been further refined over Bosnia. WP (white phosphorous) rockets have long been used as target markers by FACs, but conventional HE-tipped rockets work equally well. They can damage a target rather than warn it that it is about to come under attack. They are effective target markers, too – just look for the black smoke.

McDonnell Douglas F/A-18 Hornet

On patrol over Bosnia, a Marine Corps F/A-18D refuels from a drogue-equipped KC-135 of the 434th Wing. In many ways the Marines reinvented the Hornet, realising that the two-crew F/A-18D plus the Hornet's new nav/attack suite would make a useful replacement for its A-6Es. Thus the F/A-18D became far more than a conversion trainer and the USMC hopes to acquire up to 96 of the type. Deliveries of Night Attack F/A-18Ds began to the Marine Corps (VMFA(AW)-121) in April 1990.

Above opposite: Current USMC plans call for the establishment of six F/A-18D squadrons. One of these will be equipped with the ATARS-capable F/A-18D(RC) which will replace a reconnaissance capability the Corps (and indeed the Navy) has been lacking since its last RF-8 Crusaders were retired. These VMFA(AW)-224 F/A-18Ds, carrying a mix of Mk 83s and AGM-88s, show just how valuable the Hornet is to the Marines in providing maximum air support for troops on the ground.

(LST). The latter makes it possible for the F/A-18 crew to quickly acquire a target which has been illuminated by another Hornet, an EA-6B Prowler (these aircraft carry designators but no LGBs) or a FAC on the ground. The faster processor improves performance in a number of ways. The autotracker works better and can be set either to track the entire scene or the centroid of a target. In the air-to-air mode, the new version can search the sky ahead of the aircraft much more quickly, giving the F/A-18 a true passive track-while-scan capability. About half a dozen of the new AAS-38B pods had been delivered by early 1996.

The next step in FLIR capability will be a fly-off competition, scheduled for the summer of 1997, to select a new Gen 3 (third-generation) FLIR for the Hornet. Gen 3 IR sensors are based on focal plane array (FPA) technology rather than mechanically scanned detectors. They are more sensitive than earlier IR sensors and provide higher resolution, and are more reliable into the bargain.

The AAR-50 TINS remains in use, but is normally carried only when conditions such as a high overcast preclude the use of night-vision goggles (NVGs). NVGs give the pilot all-round night vision, and the operators prefer to use one of the side stations for an AMRAAM.

Reliable IFF

Another important sensor (which is often overlooked) is the Identification Friend or Foe (IFF) system. Kuwait was the first customer to replace the standard APX-100 with the Hazeltine APX-113 Combined Interrogator Transponder (CIT). Identifiable by the row of five short blade antennas above the fighter's nose, the APX-113 features electronic beam steering which allows it to determine the range, bearing and elevation of any aircraft which 'squawk' when interrogated by the Hornet. In early 1995, it was selected as the standard transponder for US Navy and Marine Corps Hornets. It will be fitted to all Hornets after mid-1997 and will be retrofitted to as many as 500 aircraft.

The F/A-18's digital core can also be connected to other sensors for specialised missions. The most important programme of this kind is the US Navy/Marine Corps F/A-18D(RC) – reconnaissance-capable – variant, which is due to enter USMC service later in this decade.

The reconnaissance version has had a long and sometimes difficult history. Early in the programme's history, McDonnell Douglas demonstrated that the Hornet's nose gun bay could accommodate a reconnaissance pallet, with flat camera windows in a fairing that would replace the access door. Technology and inter-service politics, however, delayed the programme.

The Marines' RF-4Cs, and the Navy's TARPS (Tactical Air Reconnaissance Pod System) pod which is carried on the F-14, use film-based cameras. By the mid-1980s, the development of electro-optical cameras, which have an array of charge-coupled devices (CCDs) in place of film, had reached a point where their image quality matched that of 127-mm reconnaissance film. This would eliminate the cumbersome task of developing film in the field or on board ship.

The ATARS saga

At the same time, there was an active debate over the role of unmanned air vehicles (UAVs) for tactical reconnaissance. Some high-level Pentagon planners favoured the UAV, but the operators were reluctant to give up their manned reconnaissance aircraft until UAVs were proven to work. The final result was a programme called Advanced Tactical Air Reconnaissance System (ATARS). Control Data Corporation was awarded a contract to develop ATARS in May 1988. It was a single EO reconnaissance system which was planned to fit in the F/A-18's nose, in a pod on the F-16, and in Teledyne Ryan's AQM-145 Medium Range UAV, in two versions: an air-launched variant for the Navy and a ground-launched version for the USAF.

The following seven years were eventful but did not, unfortunately, result in much progress. Technical problems with the system's video recorder and other components delayed the programme. Control Data transferred the ATARS contract to Martin-Marietta in 1990. The USAF cancelled its version of the AQM-145, which (in 1994) was dropped by the Navy as well. In July 1993, the Air Force terminated the ATARS programme, stating that manned tactical reconnaissance was no longer a necessary mission.

More recent experience in Bosnia and Somalia has

revived interest in tactical reconnaissance. High-altitude stand-off platforms can be rendered useless by overcast or terrain, may not equal the resolution of a short-range image unless the weather is perfect, and may not be available when a theatre commander needs them.

The Navy continued to test ATARS after the USAF withdrew, and restarted the programme in June 1994 with McDonnell Douglas as the prime contractor (the third in the programme's life) and Loral – which provides the sensors – as a lead subcontractor. Flight tests restarted in April 1995. The Navy plans to acquire an initial batch of 31 ATARS systems, which will be fitted to USMC F/A-18Ds. The modified aircraft is designated F/A-18D(RC) and retains full combat capability apart from the gun.

The first new ATARS systems should be delivered to the USMC in 1998-99. Meanwhile, once testing has been completed, some of the ATARS equipment which was built in earlier stages of the programme will be available for contingency use, and the Navy plans to buy 50 more systems for the F/A-18E/F, which will replace TARPS in its carrier air wings as the F-14 is retired.

ATARS includes a low-altitude EO sensor, a medium-altitude EO sensor and an infra-red linescan imager, all produced by Loral. The low-altitude sensor covers a 140° arc below the aircraft and is normally used at 3,000 ft (914 m) above ground level or lower. The medium-altitude sensor can gather high-resolution imagery at altitudes of 25,000 ft (7620 m), up to 5 miles (8 km) from the target, taking the aircraft out of range of AAA and small SAMs, while the IR linescan provides high-resolution imagery at night.

Computing Devices International's UK division provides the reconnaissance management system (RMS), which is based on the system developed for the RAF's Tornado reconnaissance variants. The RMS interfaces with the aircraft systems to activate the sensors automatically, according to the mission plan, and to scan and stabilise the sensor images. It processes imagery into a common recording format in real time, and compresses the data to match the data rates achievable by the Schlumberger digital recorder and the datalink. Random-access memory (RAM) in the RMS allows the pilot or backseater to rotate, 'zoom' and mark the recorded imagery on his multi-function display.

Selected images can be datalinked to a station on an aircraft or a ship. Using a high-rate X-band datalink carried in a pod, combined with software enhancements, programme officials hope that real-time imagery can be transmitted.

SAR and LOROP capabilities

The F/A-18D(RC) will be the first Hornet to have the APG-73 Phase 2 radar with a high-resolution SAR mode, as noted above. This will give them the ability to gather imagery at long stand-off ranges (up to 70 nm/130 km) in bad weather, with a probable resolution in the 1 m (3 ft 3 in) range. The only major unfunded gap in the reconnaissance Hornet's capability is the lack of a long-range oblique photography (LOROP) sensor which can acquire reconnaissance pictures from 40 nm (75 km) range. The Navy has ordered two pod-mounted versions of Loral's AVD-5 EO-LOROP sensor, with a 66 in (168 cm) focal length, which will be delivered in 1996, but has not made a production decision. One alternative might be Litton Itek

The F/A-18B remains essentially a training aircraft. Forty aircraft were acquired for the US Navy and Marines, and this example is seen wearing the markings of VFA-106 'Gladiators' which was established as the East Coast Hornet FRS in April 1984. The unit was actually assigned a mix of F/A-18A/B/C/Ds.

One thing that cannot be denied about the F/A-18 is that it is a tough bird. The design utilises a large proportion (49.6 per cent of the total materials) of high-strength aluminium alloys, with steel (16.7 per cent) for some high-load components, such as the landing gear and arrester gear. Titanium (12.9 per cent) is used around the engine bays, various plastics for the radome and canopy, and epoxy laminates (9.9 per cent) for the fins and wing skins. During ballistic tolerance testing a 20-mm incendiary shell was shot into the wing, destroying the inner wing spar. The wing remained intact and retained its limit load capability, with only a small change in deflection.

Optical Systems' DB-110, a new sensor with a 110-in (280-cm) focal length and a dual-band capability – that is, it can operate in both the visible and mid-wave IR bands. Despite its long focal length, it can fit into the F/A-18's nose bay.

While sensors such as radar and EO devices help find and locate targets, another group of avionics systems is used to detect and defeat threats to the aircraft. Like other systems on the F/A-18, the defensive electronic countermeasures (DECM) suite is in a constant process of evolution, driven by technology, the changing threat and changing doctrine.

Hornet self-defence and ASPJ

One of the original distinctions between the F/A-18 and its smaller rival, the F-16, was that the Hornet carried an internal active jamming system. This was the Sanders (later, Lockheed Sanders) ALQ-126B, an improved version of a standard Navy system that was also used on the A-6 and F-14. Even when the F/A-18 entered service, however, the ALQ-126 was becoming less capable in the face of improved Soviet radars. It remains useful against older radars, many of which are still in service worldwide, and is still used on the F/A-18. Not every F/A-18 carries an active jammer at all times; typically, the systems are installed when a squadron is preparing for a cruise away from the US. Australian, Spanish and Canadian F/A-18s are fitted with the ALQ-126B, and Spanish and Canadian aircraft also use the Northrop ALQ-162.

The planned replacement for the ALQ-126 ran into a dense thicket of problems, from which it still has not emerged. The ITT/Westinghouse ALQ-165 Advanced Self-Protection Jammer (ASPJ) was conceived in the early 1980s as an improved internal jammer for the F/A-18, F-16, F-14 and A-6. The highly automated, software-controlled system incorporates many state-of-the-art electronic technologies, including microwave monolithic integrated circuits, application-specific integrated circuits and gate arrays. Like many other jammer programmes, it ran into

serious technical problems, compounded by political troubles, and development ran years behind schedule. The USAF withdrew from the programme in 1990. At the end of 1992, the Navy terminated the ASPJ low-rate initial production programme because of the system's failure to meet all the test requirements imposed by the Department of Defense.

Some of the ASPJ's supporters within the Marine and Navy aviation communities continued to maintain that the ASPJ worked well enough to justify its production, and that the DoD had set unrealistically high performance standards that no onboard jammer could meet. Their views were clearly shared by the air forces of Finland and Switzerland, which both ordered the ALQ-165 for their Hornets after the US Navy had cancelled it – possibly the only instance in which a major system has been successfully sold for export after the prime customer has scrapped it. (Finland took delivery of its first system in November 1995.)

Relearning old lessons in Bosnia

On 2 June 1995, a USAF F-16 was shot down over Bosnia by an SA-6 radar-guided missile. Marine aviators flying F/A-18s in the theatre requested better ECM equipment. A Navy depot in Indiana held 96 ASPJ systems which had been delivered before the programme was cancelled, and some of these were rapidly fitted in 12 USMC F/A-18Ds and 12 USN F/A-18Cs. The system provides a much better detection capability against the SA-6 than the older ALQ-126B.

So far, the Navy does not plan to buy more ALQ-165s, although that option exists as long as the system is in production. Some of its components are being used in the Integrated DECM (IDECM) system for the F/A-18E/F, the B-1B and the F-15E.

The other basic element of the original DECM system was the Litton ALR-67(V)1 radar warning receiver (RWR). From 1990, this was replaced by the same company's ALR-67(V)2: these aircraft are distinguished by

additional antenna blisters on the nose, vertical tails and mid-body. The next step is the ALR-67(V)3, produced by GM-Hughes, which uses the same antennas but features a more advanced receiver. Its more powerful processor is better able to handle dense clusters of targets, particularly if they can frequency-hop, and it is better at detecting and tracking pulse-Doppler and monopulse radars. The ALR-67 (V)3 is due to enter production with the FY 1997 batch.

One change in DECM philosophy in recent years has been a revived recognition of the importance of expendable countermeasures. The original F/A-18 was fitted with two 30-tube Tracor ALE-39 dispenser 'buckets'. Starting with Finland's aircraft and 1996 Navy deliveries, however, the aircraft will have four of the improved ALE-47 dispensers for a total of 120 launch tubes. These decoys include chaff, flares and the Texas Instruments GEN-X, an active radar decoy that repeats the signal from a radar that is trying to guide a missile on to the F-18.

All these systems and more should be brought together in the F/A-18E/F and its new IDECM system. It will be based on a new Lockheed Sanders core system, with ITT and Loral as sub-contractors, and will closely integrate passive sensors, jammers and decoys. The Army's Advanced Threat Infra-Red Countermeasures (ATIRCM), also from Lockheed Sanders, may be adopted: it is designed to detect IR-homing missiles heading towards the aircraft, and to jam their seekers with steerable lasers.

Another new element of the F/A-18E/F's DECM suite will be the Raytheon ALE-50 towed decoy. Three of these units will be on board. Towed on a 328-ft (100-m) cable, the ALE-50 is designed to confuse monopulse tracking radars by generating a signal similar to the target return. The missile guidance system detects a target 328 ft (100 m) long and steers the missile towards its centroid, missing the real target. Eventually, the ALE-50 should be replaced by an improved towed decoy from Sanders and ITT, which will be towed on a fibre-optic cable.

Going hand in hand with the development of new avionics to detect targets and threats is the deployment of new weapons to negate them.

McDonnell Douglas claims that the F/A-18 is unrivalled in the variety of weapons which it is designed and cleared to carry. "We can launch anything in the inventory – black, white or grey," F/A-18 vice president Michael Sears has remarked. A wide choice of weapons is they key to the F/A-18's versatility, lethality and survivability, as it takes on an ever larger spectrum of missions.

Like the rest of the US fighter force, the Navy's F/A-18s are converting from the AIM-7 Sparrow medium-range air-to-air missile – a much refined version of a weapon designed in the 1950s – to the GM-Hughes Missile Systems Company AIM-120 Advanced Medium-Range Air-to-Air Missile (AMRAAM), known to US pilots as the 'Slammer'.

The 'Slammer'

AMRAAM is a large step forward from the AIM-7. The older missile uses semi-active radar homing (SARH), with a seeker that homes on to radar signals transmitted by the launch aircraft. The shooter must continuously illuminate the target from launch to impact. Consequently, the shooter's manoeuvres are limited by the need to keep the target within the gimbal limits of the radar; the shooter is blind to other targets when the missile is in flight; and the continuous radar beam is a beacon for hostile detectors, and an unambiguous warning to the target.

AMRAAM is an active radar homing (ARH) missile with its own radar. It also has an inertial navigation system and a datalink. Immediately before launch, the fighter's fire control system predicts where the missile will intercept the target and loads that information into the missile's memory via the MIL-STD-1760 interface in the pylon. The missile flies out towards that point. The fighter's radar continues to track the target, and as the target's track and velocity change, it computes a new intercept point and transmits it to the missile. At a certain (classified) distance from the target, the AMRAAM automatically activates its own radar

A VMFA(AW)-332 F/A-18D is seen at altitude over California. TERs (triple ejector racks) are a common sight on Hornets during training sorties, but for combat missions they would be replaced by VERs (vertical ejector racks). BRU-33/A (VER-2) ejectors carry two bombs, in a side-by-side configuration. They are more reliable than TERs because they have dual firing circuits and cartridges in addition to a higher load-carrying and release (g) capability. Like TERs, VERs are attached to the standard SUU-62/A Hornet underwing pylon, but they can also be fitted to the SUU-62/A pylon on the centreline.

A pair of MCAS
Beaufort-based
VMFA(AW)-224 F/A-18D
Hornets streams fuel
from their fintip vents.
This is not a procedure
that could be
recommended for early-
model Hornets, which
were hamstrung by fuel-
imposed range
limitations.

and locks on to the target.

The advantages are clear. The shooter's radar is free to search and track other targets throughout the engagement. In theory, the shooter's ability to launch and guide multiple missiles against multiple targets is limited only by the tracking ability of the radar, and once AMRAAM has locked on the attacker is free to manoeuvre at will.

The AMRAAM is also faster (Mach 4) and lighter than the AIM-7. One Hughes brochure photo shows an F/A-18 bristling with no fewer than 10 Slammers, although the real-world probability of such a load-out must be close to zero. However, the lower weight does have important practical applications, because it allows the F/A-18 to carry paired AMRAAMs in place of a single AIM-7 on its under-wing pylons.

After a long development period, AMRAAM entered service in 1992. Those who predicted an outcome similar to the mediocre performance of early AIM-7s in Vietnam

have been confounded. The Slammer has proven reliable and lethal. During 1993, USAF F-16Cs shot down two Iraqi fighters with AMRAAMs during Southern Watch operations over Iraq. In September 1993, AMRAAM was declared operational on the F/A-18C/D aboard USS *Theodore Roosevelt*.

The current production version is the AIM-120B, with an electronically reprogrammable signal processor which can be loaded with new software in the field to meet changing ECM threats. The AIM-120C clipped-wing AMRAAM, designed to fit the F-22A's belly weapon bays, will be standard from Lot 9 (ordered in FY95, to be delivered around 1997) and is expected to be essentially identical in performance to the original version.

BVR missile threats, today and tomorrow

Phase 3, a more radical development, has acquired more importance as the Western fighter community has appreciated

This more recent photo
of a VMFA(AW)-224
Hornet shows an aircraft
with a typical Bosnia
loadout of AIM-9s, LAU-
10 rocket launcher and a
centreline Mk 82 bomb.
In that environment,
endurance – time on
station – was more
important than warload.
Targets were often small
and fleeting. This aircraft
carries two fuel tanks at
the expense of ordnance,
but would be able to find
and attack any likely
target with its rockets
and bomb.

Hughes expects to offer the Phase 3 AMRAAM to arm the UK's Eurofighter 2000s, under Staff Requirement (Air) 1239 for a Future MRAAM (FMRAAM). Hughes' candidate combines the AMRAAM electronics and warhead with a variable flow ducted rocket (VFDR) which has been developed over the past 17 years by ARC and Hercules (now part of Alliant TechSystems). The VFDR has two air inlets in an inverted V configuration. According to Hughes, the inverted V provides good airflow in all flight attitudes and is compatible with most current AMRAAM stations, and the inlet ducts develop lift.

The USAF has a less urgent requirement for Phase 3 than other services, because the stealthy F-22 is expected to prevail in combat with the existing weapon. However, export customers and the Navy are likely to participate in such an effort.

Although the Phase 3 AMRAAM was not specifically designed as a long-range weapon, it will have a greater reach than the existing AIM-120C. To some extent, it will fill the gap left as the F-14 is retired, along with the long-range AIM-54 Phoenix missile. At the time that the Navy terminated production of the F-14D, in 1989, the Navy was pursuing development of the Advanced Air-to-Air Missile (AAAM), which would not only replace the AIM-54 aboard the F-14 but which would be compatible with the F-18 and A-12. Two teams were given AAAM study contracts: Hughes and Raytheon, with a ramjet-powered missile using a dual-mode seeker, and General Dynamics and Westinghouse, who offered a radical tube-launched missile using a pulsed rocket motor. The entire programme was cancelled in 1992, partly because the break-up of the Soviet Union had greatly reduced any near-term threat from long-range bombers with supersonic missiles.

New short-range missiles

Short-range AAMs are another area where Russian technology has given the West a shock. The highly agile, vectored-thrust Vympel R-73 (AA-11 'Archer') is considered to be the best SRAAM in the world, by a large margin, and has left the US playing catch-up. Meanwhile, the Navy's proposed AIM-9R, with an imaging daylight seeker, was

the potential of the Vympel R-77 (AA-12 'Adder') MRAAM, unveiled in 1992. Bigger than AMRAAM, the R-77 has greater energy at maximum range and is harder to evade. The USAF had set better energy-at-range as the main goal of Phase 3 as long ago as the mid-1980s.

Another Hornet on patrol over Bosnia meets the tanker – which could be US, British or French. This aircraft also carries a single Mk 82 bomb along with an AGM-65 on the outboard station one. Just visible over the nose is a GBU-16 LGB. With its NITE Hawk targeting FLIR on station four (the port 'shoulder' pylon), this Hornet should have beeen capable of finding and destroying virtually any target in Bosnia's rolling terrain.

Top: Supersonic 'somewhere over Bosnia'. The 'draggy' load on this aircraft ensures an impressive shockwave when the Hornet 'booms'.

Above: Two Deny Flight Hornets keep tabs on each other. Note the HARM/Sparrow/Mk 82/ Maverick configuration.

Below: The Corps was busy over Bosnia. Along with the USAF F-15Es deployed at Aviano, the F/A-18Ds were the most potent aircraft available to 5 ATAF – in an area where night and adverse weather attack capability counted.

cancelled in 1992 due to cost and a lack of USAF interest.

At the time of writing, Hughes and Raytheon are competing to develop a new missile, the AIM-9X, through a demonstration/validation programme. The AIM-9X is intended to combine the AIM-9's motor, warhead and safe-arm device with a new guidance and control system and control surfaces, and the plan is to produce the new missiles by modifying existing AIM-9s. It will be more agile than the AIM-9 and will have a seeker which can acquire targets at up to 90° off the missile's boresight. The Pentagon expects to award an engineering and manufacturing development (EMD) contract in early 1997, and the missile should become operational in 2002 or 2003. The F/A-18C will be the first Navy aircraft to carry it.

Meanwhile, at least two other countries have developed agile, high-off-boresight missiles. Israel's Rafale Python 4 entered service in 1994, the first AAM with a 90° seeker to do so, and the UK's British Aerospace Advanced Short-Range AAM (ASRAAM) is due to enter service in 1998. While the US services are unlikely to adopt either weapon,

they may well be of interest to export customers. McDonnell Douglas does not confirm reports that Python 4 has been fired from an F-18, but admits that the still-classified Israeli missile has been mounted on a number of its aircraft.

Air-to-surface stores

The F/A-18 also carries a wide range of air-to-surface ordnance. As a non-stealthy aircraft, stand-off weapons are important to its survival; also, the limited space for ordnance available on the carrier places a heavy premium on precision-guided weapons which can kill the target with a single shot, rather than large numbers of unguided weapons with a smaller kill probability.

One of the Hornet's most effective air-to-surface weapons is McDonnell Douglas Aerospace's own AGM-84E Stand-off Land Attack Missile (SLAM). This was originally developed as an interim weapon, pending the arrival of the then-classified Northrop AGM-137 Tri-Service Stand-off Attack Missile (TSSAM). TSSAM was a stealthy, highly accurate missile which, in its Navy version, was to carry a 1,000-lb (454-kg) penetrating warhead 115 miles (185 km) from its launch point. When development started in 1986, TSSAM was expected to enter service in 1990. As the programme slipped behind schedule, however, the Navy accepted McDonnell Douglas' proposal for a land-attack derivative of the AGM-84D Harpoon anti-ship missile (also carried by the F-18).

The SLAM programme started in 1989 and the missile was used operationally in Desert Storm, when an A-6 fired two missiles at an Iraqi hydroelectric plant. The rapid development was possible because the missile used off-the-shelf components. Instead of the Harpoon's radar seeker, SLAM has the imaging infra-red seeker from the AGM-65D Maverick, an integrated inertial/Global Positioning System navigation unit and the datalink from the Walleye glide bomb. The missile flies autonomously until it is in the vicinity of the target, when the seeker and datalink are automatically activated and transmit an image of the target to either the launch aircraft or a 'buddy' director aircraft. The operator verifies the target, selects an aimpoint and locks the seeker. SLAM is one of the most accurate missiles in existence, with a circular error probability (CEP) in single figures of feet.

Despite frantic efforts by its manufacturer, TSSAM did not recover from its problems and it was cancelled in December 1994. The Navy had already decided to cut back on its orders, and had funded development of the AGM-84H SLAM-ER (Expanded Response). This version has larger wings which increase the missile's range by 50 to 100 per cent depending on the flight profile, the Harris/Magnavox Improved Data Link which has greater range and better jamming resistance, a better warhead, and a revised nose which reduces drag and radar cross-section. SLAM-ER tests

should start in 1997 and deliveries of modification kits will begin in 1998; it will be a key weapon for the F/A-18E/F.

JSOW – the 'smart truck'

The F-18 will carry a shorter-range stand-off weapon in the shape of the Texas Instruments AGM-154 Joint Stand-off Weapon (JSOW). Originally known as the Advanced Interdiction Weapon System (AIWS), it was conceived by the Navy as a low-cost modular weapon which could replace a range of dissimilar systems including the Mk 20 Rockeye and CBU-59 cluster bombs plus the Walleye, AGM-123 Skipper and older GBU-series laser-guided bombs. Vought and TI were awarded demonstration contracts in 1991. In the following year, the USAF joined the programme, the name was changed to JSOW and TI was selected as prime contractor. The first guided drop was made in late 1994.

JSOW has been called 'a smart truck'. The nose section contains the guidance system. The mid-body is a 'strong-back' which carries a pair of high-aspect-ratio folding wings and the payload, with a fairing around it. The flight control system is located in the tail. The long wings give the missile a range of 15 miles (25 km) from a high-level launch, even without power.

The initial version of JSOW uses GPS/INS guidance and carries BLU-97 Combined Effects Munition (CEM) warheads which are effective against air defence systems, non-armoured vehicles and parked aircraft. This version is in EMD for the US Navy. A later version will have a BLU-111 hard-target warhead and precision guidance, and will replace the Navy's LGBs and Mavericks. It will have a 500-1,000 lb (227-450 kg) warhead (the choice depends on the launch aircraft's bring-back limit), an imaging infra-red seeker and the Walleye's datalink.

JDAM – the next-generation PGM

Another new bomb family will be used on the F/A-18: the McDonnell Douglas GBU-29/30 Joint Direct Attack Munition (JDAM). McDonnell Douglas was selected to develop this weapon in September 1995, and it should become operational in 1997. In its basic form, JDAM is a simple iron bomb with the addition of a tail section containing an INS/GPS guidance system and a standard 1760A interface. As in any bomb attack, the launch aircraft's weapon control system computes the bomb's trajectory and guides the pilot to the release point. With JDAM, the computer also loads the predicted trajectory

Top: A NITE Hawk-equipped F/A-18D totes a load of five 1,000-lb Mk 83 bombs, all live and ready to release.

Above: A second aircraft delivers its last pair of Mk 83s over the range. Note the empty VERs and the remaining load of eight Zunis.

McDonnell Douglas F/A-18 Hornet

Until 1987 all Hornets were fitted with the Martin-Baker Mk 10 ejection seat, known by its US designation as the SJU-5. Subsequently, this seat was replaced on production aircraft (and retrofitted to many others) by the Martin-Baker Mk 14 seat. This is also known as the NACES (Navy Aircrew Common Ejection Seat) seat, referred to by the US Navy as the SJU-17-3. Despite the stated goal of commonality, there are minor differences among the NACES seats used on the F/A-18, F-14 and T-45 meaning that each uses a different variant of the basic SJU-17.

into the bomb's guidance system, allowing it to cancel out errors caused by turbulence around the aircraft or by changes in wind velocity. The JDAM guidance system is inexpensive (around $18,000 per weapon) and requires no action by the launch aircraft after release, and has a CEP of 33-49 ft (10-15 m). The GBU-29 variant uses a 2,000-lb (907-kg) BLU-109/B penetrator warhead, while the GBU-30 will use a 1,000-lb (454-kg) bomb.

JDAM accuracy is determined to a great extent by the accuracy of the data provided by the launch platform, so the advent of a SAR mode on the APG-73 radar will lead to a significant improvement in all-weather bombing accuracy.

Vital HARM capability

As the F/A-18 continues to expand its suppression of enemy air defences (SEAD) role, it will become the Navy's main user of the Texas Instruments AGM-88 High-speed Anti-Radiation Missile (HARM). The US Navy and USAF are updating their HARM inventories with the AGM-88C Block IV, which has a more sensitive seeker, a better processor and more onboard memory, and can be updated

with new software. This variant has not been released for export, and overseas customers are taking delivery of earlier versions from US stocks.

The HARM seeker can be active while the missile is on the pylon, and is a significant source of information on threats and targets in a SEAD mission. What it cannot do is determine the range to the target. Until recently, the only platform which could launch HARM in a 'range-known' mode, which gives the missile its greatest possible range and shortest time of flight, was a dedicated SEAD aircraft such as the F-4G Wild Weasel. This has now been retired, and the USAF SEAD mission is performed by the F-16 fitted with the Texas Instruments ASQ-213 HARM Targeting System (HTS). This small pod contains a passive antenna and a compact processor. Using data from the aircraft's navigation system, it detects and identifies emitters and, using triangulation, locates them. The HTS was being tested on the F/A-18C/D at China Lake in early 1996, and may be adopted operationally.

Tactical Air-Launched Decoys

Another important but little-discussed F/A-18 store is not necessarily a weapon: the Brunswick Defense ALD-141 Tactical Air Launched Decoy (TALD). Based on the Israeli Samson, this 400-lb (180-kg) glider was used to protect Navy and Marine attack aircraft in the Gulf, and more than 4,000 were on order by mid-1991. In the Gulf, as many as 20 TALDs were launched in salvos by the lead aircraft in a strike package, which would then turn home.

I-TALD

The TALDs were pre-programmed to fly a simulated attack profile, saturating target defences and forcing enemy search and tracking radars to activate, thus increasing friendly anti-radiation missile kill probabilities. Other TALDs were modified to mask the real strike force by deploying chaff. It has been followed by Improved TALD (I-TALD) which has a small Teledyne CAE312 turbojet engine (developed for the cancelled Tacit Rainbow anti-radar missile) and can simulate a wider variety of attack profiles. The turbojet gives I-TALD a range of up to 120 nm (222 km) when launched from 20,000 ft (6096 m),

compared to TALD's range of only 68 nm (126 km) when launched from 35,000 ft (10668 m). I-TALD can be launched from heights as low as 500 ft (152 m) and at speeds of up to Mach 0.9. The first airborne launch, from an F-4 over Point Mugu, occurred in October 1995, and fit tests with the F/A-18 began in November from NAS Patuxent River.

USN/USMC operations

While McDonnell Douglas has incorporated these innovations into the Hornet, its primary users have responded by making the F/A-18 the single most important fighter in the US Navy's history.

In June 1995, the F/A-18 recorded its 2 millionth flight hour with the US Navy and Marine Corps. By that time, non-US Hornets had flown about half a million hours and the worldwide F/A-18 community was adding hours at a rate of 230,000 per year. More than 1,270 aircraft had been delivered.

The F/A-18 has also proven itself to be the most reliable, lowest-maintenance and safest tactical aircraft in Navy/Marine Corps service. The Hornet flies an average of 1.8 hours between failures, compared with 0.5 hours for the F-14 and A-6E. It requires 17.3 maintenance manhours per flight hour, compared with 46.5 hours for the F-14 and 44.4 hours for the A-6E. In the first 1.5 million flight hours in service, the Navy and Marines lost 67 Hornets in accidents, compared with 124 F-14s and 102 A-6s.

Of course, the F/A-18 certainly should be better than either the A-6 or the F-14 in all respects. The A-6E and the F-14A – which dominates the F-14 statistics – have avionics and engines which reflect the technology of the 1960s. The re-engined, digital F-14D and A-6F Intruder II would have been more directly comparable to the F/A-18, but the former was built only in small numbers and the latter was cancelled outright. As for safety, the F-14 has suffered from an engine that was never designed for its mission, and the A-6 started its career in the early 1960s, when it was not unknown for a squadron to lose seven out of 40 aircraft in a month to accidents – culture, training and technology have played parts in reducing accident rates.

From the operator's viewpoint, the fact that such comparisons may be loaded in favour of the F/A-18 matters less than the fact that the Hornet is so much more friendly to its pilots and maintainers than the other aircraft in the fleet. Another significant figure is that the Hornet's 2 million hour mark was reached after 12 years in service – an even faster accumulation of hours than the F-4 during the Vietnam era. This reflects the fact that F/A-18s generate sorties at a higher rate than other Navy tactical aircraft.

The F/A-18 has other useful attributes. Its advanced cockpit and (in later versions) MSI make it a relatively easy aircraft to fly. Engines and aerodynamics are well suited for deck landing – Hornet squadrons regularly score highest in boarding rates.

Maintainability and safety statistics also translate into hard cash. Maintenance is expensive in personnel, training and parts. The Navy/Marine Corps F/A-18 losses in the type's first 10 years of service cost well over $2 billion to replace, an amount that represents half the cost of a new carrier. The result is that the F/A-18's life-cycle cost compares very favourably with older aircraft.

VMFAT-101 'Sharpshooters' is the Marine Corps' primary F/A-18 FRS squadron for training Hornet aircrew. The squadron had long been equipped with Phantoms before transitioning to the Hornet. The aircraft nearest the camera has a typical training load of Mk 76 'blue bombs'.

VMFA(AW)-242 are the 'Batmen' from El Toro. The Batman identity is most apt for their night-attack mission. Crews train with FLIR and NVGs for precision attacks in all weathers.

Above: Even with empty bomb racks the Hornet is a threat, for it still has a 20-mm M61A1 Vulcan cannon. The gun and ammunition drum and feed system is mounted as a single unit on a pallet in the nose. The barrel is elevated by 2° to improve target tracking. The ammunition drum carries 578 rounds and the gun can fire up to 6,000 rpm. The ammunition is shielded from EMP to prevent premature detonation!

Right: The F/A-18 design service life, as far as the US Navy is concerned, is 6,000 flight hours. This would include 5,000 cycles with 2,000 catapult launches and arrested landings alone. Finnish evaluators estimated that, without the rigours of carrier operations, their Hornets may be good for up to 15,000 hours.

Opposite page: F/A-18s with the EPE powerplant can climb to 40,000 ft (12192 m) in 2.3 minutes at maximum thrust, while carrying two AIM-9s, two AIM-7s and a full tank of 20-mm ammunition. The EPE also reduces the maximum-thrust take-off roll by 10 per cent. The Hornet can be airborne within 1,700 ft (518 m) of runway, at the full fighter configuration weight of 37,000 lb (16798 kg).

Sortie generation

Reliability is an extremely important attribute for a carrier-based aircraft. A carrier's ability to put firepower on target depends not only on the range and warload of its aircraft, but also on their reliability. An aircraft that suffers a failure and cannot be launched cannot be quickly taxied off to one side and replaced, and neither can the carrier afford to launch many spare aircraft – but, given the statistics, the likelihood that one or more A-6s or F-14s in a strike package will abort for technical reasons is relatively high. On the carrier, diagnostic, repair and test facilities are limited, so reliability problems will rapidly have an impact on the rate

at which the carrier can sustain operations: after a surge of sorties, the maintenance crews may need time to deal with a backlog of problems. Fewer problems also mean that the carrier does not need to carry as many replacement parts.

Similarly, multi-mission capability has a special value aboard a carrier. The carrier air group goes to the war with the assets with which it left its home port. During a three-month cruise in 1993, the USS *Theodore Roosevelt* took part in two contingency operations in different regions. Its three F/A-18 squadrons first took part in combat air patrol (CAP) missions in support of C-130s which were air-dropping food and medicine around Sarajevo, then switched to longer CAP missions as part of Operation Deny Flight. Using their FLIR systems, they could also monitor helicopter traffic, which was exempted at the time from the United Nation's 'no-fly' ban.

Later, the carrier moved to the Red Sea, and the Hornets flew missions in support of Operation Southern Watch. In this case, there was a potential threat from Iraqi ground forces, and the Hornets carried air-to-ground munitions and (in some cases) the latest FLIR pods with laser designation and ranging capability.

While an air wing dominated by one-mission aircraft – air-combat F-14s and A-6 strike aircraft – could have covered the same missions, it would have been difficult to maintain the same sortie rates because fewer aircraft would have been available. In the case of Southern Watch, attack aircraft carrying air-to-ground weapons would probably have needed a fighter CAP to protect them from unexpected attacks, so more sorties would have been needed to perform the same basic task.

Multi-role capability is the most important new capability that the Hornet brought to the Navy. In turn, the most important feature of the F/A-18C/D was that it was a much better multi-role aircraft than the A/B. In fact, many operators (together, apparently, with the export market) believe that the most important step in F/A-18 development was the advent of the night-attack Lot 12 version, ordered in FY87 and delivered from late 1989. Commander William Gortney, who commanded one of the F/A-18C/D squadrons on the *Roosevelt* cruise, has described the night-attack version as "almost a different airplane" compared with the A/B, and "an unbelievable improvement in warfighting capability." The same assessment was made from a different angle when the US Navy sold a batch of F/A-18A/Bs to Spain: a McDonnell Douglas official said that the A/B "no longer fits in the Navy's warfighting plans."

One F/A-18 pilot describes the F/A-18A/B as "a basic day/visual bomber with some superb close-in manoeuvring capabilities," capable of defeating almost any adversary except a well-flown F-16 in a dogfight. As for bombing, "we got good hits in the day, but our night/all-weather capabilities were austere. The FLIR in the A model basically got you day accuracy with bad eyesight."

The same pilot describes the early C/Ds as "nothing to brag about. The only difference we could see was the IFEI (integrated fuel/ engine instrument display)." The real change came with the Lot 12 night-attack variants, he felt. The LTD/R upgrade to the FLIR pod "changed everything – night and day – since we can now drop a range of precision weapons. The AMRAAM made us super-competitive in the beyond-visual-range arena, and software upgrades all along have made the airplane more capable, but rapidly used up existing memory."

Hornet replaces the A-6F

It was a combination of all these factors which persuaded the Navy and Marine Corps to increase their dependence on the F/A-18 – in addition to budget cutbacks. Total US defence spending peaked in 1985 and started a slow decline thereafter, squeezing the Navy's ambitious modernisation programme. One of the first programmes to be affected was the Grumman A-6F Intruder II, intended as a replacement for USMC A-6s, which was cancelled in 1988. This also meant an end to production of the A-6, so the Navy and Marines would be short of aircraft within a few years. The Navy therefore elected to replace Marine A-6s with F/A-18Ds. Then, in 1989, planned production of the F-14D Super Tomcat was curtailed to 54 aircraft – again, increasing the service's need for the F/A-18 to fill the gap until a new aircraft would be available.

The F/A-18 does not equal the warload/range performance of either the A-6 or the F-14, but – for the time being – the Navy was willing to live with the Hornet's

The F/A-18 has four fuselage fuel tanks and two wing tanks, and runs on JP-4 aviation fuel. F/A-18C/Ds are fitted with an enhanced electronic fuel system that monitors usage and automatically adjusts the aircraft's centre of gravity as fuel is consumed. All fuel tanks are self-sealing, with a foam infill system. Canadian Hornets have been cleared to carry three 480-US gal (1818-litre) fuel tanks, which are substantially larger than the standard US Navy/Marine Corps tanks.

Seen landing at Nellis AFB during a Red Flag exercise, this VFA-37 Hornet is carrying a load of METEs: AN/ALQ-167 Multiple Environment Threat Emitters. ALQ-167 is a noise and deception jamming system with its own micro-processor-controlled threat ID 'library'. There are four METEs pods available, each working in a different way – D-band (noise jamming), E/F-band (noise jamming), G/H/I-band (noise and deception) and J-band (noise and deception). Each pod provides coverage fore and aft, and this aircraft appears to be carrying all four. ALQ-167 is regularly used as an EW training aid, in addition to being a capable 'real world' jammer.

performance rather than trying to change it. The Hornet's greater reliability and its ability to defend itself (reducing the need for escort and CAP sorties) both tend to offset its lesser warload, by enabling the carrier to put more bomb-carrying aircraft on target. The Navy has changed its tactics, stressing the use of HARM-carrying escorts and EA-6B Prowlers to suppress enemy air defences and allowing the Hornets to stay at medium altitude for a longer segment of the ingress and egress route, improving their range. (The Hornet's ability to defend itself against fighters is important in this case, as well.)

The collapse of the Soviet Union encouraged the Navy to concentrate more resources on the F/A-18, at the same time as declining defence budgets led the service to cancel modest improvements to the A-6 and reject proposals for modernised F-14s. The Soviet Union's missile-carrying bombers, submarines and even its Ekranoplans had presented the most serious long-range threat to the Navy's carriers. As it became clear that the threat was a thing of the past, and would not recover for decades, the Navy defined a new strategy of 'littoral operations', concentrating on the Navy's role in support of conflict within a few hundred miles of a sea coast. Compared with the blue-water strategies of the Cold War, it called for carriers to operate much

closer to land. Again, this made the F/A-18's range less of an issue.

The process was furthered by the cancellation of the A-12, and the continuing decline of defence budgets pushed the Navy more towards the F/A-18. Modest upgrades to the F-14 and A-6 were cancelled, and F/A-18 production plans were extended to avoid any gap between the last F/A-18C/D and the first F/A-18E/F.

The Marines over Bosnia

With the disestablishment of CVW-15 at the end of March 1995, all but one of the Navy's 10 active carrier air wings now includes two or three F/A-18C/D squadrons, leaving only two active Navy units with A/Bs. (Reserve Navy and some active Marine wings still fly the older version.) By mid-1995, three air wings were operational with a Marine F/A-18D squadron in place of the A-6.

In fact, the current showpiece of the F/A-18 fleet is the Marine F/A-18D presence in operations over Bosnia. Flying out of Aviano AB in Italy, they represent the latest standard of the Hornet – newly delivered night-attack aircraft with APG-73 radar, F404-GE-402 engines, laser designators and (since the summer of 1995) ALQ-165 ASPJ EW systems. These aircraft, like USAF F-15Es, operate

with a pilot in the front seat and a weapon system operator (WSO) in the back seat, rather than the bombardier-navigator (BN) of the A-6 which they replaced. The pilot flies the aircraft and stays head-out, while the WSO operates the radar and FLIR.

A typical load-out will be a mixed bag of weapons: two AIM-9s, one AIM-7 or AIM-120, two 500-lb (227-kg) GBU-12 LGBs, a 500-lb (227-kg) unguided bomb and a FLIR/LTD-R pod. WSOs in the Bosnia operations also carry digital cameras with zoom lenses for near-real-time reconnaissance.

'Flex' missions

In a single mission, a pair of F/A-18Ds might 'flex' among several missions. Using their radars, they would ensure that were no aircraft violating Deny Flight restrictions. They would be available to provide close air support (CAS) for UN forces on the ground, as requested by a ground forward air controller. They could also act as FACs for other aircraft, locating ground targets and talking incoming strike aircraft on to the target. Helicopters could be tracked and identified on the FLIR, and their landing sites could be photographed.

Marine F/A-18Ds flew more than 100 strike missions during Operation Deliberate Force, the raids against Serb military targets which began at the end of August 1995 and which are credited with persuading the Serbs to return to the bargaining table. Many of these operations were SEAD missions, mainly using GBU-16 1,000-lb (454-kg) LGBs. The smaller GBU-12s were used where targets were located close to centres of population and the risk of collateral damage was higher.

Weather prevented the successful use of LGBs from safe altitudes during daytime missions. As a result, more than

half the missions were flown at night, when darkness concealed the fighters from ground fire and it was safe to fly at lower altitudes, under the weather. Eventually, the Hornets hit most of their designated targets.

These missions were significant in many ways. In particular, the two-crew aircraft with its fully integrated sensors can perform a very useful mission with what would, in earlier times, be considered a very small weapon load. In fact, unloading multiple 2,000-lb (907-kg) bombs may be positively undesirable in an operation short of war, where hitting the wrong target is worse than missing the right one.

Carrier operations are still the Hornet's raison d'être. Night operations from an almost invisible deck call for a complete faith in the deck crew. Any landing, day or night, is down to the pilot and the LSO to get a good trap, on the right wire, first time.

In recent times, Canada's air force has been cut back and starved of funding to the point where it is now a shadow of its former self. Fighter Group alone has had its Hornet strength pared down to just 60 aircraft. By 1997 the air force will be 45 per cent smaller than it was in 1989. When Canadian squadrons were withdrawn from Europe they lost valuable training opportunities and exposure to other NATO personnel. Not all ties were broken, however, and Canadian aircraft returned to Europe in force for the 50th anniversary of the end of World War II. This 410 Sqn CF-188 was just one of the aircraft painted in a special scheme, this time for VE Day in 1995.

The net result is that changes in technology, tactics and geopolitics have made the most of the F/A-18C/D's good points and made its drawbacks less important. This view is apparently shared by non-US operators, who have played a major role in keeping the programme active despite declining US budgets.

Non-US operators

The Hornet has had two lives in the export market, just as it has in the United States Navy and Marine Corps. The F/A-18A/B scored three major successes in the early days of the programme, with sales to Canada, Australia and Spain. After the Spanish order was announced in May 1983, it was more than five years before a Foreign Military Sales (FMS) customer signed for another aircraft.

There were several reasons for the long drought, but one of them was the leap-frogging progress of the F/A-18 and its main rival, the F-16. The early F/A-18 customers were looking for an aircraft with beyond-visual-range missile armament and more sophisticated avionics than the F-16A/B.

In Canadian service the Hornet is primarily an air defence fighter, as evidenced by the substantial load of Sparrows and Sidewinders on this aircraft. The Canadians also pioneered the use of 'fake cockpits' on the underside of their Hornets, with the intention of disorientating an opponent in ACM.

By the early 1980s, however, General Dynamics was offering the F-16C, with a glass cockpit, higher weights and provision for modern weapons. Also, the type's earlier engine problems were mostly behind it.

The Hornet's recovery did not start in earnest with the F/A-18C/D itself, but with the night-attack version of the aircraft. Construction of night-attack Hornets for the US Navy and USMC began in 1987. Since the TINS and FLIR pods were already developed and approved for export, unlike the Martin-Marietta LANTIRN system which had been selected to perform the same functions on the F-16C/D, this gave McDonnell Douglas a useful window of opportunity during which the Hornet was the only fighter to feature a truly integrated night-attack suite – apart from McDonnell Douglas' own, much more costly and hard-to-get F-15E.

McDonnell Douglas executives believe that the night-attack capability was an important factor in Kuwait's decision to order 32 F/A-18Cs and eight F/A-18Ds, in September 1988. Most non-US customers, they observe, are buying the most capable and expensive combat aircraft that they will operate, and are keen to get as much multi-role capability as they can afford. At the time, too, world oil prices were high, and price was not a driving concern in the Kuwaiti decision. The US government supported the programme during the Iraqi occupation of Kuwait, and deliveries took place between February 1992 and August 1993.

The company faced a longer fight over Switzerland's requirement for a new combat aircraft to replace its F-5E fighters. In this case, the primary mission was interception, but the contest was complicated by a number of special considerations. Switzerland is a small, mountainous and neutral country. It needs interceptors that can reach and destroy targets before they are directly over Switzerland's main population centres, and which can operate from fighter bases tucked into mountain valleys, with small underground hangars to protect their aircraft from attack.

Points in the Hornet's favour included unusually good characteristics on approach, a legacy of its carrier-based mission. The approach speed is slow, the aircraft and engine respond well, the angle of attack on approach is low and the pilot has a good view over the nose. Folding wings, for

which most export customers care not a whit, ease handling in underground hangars.

The only major part of the initial specification that the Hornet failed to meet concerned acceleration and rate of climb – key numbers for the intercept mission. To match the performance of the F/A-18's rivals – the F-16, Mirage 2000-5 and Gripen – McDonnell Douglas and GE agreed to develop the more powerful Enhanced Performance Engine (EPE), using company funds. With the new engine on the table, the Hornet was selected in October 1988.

However, that was not the end of the story. In 1990, the contest was reopened after intense pressure from Dassault, and the F/A-18 was compared once again to the Mirage 2000-5. For a second time, the Hornet emerged as the winner – but the political controversy was such that the Swiss government decided to validate the final selection with a referendum vote. In June 1993, the Swiss population finally endorsed the choice of the F/A-18, and the programme could proceed.

Swiss Hornets

Switzerland is acquiring 26 F/A-18Cs and eight F/A-18Ds in a $2.3 billion programme which also includes technical support, training and infrastructure modernisation. The first two aircraft are to be built and tested in St Louis, and the first was due to be rolled out in February 1996 as this article was written. They will be delivered in September 1996. Meanwhile, McDonnell Douglas is delivering kits for the remaining 32 aircraft to the Swiss Federal Aircraft Company (F+W) in Emmen, where they will be assembled. The first aircraft will roll out at Emmen in January 1997 and production will be completed in October 1999.

Switzerland is not going to save any money by assembling its own Hornets. However, it does provide high-quality jobs in Switzerland, rather than Missouri, and sustains F+W's ability to assemble and flight-test advanced aircraft.

F+W is also under contract to build the ailerons and aileron shrouds for 73 Hornets in 1993-95 – just one part of what most companies call 'offsets' but which McDonnell Douglas prefers to call 'industrial participation'. According to one executive, McDonnell Douglas "realised about 15 years ago that we could either continue to sit and complain about offsets, or learn to treat it as a business, so that instead

From a peak of eight squadrons the CAF is now down to four CF-188 units. The force has been ruthlessly cut back but its taskings have not, and national defence policy decrees that two squadrons must be prepared for contingency deployment anywhere in the world. At the moment the CAF is evaluating several new weapons for its Hornets, including the 2,000-lb GBU-24B Paveway III and AGM-65G Maverick. Hand-in-hand with these weapons trials goes integration of the AN/AAS-38A NITE Hawk FLIR LD/TR system.

Top: Complete with invasion stripes, this 441 Squadron CF-188 sports another World War II commemorative scheme, this time for the 50th anniversary of D-Day in June 1994. A massive flypast involving British, American, French, Canadian, Belgian, Greek, Dutch, Norwegian, Czech and Slovak combat aircraft, warbirds and civil aircraft took place over Portsmouth on 5 June and over France the following day. All together, 11 CAF CF-188s were involved.

Above: A fully armed Spanish EF-18A+ patrols over Bosnia as part of Operation Deny Flight. Such a heavy air-to-air warload was unusual for the Spanish Hornets, which were valued for their PGM and SEAD capabilities.

Hornet's twin engines were a major factor. The Finns' preference for a twin lifted the F/A-18 and MiG-29 above other aircraft – such as the F-16, by now available with LANTIRN – and the Hornet's proven multi-role capability edged out the MiG-29 despite an attractively low price. Now, many Hornet advocates will willingly concede that engines have become far more reliable since the early days of the F-16 and F/A-18, and that the difference in safety and in predicted attrition between a single-engined and twin-engined aircraft is small. Nevertheless, McDonnell Douglas sees a continuing preference for the twin.

One reason is that a single modern fighter is a very large part of a small- to medium-sized nation's military investment. To them, losing an F/A-18 in an accident is akin to the USAF losing a B-1. Also, finding money to replace a lost aircraft may be difficult. Many smaller nations have only one funding stream for major investments in defence, which rotates every five to 10 years among the army, navy and air force. By the time the air force needs to replace a lost aircraft, the navy may be getting all the money for its new frigates.

Environment is also a factor. Like the Canadian Hornets, the Finnish aircraft will spend a great deal of time above the Arctic circle and over empty territory or cold water. A malfunction which downs the aircraft under those circumstances also leaves the pilot with a perilously slim chance of survival. Overall, the single-versus-twin argument is affected by much more than economics and engine-failure rates.

Far-Eastern Hornets

The next wave of Hornet orders has stemmed from a three-round contest in Asia. The first to sign up was Malaysia, which announced an order for eight F/A-18Ds in June 1993. The contract was smaller than McDonnell Douglas had hoped, because Malaysia split its fighter order between the Hornet and 18 MiG-29s. The reason was price: Malaysia paid $550 million for the MiGs, less than the $600 million it paid for less than half as many Hornets (and a large package of weapons), and Mikoyan offered a support package which met Malaysian concern's about the MiG-29's long-term supportability. The Royal Malaysian AF is using the MiG-29s in the interception role, and the F/A-18Ds will be used for interdiction, night attack and maritime strike. They will be delivered between October 1996 and May 1997, and McDonnell Douglas is confident that the RMAF will acquire more Hornets.

of losing money we could at least break even." The company set up an internal unit specialising in industrial participation, and enlisted the help of its suppliers on the Hornet programme – recognising that McDonnell Douglas itself makes only 22 per cent of the aircraft.

The major members of the Hornet Industry Team are powerful players in the world of industrial participation, dwarfing the manufacturing segments of many national economies. They make everything from refrigerators and power generation equipment (GE) and Cadillacs, heavy trucks and locomotives (General Motors) to airliners and helicopters (McDonnell Douglas). The team includes two of the world's five largest defence contractors. Among them, they can direct business to a wide variety of industries in the customer country.

Finnish Hornets

The next Hornet sale to be closed also includes a large element of direct industrial participation. Finland's May 1992 decision to order 64 Hornets (seven Ds and 57 single-sealers) followed the first evaluation that pitted the F/A-18 against a Russian aircraft, the MiG-29. The first of the two-seaters, all of which were assembled in St Louis, was rolled out in June 1995 and delivered to Tampere air base in Finland in November. The single-seaters will all be assembled and tested by Valmet in Finland, and will be delivered between September 1996 and August 2000.

The Finnish sale was one of several in which the

McDonnell Douglas was less successful in Singapore. Already an F-16A/B operator, Singapore evaluated the F/A-18 and the MiG-29 before settling on the F-16C Block 50 in July 1994. It had been a hard-fought contest: a major factor was Lockheed's campaign to reduce the manufacturing cost and price of the F-16, through a complete revision of its working practices and a decision to buy-in many parts which it had previously produced in-house.

The Hornet Industrial Team launched its own cost-cutting programme in response, and was able to bring a lower price to the next Asian contest, in Thailand. The Royal Thai AF announced in October 1995 that it had selected the F/A-18 as its next fighter, becoming the first F-16 operator to order the Hornet. The current plan is for the RTAF to take delivery of four Cs and four Ds, starting in 1999.

As this article is written, however, the Thailand sale is contingent upon the US government's willingness to supply AIM-120 AMRAAM missiles with the F/A-18s. The missile is not currently released for sale to Asia, and the US State Department will have to change its policy, make an exception, or persuade the Thai government to accept compromise, such as an agreement to supply AMRAAM if France or Russia sells active-radar missiles in the region. Thailand has said that it will reopen the competition to the Su-35 and Mirage 2000-5 if no agreement is reached.

A competetive package

Although it has tried to reduce its price, McDonnell Douglas has always stressed value in its F/A-18 sales campaigns. Important factors in recent contests have included the F/A-18's maritime strike capability; as a result of its Navy origins and the decision to replace the A-6 with the F/A-18, the Hornet and the APG-73 radar are very well matched to the anti-surface warfare mission. The APG-73 radar itself is newer than the F-16's radar and offers a great deal of growth potential. It appears, too, that evaluating pilots like the ease of operation of the Hornet's cockpit, with its large colour displays and multi-sensor integration technology. One increasingly important advantage is that the development and production of the Hornet and its systems are assured until at least 2010, through the F/A-18E/F programme, while the future of the F-16 beyond 2000 is uncertain.

Some deals have also got away from the F/A-18. Korea selected the Hornet for a 120-aircraft fighter programme,

but (following political upheavals) switched to the F-16. Israel carried out an extensive evaluation of the F/A-18, but was approved to acquire the F-15 instead. Likewise, the United Arab Emirates showed interest in the F/A-18 in the early 1990s, but is now evaluating the F-15E.

In early 1996, there is a lull in the worldwide fighter market, particularly at its upper end. Kuwait and Malaysia are potential candidates for follow-on orders, but otherwise there is little prospect for further F/A-18C/D sales in the next few years. Further out, Saudi Arabia has a long-standing requirement to replace its F-5s, but the timing of the deal will depend on oil prices. Currently, the Royal Saudi air force is absorbing a very large fleet of F-15S long-range strike fighters.

Another not-this-year market is central Europe – Poland, Hungary and the Czech Republic. As these newly independent countries rebuild their economies, they are likely to bolster their defences against the less stable power of Russia and align themselves with the West. Poland and the Czech Republic, too, have long-standing aerospace industries that they intend to maintain and build up.

Central Europe may be a market for new F/A-18s if economic growth is healthy and if a suitable industrial participation programme could be devised. Alternatively, these nations might acquire used F/A-18s, as the US Navy and Marines replace their A/B models and older C/Ds with newer aircraft. (Currently, only some Marine air wings and

Top: A pair of RAAF F/A-18As is seen with a mixed load of 200-lb Mk 84 and 500-lb Mk 82 GP bombs, plus Sparrow AAMs. Australia's Defence Science & Technology Organisation is developing an EO-guided glide-bomb conversion for the Mk 82, with strap-on wings, for a future RAAF requirement for a stand-off weapon.

Above: Based at Williamstown, No. 2 Operational Conversion Unit handles all Hornet training for the RAAF. Two of the four F/A-18Bs seen here are carrying SUU-30 practice bomblet dispensers.

All of Australia's Hornet squadrons were former Mirage III operators. No. 3 Squadron disbanded with its Mirages in March 1986 and was re-established with its Hornets on 1 April. It was the first front-line RAAF F/A-18 squadron to transition, and was heavily involved in formulating new air-to-air tactics for the type. The squadron markings comprise a fleur-de-lys crest on the fuselage and the five stars of the Southern Cross on the fin.

Navy reserve wings fly the A/B.)

The Spanish air force is already topping off its fleet with 24 early-model, ex-US Navy F/A-18As, with an option for six more aircraft. The first aircraft were delivered in late 1995 and will bolster the existing F/A-18A/B force until the much delayed Eurofighter EF 2000 arrives (hopefully) in 2005. The aircraft reportedly cost around $8.5 million each, plus an undisclosed sum for new F404 engines.

All three F/A-18A/B export customers (Australia, Canada and Spain) are looking at mid-life upgrades for their aircraft. The RAAF appears to be moving ahead most quickly, and could start its programme by late 1996. The main focus will be on changes to the radar and the other avionics, including the mission computer. As in the case of the F-16 Mid-Life Update programme, the immense advances in computer technology in the 1980s should make it possible to add many new capabilities to the older F/A-18s while eliminating obsolescent components.

McDonnell Douglas' strategy for the early 2000s is to keep the F/A-18C/D in production for export, alongside the Super Hornet, giving the company a better chance to win orders from budget-conscious customers who might otherwise opt for the F-16 or JAS 39 Gripen. To support this strategy, McDonnell Douglas plans to continue to improve the C/D even after Navy production ends.

All export Hornets have been built to the same standard as contemporary Navy versions. Super Hornet avionics changes, including colour displays and a new solid-state digital map, will also be offered for export. While the last Navy C/Ds may have AMLCD flat-panel displays which

An F/A-18A from No. 75 Squadron RAAF fires an AIM-7 Sparrow. Australian Hornets were delivered with a wide range of weapons including AIM-9, AIM-7, AGM-88, AGM-84 and Paveway II LGBs. Since then the Air Force has also introduced the CRV-7 rocket system and AGM-65 Maverick. As part of a projected end-of-century Hornet upgrade, Australia is seeking to acquire the AIM-120 AMRAAM.

emulate the current colour displays, future export versions may have the same large-format displays as the E/F.

The attempt to sell the F/A-18 to the Israel Defence Force/Air Force generated another new option. Although the latest F/A-18C/D configuration includes 120 dispenser tubes, the IDF wanted more. After searching for unused space on the airframe, McDonnell Douglas and Northrop designed a pair of conformal dispenser fairings which resemble ventral fins and accommodate three 30-tube ALE-47 dispensers apiece, bringing the aircraft's total capacity to 300 tubes. These were to be tested in early 1996.

With these improvements and a continuing cost-reduction programme, McDonnell Douglas can bring a range of products to the export market in the early 21st century: a relatively low-cost F/A-18C/D; the top-of-the-line, long-range F-15E; and a new-technology fighter which fits between the two and will be a competitor to Rafale and EF 2000. The last of these is the new F/A-18E/F Super Hornet.

F/A-18E/F – The Super Hornet

The Super Hornet concept dates back to the late 1980s – oddly enough, an era when the Hornet's days seemed to be numbered. The Navy had decided not to continue production of the F-14, but had not taken a final position on its

successor, and a Navy version of the Air Force's Advanced Tactical Fighter (later to become the F-22) was still under consideration. The service's biggest programme, by a large margin, was the McDonnell Douglas/General Dynamics A-12 Avenger II stealth attack aircraft.

Although the A-12 had been billed as a replacement for the A-6, it was revealed in early 1990 that the Navy planned to buy 620 of the new aircraft – almost twice as many A-12s as A-6s. Combined with the Navy ATF, they would squeeze most of the F-18s off the carrier decks by the early 2000s.

However, some officials in the Office of the Secretary of Defense had been doubtful, as far back as 1986, that there would be enough money to buy new, large and sophisticated stealth aircraft at the rates envisaged by the services. They were also concerned that they would be both too costly and too sensitive to be exported. Accordingly, in 1986, Defense Secretary Caspar Weinberger had asked McDonnell Douglas and General Dynamics to study growth versions of the F/A-18 and F-16.

McDonnell Douglas studies, known generically as Hornet 2000, covered a range of options from the addition of a dorsal fuel tank to a radically new variant with an arrow-shaped wing. By 1990, the favoured solution was neither the simplest nor most complex derivative, but a

Each of Kuwait's two Hornet squadrons has a dedicated role: No. 9 handles the air defence tasking, while No. 25, seen here, is the ground-attack unit. Each squadron operates a mix of Cs and Ds, and all aircraft (known by McDonnell Douglas as KAF/A-18s) are equipped with the searchlight for identifying intercepted aircraft at night.

The first four Hornets for Finland arrived after a non-stop flight from St Louis on 7 November 1995. Licence-manufacture has already begun, and all but the first eight F-18Ds will be produced by Valmet. They will have a range of Finnish equipment, including metric instruments.

mid-pack option with a scaled-up wing and a longer fuselage, but with a very similar overall configuration to the existing F/A-18.

As 1990 rolled on, the Navy's aviation plans began to unravel, as problems of weight growth and delays began to surface in the A-12 programme. They were compounded by the fact that the problems had not been reported to

Defense Secretary Dick Cheney. Infuriated, under pressure to restrain defence spending and unconvinced that the Navy and its contractors had a recovery programme in hand, Cheney cancelled the A-12 outright in January 1991.

This left the Navy with one current combat aircraft programme – the short-legged F/A-18 – and an inexorably ageing inventory of A-6s and F-14s. The Navy and the Department of Defense embarked on an urgent study of their options. It was agreed that a modern, long-range, stealthy substitute for the A-12 would be needed, but, after the A-12 debacle, it was unthinkable to produce such an aircraft in a concurrent development programme, in which testing and production ran in parallel. The new aircraft would not be in service before 2005.

By that time, virtually every Navy aircraft would be at or beyond its life expectancy. In order to keep the Navy's fighter/attack fleet operational and viable, the Navy needed an interim type which would have better warload and range than the F/A-18, but which could be developed and fielded quickly. Grumman proposed a variety of options based on modified F-14s, but the Pentagon had already decided to close the production line, and the heavy-handed lobbying of Grumman's political supporters had created enemies throughout the Pentagon and the Administration. At the same time, the F/A-18 was winning favour for its versatility, low costs and reliability.

E/F contract

Within months, the Navy had decided to acquire an improved F/A-18, based on the Hornet 2000 studies, on a sole-source basis and without a competition. Howls of rage from Long Island went unheard. McDonnell Douglas was given a formal contract to develop the new aircraft, designated F/A-18E/F, in June 1992.

For the F/A-18, this proved that it is indeed an ill wind that blows nobody any good; but the Hornet's run of luck

This view of E-1 alongside a standard F/A-18C graphically illustrates the subtle, but substantial, differences between the 'Super Hornet' and its forerunners. The E/F is about 25 per cent bigger, with much larger control surfaces and a new wing leading-edge dogtooth (or 'snag'). The LERXes have been redesigned and enlarged (by 34 per cent). They have also been fitted with vents at the junction with the leading-edge flaps, to allow high-energy airflow over the rear fuselage at high angles of attack. The E/F is designed to be manoeuvrable at up to 40° Alpha. To achieve this, its FCS software has been improved to increase resistance to departure at high AoAs using so-called 'Beta dot' feedback (where Beta is the rate of change of sideslip). Unlike the C/D, the E/F has no mechanical back-up for its digital FCS. Neither does it have a dorsal airbrake, relying instead on two small airbrakes positioned on top of the LERX, and flap and rudder deflection.

was not over. The A-X programme, the intended replacement for the A-12, began to take shape in late 1991 as the military mulled over the lessons of Desert Storm and the implications of the break-up of the Soviet Union. The project was still in its early stages a year later, evolving into a large, long-range dual-role fighter, the A/F-X, aimed at both the US Navy and USAF, when the 1992 election ended 12 years of hawkish Republican rule. In September 1993, the Pentagon's new leaders terminated the A/F-X, without committing to any substitute programme, leaving the F/A-18E/F as the only carrier-based combat aircraft available to the Navy before 2008-10.

At the same time, the Pentagon confirmed its support for a Navy fleet of 12 supercarriers. On present plans, some time in the early 2000s, every fighter on every one of those ships will be an F/A-18.

Development of the new F/A-18 variant has remained on budget and on schedule, drawing little of the criticism which has been thrown at the Air Force's F-22. The Navy has carefully maintained the line that the F/A-18E is a derivative of the F/A-18C – which is rather like describing a Porsche 911 as a derivative of a VW Beetle.

E/F characteristics

The F/A-18E is one-third larger than the F/A-18C. The two aircraft have no major structural parts in common. The F/A-18E's General Electric F414 engine resembles the F404 only in basic configuration. In fact, the new fighter closely resembles the F-15C Eagle in wingspan, engine thrust, empty weight and maximum take-off weight.

The crucial advantage of the F/A-18E over any new aircraft was lower risk. The new fighter would meet the Navy's needs for a more survivable strike aircraft and more long-range fighters, and, with the F/A-18C as a basis for the design, there was much less chance that unforeseen increases in weight and drag would reduce its performance. Congress was accordingly willing to support a non-competitive, concurrent development and production programme, saving years and billions of dollars and allowing the Navy to replace its A-6s in a reasonable amount of time.

The F/A-18E design is rooted in the fact that the original

F/A-18C's growth potential has been used up, and that it is limited in bring-back load and internal fuel capacity. Making the aircraft much larger lifts both these limitations. Compared with an F/A-18C, the F/A-18E has 25 per cent more wing area, weighs 28 per cent more empty, has 38 per cent more thrust and 33 per cent more internal fuel. Because it can carry a 480-US gal (1820-litre) drop tank on its centreline stores station (the F/A-18E stands higher on its landing gear than the F-18C), the Navy can adopt the larger tanks in place of the 330-US gal (1250-litre) tank used today. With three tanks, the total fuel load is increased by 38 per cent.

McDonnell Douglas says that the F/A-18E can fly 35-50 per cent farther than the F/A-18C with the same payload. This statement was questioned by some Pentagon analysts until an independent study by the Office of the Secretary of Defense confirmed the Navy's range estimates.

The F/A-18E uses about the same amount of fuel as the older aircraft in climb and descent, and both need a similar reserve at landing, so the difference between the amount of fuel available for cruise in the two aircraft is greater than the take-off-weight figures would suggest. The greater fuel load also makes 'buddy' refuelling practical, allowing the carrier to mount a smaller strike up to 850 nm (1570 km) from the

At the roll-out, E-1 was festooned with AIM-9, AGM-88 HARM, AGM-84 Harpoon, SLAM-ER and AIM-120 (to starboard) plus JDAM, JSOW, Maverick and another AIM-9 (to port).

This VMFA(AW)-332 F/A-18D is carrying a pair of Loral Laser-Guided Training Rounds (LGTRs), recently introduced by the US Navy. Instead of a warhead, the 6-ft 2-in (1.9-m), 89-lb (40.3-kg) LGTR has a smoke marker to show point of impact. It is used to train crews in LGB delivery tactics.

significant refinements such as a thicker, stiffer wing (which supports an extra pylon) with a leading-edge dog-tooth. The wing has slightly more sweepback, to reduce drag, and the leading-edge root extension is larger, having been scaled up during development to correct a shortfall in instantaneous turn performance. An unusual feature is a pair of vortex-control spoilers, located above the root extension, just in front of the spill ducts. They replace a fixed vertical strake on the C/D, and open at high angles of attack to stabilise the flow across the wing and reduce buffeting on the vertical tails. A small, separate section of wing leading-edge flap extends behind the root extension, opening up a slot at low speeds.

Engine developments

The new variant's engine stems from a systematic programme of F404 developments which started in 1983. Under this programme, GE built and tested a variety of improved fans, cores and combustors suitable for F404 derivatives. This technology was used in the F412-GE-400, a medium-bypass, non-afterburning engine which GE developed for the ill-fated A-12. It used an improved core, known as Core II, which ran 111K hotter than the basic F404 core while handling 5 per cent more airflow.

In parallel with the F412, GE studied a variety of super-sonic engines using the same core with a lower bypass ratio. These also drew on the company's experience with the YF120, an extremely advanced variable-cycle engine which was GE's contender to power the USAF's Advanced Tactical Fighter.

After the A-12 was cancelled, and as the F/A-18E/F design firmed up, these concepts coalesced into what was initially known as the F404 Growth II Plus. It used the F412 core, which had undergone four years of full-scale development, combined with an advanced low-pressure system using F120 technology. Noteworthy features include an advanced augmentor, using ceramic matrix composite materials, and a robust, efficient 'blisk' one-piece fan with a maximum airflow of 77 kg/sec, 17 per cent more than the original. The full-authority digital engine control (FADEC) system was also drawn from the F412. Thrust/weight ratio is an impressive 9:1. The Growth II

Seven E/Fs will be dedicated to the flight trials programme. Here E-1 is seen on its fourth flight from St Louis (along with a company F/A-18C), with E/F project pilot Fred Madenwald at the controls. The prototype E/F has been painted with US Navy squadron marks. The badge of VFA-131 'Wildcats' appears on the starboard fin, while that of VF-142 'Ghostriders' (currently an F-14 squadron) is seen to port.

carrier. This capability will be increasingly important as the Navy's KA-6D tankers are retired.

The new aircraft can land on a carrier with 9,000 lb (4100 kg) of fuel and weapons, compared with 5,500 lb (2500 kg) for the original. Since the fuel reserve is roughly equal, this allows the newer aircraft to come aboard the carrier with heavy, expensive weapon loads.

The F/A-18E will have similar speed, acceleration and manoeuvrability to the original, but the design includes

This is the USMC F/A-18D used for ATARS (Advanced Tactical Airborne Reconnaissance System) trials. ATARs was originally a joint USN/USAF project but has had a disjointed history. Initiated in 1982, the system first flew in 1984 yet the programme was cancelled in 1993, when the USAF withdrew. In 1994 the Navy reactivated the project with McDonnell Douglas as prime contractor (the third in ATARS's history). The USMC now hopes to acquire 31 ATARS, beginning in 1998, to equip its F/A-18D(RC)s. The Navy will fit ATARS to the F/A-18E/F to replace its TARPS pods.

Above: The Marines still retain significant numbers of F/A-18As and Bs, as well as Cs and Ds. VMFA-115 is one unit using early-model Hornets in 1996.

The cancellation of the A-6F project and subsequent conclusion of Intruder production led to the Marines adapting the two-seat Hornet for the night-attack role. Here – in anything but night or adverse weather – a pair of VMFA(AW)-533 F/A-18Ds departs the USMC's exercise base at Twentynine Palms, CA.

Plus has barely a single part in common with the F404 and cannot be interchanged with it, and has accordingly been redesignated as the F414-GE-400.

Stealth technology is another important feature of the F/A-18E. The use of stealth on the F/A-18E "does not cover all frequencies and all aspects, but it does cover terminal threats," says Sears. The objective is not to make the F/A-18E invisible. Details of the Navy's RCS requirement are classified. Generally, however, the navy wanted to see the same RCS reduction from the C/D to the new aircraft as the C/D had shown compared with the original F-18A/B. The objective is not to make the new aircraft undetectable, or to match the all-round RCS of the B-2 or F-117, but to reduce the detection and tracking range of hostile air-defence systems and to make the F/A-18E/F's towed and expendable decoys more effective.

Aligned edges

The designers incorporated RCS-reduction measures in the shape of the aircraft. Many edges, including the leading edges of the wings and the inlets, are aligned in plan view. The edges of the main landing gear and engine bay doors are serrated on the same alignments, as are the edges of smaller openings such as drain holes and vents and the boundary-layer spillways above the inlet ducts. The new straight-sided inlet eliminates the all-aspect radar reflection from the old semi-circular inlets. The inlet walls and the body sides are canted outwards at the same angle as the vertical fins.

One new feature is a baffle, superficially resembling an extra fan stage, which blocks line-of-sight reflections from the front face of the engine. (Designed by General Electric, the baffle had already been invented for an unspecified, secret development programme). The fixed baffle is de-iced

Major Joe 'Pappy' Papay, USMC, models the latest in night-vision wear. The Marine-All Weather squadrons were the first to get NVGs for the Hornet. The aircraft requires changes in cockpit lighting to make the instruments readable with NVGs.

by hot air. It does cause a small loss of engine thrust and efficiency, but the loss is half of what was predicted. Also, the baffle improves the engine's stall margin under some conditions.

On the other hand, the designers were limited in what they could do to the front of the aircraft. Because the avionics system is an evolutionary development of the F/A-18C/D suite, McDonnell Douglas decided not to

101

A VMFA-122 F/A-18A and three F/A-18Ds break for the California desert floor, with pylons empty after a day on the ranges. The F/A-18A (nearest the camera) carries an AN/ASQ-173 LST/SCAM pod, while the second F/A-18D carries a single AN/AAS-38 NITE Hawk pod.

This, by now well-worn, noseart appeared on VFA-137's 'CAG-bird' (164712/400). While McDonnell Douglas' boast of '10,000 jets for freedom' is no idle one, it is noteworthy that the F-4 (which accounts for more than half this total) is omitted and two aircraft of British origin (Hawk and Harrier, or should that be T-45 and AV-8) are included. The Hornet will add substantially to this total and McDonnell Douglas are already planning several dedicated mission versions of the F/A-18E/F. These include the F/A-18F C²W which would have new wingtip pods and an advanced integral EW/jamming suite, perhaps developed by Litton Amecon and Lockheed Sanders. The C²W is being offered as a fully combat-capable replacement for the Navy's 127 EA-6B Prowlers.

change the structure of the forward fuselage. Access panels and landing gear doors in this area are all straight-edged and treated with radar-absorbent material (RAM).

Most types of RAM in service today consist of carbonyl iron particles in paint-type polymer binders. However, the carbonyl iron is subject to corrosion when exposed to salt water. Although corrosion does not affect the material's electromagnetic characteristics, it can damage other parts of the structure if not repaired.

McDonnell Douglas and the Navy set a goal of meeting RCS requirements within strict limitations on weight and maintenance hours per flight hour. Initially, McDonnell Douglas worked on developing two types of RAM – a lightweight material, based on carbonyl iron, and a corrosion-resistant RAM using a new absorber which the company had developed.

Early in the programme's history, McDonnell Douglas expected to use both the lightweight RAM and the new corrosion-resistant material. However, tests in 1993 showed that the aircraft would have a lower RCS than the Navy required, so some of the RAM was removed from the

aircraft, including all the lightweight RAM. As a result, the F/A-18E/F uses the reduced-corrosion RAM exclusively.

The designers have also been able to remove some RAM from the outer edges of the aircraft – where it is more susceptible to damage, both in the air and on the ground – while still meeting the Navy's specifications. For example, there is no RAM either on or inside the wing leading edges. Overall, the E/F carries 154 lb (70 kg) of RAM, 88 lb (40 kg) less than the modified C/D, and its RAM requires less maintenance, but the aircraft still has a lower RCS.

McDonnell Douglas is working with Navy supportability experts on a definitive method for carrying out repairs in the field (usually, that is, at sea) and verifying that the repairs have been effective. An adhesive RAM tape is the most likely repair method. Although the Phantom Works has developed a portable RCS measurement range small enough to be set up in a carrier's hangar deck, designers hope that the RCS-reduction measures will be sufficiently robust that there will be no need for a total RCS measurement to validate a field repair.

Stealthy weapons

McDonnell Douglas is also working with the Navy on ways of reducing the RCS of external weapons. While some new weapons such as the AGM-154 are stealthy, pylons and suspension arms are not, and they will be redesigned and coated to reduce their RCS.

Because it uses relatively small amounts of RAM, the Super Hornet can be modified to reduce its RCS still further. An area where improvement is likely is the radar. One of the Navy's upgrade plans is to replace the mechanically scanned radar antenna with an active array. This eliminates the gimbals and drives, which contribute substantially to RCS.

Tests to date (including a full-scale RCS model) show that the aircraft will meet Navy stealth specifications with margin to spare. The RCS measures are focused on the front and rear sectors and are 'modular': that is, the aircraft can be built without them if the Pentagon decides that they should not be cleared for export.

Unlike a highly stealthy aircraft like the F-117, the F/A-18E has a full suite of conventional electronic warfare (EW) systems. Stealth makes them more effective in two ways: it gives the hostile system and its operators less time to recognise and counter jamming or decoy techniques, and the weaker radar echo from the target is easier to mask or to mimic.

Towed jammer

The F/A-18E has space for the ALQ-165 Advanced Self-Protection Jammer (ASPJ) or a substitute system and will carry three Raytheon ALE-50 towed monopulse decoys. (The ALE-50 is deployed on a 328-ft/100-m cable and mimics the return from the target, causing the missile to aim at the mid-point between the real target and the decoy.) The new aircraft also has twice as much room allotted for expendable decoys (120 tubes instead of 60), with room for a further 60. ("Which adds up to about half of what the Israelis consider a minimum," comments Sears.)

The F/A-18E's avionics are based closely on the F/A-18 systems. The only major electronics changes on the new version are a 6.25-in x 6.25-in (16-cm x 16-cm), flat-panel multi-colour head-down display and an imagery-compatible, touch-screen LCD up-front control.

McDonnell Douglas unveiled the F/A-18E/F on 18 September 1995. The first of seven engineering and manufacturing development (EMD) flight-test aircraft flew on 29 November, a few days ahead of schedule, and the second aircraft followed it on 26 December. All seven EMD aircraft will join the test force at the Naval Air Warfare Center at Patuxent River, Maryland, by November 1996, and sea trials are due to begin in January 1997. Low-rate initial production should start in 1997 and the aircraft is due to enter service in 2001. According to the company, the programme is on schedule, on cost and 1,000 lb (450 kg) under its target weight.

A typical carrier air wing in the early 2000s will include 36 F/A-18s – either the original or the new version – and 14 Grumman F-14s, modified into strike aircraft. Beyond 2010, the new F/A-18 will gradually replace the original versions, and the air wing is planned to comprise F/A-18E/Fs and a joint-service medium attack aircraft, developed under the Joint Advanced Strike Technology (JAST) programme.

The DoD and export customers now have firm requirements for 2,500 F/A-18s, and production will continue until 2015. It is not a bad record for an aircraft which was almost cancelled before it entered service. **Bill Sweetman**

For a US Navy pilot, the single-seat, high-performance and deadly Hornet must be one of the most prized positions in today's Navy. Allied with the two-seater's increasing sophistication as an attack aircraft, and the promise of the F/A-18E/F, the Hornet can justifiably claim to be one of the most versatile, and capable, combat aircraft in the world.

There are still many customers for the F/A-18 who will demand its advanced avionics and systems, coupled with its desirable twin-engined configuration. This, plus the pending acquisition of large number of E/Fs, means the Hornet's (and St Louis') future is secure.

F/A-18 Hornet Operators

United States of America

United States Navy

As of March 1996, the US Navy operated a total of 22 active-duty Fleet squadrons equipped with the F/A-18C. These are augmented by two Reserve squadrons which retain the F/A-18A, and a Fleet Readiness Squadron on each coast equipped with both generations of Hornet. Second-line units comprise various test and evaluation agencies, the 'Blue Angels' Demonstration team and the adversary fleet. The latter has recently been cut back dramatically, leaving one active-duty unit and two Reservist-manned squadrons. Further cuts have been threatened for 1996.

The US Navy Hornet order of battle is summarised in the following table.

*Deck crew hurry round an F/A-18C from VFA-137 as it prepares to launch from **Constellation**. The carrier has two Navy and one Marines Hornet squadron aboard.*

Designation	Nickname	Homeport	Code	Aircraft
Strike Fighter Squadrons (VFA)				
VFA-15	Valions	NAS Cecil Field	AJ	F/A-18C
VFA-22	Fighting Redcocks	NAS Lemoore	NH	F/A-18C
VFA-25	Fist of the Fleet	NAS Lemoore	NK	F/A-18C
VFA-27	Chargers	NAF Atsugi	NF	F/A-18C
VFA-37	Bulls	NAS Cecil Field	AC	F/A-18C
VFA-81	Sunliners	NAS Cecil Field	AA	F/A-18C
VFA-82	Marauders	NAS Cecil Field	AB	F/A-18C
VFA-83	Rampagers	NAS Cecil Field	AC	F/A-18C
VFA-86	Sidewinders	NAS Cecil Field	AB	F/A-18C
VFA-87	Golden Warriors	NAS Cecil Field	AJ	F/A-18C
VFA-94	Mighty Shrikes	NAS Lemoore	NH	F/A-18C
VFA-97	Warhawks	NAS Lemoore	NH	F/A-18C
VFA-105	Gunslingers	NAS Cecil Field	AC	F/A-18C
VFA-106#	Gladiators	NAS Cecil Field	AD	F/A-18A/B/C/D, T-34C
VFA-113	Stingers	NAS Lemoore	NK	F/A-18C
VFA-125#	Rough Riders	NAS Lemoore	NJ	F/A-18A/B/C/D, T-34C
VFA-131	Wildcats	NAS Cecil Field	AG	F/A-18C
VFA-136	Knighthawks	NAS Cecil Field	AG	F/A-18C
VFA-137	Kestrels	NAS Lemoore	NE	F/A-18C
VFA-146	Blue Diamonds	NAS Lemoore	NG	F/A-18C
VFA-147	Argonauts	NAS Lemoore	NG	F/A-18C
VFA-151	Vigilantes	NAS Lemoore	NE	F/A-18C
VFA-192	World Famous Golden Dragons	NAF Atsugi	NF	F/A-18C
VFA-195	Dambusters	NAF Atsugi	NF	F/A-18C
VFA-203*	Blue Dolphins	NAS Cecil Field	AF	F/A-18A
VFA-204*	River Rattlers	NAS New Orleans	AF	F/A-18A
Fighter Composite Squadrons (VFC)				
VFC-12*	Fighting Omars	NAS Oceana	AF	F/A-18A/B
VFC-13*	Saints	NAS Fallon	AF	F/A-18A/B, F-5F/F

Miscellaneous Operators

VX-9	Evaluators	NAWS China Lake	XE	F/A-18A/B/C/D
		NAWS Point Mugu (Detachment)		
NFWS	Topgun	NAS Fallon	-	F/A-18A/B
NSWC	Strike U	NAS Fallon	-	F/A-18A/B
NFDS	Blue Angels	NAS Pensacola	BA	F/A-18A/B
NAWC-AD		NAS Patuxent River	SD	NF-18A/C/D
NAWC-WD	Dust Devils	NAWS China Lake		NF-18A/B/C
USN Test Pilot School		NAS Patuxent River	TPS	F/A-18B

* = Reserve squadron
\# = Fleet Readiness Squadron

Notes:
1. VFA-27 is joining CVW-5 (NF) in March 1996.
2. VA-115 is slated to transition to the F/A-18 during summer 1996. As for now, VA-34 and VA-75 are also slated to transition. VF-14 was slated to transition, but that is now on hold.
3. All squadrons based at Cecil Field (except VFA-203) will relocate to NAS Oceana by 1999. However, two squadrons will temporarily relocate to MCAS Beaufort before moving to Oceana. VFA-203 is slated to move to NAS Atlanta.
4. VFC-13 and NFWS (Topgun) are relocating from Miramar to NAS Fallon during 1996.
5. Air wing assignments are current for early 1996; however, a large shuffle for the East Coast is planned and may come to pass because of a shortage of Hornet squadrons. VMFA-312 has been withdrawn from CVW-8, replaced by VF-14, restoring CVW-8 to a dual F-14 squadron wing.
6. Discussion is underway whether to establish a separate F/A-18E/F fleet readiness squadron, possibly to be named VFA-122.

To complete the unit picture, these are the units which have operated the Hornet in the past, but which have since deactivated.

Disestablished F/A-18 Operators

VAQ-34	Electric Horsemen	NAS Lemoore	GD	F/A-18A/B
VF-45	Blackbirds	NAS Key West	AD	F/A-18A, F-5E/F
VFA-127	Desert Bogies	NAS Fallon	NJ	F/A-18A/B, F-5E/F
VFA-132	Privateers	NAS Cecil Field	AE	F/A-18A
VFA-161	Chargers	NAS Lemoore	NN	F/A-18A
VFA-303	Goldenhawks	NAS Lemoore	ND	F/A-18A
VFA-305	Lobos	NAS Point Mugu	ND	F/A-18A
VX-4	Evaluators	NAWS Point Mugu	XF	F/A-18A/C/D
VX-5	Vampires	NAWS China Lake	XE	F/A-18A/B/C/D
NWEF Albuquerque		Kirtland AFB		F/A-18A

Above: VFA-25's CAG-bird wears a full-colour 'Fist of the Fleet' badge on the fin, with the letters 'CAG' superimposed on the multi-coloured fin-stripe.

Above: The Naval Fighter Weapons School, now at Fallon, has replaced its A-4s, F-16s and F-5s with Hornets and Tomcats. This F/A-18B carries the 'Double Nuts' Modex and an eye-catching gloss black scheme.

*Left: Partnering VFA-137 in **Constellation** is VFA-151. This unit was originally assigned to Midway before the elderly carrier's retirement.*

United States Marine Corps

The USMC active-duty Hornet force comprises five squadrons on the East Coast at Beaufort, which are transitioning from A to C modals and five (all F/A-18C) on the West Coast, the latter having recently moved to Miramar. A single A unit is at Washington, and there are three Reserve units also operating the older variant. The replacement of the A-6E in the night-attack role with six units has been completed, split between the two main bases. The single training unit remains at El Toro. The position in March 1996 is summarised in the following table.

VMFA(AW)-533 is one of six squadrons to have adopted the two-place F/A-18D for night-attack duties, replacing the A-6E in this role. Here an aircraft prepares to launch rockets over the Yuma training range.

Designation	Nickname	Base	Code	Aircraft
Marine Fighter Attack Squadrons (VMFA)				
VMFA-112*	Cowboys	NAS Fort Worth	MA	F/A-18A
VMFA-115	Silver Eagles	MCAS Beaufort	VE	F/A-18A
VMFA-122	Crusaders	MCAS Beaufort	DC	F/A-18A
VMFA-134*	Smokes	NAS Miramar	MF	F/A-18A
VMFA-142*	Flying Gators	NAS Cecil Field	MB	F/A-18A
VMFA-212	Lancers	NAS Miramar	WD	F/A-18C
VMFA-232	Red Devils	NAS Miramar	WT	F/A-18C
VMFA-235	Death Angels	NAS Miramar	DB	F/A-18C
VMFA-251	Thunderbolts	MCAS Beaufort	DW	F/A-18C
VMFA-312	Checkerboards	MCAS Beaufort	DR	F/A-18C
VMFA-314	Black Knights	NAS Miramar	VW	F/A-18C
VMFA-321	Hell's Angels	NAF Washington	MG	F/A-18A/B
VMFA-323	Death Rattlers	NAS Miramar	WS	F/A-18C
VMFA-451	Warlords	MCAS Beaufort	VM	F/A-18A

Designation	Nickname	Base	Code	Aircraft
Marine All-Weather Fighter Attack Squadrons (VMFA(AW))				
VMFA(AW)-121	Green Knights	NAS Miramar	VK	F/A-18D
VMFA(AW)-224	Bengals	MCAS Beaufort	WK	F/A-18D
VMFA(AW)-225	Vikings	NAS Miramar	CE	F/A-18D
VMFA(AW)-242	Batmen	NAS Miramar	DT	F/A-18D
VMFA(AW)-332	Polka Dots	MCAS Beaufort	EA	F/A-18D
VMFA(AW)-533	Hawks	MCAS Beaufort	ED	F/A-18D

Marine Fighter Attack Training Squadron (VMFAT)

VMFAT-101#	Sharpshooters	MCAS El Toro	SH	F/A-18A/B/C/D, T-34C

* = Reserve squadron
\# = Fleet Readiness Squadron

Notes:
1. VMFA-235 is slated for deactivation in September 1996.
2. VMFA-451 is slated for decativation in Fiscal Year 1998.
3. Former A-4M units VMFA-124 (redesignated from VMA) and VMA-131 were scheduled to transition to the Hornet, but are now slated to be deactivated by September 1996.
4. All squadrons formerly based at Kaneohe Bay and El Toro have relocated to NAS Miramar, except for VMFAT-101, which is slated to relocate there by the end of 1996. NAS Miramar will become an MCAS.
5. VMFA-142 is salted to move to NAS Atlanta when NAS Cecil Field closes in 1998.

Deactivated Squadrons

VMFA-333	Shamrocks	MCAS Beaufort	DN	F/A-18A
VMFA-531	Grey Ghosts	MCAS El Toro	EC	F/A-18A

Left: Refuelling support for the Marines Hornet force is provided by the KC-130 Hercules.

Above: VMFAT-101 trains both USN and USMC crews, hence the 'Navy' titles on this aircraft.

Carrier assignments
As of early 1996

CVW-1 'AB' *America*
VFA-82, VFA-86, VMFA-251
CVW-2 'NE' *Constellation*
VFA-137, VFA-151, VMFA-323
CVW-3 'AC' *Dwight D. Eisenhower*
VFA-37, VFA-83, VFA-105
CVW-5 'NF' (previously *Independence*)
VFA-27, VFA-192, VFA-195
CVW-7 'AG' *George Washington*
VFA-131, VFA-136
CVW-8 'AJ' *Theodore Roosevelt*
VFA-15, VFA-87, VMFA-312
CVW-9 'NG' *Nimitz*
VFA-146, VFA-147
CVW-11 'NH' *Lincoln/Kitty Hawk*
VFA-22, VFA-94, VFA-97
CVW-14 'NK' *Carl Vinson*
VFA-25, VFA-113
CVW-17 'AA' *Enterprise*
VFA-81

Tyres smoke as a VFA-137 F/A-18C takes the wire. The A model has all but disappeared from carrier decks, and soon the E will begin to appear.

F/A-18 Hornet Operators

Australia
Royal Australian Air Force

Australia selected the Hornet in October 1981, as its next-generation tactical fighter and Mirage III replacement. The US$2,788 million deal included 57 F/A-18As (AF-18As) and 18 F/A-18Bs (AF-18Bs), all but two of which were assembled at Australia's own Government Aircraft Factory. Hornets were delivered to four units between 1985 and 1990 – No. 2 OCU (re-equipped May 1985),

No. 3 Sqn (August 1986), No. 77 Sqn (July 1987) and No. 75 Sqn (May 1988). Three of these squadrons are based at Williamtown, NSW, which was refurbished to become the main base of RAAF Hornet operations between 1983 and 1985. No. 75 Sqn is based at Tindal, NT. The Aircraft Research and Development Unit (ARDU), based at Edinburgh, SA, rountinely has an AF-18A

and an AF-18B on strength for weapons and systems trials.

In February 1995 10 aircraft from No. 75 Squadron took part in Operation Western Safari. Deployed at Pearce, they exercised with several RAN vessels to test their air defences. Hornet squadrons regularly make mass deployments to other bases and FOLs.

The RAAF has lost four Hornets (two As and two Bs) in accidents. In recent years the RAAF has been underfunded compared to the Navy, which has dominated most of the procurement budget. Civilian contractors are now carrying out many second-line tasks for the RAAF; for example, Air New Zealand maintains the Hornet's F404 engines.

The RAAF is about to embark on a massive spending spree, however.

This gaggle of Hornets is from No. 2 OCU, No. 3 Squadron and (nearest the camera) No. 75 Squadron.

These three RAAF Hornets carry the blue fin flash and fuselage markings of No. 75 Squadron, the sole unit not based at Williamtown.

Competitions are currently runing to find a DHC-4 Caribou replacement and MB-326 replacement to act as a new basic and lead-in fighter trainer (for the AF-18). The Air Force will acquire 12 C-130J-30s, beginning in 1997, to replace its C-130Es and perhaps another 12 to replace its C-130Hs. The RAAF is also searching for a small number of AEW&C aircraft. Its P-3s and F-111s are the subject of avionics upgrades and the Hornet will soon be added to this list.

The AF-18 radar is due for an early upgrade to APG-73 standard and by the end of the decade a major avionics, ECM and weapons upgrade (including AMRAAM) is planned to extend their operational efectiveness to 2015.

Canada
Canadian Armed Forces

Each of the four operational CF-188 squadrons (Nos 410, 425, 441 and 433) has 15 active and three stored aircraft, with 23 assigned pilots. An additional 23 aircraft are assigned to 410 Squadron (the OTU), AETE has four, a few are used as training aids (10 FTTS at Cold Lake and CFSATE at Borden), and the rest are in either short- or long-term storage. (The ones in short-term storage are being rotated with active aircraft to 'even out' the flying hours across the fleet.)

Canadair is the contractor for the storage as well as the third-line maintenance. Interestingly, the number of CF-188s stored at Canadair's facility near Montreal is smaller than expected. Prior to the Quebec referendum in 1995, the separatist leaders stated that all Canadian government assets, including military, that were within the boundaries of Quebec would become Quebec's assets if they won the referendum. It would be one thing to fly in pilots, technicians and troops to Bagotville to remove active CF-188s, but it would be quite another to try to do the same with stored aircraft.

410 Squadron conducts two courses per year. In addition to serving as instructors, the pilots are also subject to assignment to operational units to augment them. A student is assigned to his eventual operational unit, then detached to 410 Squadron for training. In other words, students are not members of 410.

In April 1992, the Statement on Canadian Defence Policy required that the CAF be prepared to deploy two CF-188 squadrons for contingency operations anywhere in the world. This was a result of the reduction in Canada's direct NATO commitment and was in addition to the ongoing NORAD commitment.

The considerable reduction in the budget has been followed by cuts in the annual flying hours of Fighter Group's pilots. Air Command has adopted 'capability-based planning' in an "attempt to indicate to the government realistic military policy options based on existing rather than desired force structure."

Because of the current fiscal situation, Fighter Group is no longer able to keep its pilots "current in every conceivable type of air operation." Therefore, 'core skills' have been identified and given the highest priority. For the CF-188, pilots are to be kept current in "specified air-to-air roles commensurate with a medium-threat environment and limited air-to-surface roles in a low-threat environment."

Fighter Group has adopted a 'building-block' approach to deployed operations so as to achieve maximum flexibility. Known as 'flexible response', FG is developing the ability to deploy packages of up to six aircraft with their own integral support. These can be assigned to NORAD, NATO or other missions. The NORAD agreement is renewed every five years and is due again in 1996.

Five forward operating locations (FOLs) were to be built and four were completed, but work on the fifth at Kuujjuaq was deferred indefinitely and then cancelled in the 1994 federal budget.

In addition to NORAD, NATO and potential overseas missions, CF-188s are also employed in other national tasks such as counter-drug operations.

On 14 September 1990, Canada announced that a squadron of CF-188s would be deployed to the Gulf to provide air cover for Canadian ships and to augment the multi-national force already in place. The

first CF-188s (from 409 Squadron at CFB Baden-Soellingen) deployed to the Gulf under Operation Friction and were based in Doha, Qatar. They arrived on 6 October and flew their first CAP the next day. 409 was replaced by aircraft and personnel from 439 Squadron (Baden-Soellingen) and 416 Squadron (Cold Lake), which operated as a combined unit under 439 Squadron. As 439's nickname was 'Sabre-toothed Tiger' and 416's was 'Lynx', the combined unit was known as the 'Desert Cats'. They replaced 409 in mid-December 1990.

Aircraft and personnel from the other CF-188 units (409, 410, 421, 425, 433 and 441) were also assigned to augment 416 and 439 Squadrons.

A total of 40 CF-188s served in the region, although there were never more than 26 there at any one time. Two of these were added to provide coverage for aircraft undergoing maintenance. The government had authorised a total of 24 and this allowed that total to be active. (The initial 18 was increased to 24 on 11 January and was augmented later by the two additional aircraft.) On 20 February, an air-to-surface role was authorised by the Canadian government. During 56 sorties in 3.5 days, over 100 tons of bombs were dropped, most in Kuwait and along the highway north to A1 Basrah. For the added role, about half of the CF-188s were reconfigured, with the rest maintaining the air-to-air role. Fully 20 per cent of all coalition fleet defence missions were flown by Canada.

The last CF-188 returned to Baden on 21 March 1991. CANFORME (Canadian Forces Middle East) HQ and CATGME (Canadian Air Task Group Middle East) HQ both closed down on 20 April 1991.

409 Squadron disbanded on 24 June 1991. The number was later reassigned to a new Air Reserve unit 'twinned' with 414 Squadron at CFB Comox, but it was subsequently disbanded and the Reservists incorporated into 414.

421 Squadron disbanded at Baden on 1 June 1992. The political incorrectness of its name ('Red Indian') means that 421 is most unlikely ever to be reformed.

1 Canadian Air Division and 4 Wing closed down on 1 September 1992.

439 Squadron closed down on 31 December 1992. On 1 April 1993, Air Command was reorganised and wings were formed at each of its bases. 4 Wing stood up at CFB Cold Lake. CFB Bagotville (3 Wing) had its Base Flight renumbered as 439 Squadron. (The official disbandment date of 439 was 15 May 1993, so the date for the renumbering of the Base Flight was some time after that date.)

The last CF-188s departed Baden on 19 January and arrived at Ottawa on 22 January 1993. Baden closed later in 1993.

In 1988, there were 144 CF-188 pilots and they had 240 annual flying hours. By 1994, there were 92 pilots and they had down to 210 annual flying hours. The number of operational CF-188 squadrons declined from seven to four during the same period, with the number of active CF-188s declining from 96 to 60.

Following the return of the Baden-based CF-188s, the four operational squadrons in Canada took on a dual-role tasking. Each did six months as an air-to-air unit committed to NORAD operations and six months as an air-to-ground unit ready to deploy overseas, such as for NATO or other international duties. In reality, both missions were practised to some extent throughout the year, but each had a much heavier emphasis on one or the other role for each six-month period.

More recently, this has changed to a 12-month rotation, no doubt a result of the decreased annual flying hours. Fewer hours are to be wasted by having to reconvert from one role to another twice as often as is the current practice.

Current NDHQ readiness standards allow for a 30-day readiness period to prepare for participation in overseas contingency operations. A demonstration of the concept of tailoring a force for a specific mission was demonstrated in August 1992. An air-to-ground work-up was carried out by 3 Wing in preparation for a possible deployment to Italy in support of operations in the former Yugoslavia. According to Fighter Group, "despite both a cadre of resident experience in the assigned squadron and the presence of a minimum level of air-to-ground core skills among the squadron aircrew, many additional flying

The French-speaking 433 Squadron is known as the 'Porcupines' and this aircraft was painted for the unit's 50th anniversary in 1993.

This mix of CF-188A/Bs is operated by 410 'Cougar' Squadron, the CAF's Hornet training unit. It is the CAF's largest Hornet squadron, with 38 aircraft on charge.

training days were required to prepare the squadron to enter a theatre far less demanding than the former Central Europe. Thus, readiness levels have already decreased substantially in the few short years since the end of the Cold War and the repatriation of the fighters from Europe."

Fighter Group sees a quantifiable relationship between fighter force readiness and fighter force combat capability. As the capability decreases, so does readiness. Budget cuts have forced a reduced combat capability and, therefore, readiness has also been decreased. Fighter Group has decided that the major benchmark in determining the core skills is the requirement to maintain the capability to conduct four-ship operations in a defensive environment similar to that experienced in the Gulf War. However, this would still be only a minimum and pilots would need a work-up period before they could be deployed.

In the autumn of 1991, the Commander of Fighter Group commissioned a series of internal studies with the aim of recommending a fighter force structure that would see the Group well into the decade, while at the same time adhering to NDHQ force development constraints. Subsequently, the Fighter Group MultiYear Implementation Plan (MYIP) was published in May 1992.

It was decided to move toward centralising all Canadian fighter operations in a single headquarters and that, due to the reduced combat capability resulting from budget cuts, a general-purpose, multi-role fighter force would offer more flexibility. The common capability baseline provided by four identical multi-role squadrons would also result in benefits. The repatriation of the European CF-188s at the end of 1992 allowed the centralisation to go ahead (as those aircraft had been assigned to

Right: This impressive line-up of CF-188s is seen at CFB Cold Lake. Cold Lake is home to the annual Maple Flag exercises.

Canadian Forces Europe and would now come under the control of Fighter Group).

In January 1991, the proposal to raise the unit establishment (UE) of each CF-188 squadron to 18 was submitted to the Commander of Fighter Group, and this was approved that spring. While this improved the ability of the units to conduct their assigned missions, the downside was that the additional manpower and equipment would have to be found from within Fighter Group's existing assets. Therefore, an aggressive restructuring was carried out, including the amalgamation of CFB North Bay with 22 Radar Control Wing and of 21 and 51 Aerospace Control and Warning Squadrons into one unit.

An 18-aircraft UE allows a squadron to make 15 aircraft available for taskings, given historical serviceability rates of 70 per cent to 75 per cent. A UE of 18 is also compatible with many of Canada's allies. Previously, CF-188 squadrons had 13 aircraft, then 15, and the increase to 18 followed the repatriation of the Baden-based aircraft. The current idea of 15 active and three stored aircraft per squadron is a way of meeting the government-mandated total of 60 active fighters without losing the ability to deploy a squadron with 18 aircraft if a contingency occurs.

Experience has shown that a combat ratio of two pilots to one aircraft is essential and that a peacetime ratio of 1.5:1 can only be accommodated if sufficient expertise is preserved. Below this ratio, there is an unacceptable reduction in 'supervisory experience' (i.e. majors and senior captains to 'ride herd' on the younger pilots) and an attendant safety risk. Fighter Group had sad experience with this in the late 1980s/early 1990s, when there were a number of CF-188 accidents in a period of a few years.

Fighter Group states that it "presently possesses the minimum level of combat capability in both air-to-air and air-to-surface missions which is necessary to perform the

assigned tasks within the imposed readiness constraints. Further resource reductions or additional tasks will jeopardise the fighter force's ability to participate in the tasks and operations [assigned], and, perhaps more importantly, will reduce the force's ability to a level from which reattainment of the essential combat skills would not be possible."

AETE (Aerospace Engineering Test Establishment) is conducting trials of the Loral Aeroneutronic AN/AAS-38B Navigation IR Targeting Equipment (NITE) Hawk pod in conjunction with GBU-24B Paveway III laser-guided bombs and AGM-65G Maverick IR-guided missiles.

Finland
Suomen Ilmavoimat

At Soviet insistence, the Paris Treaty of 1947 limited the Finnish air force to only 60 combat aircraft, and 3,000 personnel. Treading an uneasy line between its Soviet and Western neighbours, Finland acquired a unique mix of MiG-21s and Saab Drakens. Early model MiG-21F-13s, which entered service in 1954, were replaced by MiG-21bis 'Fishbed-Ns' between 1980 and 1981. Incidentally, in all official Finnish air force documentation these aircraft are referred to as MiG-21BIS. These were complemented by Saab 35 Drakens – Valmet-built 35XS and ex-Flygvapnet 35FS versions delivered between 1974 and 1984 (Finland does not use the Swedish J/jakt prefix). The terms of the Paris Treaty were not strictly adhered to and Finland reached a peak strength of 62 (36 Draken, 26 MiG-21) front-line aircraft (not including two-seat trainer versions).

The search to replace these elderly jets (the DX competition) began in 1989 with an official request for quotations (RFQ) for 20 single-seat and five two-seat aircraft, with options on a further 20. The RFQ was transmitted to Dassault, General Dynamics and Saab and, though no specific aircraft types were mentioned, the manufacturers responded with bids for the Mirage 2000-5, F-16A/B MLU and JAS 39 Gripen, respectively. Initial submissions were made by 31 October 1990 and these were answered by a second, revised, Finnish RFQ for 60 single-seat and seven two-seat aircraft on 3 January 1991. McDonnell Douglas was included in this second round of bids, on 12 April 1991, and all four companies had responded by July. At this

point General Dynamics offered the F-16C/D. It was predicted by some that the air force would be unable to support such an ambitious expansion, as the collapse of the Soviet Union had robbed Finland of major export earnings (down from 25 per cent to 3 per cent of the total) and, like most of Europe, the country was in recession; however, the air force pressed on with plans to acquire the maximum number of aircraft. (The net result of this is that virtually all of Finland's defence acquisition funds are tied up with the Hornet, until 2000.)

A two-phase evaluation was undertaken of each type, first in the country of manufacture and then in Finland itself. Between December 1990 and December 1991 two Finnish pilots visited each of the competing nations, making about 15 to 20 flights in each aircraft. Saab gave unprecedented access to the Gripen flight test programme. Over 250 flights were

completed by the Ilmavoimat pilots at Linköping where the Gripen was being readied for Swedish service. Much of the US flying was over water, while some the French flying was over the Alps. It was felt that to fully evaluate the aircraft and avionics systems a major operational trial was required in Finland itself.

General Dynamics despatched an F-16D to Halli AFB during February 1992, while McDonnell Douglas bailed back a USMC F/A-18B in the same month. This aircraft was fitted with the uprated General Electric F404-GE-402 Enhanced Performance Engine (EPE) and wore toned-down EPE titles on the fin. It also carried an 'SF' tailcode (perhaps signifying Suomi/Finland). In March a JAS 39A and a Mirage 2000-5 arrived. All of these aircraft had Finnish pilots except the Gripen, which was flown by a Swedish test pilot who was far more familiar with its sophisticated onboard systems than the Finns. Over a two-week

period each aircraft made 15 to 20 further evaluation flights in conjunction with the Finnish command and control network and Ilmavoimat aircraft. Up to 40 aircraft were airborne on occasion, and each evaluation aircraft's radar and EW system were thoroughly tested.

Russian aircraft were also included in the trials, but at a very late stage, and they were not flown by the Finns. President Yeltsin personally instructed Russian officials in the neighbouring Karelian province (once Finnish territory) to offer the MiG-29 and the MiG-31 to the Ilmavoimat. A week prior to the final decision a Finnish air force delegation did visit Russia, but there was no serious basis on which to include the new aircraft in the competition.

By 10 March 1992 the bids portion of the evaluation was closed. A final recommendation was made in April 1992, at Finnish air force headquarters, and passed on to the Minister of Defence Elisabeth

Finland's first four F-18 Hornets were delivered to HävLLV 21, while the second batch went to HävLLV 31. Both squadrons are MiG-21bis operators but the MiGs now urgently need to be replaced.

Finland's Hornets are being equipped to a very high standard, as are the Swiss aircraft. Both nations are co-operating heavily on technical and training matters during the introduction of their new aircraft.

Rehn. Finland would acquire 57 F/A-18Cs and seven F/A-18Ds, with spares supply for three years, training and support equipment. This was three fewer than had been specified, but more than might have been expected in the prevailing financial climate. Mrs Rehn called officials in each of the countries involved to tell them of the decision. She reportedly told Secretary Dick Cheney that "she had some bad news and some good news." The bad news was that the F-16 had failed, but that she would be recommending the F/A-18 to a government council within minutes. Some sources have ascribed the F-16's failure to a perceived lack of growth potential. The Mirage 2000-5 and the Gripen were both too expensive and, additionally, the Gripen had not then been cleared to carry the AIM-120.

An offset agreement with McDonnell Douglas was signed on 19 May: the F/A-18Ds would be built in St Louis, but the single-seaters would be assembled by Valmet. Letters of Offer and Acceptance were signed on 5 June 1992, the day after the decision was officially announced by the government. Further agreements followed, including agreements to purchase weapons,

maintenance and training systems (on 20 January 1994), and the offset deal was confirmed on 21 January 1994.

Funding for the acquisition has been broken into two parts. The first Authorisation To Order (ATO) covers all 64 aircraft, funding for Valmet as sub-contractor, initial training and maintenance costs, and programme administration costs. The total bill amounts to FIM 9.5 billion from 1992 to 2000. The second ATO covers the training, maintenance and ground support systems, communications fit and weapons. It will cost FIM 4.42 billion, between 1994 to 2001.

Under the terms of a Foreign Military Sales (FMS) deal such as this, the aircraft are formally being supplied by the US Navy, which is acting as an agent of the US government. The Navy will be nominally involved in product support, with the actual work being undertaken by McDonnell Douglas.

Finland will operate the Hornet purely in the air superiority role, with the official designation F-18 as a result. Aircraft will be armed with AIM-9M Sidewinder and AIM-120B AMRAAM missiles. The F-18s

are fitted with the GE F404-402 EPE powerplant and Hughes AN/APG-73 radar. Avionics will essentially be to US Lot 17 standards and will include INS/GPS, VOR/DME and TILS. Like the Swiss Hornets, the F-18s will be fitted with the ALQ-165 ASPJ ECM system. They will also have AN/ALR-67 RWR and four AN/ALE-47 chaff/flare dispensers (US Navy aircraft routinely carry only two). A Finnish-developed datalink, as fitted to the Draken, will be added to the Hornets and then upgraded into a complete and highly advanced air-to-air/air-to-ground system by Nokia. All the instruments will be calibrated in metric. An interception/identification spotlight will be fitted in the nose, to port. Furthermore, BAK 12 mobile arrester systems are being acquired to allow the hook-equipped Hornets to undertake road strip operations.

The first F-18D for Finland flew, in the USA, on 21 April 1995, before its formal roll-out date of 7 June. The first four aircraft (all F-18Ds, serialled HN-462, -464/66) were delivered non-stop from St Louis to Tampere-Pirkkala AB, in southern Finland, on 7 November 1995. The aircraft were flown by US Navy and Finnish pilots and refuelled from a USAF KC-10 en route. Deliveries are scheduled to continue to the year 2000 at a rate as follows: seven (1995), four (1996), 10 (1997), 13 (1998), 18 (1999) and 12 (2000). Valmet plans to fly its first Hornet in May and deliver it in August/September 1996. Initially, these aircraft will be test flown and checked out by US Navy pilots. The last aircraft is due to be handed over in August 2000. The Hornet production deal should signal a turn-around

in Valmet's financial fortunes and may even launch the integration of all Finland's defence industries into a single, state-owned company.

After their delivery, Finland's Hornets were afflicted with problems with their Precision Echo-supplied WR-818 cockpit video recorders, which had to be replaced with TEAC V-80AB-F cameras. The 8-mm camera system records HUD and MFD information during the mission for playback and debriefing on the ground. The US Navy allegedly reported a similar high-failure rate (since fixed) with its PE cameras, which are an essential training aid.

The full Hornet training syllabus includes 11 months of basic training on the Valmet Vinka (45 flying hours) followed by three years of flying training on a combined Vinka and Hawk course (60 and 100 hours, respectively). One year's advanced jet and weapons training (120 flying hours) follows, before type conversion to the F-18 begins.

Ilmavoimat operations in Finland are divided among three air defence areas, each allocated a single wing. The first F-18s were delivered to HävLLv 21 (No. 21 Sqn), part of Satakunta Wing, which flies Drakens from Pirkkala. The second batch (formally part of the 1995 deliveries) was delivered on 16 February 1996 to HävLLv 31, part of Karelen Wing, which operates the MiG-21bis from Kuopio-Rissala AFB. This delivery comprised three F-18Ds (HN-461, -463, -467), again ferried non-stop from St Louis. The Hornets have been delivered to two squadrons because of the pressing need to replace Finland's MiG-21s – flown by both units. All the MiGs are due to be retired by the end of 1997. This will cause a significant shortfall in Finland's fighter force before the Hornets become fully operational. The Draken force is also being slowly reduced, and only 12 aircraft are expected to remain operational by 2000. The northernmost wing, Lapland Wing (HävLLv 11) based at Rovaniemi, will continue to operate this small number of relatively 'new' Saab 35S Drakens until then.

Kuwait
Al Quwwat al Jawwiya al Kuwaitiya/Kuwait Air Force

Kuwaiti interest in the F/A-18 was prompted, in 1987, by a perceived threat from Iran – not an unlikely one, owing to Kuwait's support for Iraq during the (first) Gulf war. Instead of reducing its air force, as once intended, Kuwait launched a substantial expansion plan to acquire 40 new 'interceptors'. Interest was expressed in the Panavia Tornado F.Mk 3, Dassault Mirage 2000 and McDonnell Douglas Hornet. The Hornet emerged as the preferred successor to the KAF's Mirage F1CKs and A-4KU Skyhawks. A $489 million order for 32 F/A-18Cs and eight F/A-18D Hornets was placed in September 1988.

The total package included 120 AIM-9L Sidewinders, 200 AIM-7F Sparrows, 344 AGM-65G Mavericks and 40 AGM-84D Harpoons, at a cost of $1.9 billion. The US expressed its concern at such a potent increase in the KAF's offensive capability by forbidding the aircraft's deployment outside Kuwait, barring any transfer to a third party, declining to provide any air-to-air refuelling equipment, and requesting the return of the A-4KUs to the United States.

The first Hornet (an F/A-18D) was due to be handed over to the KAF on 1 October 1991 in the United States, to begin crew training. The first six aircraft scheduled to be

delivered to Kuwait were due to arrive in January 1992.

Events in the region took a new turn when Iraq invaded Kuwait on 2 August 1990. The war disrupted all re-equipment plans and, while it reaffirmed the need for new aircraft and boosted US support for Kuwait (which had hitherto been lukewarm), all delivery (and payment) schedules were rearranged. Also, the nation's air base infrastructure had to be repaired and improved. The two main military air bases at Ali al Salem and Ahmed al Jaber were largely destroyed during the fighting. With substantial assistance from the US Army

Corps of Engineers, the air bases were rebuilt and prepared for the arrival of the F/A-18s. The first KAF Hornet rolled of the St Louis production line in July 1991 and was scheduled for delivery in January 1992. As an interim measure the US offered basing facilities for the aircraft until preparations in Kuwait were completed.

The first three aircraft arrived in Kuwait on 25 January 1992, on time, as originally planned. Six aircraft were in place for a flypast to commemorate the first anniversary of the liberation of Kuwait, on 25 February 1992. By May 1992, 10 aircraft had been delivered to Kuwait, with 30 remaining under the terms of the original contract. All were operating from Kuwait International Airport, as military facilities were still not yet ready. Deliveries were completed on 21 August 1993, when the final three aircraft arrived at Kuwait International, even though Ali Al Salem AB was, by then, available for use. Ahmed al Jaber AB was declared operational once more on 7 February 1994. The Hornets began their operational career flying missions as part of Operation Southern Watch over Iraq. Since then, they have engaged in regular exercise with other Gulf community air forces, including deployments to Bahrain.

Kuwaiti Hornets are operated by Nos 9 and 25 Squadrons, based at Ahmed al Jaber AB, also home to the KAF's fleet of stored A-4KUs which are up for sale. Large portions of the airfield are still off limits due to unexploded ordnance from the Gulf War, and many of the HASs remain unrepaired. Both KAF Hornet squadrons fly a mix of F/A-18Cs and Ds. McDonnell Douglas refers to the Kuwaiti aircraft as KAF-18C/Ds. No. 9 Sqn is tasked with air defence, while No. 25 Sqn has an air-to-ground role. An option to purchase an additional 38 Hornets was cancelled in 1992, but the KAF still has tentative plans to acquire an additional 12 F/A-18C/Ds. Dassault is again offering the Mirage 2000 in competition.

These KAF-18Cs belong to 9 Sqn (nearest and furthest aircraft), tasked with air defence, and 25 Sqn, whose role is solely ground attack.

Malaysia
Tentara Udara Diraja Malaysia/Royal Malaysian Air Force

On 29 June 1993 Malaysia announced a novel solution to its need for an F-5 replacement. It was decided that the air force would acquire 18 MiG-29SEs for air defence duties and eight F/A-18D Hornets for the attack role. The two-seat Hornets will be employed in the same fashion as USMC aircraft and equipped with GE F404-402 EPE powerplants and AN/APG-73 radar.

They will also be fitted with ALQ-126 ECM pods and ALR-67 RWR. An FMS contract was placed with McDonnell Douglas to supply these aircraft on 7 April 1994. Malaysia subsequently requested a bid for an additional 10 to 16 aircraft, but opted to acquire more F-16s instead. Roll-out of the first RMAF Hornet is planned for October 1996. F/A-18 deliveries are scheduled to

commence in January 1997 (four aircraft) and be completed in May (four aircraft). In advance of this, Malaysian crews began Hornet familiarisation training at China Lake in February 1994.

Malaysia's acquisition of F/A-18s prompted neighbouring Singapore to look at acquiring Hornets also, in favour of its second batch of F-16s. In the event, they

decided to proceed with the F-16 buy as planned. Armed with AGM-84, Malaysia's F/A-18Ds would provide its air force with a potent naval strike asset, unrivalled in a region where control of shipping is paramount.

It is expected that the Hornets will be based at Kuantan AB, with the added possibility that another air base in eastern Malaysia (perhaps Labuan or Kuching) might be upgraded to act as an FOL. Malaysia started work on a major new air base facility at Gong Kedah, but these plans have been scaled back and the site now houses only an air defence radar station.

Spain
Ejército del Aire

Spain selected the Hornet in 1983 after its FACA (Futuro Avión de Combate y Ataque/future fighter and attack aircraft) competition, which commenced in 1978. An initial requirement for 144 aircraft was reduced to 72, comprising 60 EF-18As and 12 two-seat EF-18Bs ('E' = España/Spain). The (little-used) air force designations are C.15 and CE.15, respectively. Deliveries began on 10 July 1986 when four EF-18Bs arrived at Zaragoza, after a non-stop flight from Lambert Field. The Spanish Hornets came from five production blocks: Lot 8 (one A and eight Bs), Lot 9 (17 As and four Bs), Lot 10 (17 As), Lot 11 (17 As) and Lot 12 (eight As). Three aircraft have been written off since then, a remarkably low accident rate.

The Ejército del Aire Hornets were delivered with AIM-9L/M Sidewinders and AIM-7F/M Sparrows. The AIM-120 AMRAAM was ordered in 1990 and the EF-18s now have the necessary software upgrades to carry the weapon. While the aircraft have a multi-role tasking within the air force, their primary mission (60 per cent of training time) is as all-weather interceptors. The Hornets also have a substantial air-to-ground role and have a variety of weapons at their disposal. These include a range of Spanish-developed ordnance such as ALD GP bombs, ASH retarded-GP bombs, BR low-drag bombs (based on the US Mk 80 series), BRP and BRP.S (special) retarded low-drag bombs (again based on the Mk 80 series), ABL-250 CBUs, BME 330 CBUs (with anti-runway bomblets), BIN napalm bombs and BRFA 330 boosted runway penetration bombs. The Hornets also have a range of US ordnance available that encompasses Mk 20 Rockeye II CBUs, Mk 80 series bombs (including 'Snakeye' retarded versions), Paveway II LGBs, AGM-65G Mavericks (with the improved IIR seeker), AGM-88 HARMs and AGM-84 Harpoons.

In 1991 Ejército Hornets had been readied for possible use in Operation Desert Storm, but the campaign ended before plans were formalised. The aircraft would have been based in Bahrain or Qatar. Instead, EF-18s, deployed at Son San Juan AB, Majorca, provided air cover for USAF B-52 operations staging through Morón.

Spanish Hornets dropped their first weapons in anger over Bosnia, as part of NATO's Operation Deny Flight (Operación Icaro to Spanish forces). On 25 May 1995 two EF-18A+s dropped 1,000-lb GBU-16 LGBs on Serb-held targets near Pale. The Hornets self-designated the targets using their Loral AN/AAS-38A NITE Hawk FLIR-LTD/R pods. A second pair of EF-18A+s provided SEAD coverage of the raid, which was carried out in conjunction with six USAF F-16Cs. The following day the target was reattacked by two EF-18A+s. Spanish Hornets also participated in the November 1995 Deliberate Force operations against the Serb air defence network and other offensive targets in Bosnia. The HARM-equipped EF-18s again provided SEAD support for NATO strike packages. For their own self-defence, Spanish Hornets are fitted with Goodyear AN/ALE-39 chaff/flare dispensers, Litton ALR-46(V) RWR and Northrop Grumman AN/ALQ-162(V) jammers, which have supplanted the earlier (Lockheed) Sanders AN/ALQ-126B on most aircraft.

On 1 December 1994 the first Spanish Hornets, eight aircraft with crews drawn

from both Grupo 12 and 15, arrived at Aviano as part of Operation Deny Flight – replacing F-15Es of the Lakenheath-based 492nd FS – under the command of NATO's 5 ATAF. The Hornet's crews came direct from Red Flag 94-4 where they had intensively practised SEAD tactics over the Nellis ranges (see *World Air Power Journal* Volume 22). The Hornets largely flew CAP missions from Aviano, although they maintained a 'swing' capability by carrying two GBU-16s along with their primary armament of AIM-9s and AIM-7s. CAPs were routinely flown for up to four hours and could be extended to five hours (with three air-to-air refuellings). The Spanish detachment flew six such sorties per day on a 'five days on, two days off' schedule. The aircraft deployed to Aviano were taken first from Grupo 15 and later replaced, on 1 April 1995, by aircraft from Grupo 12.

Between 15 September 1992 and 5 December 1994, CASA undertook a fleet-wide Hornet upgrade at Zaragoza (the first aircraft modified was CE.15-1/15-70, from Grupo 15). Upon completion of the upgrade, aircraft became redesignated as EF-18A+ and EF-18B+. The seven-phase programme

was carried out with assistance from McDonnell Douglas, which refitted the first 46 of the 69 aircraft involved. Each Hornet was withdrawn from service for between six and 12 weeks, disassembled and completely rewired. Onboard computer memory and processing capability was increased by upgrading the two central AN/AYK-14 mission computers to XN-6 standard. This allowed the AIM-120 AMRAAM and the AAS-38A NITE Hawk system to be fully integrated into the weapons computer (Spain has ordered 18 AN/AAS-38A systems). The AN/ALQ-162(V) onboard ECM system was also integrated into the aircraft's defensive suite, via a new MIL-STD 1553B databus. The first 36 Spanish Hornets were delivered with Sanders ALQ-126B ECM systems, while the second 36 were delivered with Northrop Grumman's ALQ-162(V); this more advanced CW system has been retrofitted to the earlier aircraft as part of the upgrade. A removable cartridge-based mission planning and debriefing system has also been installed. An associated upgrade which commenced in 1995 involved the replacement of the Hornet's original

US-supplied OFP-89C (operational flight programme) software with a modified OFP-94E which allows improved integration with Spanish-designed weapons.

In January 1995 Spain announced its intention to acquire 24 ex-US Navy F/A-18As, with options on a further six, under the Ejército's 'CX' programme. The Hornets will replace the CASA C.101 Aviojets temporarily allocated to Grupo 21, based at Morón, when its F-5s are transferred to Ala 23, at Talavera. These airframes have each accumulated approximately 3,000 flying hours and are judged to be good for another 6,000. They have all been re-engined with new General Electric F404-GE-400s. Deliveries began in December 1995 and are due to continue, at a rate of 12 per year, until 1998. They have received the same software upgrades as the Ejército's EF-18A/B+s.

Spanish Hornets are due to undergo an MLU between 1999 and 2002 which will most likely upgrade their radars to AN/APG-73 standard and extend their airframe service life to 2010. Most of the original batch of aircraft will have reached the 3,000-hour service mark and will have their airframe lives extended to 9,000 hours as part of the MLU.

Grupo 15

Grupo 15 was established as Ala 15, at Zaragoza, on 16 December 1985. Its first aircraft arrived the following July and deliveries were completed to the wing in 1987. Its unit insignia is a white tiger and its motto is 'Quien ose paga'. In 1989 Ala 15

Left: A Grupo 15 EF-18A+ returns to Nellis AFB after a 1995 Red Flag sortie.

Below: Red Flag exercises were an ideal preparation for Spain's participation in Operation Deny Flight. A detachment of AGM-88-capable EF-18s was based at Aviano.

was integrated into Ala 31 (the C-130/KC-130 wing that is also based at Zaragoza), becoming Grupo 15 of Ala 31. This established Spain's first combined wing, which also included the Boeing 707 tanker/transports of Grupo 45, and these units now train together for combined operations and rapid deployment overseas.

Grupo 15 has two component squadrons: 151 Escuadrón (callsign EBRO) and 152 Escuadrón (callsign MARTE). Each squadron was allocated 15 EF-18As and three EF-18Bs. When Ala 12 was forming in August 1988, Esc 152 acted as a temporary OTU (Operational Training Unit), with an increased complement of aircraft as a result (12 EF-18Bs could then be found at Zaragoza). Today Esc 151 is tasked with a primary air-to-air mission – in both offensive and defensive counter-air roles (OCA and DCA). Esc 152 has a primary SEAD tasking using AGM-88.

Esc 153 (the original Hornet OCU) was re-established in March 1995 to train new pilots for Grupo 21.

Grupo 15 still provides a regular 15-minute QRA aircraft, a duty which it shares on a bi-monthly rotation basis with Grupo 12 and the Mirage F1-equipped Ala 14.

Grupo 12

Grupo 12 was established in March 1989, at Torrejón. Its two squadrons of Hornets are 121 Escuadrón (callsign POKER) and 122 Escuadrón (callsign TENIS). 123 Escuadrón (TITÁN) continues to operate the RF-4C. Esc 121 is tasked with maritime strike missions and was assigned to NATO's Rapid Reaction Forces in 1995. Esc 122, like Esc 151, has a primary air-to-air (OCA and DCA) mission.

During the upgrade programme of 1992 to 1994, Grupo 12 handled all Hornet conversion training. A new squadron, Esc 124 (callsign MAMBO), was established on 1 November 1992 as the EF-18 UTT (Unidad de Transformación Temporal) or OCU. It was assigned most of the Ejército's EF-18Bs and undertook a nine-month, 61-sortie programme to train pilots to limited combat readiness status. Another 18 months training with the pilot's assigned front-line unit followed before he was declared fully combat-ready. Esc 124 was formally disestablished on 15 November 1994, but the UTT continued to operate from Torrejón, in de facto Esc 124 form. Operational conversion for new Grupo 21 pilots is now undertaken by Esc 153.

Centro Logistico de Armamento y Experimentación (CLAEX)

CLAEX, the Ejército del Aire's weapon and test centre, is based at Torrejón. The centre has a single flying unit, the Grupo de Ensayos en Veulo (flight test flying group), which has one EF-18A+ (C.15-13/12-01) on permanent assignment to it for weapons trials and avionics testing. Other aircraft are also assigned to CLAEX when required.

Grupo 21

Based at Morón, Grupo 21 was equipped with CASA C.101 Aviojets when it transferred the last of its F-5s to Ala 23 in 1991. This was an interim measure, prior to the acquisition of additional F/A-18As from surplus US Navy stocks. The first six of these aircraft were delivered, from NAS Cecil Field to Zaragoza, to 211 Escuadrón in December 1995. Aircraft involved are C.15-73 (161936), C.15-74 (162415), C.15-75 (162416), C.15-76 (162426), C.15-77 (162446) and C.15-78 (162471). Once in service these aircraft will be upgraded to EF-18A+ standard. The first group of Esc 211 pilots began conversion training on 15 March 1995 (with Esc 153, which was reactivated for that task).

This well-worn EF-18B is on charge with Torrejón-based Grupo 15. While Spain's Hornets were being upgraded, virtually all its EF-18Bs were based at Torrejón.

Switzerland
Kommando der Flieger- und Fliegerabwehrtruppen/Swiss Air Force and Anti-Aircraft Command

Switzerland's acquisition of the Hornet has been a long and drawn-out process, so heated that it forced a national referendum. The search for a new combat aircraft (Neue Jagdflugzeug) to replace the Mirage III (and F-5E to a degree) was launched in the mid-1980s, concurrent with the air force's F-5E acquisition which itself took 10 years to resolve. Contenders for the next-generation fighter included the (then) General Dynamics F-16, Dassault Mirage 2000 and McDonnell Douglas F/A-18. Outside contenders (at one time or another) included the IAI Lavi, Northrop F-20 and Saab Gripen. In October 1988 the Hornet was selected by the Swiss air force, which placed an initial order for 26 F/A-18Cs and eight F/A-18Bs. The aircraft would be fitted with the GE F404-202 EPE powerplant, and 13 spare engines were included in the deal. So too were AIM-7 Sparrows (the first BVR missile in Swiss service), an integrated ECM system (ultimately the ITT/Westinghouse AN/ALQ-165 ASPJ) and AN/APG-73 radar. An NVG system will be acquired, as will the AN/AAS-38 NITE Hawk FLIR. The air force plans to acquire the AIM-120 at a later date.

Dassault, and elements in the Swiss political establishment, launched a spirited defence of the Mirage 2000 once the Hornet was selected. President Mitterand made a personal appeal to the Swiss to reconsider the decision. The lessening of the perceived threat from the Soviet Union next lead some to suggest that the order could be cut back to 24 aircraft, plus 10 options. The MiG-29 was also proposed as a suitable new aircraft.

This debate culminated in a reaffirmation of the air force's decision by the Swiss Federal Council in June 1991. A formal order was not yet signed, however. The Parliament approved the Hornet acquisition bill in June 1992, but a plebiscite was needed to ensure that deliveries could commence before 2000. This vote was won on 6 June 1993 and the $2.6 billion contract was signed on 22 June.

On 25 January 1996 the first Swiss Hornet, an F/A-18D, was rolled out at St Louis. It made its maiden flight, of one hour

and 15 minutes, on 20 January. The second aircraft, an F/A-18C, was handed over in February and will remain in the US until 1997 for weapons integration testing. Formal F/A-18 deliveries are due to commence to the Swiss air force in December 1996. All of the remaining 32 aircraft will be assembled at the Swiss Aircraft and Systems Co. (F+W) at Emmen. The first of these is scheduled to fly in late

1996 and to be delivered in early 1997. Deliveries will be completed in November 1999. The air force's C-in-C, General Ferdinand Carrel, is on record as stating that a follow-on batch of Hornets may be needed for ground-attack and reconnaissance tasks.

Switzerland has a small active air force in peacetime. Only the Überwachungs-geschwader (surveillance wing) is 'full-time'

with regular air force personnel. The Hornets are intended to replace the (upgraded) Mirage IIIS allocated to the wing's two units, Fliegerstaffel 16 and Flst 17, based at Payerne. In wartime the Mirage IIIS force (but not the Mirage IIIRS units) would be commanded by Fliegerregiment 2, which would deploy the same squadrons to Stans/Buochs and Meiringen, respectively.

Despite the controversy that has surrounded it so far, Switzerland's acquisition of the Hornet seems sure to allow the air force to look to the future with confidence. Switzerland has chosen to acquire the most sophisticated option available to it – an aircraft with the EPE powerplant, APG-73 radar and ASPJ ECM system. Switzerland and Finland are remarkable for specifying the ITT/Westinghouse ALQ-165 ASPJ even after the US services had first rejected it.

Thailand
Royal Thai Air Force

Malaysia's acquisition of MiG-29s and Vietnam's acquisition of Sukhoi Su-27s (and the advanced BVR missiles supplied with them) caused Thailand to immediately approach the United States for a comparable counter. In late 1995 Washington offered Thailand additional F-16s or eight F/A-18s. The Thai government favoured AMRAAM-armed F-15s but received an unenthusiastic response. As a result, Thailand made evaluations of the Mirage 2000-5, MiG-29

and Su-27 before the US acquiesced to its demands for an advanced combat aircraft.

Thailand and the US agreed on a $578 million FMS package (via the US Navy) to supply four F/A-18Cs and four F/A-18Ds, along with AIM-9L, AIM-7M and AGM-84 missiles, AN/AAS-38 NITE Hawk FLIR system and an integrated ECM system. Contract signature was anticipated in early 1996 but this stalled upon Thailand's insistence that the Hornets be supplied with AIM-120. The US State Department refused to sanction an AMRAAM transfer (while the Pentagon supported it) but instead offered to supply the missile if Thailand was threatened. The US was reluctant to initiate an arms race in a region where the chief

protagonists were already notionally better armed than Thailand. It was suggested that Thailand remove the AIM-120 from its letter of request and the aircraft be wired for AMRAAM carriage, but delivered with AIM-7M Sparrow (and AIM-120 training rounds). At one point Thailand said it would not proceed with the deal unless AMRAAM was included and the US compromised by suggesting that firm evidence of Vympel R-77 (AA-12 'Adder') in service with Malaysia would be enough to facilitate AMRAAM delivery. An RTAF team visited Washington in late January 1996 to smooth the passage of the Letter of Acceptance which was to go before Congress in February. Once its terms had been passed

there it would be returned to Thailand for signature. Meanwhile, Dassault was lobbying the RTAF hard to supply the Mirage 2000-5 and MATRA Mica missile. During the Asian Aerospace 1996 show Dassault spokesmen expressed a belief that Thailand would not be granted the AIM-120, while Mica was available immediately.

At the time of writing it seemed certain that Thailand would circumvent formal US objections by signing separate Letters of Agreement for both the Hornet and AMRAAM missiles.

Operator Details by Richard R. Burgess, Robert Hewson and Jeff Rankin-Lowe.

Bahrain Amiri Air Force

A Photo Feature by Peter Steinemann

The Emirate of Bahrain is an archipelago in the Persian Gulf, situated between Saudi Arabia and the Qatari peninsula. Since it gained its independence from Britain in 1971, this tiny country has amassed considerable oil wealth, and the means to defend it. A small air arm was established as long ago as 1965, but today's Amiri Air Force is an expanding and well-equipped force, dedicated to the defence of the state.

Left: The massive facility of Shaikh Isa AB was built to the southeast of the main island of Sintrah, with $100 million of American assistance and US Army construction skills.

Above: This was one of the first batch of eight Block 40D F-16Cs supplied to Bahrain under the 1987 Peace Crown deal. Four F-16Ds were also included in the deal.

Below: Bahrain acquired its first AIM-9 Sidewinders (AIM-9Ps) with its F-5s, in 1985. The F-16Cs were delivered not only with AIM-9Ls but also with longer-range AIM-7F Sparrows.

Above: The F-5 was the Bahrain Amiri Air Force's first fixed-wing (and combat) type. Bahrain had originally expressed an interest in the F-20 Tigershark, and when this was refused it came close to signing an order for the BAe Hawk, in 1984. Instead, in 1985, the F-5 was acquired in the shape of eight F-5Es and four F-5Fs. This F-5E is taxiing to its 'last chance' point, before take-off, to have the safety tags removed from its SUU-20 dispenser.

Left: Conversion training for the F-16 force is provided by the Air Force's four F-16Ds.

Right: An 'armed' F-5F (note that the weapons 'chalkboard' on the nose has been filled in) taxis to the holding point with a full load of 20-mm ammunition and a practice weapons dispenser on its centreline.

Below: All of Bahrain's F-5s were of late-production standard and fitted with the flattened 'shark' nose and dorsal ILS antenna, but not the extended fin fillet. The F-16 was supposedly acquired to replace the F-5, but there is no sign of Bahrain relinquishing these valuable, versatile aircraft.

Bahrain Amiri Air Force

Above: Three of Bahrain's four F-5Fs are seen here preparing to depart Shaikh Isa AB for another training sortie. Like the single-seaters these F-5Fs wear an air-defence grey scheme, but seem to be tasked with an air-to-ground role.

Below: The Air Wing of the Bahrain Defence Force was established in 1976, with two MBB BO 105Cs. Earlier, in August 1965, the State Police was set up with two Westland Scouts, and it remains a helicopter operator to this day.

Below: The BAAF's rotary-winged fleet is chiefly tasked with policing and VIP roles. Pride of place goes to this VIP-configured UH-60A, the only one of its type in service, which is fitted out with ESSS pylons and external fuel tanks.

Right: Bahrain's para-military Public Security Flying Wing obtained 12 AB 212s which now fly in full BAAF markings, on transport and civilian policing duties. This example is fitted with emergency flotation gear on the skids.

Right: Three MBB (now Eurocopter) BO 105Cs are in service with the BAAF – one for VIP duties and two for general transport duties. The first two were acquired in 1976, with the foundation of the Bahrain Defence Force Air Wing, and the third was acquired the following year.

Below: The Bahrain Amiri Air Force, once a tiny internal security air wing, is now a well-equipped air force with a substantial support infrastructure. Its two front-line combat squadrons are well integrated into an effective C³ system, and its inventory is set to expand.

Sikorsky H-3/S-61 Sea King
Variant Briefing

The Sea King and its derivatives will go down in history as one of Sikorsky's most successful helicopters. During its long and proud service life, the Sea King proved versatile, adaptable and efficient, and this won it enormous popularity. Westland only improved on Sikorsky's fundamentally sound design, and if Sikorsky themselves failed to extract maximum potential from the S-61/H-3, it was only because they had already produced an even more capable successor in the shape of the S-70/H-60 series.

Canada's CH-124s are typical examples of the Sea King success story. Initially purchased as an anti-submarine warfare platform, the aircraft were successfully updated with modern systems including FLIR and took part in the Gulf War.

The Sikorsky SH-3 became something of a 1960s icon through its participation in the recovery of the various Gemini, Mercury and Apollo astronauts after they splashed down. Camouflaged land-based USAF H-3s were regular features of bulletins about Vietnam, and TV stardom was also conferred upon the green-painted VH-3s used by the US Marine Corps and US Army as Presidential helicopters. Few of the watching TV audience would have had any cause to realise that these disparate performers were actually variants of one and the same helicopter, or to guess that the aircraft's primary role was one of hunting submarines. This vital role was carried out well away from the glare of publicity, and out of the limelight.

During World War II, hunting submarines was made easier by the fact that they were basically submersibles, capable of faster running on the surface than under it, and needing to surface frequently to recharge batteries, or to cruise just below the surface using a 'Snort' or schnorkel. By the 1950s, nuclear-powered boats had no need to surface at all, and ran much faster underwater than on the surface. True submarines, they could recycle air or generate oxygen from the water and, as a result, were harder to detect, let alone destroy. This made them a much more deadly threat.

At the same time, naval strategy was increasingly reliant on the use of huge, highly expensive and very vulnerable capital ships, particularly aircraft-carriers, and defending these against the submarine threat was accorded a high priority. Using warships to protect against submarines was one solution, although any destroyer or similar vessel acting as part of an ASW screen could itself become a target. Land-based ASW aircraft were effective but limited a carrier to cruising within range of their land bases, while it was expensive and difficult to keep an ASW aircraft on station all the time. Attention soon focused on providing carriers and major ships with their own organic ASW capability.

The helicopter's rapid reaction capability, coupled with its ability to hover while 'dunking' a powerful sonar transducer into the water, made it potentially an extremely useful ASW tool, as did its 100-kt (115-mph; 185-km/h) speed advantage over the average target submarine. Unfortunately, early helicopters were extremely lacking in payload and range, which severely limited their usefulness since both sensors and weapons appropriate to the ASW role were heavy and bulky. The S-51, in its military R-4 Hoverfly form, could just about get airborne with its pilot and a single passenger; it was not until the introduction of the S-55 and the naval HO4S that it was even possible to carry the most limited payload. The first really effective ASW helicopter was the HSS-1N, the naval version of the S-58. Even this was limited, and the US Navy used the aircraft in hunter/killer pairs, with one carrying sensors and the other weapons.

The introduction of the free turbine or turboshaft engine brought higher power output-to-weight ratios. It was calculated that the T58 was almost as powerful as an R-1820 piston engine yet weighed only 275 lb (125 kg), while the older engine weighed 1,500 lb (680 kg). A pair of the new turboshafts thus weighed slightly more than one third as much as the piston engine, yet produced almost twice the power. The US Navy was not slow in requesting that Sikorsky should build a turbine-powered ASW helicopter that would combine hunter and killer capabilities in a single airframe. The Navy further specified the use of dunking sonar, a weapon load of 840 lb (381 kg) and a four-hour mission endurance. This payload limit allowed for the carriage of a single 550-lb (249-kg) Mk 46 homing torpedo or a nuclear depth bomb.

Sikorsky modelled the resulting S-61 (naval designation HSS-2) on the S-62, which flew first, despite its 'later' designation. The S-62 was

Above: The Sea King's ability to land on water was proudly demonstrated when it entered service. In fact, most of the wet landings were made on rivers and lakes, and pilots exercised great care when making them: several Sea Kings promptly turned upside down and sank.

Left: The HSS-2 quickly proved its capabilities by breaking three world helicopter speed records in a day. Captain Bruce Lloyd and Commander D J Roulstone, both navy test pilots, flew at an average speed of 182.8 mph (294 km/h) over a circuit of 60 miles (100 km) in December 1961.

a single-engined aircraft which retained the dynamic system of the HSS-1, while the S-61 used two turboshaft engines and introduced a new dynamic system, with 62-ft (18.9-m) diameter five-bladed main rotor. The rotor hub was only slightly larger than that of the S-58, and used much the same tried-and-tested technology, with fully articulated blades and oil-lubricated bearings. The blades themselves were similarly conventional, with a D-section aluminium alloy leading-edge spar and honeycomb-filled trailing-edge pockets. Fully automatic power-folding was incorporated to ease stowage on a crowded hangar deck. Rotor-spreading was demonstrated even during Hurricane Donna, in extremely gusty conditions. In order to imply a degree of commonality with the HSS-1 (which in fact did not exist) the new helicopter was designated HSS-2, inevitably corrupted to Hiss Two in speech. At the time, it was felt that a completely new programme would have less chance of receiving funding.

Record breakers

The use of two 1,050-shp (787-kW) General Electric T58-GE-6s conferred superb performance characteristics, and in 1961 Sikorsky used a modified early YHSS-2, flown by Lieutenant Robert W. Crafton and Captain Louis K. Meck, USMC, to set a new world helicopter speed record of 210.6 mph (338.9 km/h) over a 19-mile (30.6-km) straight line course, the first time a helicopter of single-rotor configuration had broken the 200-mph (321.8-km/h) barrier. This marked the culmination of a series of record-breaking flights. On 17 and 24 May 1961, Commander Patrick L. Sullivan and

Lieutenant Beverley W. Witherspoon of the NATC at Patuxent River used a YHSS-2 (coded 6) to set new world speed records (of 192.9 and 174.9 mph/310.4 and 281.5 km/h, respectively) over 3 and 100 km (1.8 and 62 miles). In December 1961 an HSS-2 again set world speed records in runs over the Connecticut shoreline, recording 182.8 mph (294.2 km/h) over 100 km (62 miles), 179.5 mph (288.9 km/h) over 500 km (310.7 miles) and 175.3 mph (282:1 km/h) for 1000 km (620 miles). Previous holders were respectively a YHSS-2 (174.9 mph; 281.5 km/h over 100 km), a US Army UH-1 (148.5 mph; 239.0 km/h over 500 km) and an Army H-34 (132.6 mph; 213.4 km/h over 1000 km). With the earlier 3-km (1.8-mile) record set by the YHSS-

2, this left four of five speed records in Sikorsky's hands. The fifth record, over 15-25 km (9.3-15.5 miles) was held by the Mi-6 and stood at 198.8 mph (320.0 km/h). For its second bout of record breaking, the HSS-2 was flown by Captain Bruce K. Lloyd, with Commander D. J. Jack Roulstone as co-pilot. Both officers were pilots with the NATC. In a subsequent record flight on 30 December 1961, a modified YHSS-2 (147141, with undercarriage and sponsons replaced by streamlined skids) set a new record of 199.01 mph (320.3 km/h) over 3 km, again piloted by NATC officers, this time Commander Patrick L. Sullivan and Captain David A. Spurlock, USMC.

On 6 March 1965, an SH-3A set a helicopter distance record of 2,116 miles (3405 km) by flying non-stop from the carrier USS *Hornet*, steaming near San Diego, to the carrier USS *Roosevelt* at Jacksonville, Florida. This also marked the first non-stop transcontinental helicopter flight. Operational speeds of 140 kt (161 mph; 259 km/h) were recorded routinely, and Navy pilots took the aircraft to 162 kt (186 mph; 300 km/h) during early testing. The aircraft could hover with a useful load equal to 46 per cent of its gross weight.

Perhaps more importantly, the use of twin engines conferred greater reliability, promoting increased crew confidence. The helicopter could fly on one engine at weights of up to 19,000 lb (8618 kg), nearly 2,000 lb (907 kg) over the normal gross weight. The aircraft could even take off on one engine at weights of up to 13,000 lb (5897 kg). Although an engine failure in a low-level hover was still a nightmare scenario, two engines were a decided advantage

over one, where any engine problem meant a ditching. The left-hand engine could be used to power up the accessories on the ground, without turning the rotor. These are normally driven off the tail rotor drive shaft. Both the S-61 and the S-62 used broadly the same airframe, with a boat-shaped hull, outrigger-mounted sponsons and emergency flotation bags. Although it was a relatively large helicopter, the HSS-2 followed Sikorsky's original 'penny-farthing' configuration, with a single lifting rotor and an anti-torque tail rotor. It was sufficiently compact to be used from the decks of some smaller ships, as well as from aircraft-carriers.

Despite the apparent emphasis on flotation aids, the Sea King was never intended for off-the-water operation. Instead, the watertight hull

and flotation gear were provided to keep the aircraft afloat and upright long enough for the crew to make an orderly abandonment after a forced landing and, in modest seas, to keep the aircraft afloat long enough for it to be recovered. Hosts of publicity photos shot by Sikorsky (mainly on the Housatonic River) over the years may have given the impression that off-the-water operations were (or could have been) routine, but this was never the case. Open-sea landings and take-offs were actually demonstrated following a single-engine failure, fortunately in a millpond smooth sea. The primary purpose of the outrigger sponsons was to provide a low-drag stowage for the main undercarriage when retracted, although the undercarriage bays were not covered by doors and thus remained open

The ability of a frigate to deploy a Sea King, with its tactical ASW suite gives it a quantum leap in anti-submarine capability. The Canadian navy's HMCS Nipigon carries a CH-124 in addition to its gun and homing-torpedo armament.

even with the gear up. The tailwheel was fixed. Perhaps the most obvious change in the Sea King was in the location of its engines above the cabin. The engine had been in the nose of the S-55 and S-58 and this had necessitated a horizontally stepped flight deck and main cabin, with the pilot's cockpit accessible only by ladder from the cabin, and then only with some difficulty. The new engine layout allowed straight-through level access from the cabin. Pilot and co-pilot still sat side-by-side, on seats centred 21 in (53 cm) on each side of the centreline, sepa-

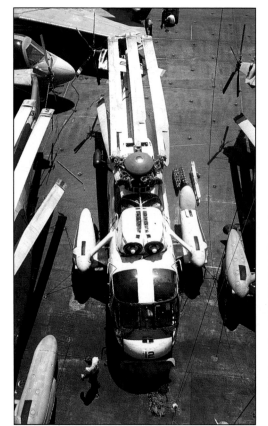

Left: Although it could hardly be classed as a small helicopter, a fully-folded H-3 has very compact dimensions indeed. The aircraft was designed from its inception to have manual tail folding and powered rotor folding, and proved its ability to be prepared even in adverse weather.

Below: The HH-3Fs of the US Coast Guard were among the last to be retired, having proved extremely successful in the search and rescue role and during anti-smuggling operations. A small number of the aircraft were converted CH-3Es but most were new-build airframes.

Many pilots flying in Vietnam owed their lives to the rescue crews of the USAF in their CH-3 and HH-3 'Jolly Green Giants'. The daring missions flown included the abortive Son Tay prison raid and a rescue of a pilot from Haiphong harbour.

rated by a central console containing ASE, radio and navaid controls.

The fuselage itself was of pod and boom construction, and was an all-metal semi-monocoque structure. The tailboom tapered gently from the rear of the cabin, without a distinctive step except at its base, where a step was visible from the cabin/tailboom underside line to the rear part of the boat hull below the cabin floor. The tailboom culminated in a modestly swept tailfin, which carried a fixed, braced half-tailplane to starboard and the five-bladed anti-torque tail rotor to port. The rear part of the tailboom, including the tail rotor pylon, could be manually folded.

Sonar detection

The key sensor in submarine detection during the 1950s was active sonar, which relied on the transmission of electrically generated high-frequency sound and the subsequent reception of its echoes to determine target bearing and range. The sonar transducer (which acted as both transmitter and receiver) could transmit in different patterns, from broad arcs to narrow pencil beams, and could rotate on the cable to 'point' in any given direction. This allowed a target's bearing to be calculated with some precision, assuming that the operator could distinguish between the echo returned by a submarine or, say, by a shoal of mackerel. Active sonar can be used by surface ships, but is usually mounted directly to the hull, which masks transmitted sound and echoes in some directions, and which ensures that the sonar is maintained at what may not be an optimum depth. The dunking sonar of a helicopter can enjoy unobstructed 360° coverage, and can be dipped to different depths to maximise range in different water conditions.

The HSS-1 had used AN/AQS-4 sonar which had a beam width of less than 10°. This meant that 36 individual samplings had to be taken, and it could take up to five minutes to traverse through 360°, far too slow against a modern submarine capable of running at 30 kt (34.5 mph; 55.5 km/h) submerged. The HSS-2 introduced Bendix AN/AQS-10 which had a wider 18° beam width, and which could traverse through 360° in less than a minute.

The effective use of sonar demands extremely accurate flying, especially in the hover, and this is extremely fatiguing, especially in marginal weather. Since the helicopter has no inherent natural stability this infers the need for a sophisticated, accurate and reliable autopilot, just to ensure the kind of hands-off flying which fixed-wing pilots have been able to take for granted for decades. In the Sea King Sikorsky integrated a Ryan APN-130 Doppler radar and radar altimeter, and a Hamilton Standard autostabilisation system. This was able to automatically transition the helicopter from the cruise into a low (50 ft/15 m) hover for sonar dipping, maintain-

ing the aircraft in the hover, motionless in relation to the dunked sonar transducer and then transitioning back to the cruise when required. Hovering lower than 50 ft was not envisaged because the rotor downwash would throw salt spray into the air to be ingested by the engines. Tilting the cable led to it picking up unwanted noise from the rotor downwash, while dragging generates its own noise. Cable trimming could be undertaken by the sonar operator by using a gyro vertical reference or by watching the water pattern underneath. Automatic transition to the hover was felt to be extremely desirable, because studies showed that making a manual transition proved difficult even for extremely experienced pilots in difficult weather conditions.

The basic Sea King's capacious cabin and excellent performance quickly led to its being adopted for a variety of roles apart from ASW. The aircraft was also designed to have a guaranteed life of 1,000 hours for all components. Sometimes adaptation has been a simple matter of stripping out ASW gear (or building an ASW-type airframe without it), but the basic airframe has undergone major redesign too. For

the US Air Force, the airframe was essentially denavalised, losing its amphibious capability and gaining a new tricycle undercarriage, with twin nosewheels and mainwheels retracting into relocated sponsons much further aft. A rear ramp was installed and the tailboom was reduced in size above this. When these helicopters were deployed to Southeast Asia they were painted in two-tone green and tan camouflage and this, coupled with their large and somewhat muscular appearance, led to their 'Jolly Green Giant' nickname, in ironic tribute to the green giant trademark of a major US manufacturer of tinned vegetables. According to one book about the Sea King (*x* by Al Adcock), these aircraft had a "2,000 lb winch carried internally to assist in the loading of bulky cargo." Civilian variants of the S-61 family introduced a stretched fuselage, sometimes with a completely fixed undercarriage, sometimes with sponsons.

The Sea King's many attributes have made it a popular aircraft with overseas customers, as well as with the US Navy, Air Force and Coast Guard. The aircraft was even built under licence in Japan, Canada and Italy, and in Great Britain, and remains in service in large numbers in each

Most navies found operations from small ships were rather awkward for the H-3 due to its size. This SH-3H is fitted with the later type MAD 'bird' on its starboard sponson, which has a single row of holes in its trailing edge.

Several navies have exploited their Sea King's versatility by arming them with missiles, including the Italian navy's combination of ASH-3Ds with anti-ship Marte Mk 2. This weapon has a range of 20 km (12.4 miles).

of these countries. Agusta in Italy and Westland in Britain actually produced significant numbers of Sea Kings for a number of export customers. The H-3 has seen action wherever the US Navy has deployed its aircraft-carriers, performing combat SAR and ASW protection duties. This has included combat operations off Cuba, Libya, the Lebanon, Grenada and Panama, as well as in larger-scale conflicts in Vietnam and during the 1991 Gulf War. The USAF's rescue- and special forces-configured H-3s have also undertaken their share of combat missions, particularly in Vietnam.

The USA's long – and ultimately fruitless and frustrating – involvement in Vietnam provided the Sea King with its baptism of fire. Intervention by foreign submarines was never likely, but the SH-3s deployed aboard the US Navy's aircraft-carriers performed sterling (if largely unsung) service in the combat SAR and VertRep roles. The USAF's H-3s roles included

CSAR and special forces insertion and support. The H-3 provided the main mount for the abortive Son Tay raid, which had aimed to recover downed USAF airmen held as PoWs by the North Vietnamese. They pioneered helicopter inflight-refuelling operations and the mid-air recovery of reconnaissance drones. The crucible of Vietnam also provided the impetus for many alterations made to the Sea King, from improved communications equipment and armour to more powerful engines better able to cope with the rigours of 'hot-and-high' operations.

Among many Sea Kings used in Operation Desert Storm were the five MH-3Es of the USAF's 71st SOS which flew from King Fahd AFB in the combat SAR and special forces support roles. As the Gulf War began the SH-60F was still not in front-line fleet service aboard any of the US Navy's carriers, so SH-3Hs went to war with HS-8 aboard the USS *Independence*,

with HS-9 aboard the USS *Theodore Roosevelt*, with HS-5 aboard the USS *Dwight D. Eisenhower*, and with other units aboard the other deployed carriers. With no perceived submarine threat, US Navy Sea Kings used in theatre were stripped of their ASW equipment and were instead equipped with equipment suitable for the mine-hunting role, and with increased defensive armament. In view of the absence of a serious submarine threat the aircraft did not operate at all in their normal assigned CV inner zone ASW protection role, but instead flew a variety of VertRep, planeguard and utility missions in addition to the mine-hunting task. Other US Navy units operated from shore bases, including the SH-3Gs of HC-2 at Bahrain's Manama International Airport, the Reserve HS-75, which operated SH-3Hs from Diego Garcia. The US Navy Sea King's were ably backed by the CH-124s of Canada's 423 Squadron aboard the frigates HMCS *Athabaskan*, *Protecteur* and *Terra Nova*.

Cold War stalwart

'Hot' wars are always more exciting and attention-grabbing than 'cold' ones, but it should be recorded that the Sea King in US Navy service made a major contribution to the deterrent posture which averted a superpower conflict for the whole of the 1950s, 1960s, 1970s and 1980s. And had deterrence ever failed, the Sea King would have played a major role in hunting the Soviet submarines that could have threatened Western nations with their nuclear-armed missile, and the submarines that would have threatened the Atlantic sea lanes which would have been so vital to keeping NATO forces in Europe resupplied. An offshoot of the Cold War was the Space Race

Among the many duties of the Sea Kings of the US Sixth Fleet, the most important was the tracking of Soviet submarines through the Mediterranean. The SH-3H was fitted with an improved tactical ASW suite and fuel system improvements, but did not have the ESM system and radar originally planned for it.

Another constant duty for SH-3 crews was flying 'plane guard' sorties, ready to rescue any pilot who ditched after a catapult launch. This SH-3H from HS-4 is lifting off from the carrier USS Carl Vinson (CVN-70) prior to fixed-wing operations commencing during a NATO exercise. The SH-3H remained in service with seven squadrons during the Gulf War.

Argentina received four S-H3Ds from Sikorsky in 1978, as well as four AS-61s from Agusta (built virtually to SH-3H standard) which were delivered in 1987. Another SH-3D was delivered in VIP transport configuration.

between the two superpowers, and the Sea King even played a vital role in this, recovering capsules when they splashed down. In fact, such recovery options were far more complicated than the public might have realised, and each involved a team of Sea King helicopters using various standardised callsigns. SWIM I and SWIM II carried the teams of frogmen dropped to assist the astronauts from their capsules, while RECOVERY I actually carried the recovered astronauts to the carrier. Since national pride was a primary consideration in the space missions, these recoveries were of course televised live, and the Sea King flotilla was usually completed by PHOTO I carrying TV cameramen and technicians and RELAY I which provided a link between the low-flying helicopters and rebroadcast stations on task force ships.

It was this unfought war that determined the evolution of the SH-3, with sensors and equipment being refined or replaced. Some new sensors and weapons were added in response to the evolving Soviet submarine threat, and to fit in better with the US Navy's ever changing and evolving ASW tactics. Perhaps the greatest challenge came with the retirement of the US Navy's dedicated ASW carriers. Suddenly, the SH-3 would have to be deployed aboard the big supercarriers, and would have to perform SAR, surface surveillance and ASV missions, in addition to its traditional ASW mission. This led to the development of the final ASW version, the SH-3H.

Sea King classification

Although British Sea Kings could fairly neatly be categorised into three generations according to engine power, with sub-species using virtually the same airframe with minor changes to windows and bulkheads, classifying the Sikorsky S-61 family is less easy. There were three basic airframes: the original SH-3 (S-61A) amphibious ASW airframe, the non-amphibious, ramp-equipped CH/HH-3 (S-61R) and the stretched airliner-type S-61L and S-61N airframe. Within these broad families aircraft differed in equipment, armament and fuel tankage. Powerplants were usually a pair of T58-GE-5s (or their equivalent), although these were uprated, and were not introduced straight away. A handful of variants also used the T58-GE-8 and T58-GE-10 engines.

And while Sikorsky's Stratford factory never rolled out a Sea King as 'improved' as, for example, the Westland Sea King Mk 2C, with its powerful engines, advanced composite rotors and modern systems, the company did use Sea King dynamics for two of its most advanced research aircraft. The first of these was the S-67 Blackhawk, an advanced attack helicopter with a slender, low cross-section fuselage seating pilot and gunner in tandem, with stub wings, an undernose gun turret and astonishing agility. This was the closest Sikorsky ever came to the

Soviet Mi-24, and the production S-67 would even have included a troop-carrying cabin. The S-67 was fitted with the engine, transmission and rotor system of the S-61R (HH-3E) and broke several world helicopter speed records, but was not selected for production. Another S-61 'Hind' was produced by Court Helicopters in South Africa, who modified at least one S-61 to resemble a Mil Mi-24 for use in the motion picture Red Dawn.

The S-72 RSRA (Rotor System Research Aircraft) was an experimental compound helicopter which combined conventional wings and TF34-GE-400 turbofans with T58 turboshafts and a Sea King derived rotor and transmission system. With these it could fly either as a helicopter or as a fixed-wing aircraft, even taking off and landing in one configuration and cruising in the other. As a major military workhorse, Sea Kings were used or requested for a huge number of experimental programmes and experiments, some of which never made it

beyond the drawing board. One such project was an Army ARPA project to produce a quiet helicopter, for which an SH-3A was to have been modified with a very slow turning 10-bladed main rotor. Unfortunately, the project was cancelled before the advantages of such a rotor could be demonstrated.

The late 1980s and early 1990s saw a dramatic decline for the H-3. The US Coast Guard has now retired the last of its HH-3Fs, and the USAF's last HH-3Es have also been withdrawn from use. While virtually all of the US Navy's front-line ASW-roled SH-3s have now been replaced by SH-60F Sea Hawks, the type remains in widespread use in second-line roles in the US Navy, and the aircraft remains in use with many of its foreign customers. It is certainly too early to write off the Sea King, which continues to add to its distinguished history, although to Sikorsky themselves the S-61 is yesterdays news, overshadowed by the newer S-70 family. **Jon Lake**

With the cancellation of the Canadian EH 101 order, the CH-124 may serve for longer than had originally been envisaged. When the last Sikorsky Sea Kings are finally retired, this design will be at least half a century old.

Sikorsky H-3/S-61 Variants

XHSS-2

The original contract for the then-unnamed Sea King called for a single prototype and six pre-production aircraft, but this was soon amended to give a trials batch of 10 aircraft. The prototype Sea King (147137) was designated XHSS-2 under the pre-1962 US Navy designation system, with HS indicating helicopter, anti-submarine, and the second S being Sikorsky's manufacturer's code. The X prefix indicated the aircraft's experimental status. In fact, the XHSS-2 differed little from the pre-production YHSS-2s and production HSS-2s which followed it. Sikorsky's engineers had done a great job with the basic Sea King, and few changes were necessary. Visually, the XHSS-2 differed from later aircraft in having a shallow box-like fairing on the starboard fuselage side, over the front part

The first HSS-2 prototype demonstrated its ability to land on water with a highly publicised display on a lake in Connecticut. The HSS-2 was the first all-weather helicopter in US Navy service.

of the door runner. This was unique to the first prototype. The XHSS-2 also had a very much smaller undernose fairing and no Doppler antenna, and had a small 'forehead' antenna fairing at the top of the central windscreen frame. These features were initially retained by the YHSS-2s.

The XHSS-2 made its maiden flight on 17 March 1959, in the hands of 'Yip' Yurrel. It was powered by a pair of General Electric T58-GE-6 turboshafts, each rated at 1,050 shp (787.5 kW). These were fed by bell-mouthed intakes, de-iced for all-weather

operation. In addition to its ASW sensors and provision for weapons, the XHSS-2 was fitted with a 600-lb (272-kg) capacity rescue winch above the cabin door, with 300 ft (91.44 m) of cable. The basic empty weight was 9,763 lb (4429 kg), although this quickly

grew to 9,953 lb (4515 kg), and normal gross weight was 17,300 lb (7847 kg). Maximum gross weight was 26,500 lb (12020 kg). Some sources indicate that the sole XHSS-2 was eventually redesignated as a YHSS-2.

YHSS-2

The remaining nine aircraft from the initial batch of 10 aircraft (147138 to 147146) were designated as YHSS-2s, the Y prefix indicating their service test status. They were later redesignated as YSH-3As following the 1962 reorganisation of the designation system. The YHSS-2s shouldered the burden of most early testing, including the Navy Board of Inspection and Survey trials at NAS Patuxent River. They were flown by Air Test and Evaluation

aircrew from the NATC's Rotary Wing Aircraft Test Directorate.

Two aircraft were used for carrier suitability trials aboard the USS *Lake Champlain* during a week-long cruise along the Atlantic Coast in early 1961. These demonstrated 100 per cent availability, automatic blade folding and spreading in winds of up to 45 kt (52 mph; 83 km/h), rotor run-ups and take-offs in winds of up to 48 kt (55 mph; 89 km/h), and demonstrated making engine starts, blade spreads and rotor turn-ups downwind; an unprecedented performance. After shutdown, the YHSS-2s

proved more than twice as quick to secure in the hangar deck (from the flight deck) than ASW types then in service. Several of the pre-production aircraft were later brought up to full SH-3A or UH-3A standards and entered productive service with front-line squadrons.

A batch of nine YHSS-2s followed the first prototype, and were used to fully validate the Sea King's versatility, reliability and efficiency in intensive flight trials.

HSS-2 (SH-3A)

The first HSS-2s weighed in at 18,000 lb (8165 kg) and were powered by a pair of 1,050-shp (787.5-kW) T58-GE-6 turboshafts. T58-GE-8B engines of 1,250 shp (937.5 kW) were introduced from the 20th aircraft, with T58-GE-8F engines on later aircraft. The increased power was welcome since gross weight had increased to 19,100 lb (8664 kg). HS-1 at NAS Key West acted as the conversion and demonstration unit, training 10 pilots and 48 enlisted personnel from the first operational unit, HS-3 at NAS Norfolk, followed by five pilots and 24 enlisted men from HS-10 at NAS Ream Field, San Diego. HS-2, another early unit, developed the technique of inflight refuelling from a destroyer, winning itself a Navy Unit Commendation.

The aircraft was redesignated as the SH-3A under the unified tri-service designation system introduced in 1962. S stood for anti-submarine, H stood for helicopter, 3 indicated that it was the third type of helicopter in use (taking 1962 as a baseline, and making third place alphabetically after the Bell H-1 and Kaman H-2), and A indicated that it was the first production variant.

An SH-3A from HS-6 releases a dummy torpedo during weapon trials. The SH-3A was the first service helicopter to combine the submarine hunter/killer functions in one airframe, greatly expanding operational effectiveness.

The first SH-3As were delivered to their squadrons in an overall midnight-blue colour scheme, to which Dayglo noses (and often tail pylons) were added fairly soon. Codes, serials and other markings were applied in brilliant white. This remained the most common SH-3A colour scheme for many years, although three-tone camouflage and overall battleship-grey schemes (with black codes) were sometimes used in Vietnam.

The SH-3A could carry a heavy weapon load in the ASW role, with up to four Mk 46 or Mk 48 torpedoes, or a single 510-lb (231-kg) Mk 57 nuclear depth bomb or 1,200-lb (544-kg) Lulu nuclear depth bomb. Bendix AN/AQS-10 sonar was fitted (though some SH-3As may have been retrofitted with AQS-13) and was the primary ASW sensor. AN/APN-130 Doppler was used to maintain a stable hover over the dunked sonar transducer. The first SH-3As were not fitted with Doppler antenna fairings and lacked flotation bags on the sponsons, but these items were usually retrofitted.

With a production total of 245 (excluding the YSH-3As), the SH-3A was the most numerous new-build Sea King. Bureau numbers ran from 148033-148052, 148964-149012, 149679-149738, 149893-149934, 150618-150620, 151522-151557 and 152104-152138. Conversions were made to CH-3A, HH-3A, NH-3A, NSH-3A, RH-3A, VH-3A, CH-3B, SH-3D, SH-3G, and SH-3H standards.

A handful of late SH-3As incorporated features normally associated with later Sea King variants. These included the AN/ASQ-81 towed MAD bird (whose winch was installed in a recontoured starboard undercarriage sponson) of the SH-3D, and

This SH-3A was fitted with large suppressors around the engines and an intake filter box during noise reduction experiments.

the SH-3H's 24 Mk 25 marine marker launch tubes in an extended port undercarriage sponson, and the 12 size A sonobuoy launch tubes in the rear cabin. One SH-3A was used for noise reduction experiments, with box-like suppressors over the exhausts and with a box-like filter in front of the intakes, similar in shape to the APME Centrisep filters used by some Westland Sea King and Commando variants.

A single SH-3A (149723) was bailed to NASA (as NASA 538) for the development of blind flying and blind landing equipment. The aircraft was fitted with a 14-in (36-cm) TV monitor in front of the co-pilot's position, with a massive box-like fairing projecting from the windscreen. This displayed imagery captured by a CCTV camera projecting from the lower left-hand cockpit window, and by an IR scanner. A second TV camera was mounted on the fuselage side

NASA used this SH-3A for a number of trials. Here it is seen with the radar of the USCG HH-3F model. Note the instrumentation boom.

just aft of the port undercarriage sponson. The same aircraft was later reserialled as NASA 735 and was used for a variety of trials, including tests of the nose-mounted radar installation designed for the Coast Guard's HH-3F.

Two SH-3As (148998 and 151544) were converted to SH-3D standards, and many more (over 150) to SH-3G and SH-3H configuration. Japan's initial aircraft, and the Canadian CHSS-2s (later redesignated as CH-124s), were broadly equivalent to the SH-3A.

After replacement in the front-line anti-submarine role by the SH-3D, many A models continued to give valuable service as utility helicopters. This aircraft of HC-6 has had engine intake filters fitted.

CH-3A

The CH-3A designation was briefly applied to three SH-3As acquired by the US Air Force from the US Navy. These were BuNos 149009, 149011 and 149012 and were reserialed as 62-12571 to 62-12573. They were used for offshore radar site support, and tripled monthly cargo and passenger totals by comparison with the fleet of nine piston-engined helicopters which the trio replaced. After the adoption

of the integrated Tri-service designation system they were soon redesignated as CH-3Bs to avoid duplication of the A suffix by the Navy and Air Force. A subsequent batch of new-build aircraft to the same standard was delivered later in 1962, and was designated CH-3B from the start. The aircraft were usually left with a polished metal finish and standard national markings and codes, as were the CH-3Bs.

The CH-3As were operated by the 551st Base Flight to support the Texas Tower radar rigs.

HH-3A

Twelve SH-3As were converted at NAS Quonsett Point to HH-3A standards for use in the combat search and rescue role. More may have been subsequently brought up to the same standards. These included 148036, 149682, 149896 (the prototype), 149903, 149912, 149916, 149922, 149933, 151531, 151552, 151553 and 151556. All ASW equipment was removed and the sonar well was covered over. The cabin floor was reinforced and armour protection was provided in the form of titanium panels in the cockpit floor and around the transmission, while the crew had armoured seats. Emerson Electric TAT-102 turrets were fitted in barbettes behind each sponson, each containing a 7.62-mm General Electric Minigun, sighted by the crewman (from bubble windows like those of the earlier RH-3A) or from the cockpit.

The HH-3A also incorporated several features already developed for the SH-3D or SH-3G. More powerful T58-GE-8F engines were fitted to cope with the increased all-up weight. The aircraft was fitted with a 'Highdrink' refuelling system with hoist, and had provision under the stub wings for the carriage of auxiliary tanks instead of the SH-3's homing torpedos. Conversions were undertaken by the US Navy at Quonset Point using Sikorsky-built kits. The first aircraft were delivered to HC-7 'Big Muthas' at Cubi Point in the Philippines at the end of 1970, for onward deployment to Vietnam. Standard SH-3As were already in

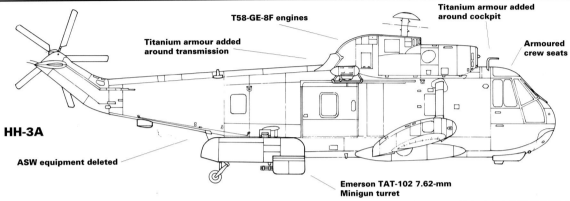

T58-GE-8F engines

Titanium armour added around cockpit

Titanium armour added around transmission

Armoured crew seats

HH-3A

ASW equipment deleted

Emerson TAT-102 7.62-mm Minigun turret

widespread use in the SAR role with other units, including VC-8, while the dedicated HH-3F was entering service with the Coast Guard. The TAT-102 barbettes caused centre of gravity problems and were soon replaced by door-mounted GAU-2B/A 7.62-mm Miniguns, each with four 1,500-round ammunition canisters. The last HH-3As were retired from HC-9 'Protectors' in 1990. Some HH-3As were converted back to ASW/utility configuration as SH-3Gs and SH-3Hs after their retirement.

HH-3As served largely in an overall dark green scheme. The cabin door usually mounted a Minigun. This aircraft was on the strength of HS-1.

NH-3A

A single SH-3A (148033) was modified for high-speed research under a joint Army/Navy contract. The aircraft gained a more streamlined fuselage, with a fully retractable undercarriage and new sponsons faired entirely into the fuselage. Two 3,000-lb st (13.35-kN) thrust Pratt & Whitney J60-P-2 turbojets were mounted on the fuselage sides, and the tail surfaces were increased in area to provide stability at higher speeds, with a low-set tailplane on each side of the fin. An adjustable rudder was also fitted. Redesignated NH-3A (S-61F), the aircraft flew in its new compound

configuration on 21 May 1965. The helicopter achieved a record speed of 242 mph (390 km/h) using a modified six-bladed main rotor with reduced torque twist. It was then further modified, with wings of 32-ft (9.75-m) span, full-span flaperons, and a new six-bladed tail rotor. The senior project engineer was George B. Chesley, ably assisted by Frederic C. DeSibert and Evan A. Fradenburgh.

The much-modified NH-3A was built for speed, with turbojets added either side of the fuselage and short wings added for extra lift. The new tail incorporated a rudder.

NSH-3A

A single SH-3A (149704/14) was converted to serve as the US Navy's only MARS- (Mid-Air Recovery System) equipped helicopter.

The system was primarily intended for the retrieval of SAMOS (Satellite and Missile Observation System) satellite camera film capsules. Twin extendable arms, equipped with grappling hooks, were intended to snag a parachute or balloon cable which

would then be reeled in. The arms pivoted down from the mid-fuselage, adjacent to the undercarriage sponsons, with a hydraulic hoist in the cabin and a remote camera on the cabin side allowing the operator to watch the final stages of a drone retrieval.

Netting was placed over the sponson/fuselage intersection, to prevent inadvertent snagging of the balloon or parachute. The MARS system was used by the USAF on CH-3C and CH/HH-3E helicopters to recover drones over Vietnam.

RH-3A

Nine SH-3As were converted to RH-3A standards for mine countermeasures duties under a $2.05 million contract placed by the Bureau of Naval Weapons as a supplement to an existing fixed-fee contract for SH-3A ASW helicopters. These included 147140 and 148038. The RH-3A was fitted with T58-GE-8B or -8F engines and had an extra full-size cargo door on the port side, and had bubble observation windows in the rear of the cabin. A special squadron, HM-12, was formed to operate the new variant. The RH-3A was the first US Navy helicopter capable of streaming and recovering its own towed minesweeping gear, previous less powerful helicopters having towed gear streamed and recovered by a surface

vessel. Three RH-3As of HM-12 operated from the mine countermeasures vessels *Ozark* (in the Atlantic) and three from the *Catskill* (in the Pacific). The remaining three aircraft were used for tests and training. Having proved the concept of helicopter mine countermeasures, but having also demonstrated little power margin thanks to the bulk of the minesweeping gear, the RH-3As of HM-12 were replaced by larger, more powerful RH-53s in 1972.

The RH-3A pioneered helicopter minesweeping operations, but the equipment for this role was really too heavy for the airframe and better suited to the later RH-53. The variant was used in its design role in Vietnam.

Sikorsky H-3/S-61 Variants

VH-3A

The first use of a helicopter by the US President dated back to 1957, when President Eisenhower needed to make a fast return from Newport, Rhode Island, to Washington. A standard Marine Corps UH-34 was summoned to transport the President to a local airport where he completed the journey in a fixed-wing aircraft. This led directly to the formation of a USAF Presidential helicopter flight equipped first with a Bell 47J, then with the H-34. With more rotary-wing experience than the USAF, the Army and Marine Corps took over responsibility for the Presidential helicopter mission in 1958.

Eight VIP versions of the S-61 were built as HSS-2Zs under a US Navy contract for use in the VIP transport role. They wore the BuNos 150610 to 150617. A ninth was produced by the conversion of SH-3A 147141. The machines were powered by a pair of T58-GE-8E engines, and had an APU or Auxiliary Power Plant (APP) in a teardrop fairing scabbed onto the upper surface of the rear part of the starboard undercarriage sponson. The aircraft were operated by the US Army and Marine Corps as those service's contributions to the joint-services Presidential air transport commitment, using the callsigns MARINE ONE or ARMY ONE when the President was aboard, or MARINE TWO with the Vice President aboard, or STATE ONE with a foreign head

of state aboard. The Presidential seal was attached to a special mounting on the door when he was aboard. Two of the aircraft (150613 and 150617) were actually painted in Army markings, but Army and Marine crews tended to man whichever aircraft was available. The aircraft were luxuriously fitted out for use in the VIP role, with carpeting from cockpit to tail, radio telephones, a wet bar, toilets and extensive sound-proofing. During the Kennedy administration the aircraft were fitted with customised chairs. The aircraft were wildly over-maintained, with all components replaced at half life. The result was astonishing reliability and great customer confidence. An HMX-1 VH-3 was used by President Nixon to make the 200-mile (321-km) overwater flight to the carrier *Hornet* to welcome the Apollo XI astronauts.

The VIP version was redesignated VH-3A when the new designation system was adopted. One VH-3A (150614) was modified with some of the features which later became standard on the later VH-3D, including the new bifilar absorber in the main rotor head, the characteristic dorsal hump and a refined tail rotor pylon with greater tail surface area and an increased area tail rotor, requiring less power input, thereby diverting less power from the main rotor. It was designated NVH-3A. When the VH-3A was replaced by the later VH-3D, one of the older aircraft was presented to Egypt's President Anwar Sadat by President Nixon.

Above: Two VH-3As wore 'Army' titles in service with the Executive Flight Detachment (HMX-1).

Below: The single NVH-3A (seen here with NAWC-AD) tested features of the VH-3D.

CH-3B

Three Navy HSS-2s (149009, 149011 and 149012) were transferred to the USAF in April 1962, configured as 27-seat transports. They were assigned to the 551st Base Flight and were used specifically for transporting men and supplies between Otis AFB, Massachusetts, to the Texas Tower radar sites in the Atlantic. They were reserialled as 62-12571 to 62-12573. These first three aircraft were initially known as CH-3A-SIs. Three more SH-3As were acquired later as CH-3B-SIs, the designation also being applied to the first three aircraft.

The second batch of CH-3s were newly-built and were serialled as 62-12574 to 62-12576. They never had US Navy Bureau numbers allocated. 62-12574 and 62-12575

were later transferred to the US Navy and were converted to SH-3H configuration for use by HS-10. All six aircraft were powered by 1,250-shp (937.5-kW) T58-GE-8B engines, and had dipping sonar, ASW

equipment and external weapons racks deleted. Sikorsky designated these aircraft as S-61As, while the USAF designated them CH-3B after the 1962 unified system was introduced. A CH-3B nicknamed 'Otis

The CH-3B was a very useful transport helicopter, despite lacking the refinements of the CH-3C. It augmented CH-3As supporting the offshore radar platforms.

Falcon' (62-12574) made history during the period 27 May to 5 June 1963 by flying across the Atlantic to Paris, France via Labrador (Canada), Greenland, Iceland and Scotland. This leisurely voyage nevertheless broke the time and distance records for a helicopter crossing of the Atlantic. Malaysia's S-61A-4s were broadly equivalent to the CH-3B, while Denmark's S-61A-4s were built basically to CH-3B standards but were fitted with larger S-61N type sponsons for extra stability on the water. One CH-3B was built for a civilian customer.

CH-3C

Sikorsky originally schemed a variant of the S-61 with a rear loading ramp in 1959, when it proposed the HR3S-1 to the US Marine Corps. This reached mock-up stage, and was demonstrated to Canada, but it remained unbuilt. The helicopter had stretched forward and rear fuselages, but retained standard S-61-type sponsons and a tailwheel. The new cabin was intended to accommodate 27 troops or up to 8,000 lb (3629 kg) of cargo. The aircraft had a large cabin entrance door forward on the starboard side, and a hydraulically actuated split rear loading ramp giving access to a hatch with vertical dimensions of 78 in (1.98 m) high and 74 in (1.88 m) wide.

The first S-61 version specifically designed for the USAF, the CH-3C was similar to the HR3S-1 in many ways, although it had redesigned and relocated sponsons well aft, and a retractable nosewheel. The sponsons faired directly into the fuselage, and were not carried on stub wings. They were unbraced and fully covered the undercarriage when retracted. They retained a high degree of buoyancy, for use in an emergency ditching, and this helped when amphibious versions of the S-61R were developed later. The CH-3C retained the internal Sikorsky designation S-61R originally allocated to the HR3S-1. Designed to meet the USAF's Specific Operational Requirement 109, the aircraft also introduced a much narrower tailboom, with a more upright and taller fin/tail rotor pylon, and with a longer-span, strut-braced tailplane. The tailboom also had a flat catwalk on the upper surface to allow maintenance access to the tail rotor and tail rotor pylon.

The new stretched cabin had a utility

cargo floor whose area was increased to 168 sq ft (15.61 m²) stressed to loads of 200 lb/sq in (1379 kPa). Internal cabin height was reduced by 0.5 in (1.3 cm) to 6 ft 3 in (1.91 m), while cabin length increased to 25 ft 10.5 in (7.89 m). Cabin volume increased to 1,050 cu ft (29.73 m³). It could accommodate 25 troops, 15 litters, two Jeeps, seven 40-in by 48-in (1.02-m x 1.22-m) pallets, or 5,000 lb (2267 kg) of freight or cargo, and the helicopter was intended to carry such loads over a distance of 206 nm (238 miles; 383 km), at a specified cruising speed of 126 kt (145 mph; 233 km/h). Range increased to 703 nm (810 miles; 1303 km) when load was reduced to 2,400 lb (1089 kg). The internal fuel capacity of the S-61R was slightly reduced by comparison with the ASW aircraft, with 340 US gal (1287 litres) in the forward cell and 310 US gal (1173 litres) in the rear cell. Two 440-US gal (1665-litre) auxiliary tanks could be carried in the cabin. A 2,000-lb (907-kg) capacity internal winch was fitted to ease cargo handling, while the external cargo hook could carry up to 6,000 lb (2721 kg) or 8,000 lb (3628 kg) with a low-response

This CH-3C took part in the first helicopter air-to-air refuelling trials with a Marine Corps KC-130F from Cherry Point, North Carolina.

sling. A 600-lb (272-kg) capacity external winch was carried, with 250 ft (76 m) of cable and a jungle penetrator. Airframe changes increased overall length (rotors turning) to 72 ft 10 in (22.20 m), or 60 ft 11 in (18.57 m) with the rotor blades folded.

The aircraft was optimised for ease of operation, and for use without extensive

ground facilities. Pressurised pre-tracked and non-folding main rotor blades were fitted to ease inspection and to simplify crack detection, while main and tail rotors were self-lubricating. The CH-3C was also fitted with a built-in Solar T62T gas turbine APU, while comprehensive built-in test equipment was also provided.

CH-3C

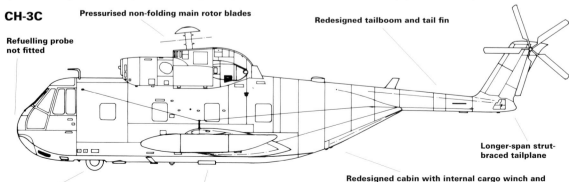

Pressurised non-folding main rotor blades

Redesigned tailboom and tail fin

Refuelling probe not fitted

Longer-span strut-braced tailplane

Retractable nosewheel

New faired sponson design

Redesigned cabin with internal cargo winch and hydraulically operated rear ramp

A letter contract for an initial 22 CH-3Cs was placed on 8 February 1963, and the first was rolled out on 6 June, three weeks ahead of schedule. The first CH-3C (Sikorsky's own demonstrator, registered N664Y, and initially painted in a civilian colour scheme) made its maiden flight on 17 June 1963, almost a month early. The initial CH-3C was formally handed over to the USAF on 30 December 1963, for joint military testing and FAA certification, which took the place of normal USAF Category 1 testing. FAA and Sikorsky test pilots flew both military and civilian S-61R versions for certification. Category 2 testing was then undertaken at Edwards, and Category 3 testing at Stead AFB. Category 3 testing was actually carried out by the ARS itself. The first examples of the new variant were delivered to Air Defense Command at Tyndall AFB for drone recovery duties in January 1964, the same month in which SAC received an aircraft to evaluate its suitability for transporting personnel and equipment to Minuteman ICBM sites.

The first operational CH-3C was handed over to the USAF's ARS on 27 May 1964. An ARS detachment was established at

Patrick AFB to support Gemini launches and other space shots, standing by to recover astronauts or equipment in the event of a launch failure or problem. Another early user was the Air Photo and Charting Service of the Military Air Transport Service, which used the aircraft for geodetic survey work. MATS also received CH-3Cs for recovering weather balloon sondes. The CH-3Cs were powered by a pair of 1,250-shp (938-kW) T58-GE-1 engines, USAF versions of the Navy's T58-GE-8. The CH-3C was used in Vietnam by the 20th Helicopter Squadron to haul millions of pounds of supplies, averaging 400,000 lb (181440 kg) per month. These included covert ('Pony Express') missions in support of US special forces troops operating against the Ho Chi Minh Trail, using black and darkly camouflaged CH-53Cs, including one (63-9676 *Black Maria*) now preserved in the USAF Museum. The NVA reportedly offered a bounty of US$50,000 to any soldier who could shoot down this helicopter, but the prize went uncollected.

A handful of CH-3Cs (reportedly a dozen) were modified for greater effectiveness in the combat SAR role, with additional armour

Most CH-3Cs wore a silver scheme with a yellow band round the rear fuselage. This later changed to three-tone camouflage as the aircraft went to war in Southeast Asia.

for the crew and transmission, and provision for M60 7.62-mm machine-guns in the doors and on the rear ramp. The aircraft were also fitted with HH-3E-type sponsons with provision for the installation of a pair of external 200-US gal (757-litre) auxiliary tanks. Additional fuel tankage was provided inside the sponsons themselves. These modified aircraft were known (unofficially at least) as HH-3Cs and included 64-14277. Four were lost in Vietnam.

Some of the CH-3Cs and HH-3Cs in Southeast Asia were fitted with MARS (Mid-Air Recovery System) gear for the inflight retrieval of Ryan reconnaissance drones launched from DC-130 Hercules aircraft. On the CH-3C/HH-3C the MARS system's grappling rods were fitted to the aft fuselage sides above the rear ramp. During the period between 1964 and 1975, MARS was used for the successful retrieval of over 2,655 drones. The MARS-equipped aircraft included 65-12800.

Seventy-five CH-3Cs were eventually built, serialled 62-12577 to 62-12582, 63-9676 to 63-9691, 64-14221 to 64-14237, 65-5690 to 65-5700, 65-12511 and 65-12777 to 65-12800. One (62-12581) was temporarily assigned to test duties under the designation JCH-3C.

Many examples were subsequently converted to CH-3E or HH-3E configuration. The conversion to CH-3E was

straightforward, entailing little more than a change of engine. At least 41 CH-3E conversions included 62-12578, 62-12580, 62-12581, 63-9676, 63-9679, 63-9683, 63-9686, 63-9687, 63-9690, 63-9691, 64-14221, 64-14223, 64-14224, 64-14225, 64-14226, 64-14228, 64-14234, 64-14235, 65-5690, 65-5692, 65-5693, 65-5696, 65-5697, 65-5698, 65-5699, 65-5700, 65-12778, 65-12779, 65-12786, 65-12788, 65-12789, 65-12790, 65-12791, 65-12792, 65-12793, 65-12795, 65-12796, 65-12797, 65-12798, 65-12799, and 65-12800. Eleven of these converted CH-3Cs including 62-12580, 62-12581, 63-9690, 64-14221, 65-5698, 65-5699, 65-5700, 65-12792, 65-12795, 65-12796 and 65-12800 were subsequently converted to JCH-3E standards and went to the US Army.

A smaller number of aircraft (at least 11) were converted to HH-3E configuration, some subsequently becoming JHH-3Es for the US Army. These conversions included 64-14230 (JHH-3E), 64-14232 (JHH-3E), 65-12780, 65-12781, 65-12782, 65-12783 (JHH-3E), 65-12784, 65-12785, 65-12787 (JHH-3E), and 65-12794.

A single CH-3C was temporarily assigned to test duties as the JCH-3C, testing avionics and equipment for future helicopters. It later became a CH-3E and subsequently became a JCH-3E. As the JCH-3C the aircraft tested the bifilar for the VH-3D, and was one of a number of CH-3Cs which tested the ice-shield/foreign object deflector subsequently fitted to the CH-3E, HH-3E, SH-3G and SH-3H. As a JCH-3C the aircraft was based at Wright-Patterson AFB and wore a smart grey and white colour scheme and the badge of Aeronautical Systems Command.

SH-3D

The SH-3D followed the SH-3A on the Stratford production line and was a refined and enhanced ASW version of the Sea King. An incomplete SH-3A was converted on the production line with a pair of uprated T58-GE-10 engines to serve as the prototype. This single YSH-3D prototype (actually the last aircraft of the last SH-3A contract, BuNo.152139) was followed by 72 production SH-3Ds. These had BuNos from 152690-152713, 154100-154123, 156483-156506. Six more (153532-153537) were built for the Spanish navy. Despite the small number of actual SH-3Ds built by Sikorsky, the type was of huge significance and importance. The S-61D-3 for Brazil and S-61D-4 for Argentina were similar to the SH-3D, while versions of the SH-3D were licence-built in Britain, Italy and Japan.

The SH-3D was powered by a pair of 1,400-shp (1050-kW) T58-GE-10 engines, with an uprated gearbox capable of absorbing a combined 2,500 shp (1875 kW). An additional 140-US gal (530-litre) tank was fitted in the fuselage and the aircraft was given a longer-span, braced horizontal stabiliser, similar to that fitted to the CH-3C. Some SH-3D conversions lacked this long-span tail, however. ASW role equipment was improved significantly. The SH-3A's AQS-10 sonar was replaced by the 180° beamwidth AN/AQS-13A sonar. Most SH-3Ds also had the new AN/APN-182 Doppler in place of the old AN/APN-130 Doppler. An AN/ASN-50 heading reference system was also fitted. Structural modifications allowed an increase in gross weight to 20,500 lb (9300 kg). Armament

was reduced to a pair of torpedoes, but these were carried on variable launch rails which allowed them to be launched from a low hover as well as from forward flight. Photographic evidence shows that some SH-3Ds were fitted with long-chord sponsons and MAD, like the SH-3H.

Some reports suggest that about six SH-3Ds were modified for the combat SAR role, in a similar fashion to the HH-3A derivative of the original SH-3A. The HH-3D designation was not allocated, however. Eleven similar aircraft were built for the VIP role as VH-3Ds (which see). The new powerplant package was used to transform the CH-3C into the CH-3E, and served as the basis for most subsequent Sikorsky-built Sea King variants.

Sikorsky started implementing a SLEP on an initial group of 26 SH-3Ds during 1987. The $100 million programme stressed reliability and maintainability improvements, and modernised aircraft were redesignated as SH-3Hs. The programme covered airframe improvements and 10 ECPs (Engineering Change Proposals) covering the retrofit of government-furnished equipment items. The SLEP was designed in the form of a kit, so that it could be incorporated at the Pensacola Naval Aviation Depot. Airframe and system changes included the replacement of key airframe frames and members, especially in the area supporting the transmission system. Changes were made to the main rotor head to reduce oil and grease leaks, with a bifilar to reduce vibration, while the main gearbox was upgraded with two new higher capacity pumps. Changes were also made to the tail rotor gearbox, drive shaft and primary servo. Crashworthy seats were installed, and a

solid-state autostab amplifier was fitted. The aircraft also received an emergency lighting system for use when the crew had to egress at night. Key systems were added, improved or replaced, with a new ASN-123 tactical navigation system, improved cockpit consoles, an AKT-22 datalink, an ARR-75 sonobuoy receiver and provision for AN/ALE-37A chaff/flare dispenser. Soundproofing was improved, and a new intake ice shield was added, while the aircraft also received a 12-chute sonobuoy launcher. The original ASN-50 compass was replaced by an A/A-24G-39 compass, the AN/ARC-159 UHF was upgraded to dual capability, and improvements were made to the AQS-13E sonar processing and display systems. The hover inflight-refuelling equipment was relocated and high-speed pumps were installed to increase the fuel dump rate from 180 to 840 US gal (681 to 3180 litres) per minute.

Many redundant Sea Kings of all variants were redirected to utility tasks once their front-line days were over. This SH-3D had its anti-submarine equipment removed, and was used in the late 1980s as a transport by HC-16.

The aircraft built for Spain were allocated under the FMS programme, becoming Z.9-1 to Z.9-6. Such was the importance of Spain's order that Escuadrilla 005 actually re-equipped with the SH-3D before any US Navy squadrons received the new variant. The squadron embarked aboard the carrier *Dedalo*, the former USN LPH USS *Cabot*. The Z.9 designation was subsequently replaced by the designation HS.9, with a corresponding change in serial prefix. The four survivors (HS.9-1, -3, -5 and -6) were subsequently upgraded to SH-3G and later SH-3H configuration, one (HS.9-1) becoming one of three Spanish ASH-3Hs modified for the AEW role in the same way as the British Westland Sea King AEW.Mk 2 and using the same mission avionics fit, including Searchwater radar. Spain also received a number of Sea Kings built to SH-3G standards.

A handful of redundant SH-3Ds were sold to Brazil to augment the navy's S-61D-3s during the 1990s, including 154108 and 154112.

The SH-3D was a vast improvement on the SH-3A, with uprated engines and additional fuel. The improved sensor capability of the AN/AQS-13 dipping sonar gave it a quantum leap in detection capability.

VH-3D

The planned replacement for the VH-3A was a VIP transport version of the larger, more powerful S-65 'Super Jolly Green Giant', but this was cancelled due to cost constraints and due to the urgent need for H-53s in Vietnam. The Presidential VH-3As were therefore eventually replaced by similarly equipped derivatives of the up-engined SH-3D. The 11 newly-built VH-3Ds (BuNos 159350-159360) were equipped with a bifilar absorber to reduce vibration, thereby improving ride comfort and reducing maintenance costs, and also featured a non-folding main rotor. Externally, the VH-3D could be distinguished by a small hemispherical fairing on the spine, in about the same location as the radomes on Westland-built ASW Sea Kings. The rear entrance was relocated from the starboard to the port side, putting both entrances on the same side of the helicopter. The interior was designed by Raymond Loewy/William Snaith Inc. of New York, using contemporary upholstery and carpeting.

The VH-3D entered service during 1976, when the Marines HMX-1 at Quantico took over sole responsibility for the Presidential helicopter mission. President Gerald Ford was the first President to use the VH-3D. The Presidential helicopter fleet was divided into two distinct parts, white-topped aircraft used by the President, Vice President and foreign heads of state, plus green-topped aircraft used for DoD VIP transport requirements. The VH-3s served alongside similarly modified Sea Stallions and Sea Knights, but these were primarily used for transporting the Secret Service, press and cargo, the Sea Kings being prized for their range, room, comfort and speed, and thus the aircraft of choice for VIP transport. A

The white-topped VH-3Ds of HMX-1 are reserved for the US President and other select VIPs. The type is being replaced by the VH-60N, which retains the very smart green and white colour scheme.

handful of UH-1s were used for those occasions when very restricted landing sites had to be used.

One VH-3D (159358) was converted to NVH-3D standards to act as the H-3 fleet structural test and demonstration aircraft, performing stress tests to determine the safe life of surviving H-3s. Externally, the aircraft remains very much a VH-3D, with its external APU, but has been painted grey overall (with Dayglo patches) and has been fitted with a nose boom containing sensors for the test instrumentation that has been installed. The aircraft is based at West Palm Beach and is crewed by Sikorsky personnel.

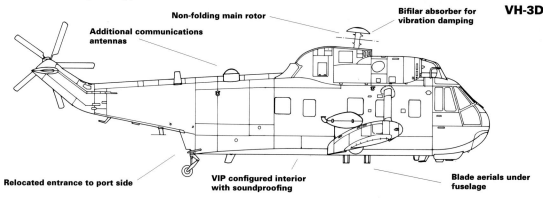

VH-3D

Non-folding main rotor

Additional communications antennas

Bifilar absorber for vibration damping

Relocated entrance to port side

VIP configured interior with soundproofing

Blade aerials under fuselage

CH-3E

Later USAF CH-3s used the T58-GE-5 engine, equivalent to the Navy T58-GE-10, and this resulted in a change of designation to CH-3E. Forty-two of these up-engined transports were built for the USAF, serialled 66-13291 to 66-13296, 67-14702 to 67-14725 and 69-5798 to 69-5812. The increased engine power brought a welcome improvement in 'hot-and-high' performance, and allowed a maximum gross weight of 22,500 lb (10206 kg). This made the type particularly useful in Vietnam, where it entered service during 1966, flying from Da Nang and from Nakhon Phanom in Thailand.

At least 41 more CH-3Es were produced by conversion of CH-3Cs. These included 62-12578, 62-12580, 62-12581, 63-9676, 63-9679, 63-9683, 63-9686, 63-9687, 63-9690, 63-9691, 64-14221, 64-14223, 64-14224, 64-14225, 64-14226, 64-1228, 64-14234, 64-14235, 65-5690, 65-5692, 65-5693, 65-5696, 65-5697, 65-5698, 65-5699, 65-5700, 65-12778, 65-12779, 65-12786, 65-12788, 65-12789, 65-12790, 65-12791, 65-12792, 65-12793, 65-12795, 65-12796, 65-12797, 65-

The CH-3E introduced the more powerful T58-GE-5 engine as well as an impressive communications and avionics fit. The TAT-102 gun turret intended for the aircraft was not adopted by the USAF. This aircraft served with Det. 5, 39th ARRW at Tyndall AFB, Florida.

12798, 65-12799, and 65-12800. Of these aircraft, about 11 were subsequently converted to JCH-3E standards, including 62-12580, 62-12581, 63-9690, 64-14221, 65-5698, 65-5699, 65-5700, 65-12792, 65-12795, 65-12796, and 65-12800.

Sikorsky designed a sponson-tip installation for the Emerson Electric TAT-102 gun pod, containing a General Electric 7.62-mm Minigun, similar to that designed for the HH-3A. The pod contained up to 8,000 rounds, enough for the 6,000-rpm gun to fire for just over a minute. This was not adopted for use by serving CH-3Es, but was fitted to at least one aircraft. Some CH-3Es were converted to full HH-3E standards, these including 63-13291, 66-13292, 66-

13296, 67-14703, 67-14704, 67-14705, 67-14706, 67-14707, 67-14709, 67-14711, 67-14712, 67-14713, 67-14714, 67-14715, 67-14716, 67-14717, 67-14718, 67-14719, 67-14720, 67-14722, 67-14723, 67-14724, 67-

14725, 69-5798, 69-5799, 69-5800, 69-5801, 69-5802, 69-5803, 69-5804, 69-5805, 69-5806, 69-5807, 69-5808, 69-5809, 69-5810, 69-5811 and 69-5812. Of these, 66-13296, 67-14715, 69-5799, 69-5801, 69-5805, and 69-95812 later became JHH-3Es. At least one CH-3E (66-13291, the first example) was used by the US Navy for drone recovery operations at NAS Point Mugu. At least one aircraft (69-5811) serving at Elmendorf AFB was fitted with the fixed braced main undercarriage units from a civilian S-61L, mounted well aft and retaining the usual nosewheel.

The standard CH-3E avionics fit initially included AN/ARC-34B UHF command radio and a TR-4A UHF backup, AN/ARA-25 UHF DF, HF-103 HF radio, FM-622 FM command radio and VHF-101 VHF command radio. Navigation equipment included AN/ARN-65 TACAN, AN/ARN-59 LF ADF compass, VOR-101 Omni Nav and AN/APN-175(V). Other equipment included AN/APX-64(V) IFF, an AN/APX-46 transponder, AN/ARN-58 ILS and an AN/APN-150 radar altimeter.

From 1989 about 10 CH-3Es (including 62-12578, 63-9679, 63-9691, 64-14234, 65-5697, 65-12788, 65-12789, 65-12791 and 65-12793) were transferred to the US Coast Guard. Five of these were subsequently converted to HH-3F standards for operational use, and the rest were employed for ground instructional training or reduced for spares.

CH-3E

T58-GE-5 engine (equivalent to US Navy T58-GE-10)

UHF, VHF and HF comms fitted

TACAN, VOR and ADF fitted

Teledyne Ryan 147 drone

Faired sponsons

Drogue chute snagging equipment

Rear loading ramp

Stabiliser drogue chute

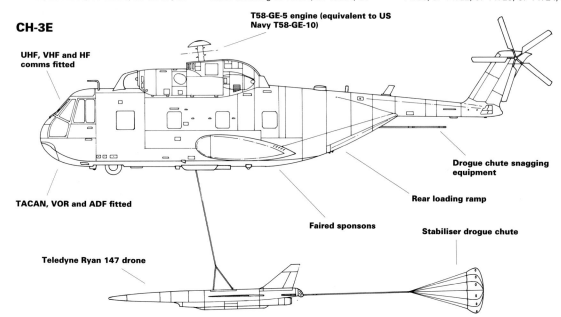

JCH-3E and QCH-3E

A number of CH-3Es were delivered to the US Army for use in its drone programme, and received the designation JCH-3E, indicating temporary test status. The CH-3Es included 62-12580, 62-12581, 63-9690, 64-14221, 65-5698, 65-5699, 65-5700, 65-12792, 65-12795, 65-12796, and 65-12800. None was actually converted to QCH-3E standards.

From 1991, about 23 surplus CH-3Es (and HH-3Es) were transferred to the US Army for conversion to drone configuration. The drones were to have been used for honing the air-to-air gunnery skills of AH-64 pilots and gunners, but the project was cancelled due to a lack of funds. Conversions would have entailed stripping out all non-essential equipment, including the refuelling booms and armour of the HH-3Es, effectively bringing them back to CH-3E standards. The aircraft would have been converted at Fort Rucker's Cairns AAF.

HH-3E

The HH-3E resulted from a USAF requirement for a dedicated aircrew recovery and combat SAR helicopter for use in Vietnam, following the successful combat evaluation of a pair of CH-3Cs by the 38th ARRS. These were obtained from an Eglin-based TAC unit. The variant was based on the CH-3C, with some further modifications to improve combat survivability and to increase range and endurance. The aircraft was fitted with self-sealing fuel tanks. The new rescue variant was initially referred to as the HH-3C, but was soon redesignated as the HH-3E, reflecting the fact that it used the same T58-GE-5 engines as the CH-3E transport version, which appeared later. About 1,000 lb (454 kg) of titanium armour plate was added in key areas, and provision was made for the installation of door guns. Provision was also made for jettisonable long-range fuel tanks under the stub wings, and a retractable telescopic inflight-refuelling probe was fitted to allow inflight refuelling from HC-130 Hercules tankers, using the probe-and-drogue method. This was proven by a probe-equipped CH-3C, which began trials with a US Marine Corps KC-130F Hercules (of VMGR-252) during 1965. The test aircraft had a non-retractable probe, braced at its base, on the centreline, but trials soon showed that the boom would be more stably mounted on the forward fuselage side, where it could also incorporate a telescopic feature. Structural improvements allowed operations at weights of up to 20,500 lb (10000 kg).

The first HH-3E was delivered to the 38th ARRS in Vietnam on 5 November 1965. The aircraft was delivered aboard a Douglas C-133 directly from the Bridgeport Municipal Airport near Sikorsky's Stratford plant. The type's record in Vietnam brought it great popularity, and resulted in the 'Jolly Green Giant' nickname. The heroism displayed by HH-3E aircrew quickly became legendary, and they effected some astonishing rescues. In one issue of its monthly newsletter, Sikorsky reported the award of an Air Force Cross to Technical Sergeant Donald Smith, after enemy fire severed his winch cable while he was recovering a downed F-100 pilot. Smith coolly directed another aircraft in to rescue him and his charge. In the same issue Sikorsky reported that Lieutenant Colonel Royal A. Brown had clocked up his 16th 'save' of his second combat tour, bringing his total to an astonishing 32. .

More HH-3Es were produced by conversion of aircraft built as CH-3Es, including 66-13291, 66-13292, 66-13296, 67-14703, 67-14704, 67-14705, 67-14706, 67-14707, 67-14709, 67-14711, 67-14712, 67-14713, 67-14715, 67-14716, 67-14717, 67-14718, 67-14719, 67-14720, 67-14722, 67-14723, 67-14724, 67-14725, 69-95798, 69-95799, 69-95800, 69-95801, 69-95802, 69-95803, 69-95804, 69-95805, 69-95806, 69-95807, 69-95808, 69-95809,

The HH-3E was the first in a long line of 'Jolly Green Giants'. The type was equipped with titanium armour, a refuelling probe, self-sealing fuel tanks and jettisonable external fuel tanks under the stub wings. This example served with the 39th ARRW's detachment at Keflavik in Iceland.

69-95810, 69-95811, and 69-95812. Further HH-3Es were converted from aircraft originally built as CH-3Cs, although these sometimes became CH-3Es first. These aircraft included 64-14230, 64-14232, 65-12777, 65-12780, 65-12781, 65-12782, 65-12783, 65-12784, 65-12785, 65-12787, and 65-12794. 65-12798 and 65-12799 have also been quoted as HH-3Es.

Above: The transition of the rescue forces from the HH-3 to the HH-60 was a long one, not completed until 1994. The aircraft served on rescue work with the Air National Guard and the Air Force Reserve, while the last active-duty user was the 1st Fighter Wing's rescue detachment at Patrick AFB, Florida. This machine belonged to the 303rd ARRS of the 403 ARRW, seen refuelling from an HC-130N in 1984.

Right: Despite its longevity, the HH-3E is best known as a Vietnam warrior. This aircraft is seen operating in support of the PJ's jungle survival school, based at Clark AB, Philippines. The long-range tanks were a necessity during long combat SAR missions deep into hostile territory.

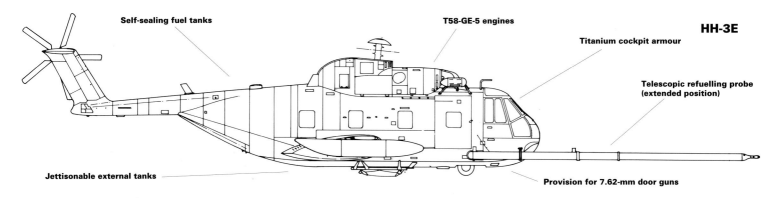

Self-sealing fuel tanks

T58-GE-5 engines

HH-3E

Titanium cockpit armour

Telescopic refuelling probe (extended position)

Jettisonable external tanks

Provision for 7.62-mm door guns

Sikorsky H-3/S-61 Variants

MH-3E

In 1990 the 71st SOS (an AFRes Special Operations squadron) based at Davis-Monthan AFB, Arizona, traded its CH-3Es for HH-3Es, redesignating them as MH-3Es (probably unofficially) in recognition of their special operations tasking. Aircraft included 66-13292, 67-14703, 67-14707, 67-14718, 67-14724 and 69-95798. Five of the aircraft (14703, 14707, 14718, 14724 and 95798) were fitted with FLIR turrets, GPS, and AN/APR-39A(V)1 RHAWS and were deployed to the Gulf for participation in Operation Desert Storm. They were specially camouflaged in a desert colour scheme of sand and brown, and received a profusion of new antennas on the top of the tailboom. Plans were made to fit AN/ALQ-144(V)3 IRCM jammers and Tracor AN/ALE-40 chaff/flare dispensers, but these did not arrive in time. The aircraft retained door-mounted M60D machine-guns when the promised M240Es failed to arrive. The aircraft routinely operated with a single 0.50-in machine-gun on the rear ramp, like that fitted to the MH-53J. This had longer reach and a heavier weight of fire than the M60Ds. Tests had been carried out using 2.75-in rockets at the Goldwater North tactical range at Gila Bend in 1985. Although these were successful, the weapon was not adopted for use by the HH/MH-3E. The HH-3Es operated from King Fahd Air Base

during the war. Several of the MH-3Es (including 67-14703, 69-5798 and 69-5802) were later handed on to the 41st RQS at Patrick AFB, still in their Desert Storm colours as late as April 1994, and served until replaced by the MH-60G.

One of the 71st SOS MH-3Es is seen shortly after its return to Davis-Monthan AFB in 1991. Some of these aircraft subsequently served with the 41st RQS, but without SOF modifications.

MH-3E

Door-mounted M60 machine-guns · T58-GE-5 engine · Refuelling probe – retracted · AN/APR-39 RHAWS · 0.50-in calibre machine-gun fitted in rear ramp · FLIR turret

VH-3E

The VH-3E designation was unofficially applied to a small number of CH-3Es used for VIP transport duties by the US Air Force, particularly by the 89th Military Airlift Wing at Andrews AFB, which also parented the Presidential VC-137. The aircraft were specially modified for the VIP transport role, and were luxuriously appointed with airline-type seats, soundproofing and other improvements. Externally, they remained virtually identical to the CH-3E, although they were differently painted. The aircraft initially wore a smart grey and white transport-type colour scheme, with a red, white and blue cheat line, but several were later painted in

full dark blue and white Presidential colours, with gold cheatlines. The aircraft used by the 1st Helicopter Squadron at Andrews included 62-12578, 63-9691, 64-14221 and 65-12793. The aircraft served until late 1989, when the unit became a single-type squadron with UH-1s. Of the VH-3Es, 64-14221 subsequently became a JCH-3E, and 65-12793 went to the Coast Guard and was converted to HH-3F standards.

65-12578 started life as a CH-3C, was then converted to a CH-3E and finally became an HH-3F before retiring. Here it is seen on the strength of the 1st HS, in VH-3E configuration.

HH-3F

The HH-3F was a dedicated extended-range SAR helicopter for the US Coast Guard based on the USAF's CH-3E, but with the same provision for external fuel and increased AUW as the HH-3E. External fuel tanks have never been used by the HH-3F, although the aircraft did frequently use its HIFR equipment for refuelling from ships at sea. The HH-3F was similarly powered by a pair of T58-GE-5 engines rated at 1,500 shp (1125 kW). The aircraft was designed to be able to fly 300 nm (345 miles; 555 km) out from base, hover for 20 minutes and return with six survivors. It could search an area of 2,100 sq miles (54386 km²) without refuelling. It had pop-out flotation gear fitted to the sponsons, to allow limited on-the-water capability. Avionics equipment was housed in a watertight compartment below the cockpit, behind the co-pilot and in the rear of the cabin. The HH-3F had an AN/APN-215 search and weather radar in

Water-landing could only be accomplished on calm seas, but did provide a capability not enjoyed by the HH-60J, the HH-3F's replacement. A boarding platform was lowered from the hatchway.

the nose with an offset thimble radome, and was equipped with LORAN C and with HF, UHF and VHF radios. The aircraft had an integrated flight director, heading/attitude reference system, automatic altitude retention system, navigation computer and gyro-stabilised Doppler system. The external hoist had a capacity of 800 lb (363 kg) and had 240 ft (73.2 m) of usable cable.

The aircraft had a flight crew of four, with swivel seats for the navigator and hoist operator and with provision for up to 15/20 passengers or six/nine stretchers in the cabin. The crew was often augmented by a trained rescue swimmer, who was also qualified as an emergency medical technician. The winch could be used with a

simple horsecollar, a rescue basket, or a Stokes litter to effect a rescue, or the aircraft could land on the water and a rescue platform could be folded out from the main door.

Sikorsky retained the S-61R designation for the new variant, the first example of which made its maiden flight on 11 October 1967 in the hands of William H. Kimes. The first deliveries were made during 1969. A competition among enlisted Coast Guard personnel resulted in the allocation of the name Pelican, the choice of ADCS Ray L. Scarborough of CGAS Port Angeles, Washington. This officially selected name has proved of limited appeal, however, and is seldom used. The Coast Guard had begun helicopter operations during World War II, acquiring the third Sikorsky R-4. It had flown its first mercy mission in 1944, rushing plasma to the victims of an explosion aboard a ship. It used the HH-3F for border patrol, law enforcement, and for support of oceanographic research and navaid calibration. The Coast Guard took delivery of 40 HH-3Fs, which were serialled from 1430-1438 and from 1467-1497. The last HH-3F was delivered on 10 July 1973.

At least nine ex-USAF CH-3Es and possibly some HH-3Es were subsequently acquired in 1989, mainly for spares. The aircraft included 62-12578, 63-9679,

HH-3F

Provision for up to 20 survivors in main cabin · T58-GE-5 engines · 363-kg capacity winch · AN/APN-215 nose radar · Flotation gear in sponsons in most aircraft · Retractable nosewheel

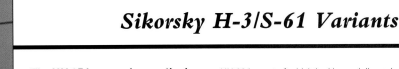

The HH-3F has now been retired after almost 30 years of service in the SAR role. The HH-3F carried radar, LORAN navigation gear and even FLIR in a few examples, and could land on water for rescues.

As such, they consisted of 2578 (62-12578), 2788 (65-12788), 2791 (65-12791), 2793 (65-12793), and 9691 (63-9691). Inflight-refuelling probes were removed from the HH-3Es, and all ex-USAF aircraft received nose radomes housing AN/APN-215 radar. They did lack sponson-mounted auxiliary flotation gear, however, providing one recognition feature. The new HH-3Fs served at Elizabeth City (three aircraft) and at Traverse City, Michigan (two aircraft). The HH-3F was replaced in the SAR role by the

HH-60J, most of which had been delivered by early 1994.

The HH-60J offered longer range, higher peformance and greater economy, although its cabin is smaller than that of the HH-3F and it is unable to land on the water. By February 1994 five examples of the HH-3F (1475, 1486, 1492, 1493, 1497) remained in use at CGAS Clearwater (St Petersburg International Airport), Florida, for OPBAT (Operations in the Bahamas, and the Turks and Caicos Islands) drug enforcement operations using powerful Nitesun searchlights and turret-mounted FLIRs. These had been retired by late 1995.

The two S-61NRs delivered to the Argentine air force are reportedly broadly similar to the Coast Guard HH-3Fs, and the type was also built under licence by Agusta in Italy as the AS-61R Pelican.

63-9691, 64-14234, 65-12788, 65-12789, 65-12790, 65-12791, and 65-12793. Five were repainted and flown in Coast Guard colours, after conversion to HH-3F

standards by the Aircraft Repair and Supply Center at Elizabeth City. These were assigned Coast Guard serials based on the last five numerals of their USAF identities.

SH-3G

The SH-3G appeared in 1970 and was intended as a more versatile utility helicopter, retaining the ASW potential of the SH-3A while being able to seat up to 15 passengers, or move bulky cargo. The aircraft was powered by General Electric T58-GE-10 engines, in place of the SH-3A's T58-GE-6s or T58-GE-8s. The SH-3A's ASQ-10 sonar was removed but retained on board the aircraft, moving with it and available for reinstallation if necessary. An initial batch of 11 SH-3Gs was converted and these were soon joined by 94 more, bringing the total to 105. A handful of SH-3Gs were produced by the conversion of SH-3Ds, and these retained their later AQS-13 sonar. All SH-3Gs originally had the basic SH-3A-style short sponsons, without MAD or smoke-marker provision, though photographic evidence shows that some aircraft had long MAD-type sponsons.

Known SH-3G conversions include the following: 148034, 148035, 148037, 148039, 148044, 148045, 148046, 148047, 148048, 148050, 148051, 148052, 148970, 148971, 148973, 148974, 148979, 148987, 148989, 148996, 149000, 149003, 149006, 149679, 149683, 149688, 149694, 149695, 149696, 149697, 149698, 149699, 149700, 149702, 149710, 149720, 149722, 149723, 149724, 149729, 149730, 149731, 149733, 149734, 149737, 149893, 149897, 149914, 149915, 149919, 149923, 149925, 149930, 149932, 150620, 151523, 151527, 151529, 151532, 151533, 151536, 151539, 151544, 151545, 151547, 151554, 151555, 152117, 152131, 152710, 154102. Several of these were subsequently converted to SH-3H standards.

Provision was made for the installation of a pair of 175-US gal (662-litre) external fuel tanks underwing, and to use the HIFR (Hover In Flight Refuelling) system. The floor was strengthened and reinforced and provision was made for the installation of a door gun. Six of the earliest SH-3Gs could mount a 7.62-mm Minigun, but most aircraft could mount only an M60 machine-gun.

HC-1 'Fleet Angels' received the first SH-3Gs, operating them in detachments aboard the USS *Coral Sea*, the USS *Hancock*, the USS *Midway*, the USS *Oriskany*, and the USS *Ranger*. The next operator was HC-2 'Circuit Riders', which had detachments aboard the USS *America*, the USS *John F. Kennedy* and the USS *Franklin D. Roosevelt*. HS-15 'Red Lions' was formed in 1971 as a training unit for Sea King supply detachments, and in 1972 deployed aboard the USS *Guam* to evaluate the SH-3G in the Sea Control Ship environment. VC-5, VC-6 and VC-8 also received SH-3Gs, as did HS-10, the Sea King RAG.

The SH-3Gs of Detachment 9, HC-1, were used for recovery of Apollo 15, the first space recovery undertaken by the SH-3G, but the 20th for the Sea King generally. Six of the 20 SH-3Gs initially delivered to HC-2 at NAS Lakehurst were fitted with gun pods for combat SAR duties. An SH-3G was used for tests of the Chesapeake Instruments Interim Airborne Towed Array Sonar System (IAIRTASS). A handful of SH-3Gs (including 148973, 149679 and 151536 used by COMSEVENTHFLT and 148989 used by VC-1) were converted for VIP transport duties, with a large VH-3D type window in the cargo door. One such aircraft (151527)

was used by HC-2 as the personal aircraft of the Commander of the US Navy's Sixth Fleet (COMSIXTHFLT) using the callsign GHOSTRIDER 741.

The SH-3Gs of HC-2 saw extensive service during the Gulf War, receiving a range of 'Duck' nicknames, including 148047 *Wild Duck*, 149731 *Desert Duck*, *Dusty Duck* and *Stealth Duck*. Some SH-3Gs were converted to SH-3H standards, but the type remains in use, augmented by transport conversions of redundant SH-3Hs.

Twelve of the Spanish Sea Kings were delivered to SH-3G standards as Z.9As (later HS.9As). Some sources suggest that these second batch Sea Kings were SH-3Ds but they had many SH-3G features, and were fitted with Canadian Marconi LN66HP search radar in an underfuselage radome. Serials ran from Z.9A-7 to Z.9A-18 (and later HS.9A-7 to HS.9A-18). US Navy Bureau numbers allocated were 158724, 158725, 159053-159056 and 161207-161212. The initial batch of six SH-3Ds was soon brought up to the same standards and all 16 survivors were subsequently brought up to SH-3H standards. The aircraft is known as the 'Sacred Cow' in Spanish service due to its complexity and size, and uses the callsign MORSA (Walrus). Two of the aircraft built as SH-3Gs (HS.9-11 and HS.9-12) joined HS.9-01 in being converted to AEW configuration by CASA between September 1985 and September 1987.

The SH-3G was also equipped for HIFR refuelling (demonstrated here by HC-2) from destroyers, allowing the aircraft to fly long-range missions over the sea.

Left: Proudly wearing its nickname Stealth Duck on the undercarriage sponson, this HC-2 SH-3G took part in the Gulf War, and is seen at its regular base of Bahrain International Airport. The SH-3Gs were instrumental in supporting the US Navy ships sailing on combat duty in the Gulf.

Below: Configured from the outset for passenger transport, it is no surprise that several SH-3Gs have been used as VIP transports. This machine, operated by HC-1 at Atsugi, was the personal transport of the Seventh Fleet commander.

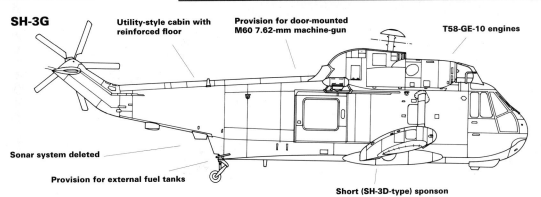

SH-3G

Utility-style cabin with reinforced floor

Provision for door-mounted M60 7.62-mm machine-gun

T58-GE-10 engines

Sonar system deleted

Provision for external fuel tanks

Short (SH-3D-type) sponson

SH-3H

The SH-3H was originally seen as little more than a SLEP for the SH-3D, but the programme was soon widened to include the provision of new equipment as well and the SH-3H came to be viewed as the first of a new generation of ASW helicopters. It was actually given significantly increased multi-role capability as well. The SH-3H received six key ASW improvements, new equipment for the anti-ship missile detection (ASMD) role, as well as 12 basic aircraft improvements, and the utility and convertability features of the SH-3G.

ASW improvements included the provision of AN/AQS-13B Miniscan sonar, a torpedo airborne pre-set mechanism and the ability to launch torpedoes in the hover by using the Mk 31 mod parachute-stabilised lanyard torpedo delivery system. The aircraft also incorporated three items of equipment also fitted to some late SH-3As, these comprising the AN/ASQ-81(V)-2 towed MAD bird (whose winch was installed in a recontoured starboard undercarriage sponson), 24 launch tubes for the Mk 25 marine markers in an extended port undercarriage sponson, and 12 size A sonobuoy launch tubes in the rear cabin. The aircraft was fitted with an AN/AKT-22(V)-2 sonobuoy datalink. ASMD role equipment included a Litton LN-66HP radar, with a 5-ft diameter scanner in a retractable underfuselage radome. General aircraft improvements included the 1,400-shp (1044-kW) T58-GE-10 engines and improved gearbox of the SH-3D and structural improvements increasing gross weight to 21,000 lb (9525 kg). Other improvements adopted from the SH-3D included KY-28 Juliet secure voice UHF radio, improved IFF, AN/ASN-50 heading reference system, and

Spain now operates a fleet of SH-3H helicopters, although these have all been modified to this configuration from SH-3Ds and SH-3Gs.

AN/APN-182 Doppler, as well as the improved pilot's instrument panel layout. The SH-3H took the improved AFCS developed for the VH-3A, and the HH-3A's increased flow rate (800 lb/363 kg per minute) fuel dump system. The radar and AN/ALR-54 ESM were eventually deleted in favour of a new attitude/heading reference system and improved sonar processing.

Other avionics equipment included AN/ARC-51A UHF radio, AN/ARC-94 VHF radio, AN/ARR-52A(V) receiver, and an AN/AIC-14 intercom. Navigation equipment included an AN/AYK-2 navigation computer, AN/ARN-52(V) TACAN, AN/ARN-59 ADF, AN/ARA-25A DF and an AN/APN-171 radar altimeter. Other equipment included an AN/APX-72 radar identification set, an AN/APQ-107 radar altitude warning system, and an AN/ASA-26B recorder group.

The aircraft also had an extra window forward on the port side, as fitted to a handful of SH-3As. SH-3G convertability/utility improvements included provision for easy sonar removal and reinstallation, provision for installing 15 troop seats, and provision for 110-US Gal (418-litre) underwing auxiliary fuel tanks. The SH-3H

also received IDF-7.5 ESM and a Model H-240 (AN/ALE-37) chaff dispenser on the port aft fuselage side. The first SH-3Hs were produced by conversion of a batch of 11 SH-3Gs by Sikorsky at Stratford in mid-1971.

The SH-3H conversion programme eventually encompassed 163 aircraft, including SH-3Gs and previously unconverted SH-3As and SH-3Ds. The former SH-3Gs differed from other SH-3Hs in that they retained the ability to carry underwing auxiliary fuel tanks.

Known SH-3H conversions include: 148035, 148036, 148039, 148042, 148043, 148045, 148048, 148049, 148050, 148052, 148964, 148965, 148966, 148967, 148968, 148969, 148971, 148972, 148974, 148976, 148977, 148980, 148981, 148983, 148984, 148986, 148987, 148988, 148990, 148992, 148995, 148996, 148997, 148998, 148999, 149005, 149006, 149010, 149684, 149687, 149688, 149690, 149693, 149701, 149702, 149703, 149705, 149706, 149708, 149711, 149712, 149713, 149717, 149718, 149719, 149722, 149724, 149725, 149726, 149727, 149728, 149730, 149735, 149736, 149738,

Graphically illustrating the hunter/killer role envisaged for the SH-3, this HS-7 SH-3H launches a torpedo while dunking sonar.

149894, 149897, 149898, 149899, 149900, 149902, 144904, 144905, 149906, 149910, 149913, 149917, 149918, 149921, 149923, 149927, 149929, 149931, 149934, 151524, 151525, 151526, 151528, 151535, 151541, 151543, 151544, 151546, 151549, 151550, 151551, 152104, 152107, 152108, 152109, 152110, 152112, 152113, 152115, 152116, 152119, 152121, 152122, 152123, 152124, 152125, 152128, 152129, 152130, 152131, 152132, 152133, 152134, 152135, 152136, 152137, 152138, 152139, 152694, 152700, 152701, 152702, 152703, 152704, 152708, 152709, 152710, 152712, 154100, 154101, 154102, 154103, 154106, 154117, 154119, 154121, 154122, 156483, 156484, 156488, 156491, 156495, 156498, 156501, 156505, 156506, 212574, 212575.

Some SH-3Hs were fitted with a new, less angular ice/FOD intake filter, which lacked the curved side pieces of the original screen used on the SH-3G. Many SH-3Hs used the SH-3G type screen, however. Another detail difference between the SH-3H and previous variants could be found in its MAD gear. The MAD bird carried by the later SH-3Hs had a slightly smaller 'cone' than that of the early SH-3H, and had only a single row of larger diameter holes at its trailing edge.

Weapons options included two Mk 46, Mk 43 or Mk 44 torpedoes, or two Mk 14 (Mod 0) or Mk 54 (Mod 1) depth bombs, or a single Mk 101 (Mod 0) depth bomb.

HS-15 was specially formed to serve as the first SH-3H squadron, and soon deployed aboard the LPH USS *Guam*. Replacement of the SH-3H by the SH-60F began in June 1989, with the re-equipment of HS-10, the West Coast FRS. This was a slow process, however, and the SH-3H was used by seven squadrons during the Gulf War. These were HS-3 aboard the *Saratoga*, HS-7 aboard the *Kennedy*, HS-8 aboard the

Left: Part of Air Wing One on USS America, HS-11 operated the SH-3H on anti-submarine warfare and SAR tasks until it was replaced by the SH-60F Ocean Hawk. This aircraft wears the squadron's 'Dragonslayer' nickname on the undercarriage sponson.

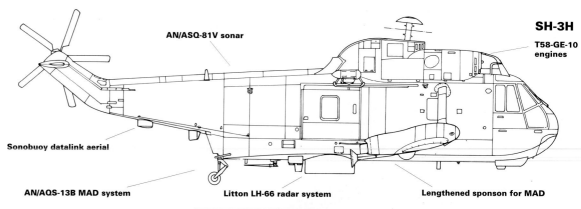

SH-3H

AN/ASQ-81V sonar

T58-GE-10 engines

Sonobuoy datalink aerial

AN/AQS-13B MAD system

Litton LH-66 radar system

Lengthened sponson for MAD

The Spanish navy converted three SH-3Hs to AEW configuration with a Searchwater radar installation.

USS *Independence*, HS-9 aboard the *Theodore Roosevelt*, HS-11 aboard the *America*, HS-12 aboard the *Midway* and HS-14 aboard the *Ranger*.

Spain's Sea Kings, delivered as SH-3Ds and SH-3Gs, were brought up to a common standard as SH-3Hs following the 16 December 1987 authorisation of an upgrade programme. They lack MAD birds and some other equipment fitted to US Navy SH-3Hs. The upgrade was carried out by CASA at Rota and included structural improvements, and modifications to the transmission, turboshafts, electrical and hydraulic systems. They were fitted with a new state-of-the-art instrument panel and with an AN/ASQ-81V sonar replacing the AQS-13B, and with a new, indigenous Ceselsa NAT-5

tactical navigator. The survivors currently serve with Escuadrilla 005 at Rota and will probably remain in use until 2015. Three have been modified to serve in the AEW role under the designation HS.9L, under the terms of a 1984 contract with Britain's Thorn-EMI Electronics. A typical carrier group aboard *Principe de Asturias* consists of five AB 212s, six SH-3Hs, two SH-3H(AEW)s, and eight AV-8 Harriers.

YSH-3J

The J suffix was used by a pair of Naval Weapons Test Centre Sea Kings used for the evaluation of weapons systems and avionics being considered for use in the LAMPS (Light Airborne Multi-Purpose System) helicopter.

UH-3H

The replacement of front-line SH-3Hs by the SH-60F left many surplus SH-3H airframes, a number of which were considerably less tired than some of the SH-3As, VH-3As, SH-3Ds and SH-3Gs serving with various second-line units. While the SH-60 offered improved ASW capability, it had a smaller cabin (385 cu ft/10.9 m³ compared to the Sea King's 1,050 cu ft/29.7m³) and lacked the Sea King's speed, range and load-carrying capacity. Additionally, procurement of the SH-60 was tightly controlled, and surplus SH-60 airframes did not exist. Some SH-3Hs were stripped of all external ASW equipment, and left with bare, empty consoles to serve with HC-16 'Bullfrogs' and some other units, but a better solution would clearly be to completely gut the former ASW aircraft. Accordingly, the US Navy converted a number of SH-3s for the utility role, chiefly by simply stripping out all ASW equipment and reinforcing the floor. The first such conversion was 148052. The UH-3H entered service with HC-2 in late 1992. Such conversions were initially informally designated USH-3H. Known UH-3H conversions include: 148035, 148042, 148052, 148977, 148986, 149684, 149687, 149702, 149703, 149706, 149708, 149718, 149722, 149899, 149918, 151549, 151550, 151551, 152129, 152135, 152694, 152704, 152708, 152709, 152710, 154103.

Large cargo door — T58-GE-10 engines — Sonar equipment deleted — Reinforced floor — VIP interior in some aircraft

UH-3H

Some UH-3Hs are in a VIP configuration similar to that used by some SH-3Gs, with an oversized window in the cargo door. These include 152704 of HSL-51's Det. 51, assigned to COMSEVENTHFLT.

The shortage of SH-60 airframes for the utility role ensured that there was still a use for any SH-3H airframes that had long airframe life remaining. Most UH-3Hs were painted in light sea grey.

S-61A-1

The S-61A designation was applied to export versions of the ASW Sea King, the SH-3A, and its utility derivative, the CH-3B. Sikorsky offered the Rolls-Royce Gnome H.1200 as an optional powerplant for the export aircraft, though, in truth, the Gnome was no more than a British licence-built version of the original T58 turboshaft. The first customer for the S-61A was the Kongelige Danske Flyvevaaben (Royal Danish Air Force), which ordered an initial batch of eight aircraft. These were serialled U-240, and U-275 to U-281, and used callsigns OV-JCA to OV-JCH. Two were written off (U-277 in January 1969 and U-281 in February 1968), although U-277 seems to have been restored to flying condition. A ninth Danish Sea King was formally designated S-61A-5, though it differed only in detail.

All of the Danish Sea Kings were based

Denmark's S-61s are easily recognised by their distinctive nose radar and enlarged sponsons. Like many of the Westland-built Sea Kings operating in Europe, they have now received a FLIR upgrade.

on the USAF's CH-3B and were optimised for the overwater SAR role. As such they received extra cabin windows (giving four on each side) and were fitted with the enlarged sponsons of the civilian S-61N, for greater stability on the water. The rearmost window on each side is a bubble-type observation blister. From the start the Danish S-61As had the long-span braced tailplane usually associated with the SH-3D, and in service were modified to virtual SH-3G standards, with intake ice deflector/filters and equipment improvements. They also received a colour weather/search radar in a nose-mounted radome, while in 1988 the air force sought

Dkr21 million ($3.3 million) to complete a mid-life update and to install a chin-mounted FLIR, preferably the Grumman Seehawk

system installed on USCG HH-65s. In the event, the aircraft were fitted with Safire FLIR and Ferranti navigation computers. The surviving Danish Sea Kings fly with Esk 722 at Vaerløse, part of Flyvemateriel Kommando, with detachments at Aalborg and Skrydstrup and, in winter, also at Ronne on the island of Bornholm.

The original silver and Dayglo colour scheme has recently given way to single-tone overall dark grey and, on other aircraft, to a dark/light grey camouflage.

The ninth Danish Sea King (U-481, callsign OV-JCI) was described as an S-61A-5. It serves alongside the surviving S-61A-1s at Vaerløse and differs only in minor details. Eskadrille 727 at Vaerløse completed its 10,000th SAR sortie on 13 September 1994, having saved 5,100 lives and having accumulated 83,000 flying hours.

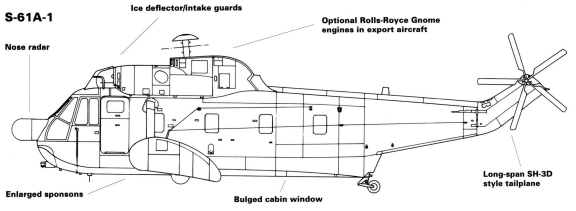

S-61A-1

Ice deflector/intake guards — Optional Rolls-Royce Gnome engines in export aircraft — Nose radar — Enlarged sponsons — Bulged cabin window — Long-span SH-3D style tailplane

Sikorsky H-3/S-61 Variants

S-61A-4

Malaysia ordered the S-61A as a utility helicopter, and its aircraft were very similar to the USAF's CH-3As, with standard SH-3 type sponsons incorporating emergency flotation gear. The aircraft were designated S-61A-4s, and were locally known as Nuris. Ten were delivered during 1967 and 1968 and six more ordered in 1970. Deliveries eventually reached 46 (and this figure excludes two Agusta-built VIP transports delivered in 1990). The aircraft were originally serialled FM1140 onwards, before the survivors were reserialled as FM1701 to FM1736 and then as M23-01 to M23-36. They are used by No.10 'Gading' (Elephant tusk) Squadron at Kuala Lumpur – Simpang and by the co-located No. 3 FTC. The type also serves with No. 3 'Wira' (Hero) Squadron at Butterworth, No. 5 'Harimau' (Tiger) Squadron at Labuan in Sabah, and No. 7 'Badak' (Rhino) Squadron at Kuching in Sarawak. The S-61As allocated for training were previously used by the Helicopter Training School at Keluang. The helicopters are used for troop transport, cargo, and SAR duties. They can carry 31 combat troops and are equipped with 250-ft (76.2 m) rescue hoists.

In 1991, the Royal Malaysian air force issued a contract to the Kuala Lumpur-based Airod to upgrade its 35 surviving S-61s. Valued at 50 million Ringit (US$19 million), the programme included structural and avionics improvements with Airod's responsibilities extending to equipment

Malaysia's S-61s are known locally as Nuris. After many years of service in the support helicopter role, the aircraft are to be upgraded with GEC Doppler, Sperry weather radar and a radar altimeter.

selection and purchase, kit fabrication and installation, integration, prototype testing and evaluation. The upgraded aircraft were fitted with a Sperry Primus 500 weather radar, a Honeywell AN/APN-209(V) radar altimeter and a GEC-Marconi ANV301 Doppler. The air force's AS-61Ns are also to be included in the upgrade.

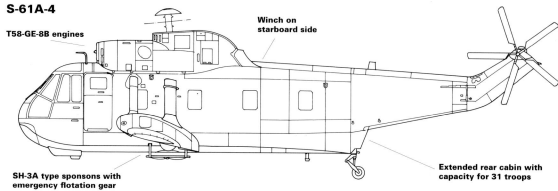

S-61A-4

T58-GE-8B engines

Winch on starboard side

SH-3A type sponsons with emergency flotation gear

Extended rear cabin with capacity for 31 troops

S-61D-3

Brazil received four S-61D-3s (N3007-N3010), broadly equivalent to the US Navy SH-3D, in 1970, later taking delivery of two more (N-3011 and N-3012). These equipped Esquadron de Helicopteros de Emprigo Geral (HS-1) at São Pedro da Aldeia and deployed aboard the carrier *Minas Gerais* (the former British carrier *Colossus*). They replaced Sikorsky HSS-1s. The six Sikorsky-built S-61Ds were augmented by four Italian-built aircraft, and later by two ex-US Navy SH-3Ds. The surviving aircraft have all been brought up to a common standard, with intake filters, undernose radar and provision for AM39 Exocet ASMs, giving a potent anti-surface capability similar to the Peruvian Sea Kings.

Brazil operates a mixed bag of Sea Kings from various sources. This is the last of the six built for Brazil as S-61D-3s, seen carrying an Exocet missile. These are known locally as SH-3As, or ASH-3A in upgraded (SH-3H) configuration.

S-61D-4

Argentina received four S-61D-4s (export versions of the US Navy's SH-3D) during 1978, as part of a major re-equipment of the Armada Argentina and the Comando de Aviacion Naval Argentina. They were serialled between 0675 and 0678 and initially equipped I Escuadron Aeronaval de Helicopteros, transferring to II Escuadron in 1978. A fifth aircraft (0696) was delivered with a VIP interior. Four more SH-3Ds were delivered in February 1987, two of them equipped with radar. Some sources suggest that the later Argentine Sea Kings were to

Argentina has acquired Sea Kings from both Sikorsky and Agusta production and in a variety of configurations. This machine (0677) was one of the original four-aircraft batch built as S-61D-4s (equivalent to the SH-3D).

SH-3H standards, others that the aircraft were Agusta-built. The truth is that the aircraft were Agusta-built, and were also to virtual H standards.

S-61L

Following the success of the HSS-2, Sikorsky designed a civilian derivative powered by a pair of General Electric CT58-100 turboshafts (civilian versions of the Navy's T58-GE-8). Sikorsky initially offered the aircraft with either two or three engines, with the third engine behind the rotor and offering improved 'hot-and-high' performance. The three-engined configuration remained unflown. The civil aircraft was given a fuselage stretch which gave a cabin length of 31 ft 11 in (9.73 m),

with a floor area of 217 sq ft (20.16 m²) and a cabin volume of 1,305 cu ft (36.95 m³). Another option offered from the beginning was a lightweight fixed land undercarriage (which saved 297 lb/135 kg). Eleven cabin windows were fitted on each side. Aircraft delivered with the simple undercarriage were later designated S-61L, although initially no distinction was made between aircraft with the different types of landing gear.

The first S-61L made its maiden flight on 6 December 1960 and was certificated by the FAA (Federal Aviation Administration) on 2 November 1961. Sikorsky retained the

prestigious Raymond Loewy Associates to design the external colour scheme and internal appointments of the civilian prototype. By comparison with the ASW SH-3A, the S-61L had a modified rotor head and a longer-span tailplane, like the SH-3D. The standard basic interior accommodated 25 passengers and a single flight attendant, with all but one of the seats facing forward. The two rearmost seats could be replaced by a toilet, and a hot-meal galley could be installed in place of the single seat opposite the main cabin entry door (which incorporated built-in air stairs). The basic layout included a 100-cu ft (28.32-m³)

baggage compartment behind the flight deck, while additional cargo space was available by moving the rear cabin bulkhead forward. With 23 passengers, an extra 149 cu ft (4.2 m³) was available, while with 20 aboard 245 cu ft (6.9 m³) of extra space was provided. A reduction to 17 or 14 passengers brought an increase of 346 or 446 cu ft (9.8 m³ or 12.6 m³), respectively.

The launch customers for the civilian S-61 were Los Angeles Airways (which ordered five 28-seaters) and Chicago Helicopter Airways (which ordered six 25-seaters, later reducing its initial order to four). LAA received its first aircraft in

November 1961, and Chicago received its initial aircraft early in 1962. LAA made its first revenue flight with the new type on 1 March 1962. Neither customer took standard aircraft. LAA designed a pair of removable baggage pods which were pre-packed and then installed in the bottom of the fuselage just behind the cockpit. They were loaded from the port side, and could be unloaded directly onto a wheeled dolly and taken to the terminal for unloading, while a second set of loaded pods could be

slid into the helicopter for the next flight. These pods were augmented by a pair of baggage bins in the hull just aft of the airstair door. Total baggage capacity was 120 cu ft (3.4 m³). The Chicago aircraft had five underfloor baggage bins with a capacity of 157 cu ft (4.4 m³) and a 45-cu ft (1.27-m³) compartment for carry-on baggage. Los Angeles Airways estimated that seat mile costs would be less than half those of contemporary piston-engined helicopters. In early 1961, Sikorsky was talking of a seat

cost per mile of between eight and nine cents, instead of the then-current average helicopter seat per mile cost of between 14 and 17 cents. An equipped price of $640,000 was widely quoted.

In 1969 the S-61L Mk I was replaced in production by the 1,500-shp (1125-kW) CT58-GE-1400-1/2 engined Mk II, which had enhanced soundproofing and new vibration dampers and which was faster, more reliable and which could lift heavier loads. The S-61L has been used as a passenger

transport, a freighter and even as a flying crane, as well as for law enforcement, border patrol and SAR duties.

One unusual S-61L was N4503E, an aircraft belonging to the Perkasie, Pennsylvania-based Carson Helicopters. This had its forward fuselage shortened, bringing it back to the same dimensions as a military SH-3. This allowed the external sling capacity to be increased from 10,000 to 11,000 lb (4536 to 4990 kg). Production of the S-61L by Sikorsky totalled 13 aircraft.

S-61N

The civilianised version of the S-61 was offered from the start with the standard Sea King-type retractable amphibious undercarriage, with sponsons attached, or with a sponson-type fixed undercarriage. With such an undercarriage fitted, and with a sealed amphibious hull, the civilian variant was designated S-61N. The S-61N prototype made its maiden flight on 7 August 1962.

A stripped-down, lightweight version of the S-61N was developed for logging, construction and other similar operations under the name Payloader. The rear air stair door was removed and the sponsons were replaced by an S-61L type fixed undercarriage. It weighed 2,000 lb (907 kg) less than the standard aircraft, and could lift an 11,000-lb (4990-kg) payload.

The S-61N Mk I was replaced on the production line by the 1,500-shp (1119-kW) CT58-GE-1400-1/2 engined Mk II in 1969. The new variant also introduced improved soundproofing and new vibration absorbers and was faster, more maintainable and able to carry more passengers than its predecessor. British civilian helicopter

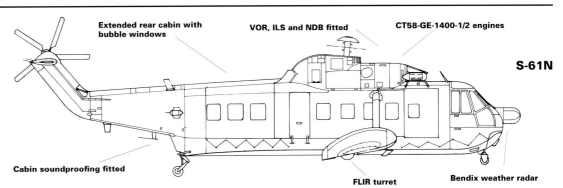

Extended rear cabin with bubble windows   **VOR, ILS and NDB fitted**   **CT58-GE-1400-1/2 engines**

S-61N

Cabin soundproofing fitted   **FLIR turret**   **Bendix weather radar**

company Bristow Helicopters, formed by a pioneering former Royal Navy helicopter pilot, has used its S-61N Mk IIs in a variety of contracted-out military roles. The S-61N Mk II usually carries 24 passengers, but is roled to carry 18 troops and internal freight in the Falklands. The aircraft are fitted with VOR, ILS, NDB, a nose-mounted Bendix weather radar and have a Helicopter Health and Usage Monitoring System, and military

VHF and UHF radios. In the Falkland Islands the 'Erics' (named after a well-known Cockney darts player, Eric Bristow) supported the British garrison on the islands from 1983, providing SAR and heavylift support. S-61N Mk IIs are also used by Bristows to fly SAR missions on behalf of HM Customs under a UK government contract. Aircraft used on this contract have a company-developed SAR equipment

package, with a fully-coupled Flight Path Control and auto-hover system, Bendix RDR 1400C colour weather, mapping, and search radar, a nose-mounted FLIR turret and a 295-ft (90-m) variable-speed rescue hoist.

The S-61N is a popular and effective SAR platform, and is used by Irish Helicopters on an Irish government SAR contract, operating from Shannon Airport (using FLIR and LN450 auto-hover systems).

S-61NR

The S-61NR designation was applied to a pair of aircraft supplied to Argentina for SAR

duties with the Fuerza Aerea Argentina. The aircraft are broadly equivalent to the HH-3F used by the US Coast Guard. These aircraft are flown by Grupo 7 (part of VII Brigada Aerea) at BAM Dr Mariano Moreno. Grupo

7's equipment also includes Boeing Vertol Chinooks, Bell 212s and UH-1Hs, a variety of Hughes 500s and 530s and fixed-wing types in the shape of the Merlin IV and Aero Commander. The S-61NRs fly with

Escuadron II, and have worn four different serials, H-01, H-02, H-71 and H-72.

S-61 interim AAFSS and S-66 testbed

Sikorsky's record-breaking demonstrator, N318Y, was converted to serve as the prototype for an interim AAFSS in

competition with modified versions of the UH-1B Iroquois and UH-2 SeaSprite, pending the service introduction of the full standard AAFSS, the Lockheed AH-56 Cheyenne. The S-61 demonstrator had already been experimentally fitted with four 10-round rocket launcher boxes, mounted above and below a tubular pylon which went through the cabin at the forward cabin window on the port side.

After testing for the AAFSS programme, N318Y was fitted out as a testbed for the S-66, complete with new tail feathers.

As the Interim AAFSS demonstrator the aircraft was painted olive drab overall and had an M6 7.62-mm quad gun turret in the nose, offset to port, with an M5 40-mm grenade launcher or an XM12 Vulcan gun pod to starboard. The aircraft had its undercarriage sponsons removed, leaving the aircraft with a fixed undercarriage like that of the S-61L or Westland Commando. Armament could also be door- and wing-mounted, the latter culminating in a short horizontal stub pylon just aboard of the undercarriage oleo.

In its Interim AAFSS configuration the aircraft could carry a pair of waist gunners,

each with a 7.62-mm or 0.50-in machine-gun, while a variety of gun and rocket pods could be carried under the wings or on their wingtip pylons. Sikorsky calculated that in one configuration the aircraft could carry 1,000 rounds of 40-mm, 12,000 rounds of 7.62-mm, and 4,000 rounds of 0.50-in ammunition, as well as 19 unguided 2.75-in rockets.

The same aircraft (with its sponsons re-fitted) was later used as a testbed for the S-66, a new compound helicopter under development by Sikorsky. It also undertook trials of the type's unique Rotoprop, a hinged tail rotor which could be used to direct the thrust from the anti-torque tail rotor as an aid to control or to provide thrust for forward flight.

Sikorsky (United Aircraft of Canada) CHSS-2 (CH-124)

The HSS-2 was finally selected to replace Royal Canadian Navy HO4S-3 (S-55) helicopters in the anti-submarine role, after a lengthy study of numerous competing helicopters, including the strongly favoured Kaman HU2K and the Boeing Vertol 107. The ageing HO4S-3s were operated from the carrier HMCS *Bonaventure*, but the new helicopters were expected to fly from high-speed destroyer escorts equipped with a 35-ft by 75-ft (10.6-m x 22.9-m) helicopter platform. In the event the Kaman was too small to carry the required systems and weapons, while the Boeing Vertol aircraft was too large to operate from a destroyer's helicopter platform. Canada therefore signed up for 41 Sea Kings, under the designation CHSS-2. They were serialled 4001 to 4041.

The Canadian aircraft was provided with automatic tail folding and a Fairey Aviation Co. (of Halifax, Nova Scotia) 'Beartrap' winch-down device. To use the winch-down system the pilot hovered 40 ft (12.2 m) above the deck, reeling out a light nylon line to which a deck crewman attached the winch cable. The helicopter then reeled in the nylon line, and the attached winch cable.

A quick-attach probe on the end of the cable was pulled into a housing in the belly of the helicopter, just ahead of the sonar aperture. The helicopter pilot maintained hover power as the winch took up slack and as the aircraft was pulled down to between 10 and 12 ft (3 to 3.66 m) above the deck. A slip clutch prevented any shock to the airframe or cable caused by sudden updrafts or downward pitching of the deck, with a quick release device which could be triggered by the pilot or if a pre-set tension limit was exceeded. From 10-12 ft the helicopter was pulled down more slowly, until the bottom of the probe locked into a securing device in the deck. When the helicopter had landed, the securing device could slide along in channels in the deck, allowing the aircraft to be moved into the hangar without releasing

Most of the first CHSS-2s were built by Pratt & Whitney of Canada, but the first three (the first is illustrated) were built by Sikorsky and were similar to SH-3Ds. The original CHSS-2s did not have radar fitted.

the lock between helicopter and ship. To take off, the helicopter was wheeled into position from the hangar, with the probe locked into the securing device. The helicopter then ran up until the rotor provided enough lift to overcome the variable tension limit (altered according to weather and launch conditions) and leapt clear of the deck.

The first three aircraft were off-the-shelf

deliveries from Sikorsky (and, with the fourth, initially lacked the automatic tail fold and winch-down device, although both were subsequently retrofitted), with the next five assembled by the Pratt & Whitney plant near Montreal. After evaluation by VX-10, the Sea Kings supplanted the HO4S-3 with HS-50. Seven of the initial eight aircraft were assigned to training aboard the *Bonaventure*, with the eighth undertaking

sea trials aboard a destroyer. Although the CHSS-2 retained the same interior layout as the basic US Navy aircraft the crew concept was different, with two pilots, a sensor operator and a Royal Navy-type observer who acted as the tactical controller and co-ordinator, and who could be the aircraft captain. US Navy practice was to have two sensor operators, with tactical control and co-ordination coming from the parent ship via the aircraft captain (always the first pilot).

The CHSS-2 was redesignated as the CH-124 on 27 July 1970 as part of a general adoption of a unified system of aircraft type designations in the wake of the integration of the armed forces. Like almost all other types in service, the aircraft were also re-serialled, using the new type designation

number 124 as the prefix, followed by the last two of the original serial. Thus they ranged from 12401 to 12441, omitting 12402, 12415 and 12427 since 4002, 4015 and 4027 had already crashed.

The operational unit HS-50 was a large one, and in 1974 it was decommissioned to form two smaller squadrons, HS-423 and HS-443, which parented detachments aboard Maritime Command's destroyers and support ships. The aircraft were originally painted light sea grey, with dark sea grey upper surfaces and a Dayglo nose, tailboom band and tailplane and with Dayglo code numbers. Before integration the aircraft carried the word NAVY in black on the tailboom and had roundels with a broad blue outer ring. Post-integration aircraft were painted grey overall, with three-digit

codes in black based on the last three, and with 'Canadian Armed Forces' above the code, and 'Maritime Command' below. On the starboard side, Canadian Armed Forces was replaced by 'Forces Armées Canadiennes' though 'Maritime Command' remained in English. The 'Band Aid' flag was carried on the rear of the tailboom.

Three CH-124s (12418, 12419 and 12425) were converted for the utility role, but officially received no new designation. The designation CH-124U has been applied unofficially, at unit level, however. Because they were frequently used for SAR and survival training, the aircraft had a 'rubber bathtub' (similar to a child's paddling pool) in the cabin. This was used for standing survivors in while they were still dripping, to prevent salt water running off over the

cabin floor and into recesses. The aircraft also carried a seven-man dinghy and were fitted with troop seats (for the survivors to sit on, once drip-dried) and a plywood false deck. One CH-124U (12418) crashed in 1973, but the others were returned to ASW configuration when they were upgraded to CH-124A standards. A fourth Sea King (12422) received similar modifications for use in the COD role, with its sonar well faired over, and was similarly restored to ASW configuration under the CH-124A conversion programme.

Some 35 surviving CH-124s were converted to CH-124A standards from 1975, the exceptions being the three aircraft lost as CSSH-2s listed above, and CH-124s 12418, 12420, and 12432, all written off during the early 1970s.

Sikorsky (United Aircraft of Canada) CH-124A and CH-124B

Under the Sea King Improvement Programme of 1975/1976, which aimed to enhance ASW capability and extend the Sea King's service life, 35 CH-124s were converted to CH-124A configuration. The new sub-type received a crashworthy fuel system, rotor de-icing and a new AN/APS-503 search radar, with a 360° scanning antenna in a thimble radome on the spine, in a similar position to the radome on early Westland-built ASW and SAR Sea Kings. The interior was also revised, with the observer and sensor operator being moved to face the starboard cabin wall in redesigned seats, with the starboard forward window being blanked out as a result. Aircraft converted were 12401, 12403, 12404, 12405, 12406, 12407, 12408, 12409, 12410, 12411, 12412, 12413, 12414, 12416, 12417, 12419, 12420, 12422, 12423, 12424, 12425, 12426, 12428, 12429, 12430, 12431, 12433, 12434, 12435, 12436, 12437, 12438, 12439, 12440, and 12441. Subsequently, 12421 became a CH-124A (OT&E) while 12401, 12424, 12430, 12434, 12437 and 12441 became CH-124Bs.

Many CH-124As have 15 prominent sonobuoy launch chutes projecting down from the rear part of the cabin. These are tubular but have the trailing edge cut away so that they resemble a 'C' in cross section. Some aircraft have a crash position indicator on the rear fuselage sides, in line with the end of the boat hull. One Sea King (12414) is maintained as the 'water bird' for practising on-the-water operation. This aircraft has had some equipment items removed, and has extra water- and corrosion-proofing, although all on-the-water training is conducted in fresh water to minimise corrosion problems. Another (12421) is permanently assigned to test duties under the designation CH-124A (OT&E). This aircraft was at one time to have received the designation CH-124, but the change was not approved.

The Sea Kings are maintained by the CFB Shearwater BAMEO (Base Aircraft

CH-124A

Crashworthy fuel system

Main rotor de-icing

AN/APS-503 radar

Westland-style rear cabin layout

Sonobuoy chutes

The most obvious feature of the CH-124A upgrade was the addition of radar. Most aircraft also received prominent sonobuoy launch tubes.

Maintenance Engineering Organisation) and are used by two Shearwater-based squadrons, HT-406 (the Maritime OTU) and HS-423 (the Helicopter ASW squadron), and by the Helicopter Operational Test and Evaluation Flight. They are also used by HS 443 across the continent at CFB Esquimalt, British Columbia. Many CH-124As have received the package of modifications developed for the Gulf War and now known as the Surveillance Mod. This is described in the CH-124C entry below. The CH-124B designation was to have been assigned to six modified Sea Kings (12401, 12424, 12430, 12434, 12437 and 12441) which were modified to serve as lead-in trainers for the EH101. These were equipped with HELTAS (Helicopter Towed Array Support) and with upgraded missions avionics and display systems. Unfortunately, the EH101,

in both its CH-148 Petrel ASW form and its CH-149 Chimo SAR form, fell victim to

defence cuts. This left the CH-124Bs with no real role to fulfil.

Sikorsky (United Aircraft of Canada) CH-124C

Canadian involvement in Desert Shield began on 10 August 1990, when Prime Minister Brian Mulroney announced that Canada would send two destroyers and a supply ship to join the multi-national operation to evict Iraqi forces from Kuwait. The 'Tribal'-class destroyer HMCS *Athabaskan* and the 'Improved-Restigouche'-class frigate HMCS *Terra Nova*, accompanied by the supply ship HMCS *Protecteur*, sailed from Halifax, Nova Scotia, as Canadian Task Group 302.3 on 24 August, reaching the Straits of Hormuz on 25 September. The operation was officially codenamed Operation Friction, and unofficially dubbed the 'Perisan Excursion'. The *Athabaskan* and the *Protecteur* sailed with their helicopters aboard (two and three Sea Kings, respectively), and these were specially prepared for their role in the Gulf. The Sea King had hitherto been carefully optimised for the ASW role, and lacked the necessary sensors and equipment for the surface search and utility roles, especially in a war zone. Accordingly, a package of 'Gulf Mods' was designed and installed on the

HS-423 Sea Kings embarked.

This package included an undernose FLIR turret housing a FLIR Systems FLIR 2000 and incorporating a vibration-damping shock mount, a spine-mounted Trimble Trimpack GPS (level with the tailwheel) and a cooling fan for the AN/APS-503 radar. The FLIR

display replaced the larger sonics display and was monitored by the AESO. A plywood floor was fitted to facilitate cargo transport. Defensive aids included a Lockheed Sanders AN/ALQ-144 infra-red jammer, a Tracor M-130 flare dispenser on the starboard rear fuselage and a Tracor

AN/ALE-37 chaff dispenser low on the port rear fuselage. The installation of the flare dispenser required a modification to the fuel dump pipe on the rear part of the starboard boat hull to ensure that fuel was vented well clear of any flares. Dalmo-Victor AN/APR-39 RWRs were installed under the tailboom and fuselage, and on the sides of the nose. The aircraft was also fitted with a SLIPAR Industries laser warning receiver on

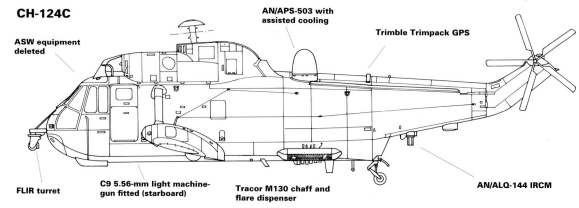

CH-124C

ASW equipment deleted

AN/APS-503 with assisted cooling

Trimble Trimpack GPS

FLIR turret

C9 5.56-mm light machine-gun fitted (starboard)

Tracor M130 chaff and flare dispenser

AN/ALQ-144 IRCM

The Gulf War modifications made to the CH-124A led to the unimplemented designation CH-124C. Improvements included IRCM, AN/ALE-37 chaff and flare dispensers (being demonstrated here), a light machine-gun in the cabin and a FLIR 2000 turret.

and installed by the Canadian Armed Forces and the DND, with an Installation Control Team at Shearwater co-operating closely with the Aircraft Maintenance Development Unit at Trenton, the Aerospace Engineering Test Establishment at Cold Lake and IMP Aerospace, the civilian contractor responsible for civilian engineering and technical support for the Sea King fleet.

Ernst Leitz (Canada) (now Hughes Leitz Optical Technologies) NVGs were issued to each observer and AESO, while all crew members received ARO Canada Inc. AC-4 chemical defence respirators and Exotemp aircrew cooling vests. The latter were water-cooled vests similar to those used by racing drivers in the southern states of the

USA. Crews also had desert survival kits, including desalination equipment. All aircrew were issued with gyro-stabilised binoculars, bullet-proof vests and anti-laser goggles.

Six aircraft were modified initially (one, 12426, for follow-on testing at HOTEF), followed by two more (12405 and 12438). The deployed aircraft (12404 *Persian Pig*, 12410 *Chicken Hawk*, 12412 *Hormuz Harry*, 12413 *Lucky Louie* and 12417 *Big Bird*) were used primarily for assisting in the maintenance of sanctions before the war, intercepting and boarding ships suspected of trying to run the blockade of Iraq.

Since the Gulf War, the equipment package has become known as the surveillance mod and several more aircraft have been retrofitted with some or all of its elements. The CH-124C designation requested for the eight aircraft modified for Operation Friction was not officially approved, since the scope of the modifications was felt to be too modest to justify allocation of a new designation, and the aircraft remain known by the original designation.

the windscreen and provision for an indigenous C-9 5.56-mm light machine-gun in the cabin door. The AN/ALQ-144, AN/ALE-37 and AN/APR-39 came from inventory stocks, but the rest of the equipment was newly procured. Finally,

existing ASW equipment was removed (though it was carried aboard the *Protecteur*, ready for reinstallation if needed), and Kevlar armour was fixed to the crew seats.

The modification package was designed

Mitsubishi HSS-2 and HSS-2A

Having already operated the HSS-1, the JMSDF was a natural customer for the Sea King in light of the perceived threat from the large Soviet Pacific submarine fleet which regularly appeared off the Japanese coast. Japan's growing indigenous aircraft industry made the lure of licence-manufacture a strong one. A licence agreement between Sikorsky and Mitsubishi Jukogyo Kabushiki Kaisha (Mitsubishi Heavy Industries) was signed in May 1962, and was sealed with an initial JMSDF order for 11 HSS-2s. The original Japanese licence-built Sea King was a standard S-61B, broadly equivalent to the US Navy SH-3A. The first was Sikorsky-built and was delivered complete, while the second and third were assembled from major sub-assemblies. Subsequent aircraft were built by Mitsubishi using an increasing proportion of indigenous components. The

Japan is one the largest licence-builders of Sea Kings, the first of which were HSS-2s which were broadly equivalent to the SH-3A. All of this batch have now been retired after the UH-60J was introduced.

aircraft was powered by a pair of Ishikawajima-Harima T58-IHI-10 turboshafts, these being licence-built versions of the T58-GE-10. Production by Mitsubishi totalled 55, serialled 8001 to 8055. The first example was delivered to the JMSDF on 24 March 1964. The first Japanese Sea Kings were delivered in the then-standard US Navy colour scheme of gloss midnight blue with Dayglo noses and tails, but overall dark grey soon took over before the JMSDF standardised on the grey and white scheme

still used on the HSS-2B today. The type equipped five squadrons, for use aboard 'Hatakaze'-, 'Shirane'-, 'Haruna'- and 'Hatsuyuki'-classes vessels, which were fitted with the Canadian 'Beartrap' helicopter landing aid. The 'Shirane'- and 'Haruna'-classes were noted for their capability to carry three HSS-2s, an impressive achievement in a 5,000-tonne hull. The

HSS-2 had been withdrawn from use by 1986, having spent the last few years of its career in the liaison, utility and training roles.

The HSS-2A, also known as the S-61B-1, was broadly equivalent to the US Navy's basic SH-3D, with dipping sonar but without towed MAD gear. The aircraft retained the first short, unbraced tailplane of the original SH-3A. Twenty-nine were built, serialled 8056-8083. The HSS-2A was fitted with station keeping equipment and had provision for hover refuelling inflight. The HSS-2A was delivered from late 1974, but has now been retired with the introduction of the UH-60J.

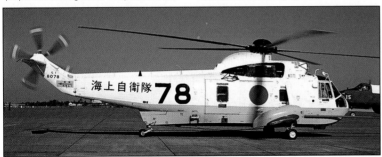

Essentially similar to the SH-3D, the HSS-2A could hover-refuel. This example served with 51 Kokutai, the JMSDF's trials unit.

Mitsubishi HSS-2B

The Mitsubishi HSS-2B was designated S-61B-2 by Mitsubishi and Sikorsky and was closely equivalent to the US Navy SH-3H. Eighty-three of these advanced ASW helicopters were produced, serialled 8084-8167. They were fitted with extended sponsons housing MAD to starboard and smoke marker launch tubes to port. The new variant had a forward-folding sonobuoy datalink antenna on the centreline, at the back of the boat hull, and sonobuoy launch tubes could be used for launching active and passive buoys. The aircraft also had a new ESM suite. The HSS-2B had provision for search radar, with a small retractable radome on the centreline, well aft, but this option was not always exercised by the JMSDF. The most

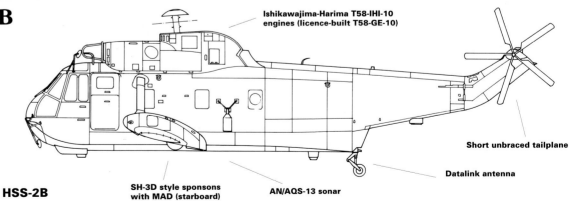

Ishikawajima-Harima T58-IHI-10 engines (licence-built T58-GE-10)

Short unbraced tailplane

Datalink antenna

HSS-2B

SH-3D style sponsons with MAD (starboard)

AN/AQS-13 sonar

obvious external feature of the HSS-2B was the unusual intake guard arrangement

An HSS-2B of 124 Kokutai is seen during a visit to Antwerp in 1991. Similar to the SH-3H, the HSS-2B has a MAD bird in the starboard sponson, but no radar. This aircraft is not fitted with the distinctive intake guards normally associated with this variant.

adopted during service. Five squadrons operated the type (101, 121 and 122 Kokutai of 21 Kokugun (Air Group) at Tateyama and 123 and 124 Kokutai of 22 Kokugun at Omhura). 122 was first to convert to the SH-60J, moving to Omhura, followed by 123 and 121. By 1996 the HSS-2B served only with 101 Hikotai and 124 Hikotai at Tateyama, and with 211 Hikotai, the training unit, at Kanoya. It also equipped the Kure, Sasebo and Ominato Chihotais (naval district flights).

Mitsubishi S-61A and S-61AH

Two Mitsubishi-built S-61As (8181 and 8182) were delivered in 1965, with another (8183) and an S-61A-1 (8184) following soon afterwards. These were procured for use aboard the icebreaker *Shirase* and its replacement, the *Fuji*. These vessels, and their helicopters, supported Japanese operations in the Antarctic. Twelve more locally-built S-61A-1s, equipped for SAR duties, were procured as S-61AHs to replace S-62Js from late 1983. The aircraft were externally similar to the HSS-2B, with the same distinctive intake filters, but without extended sponsons, sonar cut-outs or radar. These aircraft were serialled from 8941 to 8952 and equipped SAR units at Atsugi, Hachinohe, Kanoya and Oluki, but were replaced by UH-60Js at Shimofusa, Hachinohe and Atsugi during 1994-95, so that by 1996 the type served only with the SAR Kokutais of the Tokushima Kyoiku Kokugun and Oluki Kyoiku Kokugun, and with the SAR Hikotai at Kanoya. The S-61As and S-61A-1 served with the Yokosuka Chihotai for operations aboard the icebreaker *Shirase*. The S-61AHs wore a distinctive colour scheme with brick-red undersides and medium grey upper surfaces, and were festooned with mirrors above and below the cockpit. A searchlight (or later a FLIR or TV camera) could be carried on an articulated pylon aft of the port mainwheel sponson.

Painted with large Dayglo patches for conspicuity over ice, this S-61A served with 101 Kokutai for service aboard Japan's icebreakers. The Dayglo panels are for conspicuity, while the aircraft wears a penguin badge.

Wearing a bright SAR scheme, this is one of the S-61AHs procured to equip base rescue flights. Note the fuselage-mounted searchlight.

Agusta/Sikorsky AS-61A-4

The AS-61A-4 was a multi-role variant developed and built for export and suited equally for SAR, trooping and freighting. Four such aircraft (EV-8437 to EV-8440) are used by Venezuela's Aviación del Ejercito, these serving in the tactical transport role with the 811 Grupo at BA Generalissimo Francisco de Miranda at La Carlotta, Caracas. The Venezuelan aircraft are augmented by a single Sikorsky-built SH-3D.

Iranian aircraft were similarly designated AS-61A-4 but may have been ASW-configured, since the first batch (8-2301 to 8-2314) was externally similar to the second batch of Italian navy ASH-3Ds. They retained a sonar cut-out below the fuselage, and had nose-mounted search radar and undernose Doppler. When delivered they were painted in the same dark blue-grey colour scheme, with Dayglo tails and noses. Later aircraft (8-2315 to 8-2320) were similar in configuration to the first batch of Peruvian aircraft, with the same grey and white colour scheme and with an underfuselage radome well aft. Some sources suggest that the later aircraft served with the IIAF, and the older aircraft with the IINA. Only about 10 Iranian Sea Kings are believed to be in service today with the Islamic Republic of Iran navy, with most of the fleet having been cannibalised for spares. The much smaller fleet of RH-53Ds is believed to have been entirely withdrawn, and some reports suggest that the Iranian Sea Kings may have been modified for the mine counter-measures role.

EV-8437 was the first AS-61A-4 for Venezuela, used in the utility transport role.

Iran received 20 AS-61A-4s for maritime roles, equipped with search radar in a prominent nose radome.

Agusta/Sikorsky AS-61-TS

The Italian air force uses two VIP-configured AS-61s (MM80972, MM80973) with nose-mounted weather radar (offset to port) and with an external VH-3 type APU mounted above the starboard undercarriage sponson. These were initially designated ASH-3D-TS (Transporto Speziale) and serve with the 31º Stormo's 93º Gruppo at Rome Ciampino in the VIP transport role. Among the duties of these plush machines is providing transport for the Pope within Italy, most notably to and from the Vatican and his summer retreat at Castel Gandolfo. Dedicated VIP versions of the AS-61A-4 were also exported to Iran (6-9294/5 for the air force), Iraq (at least three and possibly up to six, known serials including YI-001, YI-002, and YI-005), Libya (one aircraft) and Saudi Arabia (121-123).

The AS-61-TS has appealed to several foreign customers, in addition to the home market. Saudi Arabia operates three with No. 1 Squadron, two of which are seen here. Like the AMI aircraft, they have nose radar.

Agusta/Sikorsky ASH-3D

Italy was a natural customer for the Sea King. US Navy Sea King operations with the Sixth Fleet in the Mediterranean had been watched with great interest, while the MMI had operated the Sea King's immediate predecessor, the Sikorsky HSS-1. Aircraft for the Italian navy were broadly analogous to the ASW-optimised Sikorsky SH-3D (S-61D), but with an improved tailplane, 1,500-shp (1125-kW) T58-GE-100 engines, and radar. The first entered service in 1968, following the 1967 order for 24 aircraft. The SH-3Ds entered service with the 10 Grupelicot of the Maristaeli Luni, and with the 30 Grupelicot of the Maristaeli Catania.

The first nine aircraft (MM5003N-MM5011N, coded 6-01 to 6-09) were initially delivered without radar, but were subsequently fitted with a 360° AN/APN-182 radar in a ventral radome mounted well forward, under the cockpit. Initially, at least, these aircraft went to the 3rd Grupelicot. The next 15 aircraft (MM5012-MM5026, coded 6-10 to 6-25) had a nose-mounted AN/APN-195 search radar.

All Italian navy Sea Kings have now been upgraded to ASH-3H standards, as described below. MM5005N (coded 6-03) served as a testbed, and was unique in having a nose-mounted APN-195 radome in addition to its belly-mounted APQ-706.

Agusta-built ASW Sea Kings proved popular in Latin America. Four AS-61Ds were delivered to the Servicio Aeronaval de la Marina Peruana in 1978 as HA-430 to HA-433. Two more (HQ-490 and 491 were delivered in 1979 and four more were ordered in 1984. Four ASH-3Ds (N3013-N3016) went to Brazil in 1984, augmenting existing Sikorsky-built S-61D-3s. These have subsequently been upgraded to ASH-3H standards, known locally as ASH-3As.

The Italian ASH-3D could fire short range AS12 or medium range AM39 Exocet and Marte Mk 2 missiles (illustrated). This aircraft, 6-03, served as a testbed for the fleet, later gaining nose radar.

Agusta/Sikorsky ASH-3H Sea King

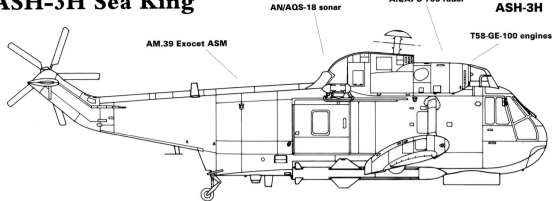

AM.39 Exocet ASM   **AN/AQS-18 sonar**   **AN/APS-705 radar**   **ASH-3H**

T58-GE-100 engines

The demonstrated success of the Sikorsky-built SH-3H in US Navy service prompted the Italian navy to upgrade the specification of the remainder of its planned Sea King buy to virtual SH-3H standards. As such, later Italian navy aircraft (MM81111-MM81116, coded 6-26 to 6-31, MM81183-MM81187 coded 6-32 to 6-36, and MM81200 coded 6-37) are sometimes referred to as ASH-3Hs.

The primary ASW sensor of the ASH-3H was the AQS-18 sonar with 360° simultaneous search capability. This was based on the AN/AQS-13B/E indicator and receiver combined with a new adaptive processor and a new wet end, which could extend to a depth of 950 ft (290 m). Moreover, the hydrodynamically streamlined transducer and its small-diameter low-drag triaxial cable could be reeled in and out very quickly, allowing a quicker dip cycle to the full depth (in 130 seconds) than was possible to 450 ft (137 m) with the AQS-13B/E.

These aircraft used AN/APS-705 radar in an underfuselage radome mounted well forward. The ASH-3Hs were also fitted with a Colibri integrated ESM/ECM suite, with ELT-161 ESM/RWR, an ELT-562 deception jammer and an ELT-361 noise jammer. The aircraft also had an 8,000-lb (3628-kg) capacity external load hook and a 600-lb (272 kg) capacity rescue winch.

Italy's earlier Sea Kings have been brought up to a similar standard to the ASH-3Hs. The first nine ASH-3Ds were retrofitted with underfuselage AN/APQ-706 targeting/missile command radar for use in the ASV role, in conjunction with AM39 Exocet or ASM Mk 2A Marte missiles. The next 15 ASH-3Ds had their nose-mounted APN-195 replaced by belly-mounted APS-705 during the mid- to late 1980s, like that fitted to the ASH-3Hs. All aircraft (ASH-3D and ASH-3H) could also carry up to four AS12 missiles on outrigger pylons which projected horizontally from the fuselage sides.

Today, the ASH-3Hs serve with 10 Grupelicot at La Spezia/Luni, 30 Grupelicot at Catania/Fontanarossa and alongside

The ASH-3H is still in widespread service with the Italian navy, recently upgraded with ESM equipment.

Among Peru's Sea King fleet are Exocet-capable Agusta-built aircraft virtually identical to the ASH-3H.

AB212s with 40 Grupelicot at Taranto/Grottaglie. In their most recent operational configuration, the AS-61Bs have a comprehensive array of RHAWS and MAWS antennas on the nose, undercarriage sponsons and on a fairing under the tailboom, providing 360° coverage. The aircraft can carry a pair of Marte missiles slung off the lower fuselage corners, or

Mk 44, Mk 46, A244/S or Sting Ray torpedoes. The A244/S is a derivative of the Mk 44, with a sophisticated active/passive/mixed homing system and pre-selected circle or snake-type attack paths. The Italian navy will replace its Sea Kings with the Anglo-Italian EHI EH101.

All but the first four Peruvian Sea Kings were built to the same standard as the later

Italian navy aircraft, with forward-mounted underfuselage radomes and with full Exocet compatibility. It is not certain whether the initial Peruvian Sea Kings carried Exocets. Another four AS-61s went to Argentina in 1987, upgraded to virtually full SH-3H standards and sometimes known as ASH-3Hs. These were serialled 0794-0797. The first two were lost on 30 January 1989.

Agusta/Sikorsky AS-61N-1 Silver

The AS-61N was a civilian version of the Sea King, combining features of the S-61N with the shorter fuselage of the S-61A/S-61B, and carrying up to 23 or 24 passengers. The shorter fuselage was achieved by removing a 50-in (1.27-m) plug from the forward fuselage. The aircraft had seven cabin windows, large S-61N type sponsons, an S-61N type tailfin and a nose radome. They also had a 3400-litre (920-US gal) fuselage fuel tank. Two military AS-61N-1s were delivered to Malaysia as AS-61NSs in 1990, serialled M39-01 and M39-02. They serve with No. 10 Squadron.

Agusta/Sikorsky AS-61R Pelican

As well as its ASW S-61B derivatives, civilian S-61Ns and multi-role S-61As, Agusta also produced the S-61R under licence. The US Coast Guard's HH-3F formed the basis of the Agusta-Sikorsky AS-61R and even gave the Italian aircraft its Pelican name. The type was selected by the Aeronautica Militare Italiana to replace the amphibious fixed-wing Grumman HU-16 Albatross in the SAR role, and an initial batch of 20 was ordered. These were serialled MM80974-MM80993, and were coded between 15-01 and 15-24, omitting 08, 09, 17 and 18. The first aircraft arrived at Ciampino on 12 August 1977, and the 15° Stormo HU-16 *Gruppi* successively re-equipped with HH-3Fs.

A second batch of 15 HH-3Fs was serialled MM81337-MM81351, coded 15-25 to 15-39. These were ordered as recently as 1992. Some of these aircraft were delivered in a green and grey camouflage instead of the overall white worn by the original batch. These aircraft had a Dayglo tailfin and black-edged yellow rear fuselage band and nose, for maximum conspicuity.

All 35 AS-61Rs serve with the 15° Stormo 'Stefano Cagna', headquartered at Roma-Ciampino. This is part of the Comando Trasporti e Soccorso Aereo (Air Transport and Rescue Command) and parents four HH-3F equipped *Gruppi*. These are 82° Gruppo at Trapani-Bergi, 83° Gruppo at Rimini-Miramare, 84° Gruppo at Brindisi and 85° Gruppo at Roma-Ciampino.

With an increasing combat SAR commitment, practised in Somalia and potentially useful for operations over Bosnia, an upgrade is being applied to Italian S-61Rs. They are receiving new RWRs, chaff/flare

dispensers and the warlike dark green and grey camouflage colour scheme applied to some of the aircraft from the second batch. The aircraft are also receiving an NVG-compatible cockpit and the old Ecko 290M nose radar is being replaced by an improved AN/APS-717 with better range and discrimination.

The AS-61R is similar in configuration to the US Coast Guard HH-3F, but has been extensively modified with the addition of an NVG-compatible cockpit, new radar and RWR. Tactical camouflage is now worn.

NVG-compatible cockpit

Capacity for 20 survivors in rear cabin

AS-61R

Ecko 209M radar (being replaced by AN/APS-17)

HH-3 style fuselage and tailboom

Retractable nosewheel

RWR aerials

Kubinka

Carrier air wing detachment

Photography by Yefim Gordon

The air wing for the carrier *Admiral Kuznetsov*, based at Severomorsk near Murmansk, has been working up at Kubinka air base. The detachment to Kubinka allowed the wing to hone its skills prior to its operational debut in the Adriatic Sea, where the carrier is now deployed in support of IFOR.

Left: This view of the tail end of the Su-27K shows the large arrester hook between the jet pipes. The Su-27K has a completely new system of trailing-edge control surfaces.

Below: As well as the naval 'Flankers' on the apron at Kubinka, three MiG-29 'Fulcrums' (two of them in the colours of the 'Swifts' aerobatic team) can be seen outside the hangar to the left of the picture, as well as three air force 'Flankers'. The huge wingspan of the Su-27K can be gauged by the tanker in front of the aircraft.

Left: This Su-27K shows its naval modifications as it touches down. The nosewheel has a much smaller debris guard than its air force counterparts, as it will presumably only operate from well swept decks. The tail cone is slightly shortened to ease high-alpha landings.

Right: A pair of Su-27Ks make a pairs take-off from Kubinka. All the aircraft seen at the base were in unarmed configuration. The aircraft can carry the powerful 'Moskit' anti-ship missile, derived from the ship-launched 3M-80.

Below: Looking down at this pair of Su-27Ks, the large canard foreplanes are very prominent, as are the leading-edge flaps. The huge lifting surfaces and excellent control system make the Flanker eminently suitable for operations from aircraft-carriers.

Above: The massive heat haze behind this Su-27K gives an indication of the power that allows take-offs from a carrier without the need for catapult launches. The Su-27K also has a very long range, even without the external fuel tanks that it can carry (unlike land-based 'Flankers'). The large size of the flaps is very clear in this picture.

Below: The crew of a Ka-27PL 'Helix-A' stand proudly in front of their aircraft, which carries the submarine hunter badge shown opposite. The Ka-27 normally carries a three-man crew in the ASW role, with a pilot, observer/navigator and an aircrewman in the rear. For the search and rescue role, the carrier will probably also carry at least one Ka-27 'Helix-D'.

Above: The pilots of the Severomorsk wing have the distinction of being at the cutting edge of naval aviation: the blue and white T-shirts were formerly worn by the elite naval infantry. The pilot's helmets all have the fitting for attachment of helmet-mounted sights, allowing high off-boresight engagements with the Vympel R-73 missile. The navy aircrew have been perhaps more fortunate in their allocation of flying hours than their air force and air defence force counterparts, who have been flying as little as 20-50 hours annually. The average age of the aircrew here shows that the navy required very experienced crews to form its first naval 'Flanker' wing.

Right: This badge worn by the Ka-27 'Helix' denotes the successful tracking of a Western nuclear submarine, a likely scenario given that Severomorsk is not far from the Northern Fleet base at Murmansk which still receives the attentions of NATO submarines on surveillance missions. The quality of Russian-made ASW equipment has steadily improved, much of it benefiting from information gleaned from NATO sonobuoys.

Below: The Ka-27PL 'Helix-A' will form the main ASW screen for the Admiral Kuznetsov, equipped with active/passive dipping sonar, sonobuoys and magnetic anomaly detection gear. Although Kuznetsov's SSN-19 'Shipwreck' missiles are capable of mid-course guidance, it is not known whether the Ka-27PL can perform this role like the Ka-25 'Hormone-B'.

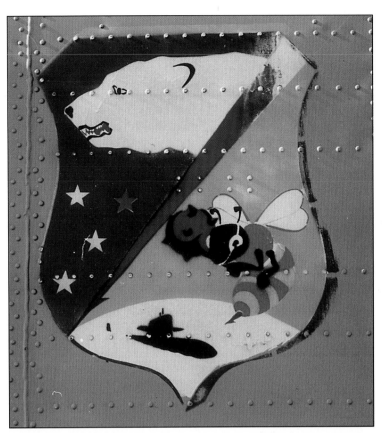

Brazil

Brazil is the largest nation in South America and has armed forces to match. The Força Aérea Brasileira is well equipped and has the backing of a worthy indigenous aviation industry. The FAB maintains sophisticated combat aircraft, whilst also attending to the many demands placed on it by Brazil's diverse population and sprawling geography. Brazil's naval air arm, while a far less potent force, is also an experienced and competent service. Despite previous bitter rivalry, the two forces now work smoothly in tandem.

Força Aérea Brasileira (Brazilian air force)

With by far the largest land area in Latin America, exceeding the size of the Continental US or the whole of Europe, and the fifth largest country in the world, Brazil inevitably also has the biggest armed forces in its area. Supported by about 700 aircraft of the Força Aérea Brasileira (FAB), including 200 or so combat types, manned by 59,000 personnel, these forces have the job of defending Brazil's frontiers with no fewer than 10 South American countries, encompassing all except Chile and Ecuador, as well as 7412 km (4,606 miles) of Atlantic coastline. Brazil's population of 153 million occupies an area of around 8.5 million km² (3.29 million sq miles), including 55457 km² (21,412 sq miles) of inland water.

Despite the country's size, its annual defence expenditure is a fraction of most Western nations. In 1994, the $4.6 billion Brazilian defence budget represented only about one per cent of gross domestic product, as against $4.4 billion in 1993 and $2.12 billion in 1992. Until recently, the Brazilian economy and FAB procurement have been bedevilled by inflation rates which reached 934 per cent in 1988. Fortunately, in recent years, these have progressively fallen to 50 per cent, and have now reached single figures. Their effects have nevertheless inevitably been reflected in many FAB programmes and operations, with cuts in fuel allocations, for example, reducing regional transport flying by up to 90 per cent of the total hours achieved five years ago. Equipment orders have been limited, and existing programmes stretched because of funding shortages.

Command structure

With a long and distinguished history, including active participation in World War II on the side of the Allies, the FAB has independent status among the Brazilian armed forces. In addition to its major commitments to national defence, the FAB also has vital support roles in opening up the vast hinterland for economic development. It currently comprises five of the six components administered by the Ministerio da Aéronautica, the exception being Departamento de Aviação Civil (Civil Aviation Department). The Comando Geral do Air (COMGAR), or General Air Command, with HQ in Brasília, supervises most of the flying operations of the FAB. Its parallel organisations, which also report directly to the

Ministry of Aeronautics, comprise the Comando Geral de Apoio (**COMGAP** or Support Command); Comando Geral do Pessoal (**COMGEP** or Personnel Command); Departamento de Pesquisas e Desenvolvimento (**DEPED** or R&D Department); and Departamento de Ensino (**DEPENS** or Training Department). As the main FAB flying element, **COMGAR** administers several sub-formations in the form of seven Comandos Aéreos Regionais (**COMAR**s or Regional Air Commands); three Forças Aréas (FAes or Air Forces); a Comando Aéreo de Treinamento (**CATRE** or Air Training Command); and the Nucleo do Comando de Defesa Aéroespacial Brasileiro (**NuCOMDAER** or HQ Brazilian Aerospace Defence Command). At unit levels, Grupos de Aviaçãos (GAv) or wings usually comprise anything from one to five consecutively-numbered Esquadrãos (squadrons), each with varying numbers of aircraft from half a dozen to 12 or more, smaller formations being known as Esquadrilhas (flights).

The FAB has its own aircraft designation system, based on the US pattern, with a role prefix letter(s) and type number. The T-27 Tucano, for example, is the 27th trainer type to be operated by the FAB. In the case of imported aircraft, the latter is occasionally allocated irregularly to match the original designation.

Maritime operations commitments

Most FAB flying elements, apart from training and regional transport units, are operated by COMGAR's three (originally five) subordinate air forces, which have specific individual tasks. The Segunda Força Aérea (IIa FAe), with HQ in Rio de Janeiro, undertakes maritime patrol, ship-borne ASW, SAR and related roles, as well as helicopter tactical support and observation tasks in co-operation with the Brazilian army. It therefore has dual inter-service commitments, since its 1º Grupo de Aviação Embarcada (1º GAE) at Santa Cruz is responsible for operating the FAB's Grumman S-2E (P-16E/H) Tracker fleet for both land- and carrier-based ASW roles.

The FAB acquired 13 Grumman S-2As (serialled 7014-7026) and eight S-2Es (7030-7037) from the US in 1961, to operate from Brazil's recently-acquired light fleet carrier *Minas Gerias*. Its initial crews were trained with the USN at NAS Key West, Florida. The FAB has continued the responsibility of manning and operating the sole

fixed-wing aircraft serving with the navy ever since, although only five or six S-2Es are still active. A similar number of S-2As are held in reserve storage at Campo Marte, in São Paulo. 1º GAE also operates a single P-16H Turbo Tracker with PT6A-67CF turboprops in place of its original Wright R-1820-82C piston engines and improved avionics. This was the prototype from a $40 million upgrade contract placed by the FAB in 1988 with the Canadian IMP Aerospace Group in Halifax, to convert the rest of its S-2E force in Brazil by Motortec for a further $15 million to Turbo Tracker standard. The Thomson-CSF TRES ASW system was chosen in late 1989 for the associated avionics update, with VARAN radar, MAD, DR2000A/1000A ESM and FLIR, for installation by EMBRAER. After its initial PT6-powered flight in June 1990, the prototype continued its flight trials in Brazil from December of that year. Technical and funding problems combined to frustrate these programmes, which were cancelled in 1993 by the Ministry of Aeronautics. Although still nominally active with 1º GAE, the P-16E rarely flies, each sortie apparently requiring individual IMP Group authorisation. The Tracker upgrade requirement nevertheless still appears to exist, since Brazil has so far revealed no plans to retire the now-ageing *Minas Gerais*. In addition to active or passive sonobuoys released from rear engine-nacelle stowage, Tracker armament includes bombs, depth charges, torpedoes or underwing rockets.

When it is in commission, 1º GAE (radio callsign CARDEAL), whose squadron motto Deixe Comigo means 'Stay With Me', normally undertakes 10-day deployments at sea with four or five Trackers every two months. Between times, a dummy deck painted on the Santa Cruz runways and a mirror deck-landing sight allow the FAB crews to maintain their ship-board proficiency. At sea, either catapult or free take-offs may be employed, although the latter require the full length of the deck, plus a headwind of at least 10 kt (12 mph; 19 km/h) and a minimum ship speed of 30 kt (35 mph; 56 km/h).

FAB's other maritime assets

Sharing the enormous 270 x 50 x 58-m high (823 x 152 x 177-ft) Zeppelin hangar, built in 1934-36 for Germany's transatlantic services with the Hindenberg, which dominates the Santa Cruz Air Base skyline, three EMBRAER EMB-111A (P-95A) Bandeirante Patrulha or 'Bandeirulha' turboprop twins also operate with 1º GAE on maritime patrol and reconnaissance duties. The EMB-111 was developed in the mid-1970s from the Bandeirante transport at the request of the FAB's Comando Costeiro (Coastal Command) to replace its 14 ageing Lockheed P2V-5 Neptunes. It features fixed tip-tanks for 140 Imp gal (636 litres) of extra fuel, airframe reinforcements for four underwing stores pylons, an increase in maximum take-off weight to 7000 kg (15,432 lb), and uprated (to 750 shp/559 kW) PT6A-34s. The starboard wing leading edge also accommodates a 500-million candlepower searchlight, to supplement the Eaton/AIL AN/APS-128 Sea Patrol radar as primary sensor in the large nose radome. Provision is made for a crew of six, comprising two pilots, a tactical navigator, flight engineer, ESM operator and observer/photographer, for missions averaging five to six hours. Twelve P-95As (now serialled 7050-7061) were built by

The VIP fleet of the Grupo de Transporte Especial (GTE) operates outside the regular FAB command structure. This is one of its two Brasília-based VC-96s (Boeing 737-2N3 Adv).

This was the final Learjet 35A delivered to the GTE, in 1989, under the service designation VU-35A. The Learjets are markedly more economic to operate than the HS 125s.

Above: The GTE operates three HS 125-403Bs (seen here) as VU-93s, alongside two older HS 125-400As with the same FAB designation.

The FAB's display team, 'Esquadrilha de Fumaca', is not assigned a parent unit, but reports directly to the Ministry of Defence.

Helibras is a subsidiary of Eurocopter France and has a long tradition of supplying Eurocopter (Aérospatiale) helicopters to the FAB, such as this licence-built CH-55 Esquilo Bi (AS 355).

1º ETA of COMAR I flies the EMBRAER C-95B Bandeirante, from Belém. Its unit motto is Devagar mas chego la (slow, but I will arrive). 1º ETA also operates the C-98 Caravan I.

Left: 3º ETA, of COMAR III based at Galeão, includes Rio de Janeiro in its operational area. The unit flies early-model, short-fuselage, C-95 Bandeirantes in addition to C-95Bs.

Above: 2º ETA of Recife-based COMAR II operates the C-95A Bandeirante, which is equivalent to the commercial-standard EMBRAER EMB-110P1K.

EMBRAER, the first three being delivered on 11 April 1978 in an overall grey paint scheme, to the 1º Esquadrão of the 7º Grupo de Aviação 'Orungan' (1º/7º GAv) of IIª FAe, at Salvador air base, in Bahia province.

Two other 7º GAv units, comprising 2º/7º GAv 'Phoenix' at Florinapolis, in the southern Santa Catarina state, and 3º/7º 'Netuno' at Belém, in the northern Para province, were also eventually equipped with EMB-111s, following additional orders for another 10 'Bandeirulhas' (7101-7110). Costing $30.77 million, these were EMB-111Bs or P-95Bs with upgraded tactical avionics, partial 'glass' cockpit and a Thorn/EMI Super Searcher radar, although with no search-light. Five each of these aircraft re-equipped 1º and 2º Esquadrões from 1990, leaving 3º/7º with the remaining P-95As. Most of the P-95Bs have been given individual names, including 7102 *Cormorao*, 7013 *Flamingo*, 7104 *Fregata*, 7105 *Guara*, 7106 *Jacana*, 7107 *Maguari*, 7108 *Soco* and 7109 *Tacha*.

Completing the FAB's maritime assets is a fleet support unit retaining the title of several long-disbanded FAB organisations known as Liaison and Observation Flights (Esquadrilha de Ligacao & Observacao). As the sole surviving example of its type, 2ª ELO 'Duelo' is now an independent unit within IIª FAe, operating until recently half a dozen armed EMBRAER EMB-312 Tucano AT-27 turboprop trainers from the naval air base at São Pedro da Aldeia, near Rio de Janeiro. These were ostensibly employed on a variety of jobs, including target facilities, observation, attack training and so on, in support of naval operations. In fact, they spent much of their time on drug-smuggling aircraft interdiction patrols, which duties they are now continuing from Santa Cruz.

SAR and army support

Another Bandeirante variant operated within IIª FAe is the EMB-110P1K or SC-95B, five of which (6542-6546) have equipped the second squadron of 10º GAv (2º/10º 'Pelicano') at Campo Grande in Mato Grosso since late 1981 for dedicated search and rescue roles. This small unit is intended to cover Brazil's entire vast inland area and coastal waters, and its SC-95s, delivered in 1981 to the FAB's Comissão de Fiscalizacão e Recebimento de Aéronaves (COMFIREM), or Air Force Inspection and Acceptance Commission, are equipped with GPS and VLF Omega precision navigation equipment, as well as having bulged rear cabin windows for surface observation. Their crews of eight comprise two pilots, a loadmaster, one flight engineer and four observers who are also trained as paramedics. Dinghies and survival packs are carried to be dropped to survivors, and provision is made for up to six stretcher patients. Maximum endurance is about six hours.

For shorter-range and specialised SAR roles, 2º/10º GAv is also equipped with six Bell UH-1H Iroquois utility helicopters. The FAB received its first Iroquois in 1967 in the form of six SH-1Ds (8530-8535) for SAR, followed by eight UH-1Ds (8536-8543), most of which were later re-engined to UH-1H standard. Twenty-six of these later versions known locally as 'Sapaos' (or 'big frogs'), were then acquired by the FAB from the US from 1972, supplemented in 1982 by a further five, plus three Agusta-Bell 205 versions bought from Israel, serialled sequentially from 8650 to

8683. The Iroquois can be quickly fitted with a rescue hoist when required and, with the SC-95s, operate a 24-hour per day standby service. They are particularly useful for jungle and mountain rescues in the Maracaju range in the Pantanal area. UH-1Hs are also operated by some of the five squadrons in IIª FAe's 8º Grupo, which is mainly concerned with army support, and flies most of the FAB's helicopters, although it is additionally equipped with fixed-wing types. At Belém (Para), 1º/8º GAv 'Falcão Pioneiro' is the sole FAB unit to operate the Aérospatiale AS 355M Twin Ecureuil or CH-55 Esquilo in attack and observation roles. Eleven Ecureuils were assembled in Brazil by Helibras, including eight armed versions for 1º/8º (8810-8817), and three VH-55s in VIP configuration (8818-8820) for the Special Transport Group (GTE) at Brasília. Several have since been lost in accidents. At Recife, in Bahia state, 2º/8º GAv 'Poti' is equipped with about 10 single-turboshaft HB-350B Esquilo (UH-50) helicopters from 30 (8760-8789) assembled by Helibras in 1986-87 to replace Bell H-13G/Hs. Those at Recife are used for observation and light transport as well as SAR roles, with provision for a rescue hoist and under-fuselage searchlight.

In a mixed inventory, 2º/8º also operates five indigenous Neiva T-25C Universal two-seat basic trainers from 150 built (1830-1979) from 1968, and now used for liaison and observation. As 8º Grupo's third squadron, 3º/8º GAv 'Puma' at Campo dos Afonsos uses eight Eurocopter AS 332M Super Pumas (CH-34s, 8730-8738) of nine ordered by the FAB in 1985 for general and assault transport roles. The Super Pumas have provision for machine-gun and other armament, although they may also be fitted with a rescue winch for secondary SAR tasks, and replaced six FAB SA 330 Pumas (CH-33s, 8700-8705) bought back by Aérospatiale in a part-exchange deal in mid-1987.

3º/8º GAv is further equipped with three indigenous two-seat Neiva Regente high-wing liaison aircraft from 41 delivered from 1968 (3120, 3210-3249). In a camouflaged finish, these aircraft are now operated for army observation and forward air control roles. For such taskings, they have provision for underwing rockets or other light stores for target marking. With a 210-hp (156-kW) Continental IO-360D engine, the sturdily-built T-42 is said to be slightly under-powered for tropical operation, and to be a bit of a handful in cross-winds, despite its tricycle undercarriage. About four are also operated in similar roles by 5º/8º GAv 'Pantera' from Santa Maria, in Rio Grande do Sol near the Paraguayan border, in conjunction with eight Bell UH-1Hs and four EMBRAER EMB-810 U-7s, better known as the locally-built Piper Seneca II/III six-seat light twin. In 1978 EMBRAER began delivering 35 (2600-2634) turbo-supercharged U-7 and U-7A Senecas, the latter with Robertson STOL modifications; they have provided low-cost and efficient transport to the FAB. UH-1Hs and U-7s are similarly operated by the last of 8º Grupo's squadrons, which is 7º/8º GAv 'Falcão', in the Amazon region at Manaus, in northwestern Brazil.

Brazil's air combat units are grouped within the Terceira Força Aérea (IIIª FAe), with HQ in Brasília, although also integrated with the independent Comando Geral de Apoio (CGA), or

General Support Command. From its Rio HQ, this command manages the national air defence system, which is further integrated through COMGAR's NuCOMDAER HQ in Brasília. Through CGA auspices, Brazil's integrated air defence system has been progressively established over the past two decades through the DACTA I and II programmes to provide an initial network of detection, control and reporting radars, communications and computer elements, all from an $83 million contract with Thomson-CSF in France to cover the key areas in the Rio-São Paulo-Brasília triangle. As CINDACTA I, this is now one of three national air defence regions. A further $195 million DACTA III programme, which was completed in 1985, extended this system to provide coverage for the entire southern area of Brazil, plus parts of Uruguay and Argentina, as CINDACTA II. A fourth DACTA contract placed with Thomson-CSF in 1984, for the north-eastern areas, completed the national air defence coverage as CINDACTA III, at a further cost of $48 million. It was integrated with 50 army-operated Euromissile ROLAND 2 mobile SAMs on Marder tracked launch vehicles delivered in 1977.

SIVAM and ALX

Major augmentation of Brazilian air defence is now planned from a $1.4 billion contract placed in August 1994 with the US Raytheon Corp. after intense competition with Thomson-CSF, as prime contractor for a new surveillance system of the 5.2 million km² (2 million sq miles) Amazon basin region. Known as SIVAM – Sistema de Vigilancia da Amazonia – this will comprise integrated ground and airborne radars, plus other sensors and communication systems, including already-launched Brazilian space satellites. SIVAM is intended to monitor the vast and remote areas of the Amazon for drug trafficking, illegal mining and logging, plus unauthorised destruction of the rain forests, apart from providing early warning, air defence and air traffic control facilities.

For its airborne sensors, the FAB, with Swedish Export Credit Agency backing, has selected Sweden's Ericcson Erieye planar phased-array radar, mounted above five EMBRAER EMB-120EW Brasilia twin-turboprop transports, in a similar manner to the Saab 340AEW. Unlike the Swedish air force, however, which plans to use only one airborne radar operator to pass most of its sensor data for ground processing, the FAB is specifying three operator stations, in addition to two pilots, for onboard command and control of the radar and its wider roles. These will also require some optimisation of the Erieye radar for slower-speed targets. Given the funding, three EMB-120SR versions are also planned for eco-system SIVAM surveillance with different sensors, including synthetic aperture radar, infra-red line-scanning and FLIR/TV cameras.

Additional airborne components planned for SIVAM include Raytheon/Hawker 800s for logistic support, and 100 EMB-312H Super Tucanos in single-seat A-29 and two-seat TA-29 armed trainer versions. The latter will come from an original requirement for 170 for the FAB's ALX light ground-attack requirement to police the Amazonian area. Developed from EMBRAER's unsuccessful submission for the US Joint Primary Trainer Aircraft System (JPATS)

Iº ETA is based at São Paulo/Cumbrica AB, as part of COMAR IV. It too operates the 1973-vintage C-95 Bandeirante on its services throughout São Paulo and Mato Grosso provinces.

Displaying yet another Bandeirante colour scheme, this C-95C is flown by 6º ETA from Brasília. 6º ETA is a specialist VIP unit attached to COMAR VI which shares its home in the nation's capital with the GTE.

Above: COMAR VI shares the FAB's six VU-9 Xingus with the co-located GTE.

Below: 6º ETA also operates a small number of VIP-dedicated VC-97 Brasilias.

7º ETA is the only COMAR unit to have a combat role. 1º Esq/7º ETA and 2º Esq/7º ETA both operate armed Tucanos for SIVAM surveillance (drug interdiction) missions. This 2º Esq/7º ETA T-27 wears the 'PV' tailcode of Porto Velho.

Above and right: 1º GAE is an FAB unit attached to the Brazilian navy. It is one of the very last operational users of the S-2E Tracker (P-16E). A single aircraft has been upgraded to P-16H standard with PT-6 turboprops but the remainder all rely on their original Wright R-1820 Cyclone piston engines.

Below: When not aboard the Minas Gerias, 1º GAE is based at Santa Cruz AB, with its awe-inspiring Zeppelin hangar – an immense relic from the 1930s.

Small numbers of rugged and versatile Cessna Model 208 Caravan Is (service designation C-98) are in service with various COMAR units, most notably 1º ETA and 7º ETA.

programme, the two stretched EMB-312H prototypes are undergoing further modifications for weapons delivery, in addition to their earlier installation of 1,600-shp (1190-kW) Pratt & Whitney Canada PT6-68/1 turboprops. They are being fitted with five underwing weapons pylons and associated nav/attack systems, head-up and multi-function displays, cockpit armour and night-vision systems to precede production A-29s and two-seat AT-29s by the turn of the century. The Super Tucanos will then operate under the control of the EMB-120EWs in the Amazon area, and take over the FAB's covert drug-smuggling aircraft interception role. That role is currently performed by detached flights each operating four armed AT-27 Tucanos from the 1o Esquadrilha of the misleadingly-named 7o Esquadrão de Transporte Aéreo (ETA) at Boa Vista, in Rondonia, and 2º/7º ETA from Porto Velho in the neighbouring Amazonas province. With Manaus, these bases, which are currently administered through COMGAR's Regional Air Command, will also house SIVAM monitoring and data processing stations. Other A-29/AT-29s will replace some of the 90 or so ageing AT-26 (EMB-326GB) Xavantes in current FAB service for weapons and proficiency training.

Air defence fighters

FAB's former Air Defence Command is now represented by only a single wing – 1º Grupo de Defesa Aérea (1º GDA) – with a single squadron (1º/1º GDA 'Jaguares') of Dassault Mirage IIIEs. They operate within III FAe, based at Anapolis in Goias province, for protection of the capital of Brasília. Twelve multi-role Mirage IIIEBRs (F-103Es, 4910-4921), of which at least three have now been written-off, and six two-seat IIIDBR (F-103Ds, 4900-4905) combat trainers (four written off) were delivered from France from October 1972. These were followed in 1979-80 by another five IIIEBRs (4922-4926) to equip two squadrons.

In October 1988, delivery started from Dassault's Bordeaux factory of six more ex-French air force Mirage IIIEs (4927-4930 as single-seaters, costing $17.9 million) ordered by the FAB in 1987, and completely refurbished and upgraded. This modification included canards and accompanying lateral strakes at the pitot/radome junction, which increase the usable AoA in combat from 28° to 40°; single-point pressure fuelling reducing filling times for internal tanks from 15 to three minutes; fitment of two 30-mm DEFA internal cannon; and provision for MATRA R530 radar-guided AAMs. Cockpit improvements were limited to the installation of HOTAS controls, with little in the way of upgraded avionics. In addition to being stripped down, rewired and given new systems, those Mirage IIIEs with more than 4,000 hours total flying were rewinged. Two of the six 'new' Mirages were also converted as two-seat trainers (4906,4907) for $9 million, with the same single-seat upgrades, and were delivered by FAB C-130s at the rate of one per month.

The FAB's remaining Mirages, comprising 10 IIIEBRs and two IIIDBR trainers, were modified from 1989 to similar standards in Brazil with the assistance of Dassault technicians, from kits supplied by AMD. They were then cleared for a further 2,500-3,000 flying hours. One F-103E (4929) was equipped for air refuelling, including a detachable nose probe and the necessary plumbing,

but the FAB was apparently unable to fund this upgrade for the rest of the fleet.

By late 1995, a dozen F-103E and four F-103D Mirage IIIs remained in FAB service, mainly for interception roles. The aircraft were finished in a low-visibility scheme after their upgrade instead of their original overall silver. They also retain their original ground-attack capabilities, for which the FAB developed an ingenious modification by which four multi-purpose bombs could be attached to each of the Mirage's underwing drop tanks. Two Mirages are maintained on a five-minute alert throughout each 24 hours at Anapolis, where its impressive 4000-m (13,123-ft) runway is regarded as no luxury in view of its 914-m (3,000-ft) altitude and near-constant summer temperatures above 30° C (86° F).

FAB Mirages are currently scheduled to remain in service until about 2005. Following serious evaluation in the late 1980s of the Chinese F-7M development of the MiG-21, Brazil has expressed interest in acquiring ex-USAF F-16s – if the US relaxes its restrictions on the supply of advanced aircraft to Latin America, and the necessary finance can be found. Meanwhile, no decision has yet been made concerning further Mirage upgrades which have been under consideration. Like most FAB combat aircraft, the Mirages have large two-letter codes on their tailfins to indicate their operating base.

1º GDA also has several support and training aircraft on its establishment, including three AT-27s for instrument and weapons training, plus a single UH-50 (HB-350B) Esquilo, and a base flight with a pair of Neiva U-42 Regentes.

FAB's tactical force

Three squadrons of Northrop F-5 fighter-bombers are now operated within IIIª FAe, following initial deliveries between March 1975 and February 1976 of 36 new F-5Es (4820-4855) and six two-seat F-5Bs (4800-4805) costing $111 million. These equipped two multi-role squadrons of the FAB's historic 1º Grupo Aviação de Caca (Fighter Air Wing) at Santa Cruz. 1º/1º GAvCa retained its World War II predecessor's famous radio callsign of JAMBOCK, dating from the unit's 1944 to 1945 operations of Republic P-47Ds in Italy with the 12th US Army Air Force. Its aircraft are pooled with 2º/1º 'Pif Paf', the badge of the former squadron being painted on the port side of the fin and that of the latter unit to starboard. No base letter codes are currently displayed on the Sante Cruz F-5s.

Deliveries in 1988-89 of 24 ex-USAF F-5Es (4856-4879) and four two-seat F-5Fs (4806-4809) allowed the formation of a third squadron, 1º/14º GAv 'Pampa' at Canoas/Porto Alegre. This unit operates solely in air defence roles with aircraft armed with first-generation AIM-9B Sidewinders. Like the Mirages, they were to have been equipped with more advanced indigenous Piranha IR-homing air-to-air missiles developed by the Instituto de Atividades Espacia division of the Centro Tecnico Aérospacial, but this project has so far failed to reach the production stage.

Formerly operated by the USAF's 57th Fighter Wing for aggressor combat training from Nellis AFB, and by the 4th Tactical Fighter Training Squadron at Williams AFB, the first six single-seaters were flown from Kelly AFB in October 1988. Unlike their camouflaged FAB predecessors, all aircraft retained their original overall-grey

colour scheme, and also differed in lacking air refuelling probes and systems. These are fitted as standard to all the F-5Es of the 1º Grupo, as part of earlier upgrade programmes, and contacts are regularly practised with the FAB's Lockheed KC-130 and Boeing KC-137 tankers of 2º/2º GTE. The Santa Cruz-based F-5s also train for live bombing and strafing practice on the nearby Maram Bahia range only 12 km (7.4 miles) away, while their F-5Bs were used to tow flag targets for air-to-air gunnery sorties until withdrawal of the last two at the end of 1995. Each of the three F-5 squadrons also has three AT-27 Tucanos for instrument and weapons proficiency training, together with a couple of base flight U-42s.

According to Brazilian Defence Minister General Benedito Leonel in late 1995, a decision in principle has been made to upgrade the FAB's 50 or so F-5E/Fs with new avionics and structural components to extend their useful lives well into the next century. Discussions are being held with some of the international F-5 upgrade specialists, and EMBRAER has been talking to Northrop about the possibility of installing some of the AMX avionics and systems. This would include the SCP-10 radar being developed by SMA/Technesa for a proposed maritime strike version of the AMX, and the Israeli El-Op HUD.

Ground attack and recce elements

Dedicated long-range ground attack and interdiction are the roles of the FAB's latest combat equipment, in the form of the Rolls-Royce RB.168 Spey Mk 807-powered Alenia/EMBRAER AMX, or A-1, now in operational service alongside 1º Grupo GAvCa's F-5s at Santa Cruz. EMBRAER builds 29.7 per cent of all AMXs, as well as undertaking final assembly of those for the FAB.

Following flight development with seven single-seat YA-1 prototypes (4200-4206) from May 1984, Brazil's first two production A-1s were delivered in October 1989 to a new unit, 1º Esquadrão of 16º Grupo de Aviação, at Santa Cruz. This was at least one year later than planned and was caused by earlier delays, resulting in short-term upgrade requirements emerging for the FAB's F-5s and Mirage IIIs. Under the original schedule, six aircraft were due for delivery in 1989 followed by the remainder at 1.2 per month until 1995; this was intended to meet FAB orders for 65 (5500-5564) single-seat A-1s plus 14 two-seat AMX-T TA-1 (A-1B) combat and training versions (5650-5663) totalling 79 in all, to equip up to five squadrons. Prolonged defence economies, however, have resulted in extensive delays in deliveries, to the point where by the end of 1995 the FAB had received only 29 A-1s and four two-seat TA-1s.

Retaining full operational capabilities, EMBRAER's first TA-1 made its initial flight on 14 August 1991, and entered FAB service on 7 May 1992. A second AMX squadron is now in process of formation in 16º GAv, and is intended to take over some of the ground-attack roles now performed by AT-26 Xavante armed trainers.

While the FAB's AMXs share many common equipment features with their Italian air force counterparts, their fixed-gun armament comprises two 30-mm DEFA 664 cannon in the lower nose instead of a single 20-mm M61 cannon in the AMI versions. The A-1s also carry more internal fuel and are equipped with fixed air-refuelling

The FAB's second maritime asset is the P-95 Patrulha. This is a P-95A of 1º GAE.

Below: 8º GAv is the FAB's army support wing. This is a UH-50 of 2º Esq/8º GAv.

Above: 7º GAv is the FAB's second dedicated maritime unit. Its three squadrons fly a mix of P-95A/B Patrulhas. This armed P-95B is operated by 1º Esq/7º GAv, from Salvador.

Below: 8º GAv, the army-dedicated support wing, maintains five squadrons (the largest of any FAB wing) equipped mostly with helicopters. This UH-1H is from 5º Esq/8º Gav.

Above: As the CH-34, the AS 332M Super Puma has replaced earlier CH-33s (SA 330s) with 3º Esq/8º GAv.

Below: 8º GAv is one of many FAB units to operate the Neiva L-42, but is alone in using the type for FAC missions.

Above: Five SC-95Bs were produced for inland and overwater SAR missions. They can carry up to six stretchers for medevac duties or air-droppable dinghies. All are in service with 2º Esq/10º GAv, at Campo Grande.

Above: Flying alongside the SC-95s of 7 GAv are a number of camouflaged Bell UH-1Hs also used for SAR duties.

Right: 2º ELO is a one-time naval unit, now part of IIª Força Aérea, tasked with armed surveillance missions.

probes for extended-range operations. Armament includes AIM-9Ls, as well as a variety of bombs, napalm, rockets, gun-pods, reconnaissance equipment or external fuel tanks. A typical 3800-kg (8,377-lb) combat load comprises six 500-lb Mk 82 HE bombs and two 127.6-Imp gal (580-litre) drop tanks; in dissimilar combat exercises with USAF F-16s, A-1 pilots have been satisfied that they could out-turn their potent adversaries.

IIIª FAe ground-attack and reconnaissance forces also include three squadrons equipped with RR Viper 20-powered two-seat EMB-326GB or AT-26 (Ataque Treinamento) Xavante armed jet trainers. About 100 remain in the current FAB inventory from 166 (4462-4627) built under Aermacchi licence by EMBRAER for service from 1971 as T-33 replacements. Two of these units, comprising 1º/10º GAv 'Poker' and 3º/10º GAv 'Centauro', operate within 10º Grupo from Santa Maria in Rio Grande do Sul. Tasked with tactical reconnaissance roles, 1º/10º GAv is equipped with a dozen or so RT-26 (Reconhecimento) Xavante versions, which carry a Vinten camera pod under the port inboard pylon (of six available), as an alternative to the normal armament. The RT-26s are also equipped with a locally-developed fixed inflight-refuelling probe on the starboard forward fuselage. They can carry up to 4,000 lb (1814 kg) of weapons, which includes 0.5-in Browning M3 machine-gun or 30-mm cannon pods, as well as bombs, rockets, etc. Although based well inland, 3º/10º GAv's primary role is anti-shipping strikes, apart from additional close-support tasks.

These, plus operational conversion unit and tactical training roles, are also undertaken in northeastern Brazil by IIIa FAe's third Xavante unit, which is 1º/4º GAv 'Pacau' at Fortazela, in Ceara province. A few RT-26s are also operated by 1º/4º, as well as one or two UH-50 Esquilo helicopters for SAR, alongside the base flight's Neiva T-25 communications lightplanes. While minor upgrades have helped to maintain the Xavante's operational capabilities, its replacement is now becoming well overdue.

As IIIª FAe's final unit, the activities of 1º/6º GAv 'Carcara' at the FAB's most easterly air base at Recife are officially classified – although nominally involving photographic survey, ground-mapping and reconnaissance. For these roles, the unit has been equipped since August 1977 with six camouflaged EMBRAER EMB-110B (R-95) Bandeirantes for medium-/low-level photography with vertical and oblique cameras in the aft fuselage behind sliding panels. High-altitude photography and surveillance is undertaken by the unit's three pale green R-35A Learjets (6000-6002), also with fuselage-mounted sensors, which replaced three adapted RC-130 Hercules previously used for these roles in December 1987. Although officially inaugurated as an FAB base only in 1954, Recife was extensively used as a staging post and for ASW operations by the USAAF in World War II, commemorated by its SB-17G gate guardian. It is also the location for third-level maintenance of the FAB's AT-26s and Learjets.

Transport support for the FAB's combat forces is provided by the Quinta Força Aérea (Vª FAe) from its HQ in Rio de Janeiro, through seven squadrons in five air wings. Most of these are also housed in the Rio area at the historic bases of Campo dos Afonsos and Galeão. Heavy logistic support is provided by 1o Esquadrão of the 1º

Grupo de Transporte de Tropos (1 Troop Transport Wing) (1º/1º GTT 'Gordo') at Campo dos Afonsos. This unit operates four Lockheed C-130E Hercules on mainly cargo movements, from 11 aircraft delivered (2450-2460) between 1965-68. Troop transport and paratrooping missions are usually undertaken from the same base by de Havilland Canada DHC-5A Buffalos operating with 2º/1º GTT 'Cascavel'; five Buffalos remain from 1968-70 deliveries of 24 (2350-2373, of which at least four have crashed). Retaining their original Canadian C-115 designation, the Buffalos are also used to fly passengers, freight, vehicles and other supplies into remote villages and army bases in Amazonia. Seventeen C-115s remain in service, including up to 10 with 1º/9º GAv 'Arara' sharing similar duties from Manaus, the sole FAB air base in the vast Amazon province.

In fact, the FAB has only eight dedicated military air bases – comprising Alcantara, Anapolis, Campo dos Afonsos, Canoas, Guaratingueta, Pirassununga, Santa Cruz and Santa Maria – throughout Brazil's entire enormous area. It operates from many more joint-user military/civil airfields, however, which makes economic sense to share facilities, equipment and operating costs.

In 1984 the FAB also received eight C-130Hs (2461-2468), including two KC-130Hs (2461/2) equipped as aerial tankers, plus another three in 1987 (2466-2468). One of these was soon lost in an accident, as were four of the C-130Es over their years of service, but the remaining seven C/KC-130Hs and three SC-130E search and rescue versions are now operated by 1º/1º Grupo de Transporte (1º/1º GT 'Coral') from Galeão.

Following 1988 delivery from Boeing Military Airplanes of the FAB's two 707-based KC-137 tankers, converted at a cost of $24 million, the two KC-130s were reportedly converted back to cargo configuration. At least one of these, however, was still operating in the tanker role at the end of 1989 for AMX air-refuelling trials. One KC-130H has also recently been held in short-term storage through lack of overhauled T56s.

Like the FAB's Buffalos, its Hercules spend much of their time on domestic supply flights, often into semi-prepared airstrips, but are also kept busy on long-haul flights, including frequent transatlantic services via Las Palmas to Lyneham in the UK and Paris/Orly carrying spares, life-expired and overhauled engines and equipment. More experienced crews in the FAB's C-130 fleet also schedule seven flights per year into the Antarctic in support of scientific surveys from the Brazilian base of Comandante Ferraz, routing via Punta Arenas in Chile, and further south, where they operate from frozen airstrips.

Other FAB transport elements

Long-range operations are also undertaken by the four grey-painted ex-VARIG airline Boeing 707-320Cs (KC-137s 2401-2404). These aircraft are the sole equipment of 2o Esquadrão of 2º Grupo de Transporte (2º/2º GT 'Corsario') from Galeão, although their main activity is to act as tankers in support of the FAB's combat aircraft force. For this, they are fitted with underwing tip-mounted Beech 1800 hose-drum refuelling pods, each with a trailing drogue for probe-equipped aircraft, and the necessary internal fuel-transfer plumbing, an APU, folding air stairs, plus provision for extra fuel tankage. They therefore have a dual air-refuelling capability, although one

of the four KC-137s (2401), in airline-type livery, is normally employed without this equipment on Presidential and government passenger services.

Among the FAB's remaining transport units, 1º/2º GT 'Condor' at Galeão is unique in operating its 12 Avro/Hawker Siddeley (now BAe) 748 Series 2/2A (C-91, 2500-2511) twin-turboprop transports for 33 years without a single loss. This is particularly creditable in that, during that time, the smart white-topped C-91s have been one of the mainstays of the Correio Aéreo Naçional (National Air Mail Service), which involves night and all-weather operations, as well as moving large numbers of passengers and freight items, for which task the Series 2A has a large cargo door.

VIP transport

As the FAB's VIP and government transport unit, the Grupo de Transporte Especial (GTE) is not administered by Vª FAe, being an independent unit reporting directly to the Aeronautical Ministry in Brasília, where it is naturally based. It includes the Presidential Flight, equipped with two Boeing 737-200s (VC-96, 2915/6) delivered in April 1976, plus six of seven delivered EMB-121 Xingus (VU-9, 2650-2656) which have been in GTE service since April 1978. Eight of 13 HS 125 Series 3B/RC and 400 (VC/EC/VU/EU-93, 2117-2129) seven-passenger light jet transports bought by the FAB have given sterling service with the GTE since 1968, having completed 110,000 flying hours by their 25th anniversary on 23 November 1993. GTE's light jet squadron is supplemented by nine more recent (1988-89) VU-35A Learjets (2710-2718), with which two of the later VU-93s now have common avionics, including GPS. GTE would like some new Raytheon Hawker 800s to replace its fuel-thirsty VU-93s, but currently has no funds for this. GTE's aircraft inventory is rounded off by two VH-55 Twin-Esquilo light helicopters (8818/19), which now comprise the unit's only rotary-winged types following apparent disposal of six Bell Jet Rangers (VH-4s, 8570-8572, 8590-8592) in the early 1990s.

Light transport support in the Mato Grosso area within Va Força Aérea is provided from Campo Grande by the 1º/15º GAv 'Onca', which in January 1981 traded its four C-115 Buffalos for a few more C-95Bs. These have a good short-field capability, and are also used for parachute supply-dropping roles.

Brazil's Bandeirante

In all, a total of 134 Bandeirante transports from overall production of 500 EMB-110/111s were built for the FAB, including the two EMB-100 YC-95 prototypes (2130/1), plus 56 C-95s (2132-2176, 2179-2189); two EMB-110A EC-95s (2177/78), and two EMB-110P1 EC-95B (2190/91) navaid calibration variants; six EMB-110BR-95s (2240-2245) for aerophotogrammetry; 20 EMB-110K1 C-95As (2280-2299); 29 EMB-110P1K C-95Bs (2300-2328, including 2315 modified as the prototype XC-95B for artificial rain research); 12 C-95Cs (2329-2341); and another five K1s produced as SC-95Bs (6542-6546) for SAR roles. Differences were largely internal, according to role, although the C-95A introduced a 0.85-m (2.76-in) forward fuselage stretch, a ventral fin to balance the extra side area, uprated PT6A-34 turboprops developing 750 shp (559 kW) instead of the earlier 680-shp (505-kW) PT6A-27s,

Above: EMBRAER-built PA-34 Senecas (U-7s) serve as liaison aircraft with several units, including 2º ELO.

Below: Mirage-equipped 1º GDA also has its own attached liaison aircraft in the shape of the UH-50 (AS 350).

2º ELO's armed AT-27s pursue an aggressive anti-drug and anti-smuggling campaign from their FOL at Santa Cruz. EMBRAER is now developing a version of the EMB-312H Super Tucano to fulfil the FAB's ALX (service designation A/AT-29) requirement for an even more capable light attack and surveillance aircraft for use over Brazil's huge Amazon interior.

Above left: 1º GDA has a number of standard, camouflaged T-27 Tucanos on strength for continuation and instrument training.

Above: Anapolis-based 1º GDA is the air force's primary interceptor/air defence unit. It flies the Dassault Mirage IIIEBR (F-103E).

Above: Elderly Neiva Regentes serve with the Anapolis base flight, on behalf of 1º GDA. The Regente first flew in 1961 and was sold exclusively to the FAB, though some have since appeared on the Brazilian civil register.

Left: Four Mirage IIIDBRs (F-103Ds) remain in service with 1º GDA. Like their single-seat siblings thay have all been upgraded by Dassault and by FAB technicians in Brazil.

The F-103Es of 1º GDA were upgraded between 1988 and 1989, receiving detachable refuelling probes, fixed canards, vortex-generator strakes, pressure refuelling and an improved cannon.

an upward-opening rear cargo door and increased take-off weight. The C-95B is similar, with the addition of Omega long-range navigation equipment. A dihedral tailplane was added to the C-95C, among other minor changes, and the last of the 500 Bandeirantes built was also the FAB's final EMB-110P1K (C-95C, 2341), delivered in 1990. It seems that the FAB finished up with more Bandeirantes than it needs, since in July 1994 19 were auctioned off in Rio, along with 20 spare PT6A-27 turboprop units, to raise some cash for Brazil's hard-up air force.

FAB's Regional Air Commands

In addition to its three operational air forces, the FAB has a superimposed Regional Air Command administrative structure, comprising seven Comandos Aéreos Regionais (COMARs), covering all 20 or so provinces of Brazil. These are also aircraft-operating units, each regional HQ having its own similarly numbered light transport and tactical support squadron (Esquadrão de Transporte Aéreo – ETA), which are the FAB's main users of the C-95 Bandeirante in its various versions.

1º ETA, serving COMAR I HQ at Belém, is typical in operating six C-95Bs, plus two single-turboprop Cessna C-98 Caravans, to cover its 'parish' of Para and Amapa provinces along the borders of Guyana, Suriname and French Guiana in northern Brazil. The FAB was one of the first foreign operators of the 14-seat (or 3,500-lb/1588-kg payload) Cessna 208A Caravan, of which deliveries of seven (2701-2707) started in 1987.

COMAR II, covering Bahia, Piaui, Maranhão and Ceara provinces in northeastern Brazil, has its HQ in Recife. The unit operates seven C-95As through 2o ETA from the Pernambuco air base there, while also supporting Fortaleza and Salvador airfields. The Rio de Janeiro area, plus Espirito Santo and Minas Gerias provinces, is covered by COMAR III and 3º ETA, operating five C-95s and C-95Bs from Galeão, into half a dozen other air bases. São Paulo and Mato Grosso provinces come under the aegis of COMAR IV and 4º ETA with a few C-95 and C-95As at the former state's Cumbica Airport, and covers Campo Grande, Guarulhos, Pirassanunga, São José and Santos.

In the extreme south of Brazil, COMAR V has three air bases in Parana, Santa Catarina and Rio Grande do Sul provinces. These include Florianapolis and Santa Maria, as well as Porto Alegre/ Canoas, from where 5º ETA operates its five C-95A/Bs. Anapolis and Brasília air bases in Goias province are administered by COMAR VI, the latter's international airport also housing a varied fleet of VU-9s, C-95Cs and VC-97s operated by 6º ETA. This unit has three of the seven VU-9 Xingus delivered to the FAB, together with a similar number of the five EMB-120 Brasilias (VC-97, 2000-2004) received in 1986-88, the latter augmenting when required the VIP fleet of the FAB's Grupo de Transporte Especial at Brasília. For this role, two VC-97s have a 12-seat luxury layout, while the third has 28 seats in a more normal airline configuration. Three other Xingus previously operated by 6º ETA are now in storage. The Brasília-based unit is unique in the FAB in operating the C-95C Bandeirante, which features a Collins EFIS cockpit, an enlarged cargo/parachute door and a dihedral tailplane.

COMAR VII's 7º ETA, with HQ at Manaus, covers Brazil's most westerly Amazonas and Acre provinces, as well as the most northerly Roraima state and Rondonia flanking Mato Grosso, bordering Guyana, Venezuela, Colombia, Peru and Bolivia. As already mentioned, COMAR VII has rather different roles from the other Regional Air Command units. In addition to its two flights of armed and grey-camouflaged AT-27 Tucano trainers – comprising 1º Esquadrilha of 7º ETA detached to Boa Vista and 2º/7º ETA at Porto Velho for SIVAM support – its HQ unit continues to operate six C-95/C-95Bs in normal COMAR roles. Each of the detached flights also has a single Cessna C-98 for support roles. The Porto Velho-based AT-27s carry MPVN fin-codes.

Non-COMGAR air units

Although Brazil's Comando Geral do Ar (COMGAR) flies most of the FAB's operational and support aircraft, all but one of its parallel departments under the Ministry of Aeronautics have small units with a variety of aircraft. The Comando Geral de Apoio (COMGAP), or Air Support Command, for example, controls the Grupo Especial de Inspecção em Voo (GEIV), or Special Flight Inspection Wing, responsible for checking and calibrating the FAB's ground-based navigation and approach aids. It operates four specially-equipped EC-95/B Bandeirantes, and two EU-93 HS 125s from its base at Rio's downtown Santos Dumont airport.

COMGAP also provides depot-level maintenance for FAB aircraft and helicopters in six regional Parques de Materiels Aéronauticas or Aeronautical Equipment Parks (PAMAs). These comprise PAMA-AF at Campo dos Afonsos, Rio de Janeiro, for VU-9s, C-95s and helicopters; PAMA-GL, at Galeão, RJ for C-91s, VU-93s, C-130s and C-137s; PAMA-SP, for C-115s and P-16s at Campo de Marte, São Paulo; PAMA-BE, for C-95s and helicopters at Belém, Para; PAMA-RF, for AT-26s, C-95s and R/VU-35As at Recife; and PAMA-LS, for C-115s, C-95s, T-25s and T-27s at Lagoa Santa and Belo Horizonte (also an aircraft storage unit), in Mato Grosso. Some of the listed FAB transports, including C-95s and C-115s, are used in small numbers by the PAMA flights to ferry spares and equipment around the main FAB bases.

FAB flight test division

An important FAB unit operated by the Departamento de Pesquisas e Desenvolvimento (DEPED), or R&D Department, is the Centro Tecnico Aéroespacial (Aerospace Technical Centre) located at São José dos Campos, São Paulo. As the FAB's equivalent of Boscombe Down, the CTA undertakes service trials and more basic research with a variety of aircraft which currently include examples of the XC-95 Bandeirante, XT-27 Tucano, YT-27 Tucano, YTA-1 AMX trainer, XC-97 Brasilia, AT-26 Xavante, XU-93 HS 125 radar testbed, U-7 Seneca and U-42 Regente. The X or Y prefixes to many of the designations indicate their use in test or research flying, although the CTA also undertakes certification and service clearance of new aircraft, equipment and weapons. An associated DEPED unit is Centro de Lancamento de Alcantara or CLA, which is responsible for telemetry equipment used in association with Brazil's participation in the Ariane space programme, and the rockets and satellites launched from French Guiana. To support this operation, a single Cessna C-98 is based at São Luis de Maranhoa airfield in north-eastern Brazil.

One other independent unit which has now achieved considerable fame is the Esquadrão de Demonstração Aéreo (EDA), better known as the 'Esquadrão da Fumaca' – literally, the 'Smoke Squadron'. Brazil's national aerobatic team of nine bright red-and-white Tucanos, plus at least two spare aircraft, was formed in September 1983. This was at the same time as the first T-27s arrived for the FAB's Air Academy, with which the team shares base facilities at Pirassununga, near São Paulo. The 'Esquadrão da Fumaca' performs about 30 displays through Brazil every year, but has also made many other international appearances in both South and North America, as well as at the Paris air show. All its pilots are full-time members of the team, which gained its name from the white smoke trails which mark its display manoeuvres and which are generated from the injection of diesel oil into the jet pipes of its PT6A-25Cs. Coloured smoke is apparently not used, because its dyes would stain the Tucanos' immaculate finish.

FAB training organisation

Aircrew training in the FAB is administered by the Departamento de Ensino (DEPENS) as one of the five air force commands reporting to the Ministry of Aeronautics, although another of these – the Comando Geral do Ar (COMGAR) – also has a subordinate Comando Aéreo de Treinamento administering operational conversion. DEPENS operates several ground instructional units, notably the Escola do Especialistas de Aéronautico at Guaratingueta, which uses a C-95 in connection with training technicians and air traffic control NCOs. All FAB pilots undergo a four-year academic and flying training course at the Academia da Força Aérea (AFA), or Air Force College, currently commanded by Brigadier Lencastre, and located at São Paulo's sprawling Pirassununga Air Base.

Covering an area of more than 215000 m² (2.31 million sq ft), this base actually comprises two (east and west) airfields, with three parallel runways. The east field has a single 1300-m (4,265-ft) runway for light aircraft operation, while twin 2300-m (7,546-ft) strips in the western area accommodate turboprop and visiting jet movements. Together, the airfields house over 100 aircraft, plus simulators, other training aids, classrooms and extensive infrastructure facilities, including an Olympic-size swimming pool.

About 350 students pass through the Academy at any one time, a figure which also includes personnel from many other Latin American air force – notably Bolivia, Ecuador, Guatemala, Paraguay and Peru – as well as from far afield as Iran. All instruction is in Portuguese, although all cadets are also taught English, but only about 30 per cent will eventually graduate from the completed course. Most of the failures result in the early stages of the training programme from an initial 16 hours of grading instruction, given on the AFA's now-venerable Neiva T-25 Universal basic trainers powered by 300-hp (223-kW) Lycoming IO-540K-1D5 piston engines. No further formal flying training is undertaken during the first two years of the course, although cadets are encouraged, in what little spare time they have, to participate in the activities of the AFA's micro-light and gliding clubs (Clube de Ultraleves/CU and Clube de Voo/CV). Between them, these

Above: Like the FAB's other front-line combat units, 1 GAvCa operates a number of A/T-27s with which its F-5 pilots maintain their flying hours and overall proficiency.

Above: 1º GAvCa 'Senta a Pua' is Brazil's most famous air force unit. It can trace its lineage back to World War II when it fought in Italy, as a P-47 unit, alongside the Allies.

Right: 1º GAvCa was an early F-5E customer and so it recieved the F-5B as a trainer because the F-5F was not then available. The badge of 2º Esq/1º GAvCa is worn, to port, on the fin.

6º GAv is the FAB's most secretive unit, undertaking survey and reconnaissance missions from the FAB's most easterly base, Recife. Its three high-flying R-35A Learjets are capable of carrying LOROP cameras, SLAR and a wide range of standard camera fits.

The R-95 has a ventral camera pallet equipped with a sliding door that reveals a Zeiss aerial mapping camera. The R-95 was also delivered with a Decca 72 Doppler navigation system. Only two civil-standard EMB-110Bs were delivered to other customers and the six FAB aircraft are ideal platforms for long focal length cameras, or even cabin-mounted SLARs.

Partnering 6º GAVs R-35As are six EMBRAER R-95 Bandeirantes, military versions of the civilian EMB-110B photo survey model.

Neiva followed its Regente design with the N-621 Universal primary trainer, which serves with the FAB as the T-25. Most are in the hands of the Air Force Academy but some, like this 14º GAv example, also serve as squadron hacks.

Brazil's second F-5 unit is the air defence-tasked 14º GAv 'Pampa', based at Canoas. Its single squadron was formed with ex-USAF F-5Es in 1988 and thus its aircraft retain an 'aggressor grey' camouflage scheme and lack refuelling probes. Brazil is currently investigating various upgrade options for its three F-5 squadrons.

operate 30 aircraft of seven different types, comprising 11 single-seat and three two-seat Microleve MXLs (T-8A/B), and five elderly two-seat Let L-13 Blaniks (TZ-13), plus seven indigenous TPE KW 1b2 (Z-16, originally 8150-8159) Quero Queros, and one each Glasfluegel 201B Libelle (Z-15, 8100) and Schleicher ASW-20 (Z-20, 8120) single-seat sailplanes. Two of three EMBRAER EMB-201R Ipanemas (U-19, 1051-0153) originally delivered to the AFA in 1976 are used to launch the gliders.

Flight training sequence

Before starting formal instruction at the beginning of their third year, AFA students should have a useful amount of ultra-light and glider experience, while in small groups they will also have made a number of visits to some of the FAB's operational bases in the College's own C-95 Bandeirante. Sixty-five hours of basic training is then flown during the third year on the AFA's 60 or so Neiva T-25s, which are operated by the resident 2° Esquadrão de Instrução Aérea (EIA) 'Apollo'. This unit operates both T-25As and lesser numbers of T-25Cs, the latter with more modern instrumentation to full IFR standards, used for about five hours of instrument training procedures within the basic syllabus. This stage includes normal handling, cross-country, aerobatic and formation flying exercises, prior to fourth year conversion to the EMB-312 Tucano for advanced instruction.

About 40 T-27s are operated by the AFA from 118 (1300-1417) originally delivered to the FAB between September 1983 and September 1986. Funding problems prevented FAB options for 50 more Tucanos being exercised, but follow-up orders for 10 in 1990 (1418-1427) and five in 1992 (1428-1432) increased total procurement to 133, plus four attrition replacements. These replaced the FAB's remaining Cessna T-37Cs from 65 originally acquired (0870-0934) from 1967 and retired in 1981 because of spares problems. The FAB also withdrew the last of its 76 original Aerotec A-122A Uirapuru (T-23, 0940-0999 and 1730-1745) primary trainers in the mid-1980s.

With a high-visibility orange-and-white paint scheme, the AFA's Tucanos in 1° EIA 'Cometa' provide fourth-year cadets with 110 hours of advanced training, including day and night formation flying, instrument flying and aerobatics. A further 16 hours or so is allocated to instrument procedure instruction in the AFA's Tucano flight simulator. In recent months, budget economies have resulted in about 25 per cent of the AFA's Tucano fleet being grounded at any one time, awaiting funding for the return of their overhauled PT6A turboprops. The AFA also has a number of support aircraft, including two EMBRAER EMB-810D (Piper PA-34-220T Seneca III) U-7 light twins, the C-95A and two UH-50 Esquilo helicopters used mainly for SAR roles.

Final training stages

From the Air Force College, successful students change commands from DEPENS to COMGAR's Comando Aéreo de Treinamento or CATRE, which has its HQ in Natal, on Brazil's northeastern tip. The Natal base flight operates three U-42s for liaison duties and range support tasks, together with a single C-95B, and a UH-50 SAR

helicopter on detachment from 2°/8° GAv, at Recife.

Some pilots are streamed at this stage, those selected for helicopter training being posted to 1°/11° GAv 'Gavião' at Santos, near São Paulo, to convert to the Aérospatiale/Helibras HB-350B (UH-50) Esquilo. All the remaining personnel then continue to the next stage of a year's tactical and weapons training on armed AT-27 Tucanos of the resident former 5o Grupo at Natal. This is currently being reorganised and possibly redesignated, although for the moment its component squadrons are still referred to as 1°/5° 'Rumba' and 2°/5° 'Joker' GAv, for identification purposes. During the AT-27 course with 1°/5°, students are progressively assessed for their suitability as potential fast-jet combat pilots, some being judged more suitable for transport flying. Hitherto, 5° Grupo had a third squadron, 'Daedalus', with four C-95s to provide multi-engine conversion training. Its disbandment because of defence economies transferred this role to the regional air transport squadrons (ETAs), where light transport experience is gained before qualifying as a co-pilot on heavier types.

Fast jet students then move across to 2°/5° GAv, still at Natal, to complete their 18-month operational conversion on its 25 or so two-seat AT-26 Xavante light ground-attack aircraft. Like the AT-27s, the Xavantes are finished in a USAF Vietnam-style green and tan camouflage scheme, and carry a full range of weapons, including bombs, rockets and a 7.62-mm machine-gun pod, for armament training on their six underwing hard points. Great attention is also paid to air combat training, which includes air-to-air firing against banner targets towed by other AT-26s. The surviving candidates can then call themselves fully-qualified jet fighter pilots, but they then have to serve a minimum of another two years on Xavantes with either 1°/4° GAv at Fortaleza or 3°/10° at Santa Maria, both in IIIª FAe, to increase their general combat experience, before being considered to join the big league FAB A-1, F-5 or Mirage units.

The Xavante is now considered obsolete by the FAB, which is planning its replacement in 2°/5° by the new ALX Super Tucanos, trading jets for turboprops. All FAB AT-26 units have tail markings comprising the fighter insignia of a double arrow and the stars of the Southern Cross on a coloured fin band which, in the case of

2o/5o, is light blue. Fighter pilots also wear gold stars on the left breast of their flying suits, each star signifying 100 hours of fighter flight-time. Instructor pilots at Natal require a minimum of 400 hours of fighter time, which means nearly three years of combat unit experience, and are qualified to lead a four-aircraft formation.

John Fricker

FAB Type Designations

A-1	AMX
A-1B	AMX-T (see also TA-1)
A-29	EMB-312H 'ALX' Super Tucano (single-seat)
AT-26	EMB-326GB Xavante (licence-built Aermacchi MB.326)
AT-27	EMB-312 Tucanao (armed trainer)
C-91	HS 748 Srs 2/2A
C-115	DHC-5A Buffalo
CH-33	SA 330 Puma
CH-34	AS 332M Super Puma
C-35A	Learjet 35A
C-95A	EMB-110K1 Bandeirante
C-95B	EMB-110P1K Bandeirante
C-95C	EMB-110 Bandeirante
C-98	C.208A Caravan I
CH-55	AS 355M Twin Ecureuil
EC-93	HS 125-3B/RC
EC-95/B	EMB-110A/P1 Bandeirante (calibration)
EU-93	HS 125-403B (calibration)
KC-137	Boeing 707-320C (tanker configuration)
F-103D	Mirage IIIDBR
F-103E	Mirage IIIEBR
P-16E/H	S-2E/H Tracker/Turbo Tracker
P-95A	EMB-111A Patrulha
P-95B	EMB-111B Patrulha
R-95	EMB-110B Bandeirante (photo-recce configuration)
RT-26	EMB-326 (photo-recce configuration)
SC-95B	EMB-110P1K Bandeirante (SAR)
SC-130E	C-130E Hercules (SAR)
SH-1D	UH-1D Iroquois
SH-1H	UH-1H Iroquois
T-8/A	Microleve MXL
T-23	A-122A Uirapuru
T-27	EMB-312 Tucano
TA-1	AMX-T (see also A-1B)
TA-29	EMB-312H 'ALX' Super Tucano (two-seat)
TZ-13	Let L-13 Blanik
U-7/A	EMB-810 (licence-built Piper PA-34 Seneca)
U-19	EMB-201R Ipanema
UH-50	Helibras AB-350B (licence-built Aérospatiale AS 350B)
VC-93	HS 125-3B/RC
VC-96	Boeing 737-2N3 (VIP)
VC-97	EMB-120 Brasília (VIP)
VH-4	B 206B Jet Ranger
VH-55	AS 355M Twin Ecureuil (VIP)
VU-9	EMB-121E Xingu
VU-35A	Learjet 35A
VU-93	HS 125-400A/-403B
Z-15	Glasflugel 201B Libelle
Z-16	TPE KW 1b2 Quero Quero
Z-20	Schleicher ASW-20

Força Aérea Brasileira Order of Battle

Estrutura do Ministerio da Aéronautica comprises:
Comando Geral do Ar– COMGAR (Air General Comand, FAB)
Comando Geral de Apoio – CDMGAP (Support General Command)
(with Material, Engineering, Electronics and Flight Safety directorates)
Comando Geral do Pessoal – COMGEP (Personnel General Command)
(with Personnel, Medicine, Administration and Welfare directorates)
Departamento de Pesquisas e Desenvolvimento – DEPED (Department of Research and Development)
Departamento de Aviação Civil (Department of Civil Aviation)
Departamento de Ensino – DEPENS (Department of Training)

Reporting direct to Minister of Defence

Grupo de Transporte Especial (GTE)	VU-9, VU-35A, VU-93 VC-96, VH-55	Brasília
'Esquadrão da Fumaca'	T-27	Pirassununga

COMANDO GERAL do AR (Air General Command)

UNIT	TYPE	BASE
Comando Aéreos Regional		
COMAR 1 (1° Comando Aéreos Regionais), Belém AB		
1 Esquadrão de Transporte Aereo (ETA)	C-95B, C-98	Belém
COMAR 2 Fortaleza, Recife & Salvador AB		
2° ETA	C-95	Recife
COMAR 3 Afonsos, Galeão & Santa Cruz AB		
3° ETA	C-95, C-95B	Galeão
COMAR 4 São Paulo/Guarulhos, Campo Grande		
4° ETA	C-95, C-95A	São Paulo/Cumbica AFB

Above: 14° GAV took delivery of four F-5Fs and all its Tigers wear prominent tail-codes.

Right: A sharkmouthed F-5E taxis in at Canoas adorned also with various Tiger II logos.

Above: To the FAB, the AMX is known as the A-1. 16° GAv's single squadron will soon be joined by a second.

Below: Brasil's four remaining C-130Es are all operated by 1° Esq/1° GTT, at Afonsos, as part of Vª Força Aérea.

Above: This 1° Esq/16° GAv A-1 is surrounded by an array of Avibras AV-BAFG HE bombs, rocket pods and an M61A1 Vulcan cannon. Under the fuselage and wing hardpoints are AV-BI napalm canisters.

Below: During August and September 1989 AMX prototype 006 undertook AAR trials with a KC-130H from 1° Esq/1° GT, and KC-137 from 2° GT. Ninety 'prods' were carried out – the majority of real fuel transfers with the KC-130H.

Five de Havilland Canada DHC-5A Buffalos (FAB service designation C-115) remain in service with 2° Esq/1° GTT, based at Afonsos, along with 17 in the hands of 1° Esq/9° GAv, based at Manaus.

2° Esq/2° GT operates four ex-VARIG Boeing 707-320Cs as KC-137 tanker/ transports. Three of these are grey-painted dedicated tankers fitted with Beech 1800 podded HDUs, but one aircraft retains a polished livery and interior for Presidential and governmental transport tasks.

The Hawker Siddeley HS 748 has provided the FAB with 33 years of sterling service in the shape of 12 C-91s (HS 728 Srs 2/2A), not one of which has been lost in over three decades of flying. The C-91s are today flown by 1° Esq/ 2° GT, alongside the same wing's KC-137s, at Galeão.

COMAR 5 Canoas, Florianapolis, Santa Maria AB
5º ETA	C-95A	Porto Alegre/Canoas

COMAR 6 Anapolis, Brasília AB
6º ETA	C-95C, VC-97, VU-9, VC-97	Brasília

COMAR 7 Boa Vista, Manaus, Porto Velho AB
7º ETA	C-95C	Manaus
1º Esquadrilha/7º ETA.	AT-27	Boa Vista
2º Esq/7º ETA	AT-27	Porto Velho

Both units also have one C-98 as base flight.

IIª FORÇA AÉREA (2nd Air Force), Rio de Janeiro

1º Grupo de Aviação Embarcada (GAE)
1º GAE	'Cardeal'	P-16E, P-95A	Santa Cruz

7º Grupo de Aviação (GAv)
1º Esq/7º GAv	'Orungan'	P-95B	Salvador
2º Esq/7º GAv	'Phoenix'	P-95B	Florianapolis
3º Esq/7º GAv	'Netuno'	P-95A	Belém

8º Grupo de Aviação
1º Esq/8º GAv	'Falcão Pioneiro'	CH-55	Belém
2º Esq/8º GAv	'Poti'	UH-50, T-25C	Recife
3º Esq/8º GAv	'Puma'	CH-34, L-42	Afonsos
5º Esq/8º GAv	'Pantera'	UH-1H, L-42, U-7	Santa Maria
7º Esq/8º GAv	'Falcão'	UH-1H, U-7	Manaus

10º Grupo de Aviação
2º Esq/10º GAv	'Pelicano'	SC-95B, UH-1H	Campo Grande

2º Esquadrilha de Ligação & Observação (ELO)
	'Duelo'	AT-27	São Pedro da Aldeia

IIIª FORÇA AÉREA (3rd Air Force), Brasília

1º Grupo de Defesa Aérea (GDA)
1º Esq/1º GDA	'Jaguares'	F-103D/E, AT-27, UH-50	Anapolis

1º Grupo de Aviação de Caca (GAvCa)
1º Esq/1º GAvCa	'Jambock'	F-5B/E, AT-27	Santa Cruz
2º Esq/1º GAvCa	'Pif Paf'	F-5B/E, AT-27	Santa Cruz

4º Grupo de Aviação
1º Esq/4º GAv	'Pacau'	AT-26, RT-26, UH-50	Fortaleza

6º Grupo de Aviação
1º Esq/6º GAv	'Carcara'	R-35A, R-95	Recife

10º Grupo de Aviação
1º Esq/10º GAv	'Poker'	RT-26	Santa Maria
3º Esq/10º GAv	'Centauro'	AT-26	Santa Maria

14º Grupo de Aviação
1º Esq/14º GAv	'Pampa'	F-5E/F, AT-27	Canoas

16º Grupo de Aviação
1º Esq/16º GAv	'Adelfi'	A-1	Santa Cruz
2º Esq/16º GAv (now forming)	A-1	Santa Cruz

Vª FORÇA AÉREA (5th Air Force), Rio de Janeiro

1º Grupo de Transporte de Tropos (GTT)
1º Esq/1º GTT	'Gordo'	C-130E	Afonsos
2º Esq/1º GTT	'Cascavel'	C-115	Afonsos

1º Grupo de Transporte (GT)
1º Esq/1º GT	'Coral'	SC-130E, K/C-130H	Galeão

2º Grupo de Transporte
1º Esq/2º GT	'Condor'	C-91	Galeão
2º Esq/2º GT	'Corsário'	KC-137	Galeão

9º Grupo de Aviação
1º Esq/9º GAv	'Arara'	C-115	Manaus

15º Grupo de Aviação
1º Esq/15º GAv	'Onça'	C-95B	Campo Grande

Comando Aéreo de Treinamento (CATRE)

5º Grupo de Aviação
1º Esq/5º GAv	'Rumba'	AT-27	Natal
2º Esq/5º GAv	'Joker'	AT-26	Natal

11º Grupo de Aviação
1º Esq/11º GAv	'Gavião'	UH-50	Santos

(5º Grupo no longer exists, but squadrons still known as 1/5 etc)

Comando Geral de Apoio (COMGAP)

Directoria de Eletronica E Prot. Ao Voo
Grupo Especial de Inspeção em Voo (GEIV)
	EC-95, EU-93	Santos Dumont

Departamento de Pesquisas e Desenvolvimento (DEPED)

Centro Tecnico Aéroespacial (CTA)
XC-95, XC-97, T-25, T-27, U-42, XU-93	São José Dos Campos

Departamento de Ensino (DEPENS)

Academia da Força Aérea/AFA (air force academy), Pirassununga
1º Esquadrão de Instrução Aérea (EIA)	T-27	Pirassununga
2º EIA	T-25A/C	Pirassununga

Clube de Voo a Vela (CVV)	U-19, Gliders	Pirassununga
Clube de Ultraleves (CU)	T-8A/B, Microlights	Pirassununga

Support	C-95A, UH-50, U-7

Escola do Especialistas de Aéronautica (EEAR)
C-95	Guaratingueta

Nucleo do Comando de Defesa Aéroespecial Brasília (NUCOMDABRA) – Brazilian aerospace defence headquarters no aircraft on strength

As a trial some bases have painted code letters on some of their aircraft.
Those noted to date are:

AN – Anapolis (all AT-27 & F-103 Mirage)
ES –
CN – Canoas
NT – Natal (one AT-26 only)
PV – Porto Velho
SC – Santa Cruz (some A-1, but no other types)

Unit abbreviations listed above are as follows:

AFA	Academia da Força Aérea (Air Force Academy)
CATRE	Comando Aérea de Treinamento (Operational Training Command)
CTA	Centre Tecnico Aérospacial (Aerospace Technical Centre)
CU	Clube de Ultraleves
CVV	Clube de Voo a Vela (Gliding Club)
EEAR	Escola do Especialistas de Aéronautica (Aeronautical Specialist School)
EIA	Esquadrão de Instrução Aérea (Air Training Squadron)
ELO	Esquadrilha de Ligação & Observação (Liaison & Observation Sqn)
ETA	Esquadrão de Transporte Aéreo (Air Transport Squadron)
GAE	Grupo de Aviação Embarcada (Embarked Aviation Wing)
GAv	Grupo de Aviação (Air Wing)
GAvCa	Grupo de Aviação de Caca (Fighter Air Wing)
GDA	Grupo de Aviação de Defesa (Air Defence Wing)
GEIV	Grupo Especial de Inspeção & Vigilancia (Special Inspection & (Navaids) Checking Wing)
GT	Grupo de Transporte (Transport Wing)
GTE	Grupo de Transporte Especial (Special Transport Wing)
GTT	Grupo de Transporte de Tropos (Troop Carrier Wing)

Força Aéronaval da Marinha do Brasil (Brazilian naval aviation)

Brazilian naval aviation can trace its history to 23 August 1916 when the Escola de Aviação Naval (Naval Aviation School) was founded, equipped with Curtiss Model F flying-boats. This naval air arm expanded during the 1920s, until it warranted a reorganisation as the Corpo Aviação (Navy Aviation Corps) on 3 October 1931. However, independent naval aviation came to an end in January 1941 with the foundation of the Ministry of Aeronautics, which unified all military flying under the aegis of the Forças Aéreas Naçionas (National Air Forces) which, within four months, became the Força Aérea Brasileira.

Not until 1958 did aircraft once again wear the colours of the Brazilian navy. Moves to re-establish a small naval air arm began in 1957 with the acquisition of two Bell 47J helicopters. Subsequently, three new Westland Widgeons were obtained from the UK and SH-34Js were transferred from the FAB. A new naval Centrão de Instrução e Adestramento Aéro-Naval (Air-Naval Training Centre) was established in Rio de Janeiro along with a sizeable naval air station

development at São Pedro da Aldeia. The small helicopter force was also deployed aboard the navy's 'Brooklin'-class cruisers and survey ships.

Brazil took the major step of acquiring an aircraft-carrier when it bought the 'Colossus'-class HMS Vengeance from the Royal Navy on 14 December 1956. The 'new' carrier was refitted at Rotterdam between 1957 and 1960 with new boilers, a modified island, an 8.5° angled deck with mirror deck-landing system, steam catapults, and an arrester wire system. In Brazilian service the vessel was named *Minas Gerias*, and it was commissioned on 6 December 1960. *Minas Gerias* arrived in Brazil with two new Westland Whirlwind Series 3s and two Grumman TBM-3 Avengers, which had been donated by the Dutch government. The Avengers were in such poor condition that they could only be taxied around the carrier's deck.

To equip the *Minas Gerias*' air wing, the FAB founded the 1º Grupo de Aviação Embarcada (GAE) at Santa Cruz AB on 1 November 1958. This unit began training with T-6Ds and B-25Js,

in preparation for its operational force of 13 newly-delivered S-2A Trackers and six Sikorsky SH-34J Seabats, courtesy of the United States' MAP programme. 1º GAE's (air force) personnel were extensively trained in the US, including actual carrier operations, and Brazilian navy officers were trained alongside them with the obvious intention of taking over the unit for the navy, in the future.

The Força Aérea Naval was founded on 17 April 1962, comprising the *Minas Gerias* and 1º GAE. At that time 1º GAE maintained a fixed-wing anti-submarine squadron, a helicopter anti-submarine squadron and a fighter squadron. Three additional units were planned, as was a Marine Corps aviation command. This 'paper' expansion fuelled intense inter-service rivalry (and some disquiet in the government), particularly as the navy had begun to obtain aircraft in a clandestine fashion. The situation reached its peak when the FAB launched several low-level T-6 photo-reconnaissance sorties against the navy to confirm reports of six Pilatus P-3 trainers and 12

Above: 15º GAv provides **STOL** transport and airdrop capability for Vª Força Aérea.

1º Esq/5º GAv's **AT-27s** are part of **CATRE**'s weapons training programme at Natal.

Above: The **FAB**'s long-serving **AT-26 Xavantes** are now concentrated with **CATRE** training units at Natal.

Below: The **GEIV** operates two **EC-95s** configured for navaid and runway calibration from its base at **Santos Dumont**.

Above: **EMBRAER**-built **AT-26s (EMB-326GC)** can carry a podded gun system similar to the camera pods fitted to the **FAB**'s reconnaissance-configured **RT-26 Xavantes**.

This **EU-93 (HS 125-3B/RC)** is one of two on strength with the **GEIV (Grupo Especial de Inspecção em Voo)**, at Rio de Janeiro's **Santos Dumont** airport.

Below: As part of **DPED**, the air force research and development arm, the **Centro Tecnico Aéroespecial (CTA)** conducts service trials with a wide range of **FAB** aircraft, including this **XC-95B Bandeirante**.

North American T-28s which had been discreetly acquired and were being assembled at Rio de Janeiro. These aircraft were later trucked to São Pedro da Aldeia and began serious flying operations. The navy continued acquiring more aircraft (chiefly lightplanes), and even began building its own, when a Presidential decree stopped it in its tracks.

On 26 January 1965 responsibility for any fixed-wing operations by the navy was removed and placed entirely with the air force. 2º ELO, which had been flying the P-3s and T-28s, was transferred to the FAB where it remains today as an armed Tucano unit. The navy formally acquired the FAB's SH-34J Seabats but became an exclusively helicopter-equipped force, with the resultant loss of prestige and operational capability. 1º GAE continued to work with the navy, and deploys regularly aboard the *Minas Gerias*. The S-2As were augmented by S-2Es in 1960. (More details of 1º GAE's current operations can be found in the Força Aérea Brasileira entry.)

Today, the Força Aéronaval de Marinha do Brasil operates 55 helicopters, spread among eight units at four bases. In addition, the navy has a sizeable number of helicopter-capable vessels including, still, the carrier *Minas Gerias*. This ship is now the oldest aircraft-carrier in service in the world. Argentina's *Veinticinco de Mayo* (the former HMS *Venerable* and HrMS *Karel Doorman*) was launched two months prior to *Minas Gerias*, in December 1943, but the Brazilian ship was laid down two weeks before the '*de Mayo*', in November 1942 . India's *Vikrant* (the former HMS *Hercules*) dates from 1943, and *Viraat* (the former HMS *Hermes*) was laid down in 1943 but not launched until 1953. France's *Clemenceau* and *Foch* are relative youngsters, having been launched in 1957 and 1960, respectively.

Maintaining a carrier force

In 1972 the *Minas Gerias* was refitted with more modern engines, radar and communications. The catapult and arrester system was also replaced. The Argentine experience with its own similar carrier convinced Brazil that it needed a more potent carrier air wing and so, in 1984, the navy announced its intention to acquire 22 A-4s. Ex-Kuwaiti or Israeli aircraft were mooted, until the United States persuaded Brazil that such an expansion was unwarranted. The *Minas Gerias'* air wing remained firmly an ASW force – in a region where there is virtually no submarine threat.

Today, *Minas Gerias* is at sea between 80 to 100 days per year. Regular exercises are held with the US Navy and other South American navies, such as the Araex '94 exercise with Argentina's Super Etendards. *Minas Gerias'* catapults are not strong enough to launch such high-performance aircraft and the Etendards limited themselves to practising 'touch-and-goes'. On 12 December 1994, one Super Etendard (the aircraft which had sunk HMS *Sheffield* in 1982) caught a wire by accident and was unceremoniously dumped onto the deck. The stricken aircraft could not be removed until *Minas Gerias* returned to port.

The Marinha's oldest aviation asset is the Sea Kings of Esquadrão de Helicopteros Anti-Submarino 1 (HS-1). This unit was activated with SH-34Js (HSS-1s) in 1965. The Seabats were replaced in 1971 by four Sikorsky S-61D-3s (equivalent to US Navy SH-3Ds), four Agusta-built S-61D-3s (in 1984), and, subsequently, two

ex-USN SH-3Ds – all of which received the service designation SH-3A. Seven of these original Sea Kings survive in service, all have been maintained and upgraded by Agusta, and the fleet is currently being modified to ASH-3A (SH-3H) standard. All aircraft are AM-39 Exocet-capable and are fitted with undernose search and targeting radar, plus engine intake filters. Other weapon options for the ASH-3As include two Mk 46 torpedoes or four depth charges, and they are the prime ASW asset when deployed aboard *Minas Gerias*, with a secondary anti-shipping role. Normally, three to four aircraft are assigned to the carrier when it is at sea. The Sea Kings can also be accommodated by the assault ships *Rio de Janeiro* and *Ceará*. HS-1 has an additional SAR and medevac role and its Sea Kings can be fitted with 12 stretchers or carry up to 25 passengers. Between January and March 1996, HS-1 took delivery of three new ex-US Navy SH-3H Sea Kings (service designation ASH-3B) in addition to two SH-3Ds, for spares use.

The real teeth of the Marinha are the Westland Lynx Mk 21s (SAH-11s) of Esquadrão de Helicopteros de Esclarecimento e Ataque 1 (HA-1). HA-1 stood up at São Pedro da Aldeia in 1978 with the delivery of the first of nine SAH-11s, of which four have since been lost in accidents. The Lynx operate regularly from the six 'Niterói'-class frigates (Vosper Thorneycraft Mk 10 design), but can also be flown from any of the navy's diverse destroyer and frigate fleet. The Lynx can be armed with up to four Sea Skua anti-ship missiles, two Mk 46 torpedoes or two Mk 9 depth charges. Despite its accident rate it is the most popular helicopter among naval pilots, who praise its speed while disliking its noise and vibration. In 1991 a follow-on order for nine Super Lynx Mk 21As was placed with Westland. These aircraft will be equipped with Seaspray 3000 360° search radar, an RNS252 INS and Doppler 71 navigation fit, with provision for reconnaissance pods, FLIR or a dipping sonar. Deliveries are due to commence later in 1996. The original Lynx Mk 21s, with their Sea Spray Mk 1 radars, will be upgraded to Mk 21A standard by Westland.

Main helicopter fleet

The majority of the Marinha's helicopter force is devoted to transport duties, although some have a secondary armed role. Between them, Esquadrão de Helicopteros de Emprego Geral 1, 3, 5 and 5 (HU-1, -3 -4 and -5) operate 17 licence-built Aérospatiale (Eurocopter France) Squirrels and Twin Squirrels. Since 1979 Helibras has been assembling and delivering Aérospatiale helicopters in Brazil. The navy operates eight (of 11 ordered) single-engined UH-12s (Helibras HB-350/AS 550U2) and nine twin-engined UH-13s (Helibras HB-355F/AS 555U2). Both versions are known as Esquilo (ecureuil/squirrel).

Founded on 17 April 1962, HU-1 is the oldest aviation unit in the Marinha and the only Esquilo operator based at São Pedro da Aldeia. HU-1 is tasked with armed reconnaissance, surveillance, special forces insertion and SAR missions. Its aircraft can be fitted with door-mounted 7.62-mm machine-guns or seven-round 70-mm rocket pods. In 1994 HU-1 helicopters conducted 'psyops' missions over downtown Rio in support of the police, during street fighting against drug gangs. Some of its UH-13s have Dayglo panels

for Antarctic operations at Brazil's Teniente Rodolfo Marsh polar base, on King George Island, in addition to deployments aboard the survey ship *Ary Rongel*.

HU-3 is based at Manaus in the Amazon, and at HU-4 at Ladário, near Bolivia, in the Pantanal nature reserve. HU-5 was activated only in early 1996, at Rio Grande in southern Brazil. HU-3, HU-4 and HU-5 are equipped solely with UH-12s and often fly in support of the Fuzileiros Navais (Marines). The UH-12 is reportedly unpopular among pilots despite its speed and maneouvrability, and it has a reputation for tricky handling and instability.

The Eurocopter AS 332M Cougars (UH-14s) of HU-2 provide heavy-lift capability for the Marinha, in addition to troop transport and SAR duties. The first five, of seven, UH-14s were delivered in September 1986, finally replacing the remaining Westland Whirlwinds. Two more followed in 1993. The large UH-14s can only be deployed aboard the *Minas Gerias* or the two 'Mattoso Maia'-class assault ships, and the Marinha would undoubtedly like more of these versatile and sophisticated helicopters.

Pilot training

All Marinha helicopter pilot training is undertaken by the navy itself. Before being accepted as a pilot cadet, a prospective candidate must complete the regular naval training course. This multi-year task requires four years' study at the Naval Academy, followed by a year at sea with the training ship fleet and then another two years on a warship. Only then can the student pilot join the aviation school at São Pedro da Aldeia.

A course with Esquadrão de Helicopteros Instrução 1 (HI-1) takes 14 months, of which five are in ground school. HI-1 has 20 rated instructors flying Bell 206B Jetranger IIIs (IH-6B). Sixteen IH-6Bs were delivered between 1985 and 1987 to replace earlier Bell 206A Jetranger IIs (IH-6As). The IH-6Bs can be armed with 7.62-mm gun pods or 70-mm rocket pods, with the addition of a removable gunsight in the cockpit, and special (windowless) side cabin doors.

Students undertake a 120- to 140-hour flying course that includes basic flying training, navigation (VFR and IFR) and formation flying. The course later progresses to operations on mountainous terrain, night flying and deck landing, with weapons training also. The final element of the course involves long-range navigation flights and SAR training. Between 1986 and 1992, HI-1 trained pilots for the Brazilian army and still trains exchange students from Venezuela and Peru. In future, HI-1 will also undertake all Argentine navy helicopter pilot training too.   **Robert Hewson**

Força Aéronaval da Marinha do Brasil

UNIT	TYPE	BASE
HA-1	SAH-11 (Lynx Mk 21/B)	São Pedro da Aldeia
HI-1	IH-6B (B 206B Jetranger III)	São Pedro da Aldeia
HS-1	ASH-3A (SH-3H Sea King)	São Pedro da Aldeia
HU-1	UH-12/-13 (HB-350B/HB-355F)	São Pedro da Aldeia
HU-2	UH-14	São Pedro da Aldeia
HU-3	UH-12 (HB-350B Esquilo)	Manaus
HU-4	UH-12 (HB-350B Esquilo)	Ladário
HU-5	UH-12 (HB-350B Esquilo)	Rio Grande

The CTA is yet another HS 125 operator, this time in the shape of an XU-93 radar testbed. The FAB uses an 'X' or 'Y' prefix to denote permanent or temporary involvement in test duties.

The Academia da Força Aérea (AFA) is based at Pirassununga and undertakes air experience and basic flying training for the FAB and other air forces. It has a single squadron of T-27A/C Tucanos – 1º EIA.

Above: The AFA's second active squadron is 2º EIA (Esquadrão de Instrução Aérea), which flies the T-25 Universal.

Below: The Escola do Especialistas de Aéronautica (EEAR) flies this C-95A, based at Guaratingueta, in association with the AFA.

Above: The AFA uses two EMBRAER EMB-210 Ipanema 'Ag-planes' (U-19s) as glider tugs.

The AFA maintains an eclectic selection of gliders and microlights. This is a TPE KW 1b2 Quero Quero.

Above left: The Marinha operates five squadrons of HB-350B Esquilos (plus some HB-355s) for shipboard, transport and SAR duties.

Left: Westland supplied nine Lynx Mk 21s (SAH-11s) in 1978 and a further nine Super Lynx were ordered in 1991. The Lynx are flown by HA-1.

Above: The Marinha's most potent airborne assets are its Exocet-armed SH-3Ds (as seen here) and its more recently delivered SH-3Hs.

Picture acknowledgments

Front cover: Peter Steinemann. **4:** Werner Greppmeier, Alex Mladenov. **5:** P. Soukop via J. Spacek, Werner Greppmeier (two). **6:** Carlo Marcora, Werner Greppmeier (two). **7:** A. Sakisyan (MAPO) via Georg Mader. **8:** via Werner Greppmeier (two), Alan Bayliss. **9:** Jeremy Flack/API, David Donald. **10:** McDonnell Douglas, Kevin L. Patrick, Robbie Shaw. **11:** Paul Jackson (two). **12:** Fokker, Patrick Laureau. **13:** Lockheed Martin, N. Dunridge. **14:** Boeing/Sikorsky. **15:** Carey Mavor, McDonnell Douglas, Wernge Winzenmaier. **16:** G.R. Stockle, Keith Riddle (two). **17:** David F. Brown, Vance Vasquez/US Navy. **18:** Tieme Festner, Frank Rozendaal (two). **19:** Frank Rozendaal (four). **20:** Martin Baumann, Werner Greppmeier, Tieme Festner, Frank Rozendaal. **21:** Frank Rozendaal (two), Tieme Festner (three). **22-23:** Georg Mader. **24-27:** Dragisa Brasnovic. **28:** Robbie Shaw, Alec Molton. **29:** AIDC/Feng (two), AIDC, Associated Press. **30:** AIDC, Shoki via Chris Pocock. **31:** Robbie Shaw, AIDC. **32:** Alec Molton, Robbie Shaw via Jon Lake. **34:** Robbie Shaw. **35:** Martin-Baker, via Defence International (two). **36:** AIDC. **38-41:** Robbie Shaw. **42:** Steve Harding. **43:** Ted Carlson/Fotodynamics, Steve Harding. **44:** Steve Harding, Matthew Olafsen. **45:** Steve Harding (two), Matthew Olafsen. **46:** Ted Carlson/Fotodynamics, Matthew Olafsen. **47:** Matthew Olafsen, Steve Harding (two). **48:** Ted Carlson/Fotodynamics, Matthew Olafsen (two). **49:** David F. Brown, G.R. Stockle (two). **50-51:** Stefan Petersen. **52:** Neville Dawson, Ted Carlson/Fotodynamics. **53:** Rick Llinares. **54:** Ted Carlson/Fotodynamics, Joe Cupido. **55:** Joe Cupido. **56:** Joe Papay, Joe Cupido, McDonnell Douglas. **57:** Frank B. Mormillo, McDonnell Douglas. **58:** F. Lert (two), Luigino Caliaro. **61:** Warren Thompson (two), Ted Carlson/Fotodynamics. **68:** David Evans via Jim Winchester (two), Luigino Caliaro, Tim Ripley, Ted Carlson/Fotodynamics, Joe Papay, Randy Jolly (two), Jose M. Ramos. **69:** Hughes. **70:** Ted Carlson/Fotodynamics, Luigino Caliaro. **71:** Frank B. Mormillo, Robbie Shaw. **72:** Gary Bihary, Ted Carlson/Fotodynamics. **73:** Ted Carlson/Fotodynamics, McDonnell Douglas. **74:** Gert Kromhout, Richards, Ted Carlson/Fotodynamics. **75:** Ted Carlson/Fotodynamics. **76:** Joe Cupido. **77:** Randy Jolly. **78:** Yves Debay. **79:** Ted Carlson/Fotodynamics. **80:** Frank B. Mormillo. **81:** Ted Carlson/Fotodynamics. **82:** Randy Jolly, Joe Papay. **83:** Yves Debay. **84:** Joe Papay (three). **85:** Randy Jolly (two). **86:** Frank B. Mormillo. **87:** Randy Jolly, Joe Cupido. **88:** Ted Carlson/Fotodynamics, Douglas R. Tachauer. **89:** Randy

Jolly. **90:** Ted Carlson/Fotodynamics (two). **91:** Jose M. Ramos, Luigino Caliaro. **92:** via Neville Dawson, Mike Rondot. **93:** Jeff Rankin-Lowe. **94:** Mike Reyno, Salvador Mafé Huertas. **95-96:** RAAF. **97:** Peter Steinemann, McDonnell Douglas. **98:** McDonnell Douglas (two). **99:** McDonnell Douglas, Ted Carlson/Fotodynamics. **100:** McDonnell Douglas (two). **101:** Randy Jolly (three). **102:** Randy Jolly, Jody Louviere. **103:** Jose M. Ramos, F. Lert. **104:** Jose M. Ramos, Ted Carlson/Fotodynamics. **105:** Randy Jolly (two), Rick Llinares, Ted Carlson/Fotodynamics. **106:** RAAF (two), Jeff Rankin-Lowe. **107:** Neville Dawson, Andrew H. Cline, Hasse Vallas. **108:** Hasse Vallas, Andrew H. Cline. **109:** Jim Dunn, Luigino Caliaro. **110:** Ian Black. **111:** McDonnell Douglas (two). **112-115:** Peter Steinemann. **116:** Mike Reyno. **117:** Mike Reyno, Sikorsky. **118:** Jeff Rankin-Lowe, Carmine di Napoli, Barry D. Smith. **119:** Jerry Scutts, Peter B. Mersky. **120:** Agusta, Di Napoli/Mancini, Frank B. Mormillo. **121:** Agusta, Andrew H. Cline. **122:** Sikorsky (two), via Michael Stroud, Bob Burns Collection, US Navy via Peter B. Mersky, Robert E. Kling. **123:** Sikorsky (two), Robert E. Kling. **124:** Howard Levy, Alex Hrapunov, Aerospace, Sikorsky. **125:** USAF, David Donald, US Navy via Peter B. Mersky. **126:** Dougie Monk, Chris Ryan. **127:** T. Malcolm English, Douglas R. Tachauer, Don Logan. **128:** B. Knowles via C. di Napoli, USAF, USCG. **129:** Aerophoto, David Donald, Tadao Imazumi via Ted Carlson, US Navy via Peter B. Mersky. **130:** US Navy, Salvador Mafé Huertas, Yves Debay. **131:** Salvador Mafé Huertas, Ted Carlson/Fotodynamics, Jan Jørgensen. **132:** Peter Steinemann, Aviation Photo Agency, MAP. **133:** Sikorsky, Robbie Shaw. **134:** Peter R. Foster. **135:** Terry Panopalis, Mitsubishi, Di Napoli/Mancini, Gerd Kromhout. **136:** Peter R. Foster (three), MAP, Jelle Sjoerdsma, Agusta. **137:** Yves Debay, Agusta, Marco Amatimaggio. **138-141:** Yefim Gordon (six). **143:** Robbie Shaw (seven), Alvarez. **145:** APA-Rob Schleiffert, Robbie Shaw (five), APA-Corné Rodenburg, Mario Roberto v. Carneiro, Alec Moutlon. **147:** Robbie Shaw (five), Mario Roberto v. Carneiro (two), APA-Corné Rodenburg (two). **148:** Mario Roberto v. Carneiro (two), Robbie Shaw (four), APA-Rob Schleiffert, Peter R. Foster. **153:** Mario Roberto v. Carneiro, Robbie Shaw (three). **151:** APA-Rob Schleiffert (two), Robbie Shaw (three), Mauro César Mezzacappa, EMBRAER, Peter R. Foster. **153:** Peter R. Foster, Mario Roberto v. Carneiro, Robbie Shaw (four), APA-Rob Schleiffert, John Fricker, David Donald. **155:** APA-Corné Rodenburg (two), Robbie Shaw (five). **157:** Robbie Shaw (four), Mauro César Mezzacappa, Louis Vosloo, Aerospace, APA-Corné Rodenburg.